Fragmentation and Redemption

Fragmentation and Redemption

Essays on Gender and the
Human Body in Medieval Religion

Caroline Walker Bynum

ZONE BOOKS · NEW YORK

1992

© 1991 Urzone, Inc.
ZONE BOOKS
40 White Street, 5th Floor
New York, NY 10013

Printed in the United States of America.

Distributed by The MIT Press,
Cambridge, Massachusetts, and London, England

Library of Congress Cataloging in Publication Data

Bynum, Caroline Walker.
    Fragmentation and redemption: essays on gender
and the human body in medieval religion / by Caroline
Walker Bynum.
        p.   cm.
    Includes bibliographical references.
    Includes index.
    ISBN 0-942299-63-9 (pbk.)
    1. Body, Human–Religious aspects–Christianity–
History of doctrines–Middle Ages, 600–1500. 2. Sex
role–Religious aspects–Christianity–History of doctrines–Middle Ages, 600–1500. 3. Women (Christian
theology)–History of doctrines–Middle Ages, 600–
1500. 4. Women in Christianity–History. I. Title.
BT741.S.B95   1990
233'.5–dc20   90-12451
                                                         CIP

Contents

Acknowledgments

The essays in this volume first appeared as follows: "Women's Stories, Women's Symbols: A Critique of Victor Turner's Theory of Liminality," in Frank Reynolds and Robert Moore (eds.), *Anthropology and the Study of Religion* (Chicago: Center for the Scientific Study of Religion, 1984), pp. 105–25 (reprinted by permission); "The Mysticism and Asceticism of Medieval Women: Some Comments on the Typologies of Max Weber and Ernst Troeltsch," in German in Wolfgang Schluchter (ed.), *Max Webers Sicht des okzidentalen Christentums: Interpretation und Kritik* (Frankfurt: Suhrkamp, 1988), pp. 355–82; "The Body of Christ in the Later Middle Ages: A Reply to Leo Steinberg," in *Renaissance Quarterly* 39.3 (Autumn, 1986), pp. 399–439 (reprinted by permission); "Women Mystics and Eucharistic Devotion in the Thirteenth Century," in *Women's Studies* 11 (1984), pp. 179–214; " '... And Woman His Humanity': Female Imagery in the Religious Writing of the Later Middle Ages," in Caroline Walker Bynum, Stevan Harrell, and Paula Richman (eds.), *Gender and Religion: On The Complexity of Symbols* (Boston: Beacon Press, 1986), pp. 257–88 (reprinted by permission); "The Female Body and Religious Practice," in *Zone* 3: *Fragments for a History of the Human Body*, Part 1 (New York: Urzone, 1989), pp. 160–219. The final essay, "Material Continuity, Personal Survival and the Resurrection of the Body: A Scholastic Discussion in Its Medieval and Modern Contexts," contains material that appears under the same title in *History of Religions* (forthcoming, 1990); it is reprinted by permission of the University of Chicago Press, which holds the copyright to the original article. Both the Introduction and Chapter 7 contain some material that is included in "Bodily Miracles and the Resurrection of the Body in the High Middle Ages," Thomas Kselman (ed.), *Belief in History* (Notre Dame, IN: University of Notre Dame Press, forthcoming, 1990). I am grateful to the editors of these journals and collections for permission to republish and for the good advice they gave about the essays in their original form.

I have done minor rewriting in all the essays, and have added recent bibliography to the footnotes, indicating it in square brackets. The piece on Max Weber, which was prepared for a conference in Germany in 1986, appears here in English for the first time. The final essay is an amalgamation of two pieces I wrote in 1988 and has been expanded beyond either of the original articles. Material from art history has, moreover, been added to Chapters 6 and 7. Nonetheless, the earliest of the essays republished here (Chapters 1, 3, 4 and 5) have not been substantially rewritten. They conceptualize problems as I saw them in the early eighties. To rewrite them now would have meant in some cases to enter into conversation with arguments they themselves generated. I found it impossible to do that without destroying the original articles. I have, moreover, not wanted to eliminate all repetition between essays. Some overlapping documentation has been replaced with cross-references. But, in several cases, I found that later essays relied on arguments in earlier ones that are still unfamiliar, controversial and even distasteful to contemporary historians. To assert my own, still debatable and debated positions, without proof or elaboration, as if they represented an established scholarly consensus, seemed to me a less agreeable alternative than repeating a bit of evidence or explaining a previous insight. So I have let some repetition remain. I argue below that historians can never present more than a part of the story of history and that these parts are true fragments, not microcosms of the whole; but such a conception of the historian's task does not, after all, preclude making each fragment as comprehensible and self-contained as possible.

When they originally appeared, two of these essays were dedicated to individuals who have contributed much to my intellectual development over the years: Donald J. Wilcox and my husband, Guenther Roth. I thank them again. Each has helped me think about what it means to do history. In addition, Guenther Roth has read the entire manuscript with an eye to curtailing my exuberant adjectives and has scoured museums with me, looking for bones and apocalypses. I also thank several friends who have influenced my ideas far more profoundly than this cursory alphabetical listing can indicate: Peter Brown, Giles Constable, Stephen Greenblatt, Jeffrey Hamburger, Stevan Harrell, Thomas Head, Frank Reynolds, Judith Van Herik and Stephen D. White. I am especially grateful to Lynn Hunt, whose example both as a practicing historian and as a commentator on the current state of the historical profession has been of the utmost importance in shaping my ideas and giving me the confidence to voice them. For stimulating conversation and trenchant criticism, I thank Alan Bernstein, Gillian Brown, Anna Kartsonis, Richard Kieckhefer, Robert Lerner, Steven P. Marrone, Barbara Newman, Fred Paxton and Harvey Stahl. Patricia Fortini Brown, Laura Dushkes, Clare Kudera, James Marrow, Ruth Mellinkoff, Karen Scott, Jan Westfall and Steven Wight helped with particular texts and pictures. Several of the early essays were typed by my friend Elizabeth Goolian. Ted Byfield, Rennie Childress and Meighan Gale helped at every stage of production and contributed much to the beauty and accuracy of the book. I owe special thanks to my editor at Zone Books, Ramona Naddaff, for her efficiency, her marvelous suggestions and her sense of humor.

While I was writing the last two essays collected here, I was the recipient of a residential fellowship as a Senior Scholar at the Getty Center for the History of Art and the Humanities in Santa Monica, California, and of a five-year fellowship from the John D. and Catherine T. MacArthur Foundation. Both fellowships were intended to provide recipients with the opportunity to pursue new interests. I hope I have used my freedom responsibly and creatively. I am grateful for the confidence expressed in my work and for the lively community provided both at the Getty Center and at the occasional but very fruitful MacArthur reunions. I would also like to thank my new colleagues at Columbia University, especially Malcolm Bean, Eric Foner, William Harris, Martha Howell, Natalie Kampen, Miranda Pollard, Wim Smit, Robert Somerville and Yosef Yerushalmi. In the midst of the dirt, the confusion and the poverty that New York City is today, my fellow historians at Columbia have been, not an island, but an engaged community, characterized by civility, intellectual curiosity, pedagogical responsibility and a sense of the relevance of scholarship.

I argue below that the writing of history must come to terms gracefully with the incomplete, that it must be a conversation open to new voices, that its essential mode is a comic one. I suggest that the pleasure we find in research and in storytelling about the past is enhanced both by awareness that our own voices are provisional and by confidence in the revisions the future will bring. Therefore, I dedicate this volume to my students. May they find that the comedy of history welcomes them, both as actors and as authors.

New York City
September, 1989

In Praise of Fragments:

History in the Comic Mode

In the early years of the twelfth century, the monk Guibert of Nogent wrote a treatise on relics that has been lauded by historians as the beginning of scientific hagiography, a precursor of Valla or Erasmus or Mabillon. Guibert criticized credulous veneration of remains simply because miracles happened there. He insisted that relics be properly documented and that miracles be approved by church authorities. But Guibert is not, in fact, a forerunner of source criticism, of scientific history, of modernism or of ecclesiastical centralization. His concern was not with methods of research and authentication and control. What disturbed Guibert was the practice of moving and dividing the bodies of the saints. Fragmentation was, to Guibert, the ultimate insult and scandal; aiding and abetting it by translating and mutilating holy cadavers struck him as obscene.[1]

The occasion for Guibert's *De pignoribus* was the claim of the monastery of St. Médard to possess the tooth of Christ. Against this claim, Guibert's fundamental argument was theological. He expressed horror and outrage at the notion that any part of Christ (tooth, umbilical cord or foreskin) could be left on earth to suffer decay. Christ's resurrected body is the paradigm for ours, wrote Guibert; if so much as a drop of his blood or a hair of his

11

head is left behind, how shall we believe that we will rise again
at the sound of the trumpet? The martyrs bear up under unspeakable tortures (splittings of fingernails, hanging by genitals, flaying
and severing) because they know every particle will return in the
end. The eucharistic host, fragmented by human teeth and diges-
tive processes yet in every minute crumb the whole body of Christ
is, argued Guibert, the guarantee that wholeness – non-partibility
and non-passibility – is God's ultimate promise to humankind.
So crucial to salvation was wholeness for Guibert that he used
rhetorical theory to argue that synecdoche, *pars pro toto*, must be
literally true.[2]

Later in the twelfth century, the abbess Herrad of Hohenbourg
directed the compilation of a vast compendium of theological
and scientific information, the *Hortus deliciarum*. Herrad collected with care passages from Peter Lombard and Honorius
Augustodunensis concerning the reassembling of human bodies
at the end of time. Fascinated, as was Guibert, by matters that
appear decidedly odd to modern taste, Herrad queried whether
aborted fetuses, severed limbs and pared fingernails will rise from
the dead.[3] To illustrate such questions she, or her artist-col-
laborators, chose an iconographic program historians have called
the Byzantine Last Judgment (see Figures 7.9, 7.10, 7.11, 7.12).[4]
The wonderful miniatures of the *Hortus deliciarum* have survived
only through the drawings made by scholars who studied them
before the destruction of the manuscript in the bombardment of
Strasbourg in 1870.[5] But even the recent scholarly reconstruction
makes it clear that, just as the *Hortus deliciarum* pieces together
somewhat incongruous elements from the Lombard and Honorius
in order to discuss exactly how bodies will appear at the Last Judgment, so it uses available artistic motifs to depict a resurrection
in which part returns to wholeness without losing its individuality. The miniatures show resurrection as three distinct moments:

body parts are vomited up from the depths of the sea and the craws of birds and beasts; bodies, drawn enfleshed but labeled "ossa mortuorum," emerge whole from their tombs; the saved appear before God shining with the specific characteristics of their religious accomplishments – that is, as martyrs, monks, virgins and so forth.

In the writings and pictures of Guibert and Herrad, the torture and fragmentation to which these authors were drawn with prurient horror are redeemed by a vision of last things in which not just wholeness but reassemblage is the ultimate promise. In this vision, Herrad and Guibert were not alone. The twelfth and thirteenth centuries in western Europe saw renewed debate over dozens of theological matters (such as the eucharist, the transmission of original sin, the nature of the body–soul nexus) in which the relationship of part to whole is crucial, and a new emphasis on miracles (such as stigmata, bleeding hosts, miraculous fasting, incorrupt cadavers) in which bodies are the mediators between earth and heaven. It was a period in which the overcoming of partition and putrefaction – either through reunion of parts into a whole or through assertion of part *as part* to *be* the whole – was the image of paradise.[6]

Guibert and Herrad can serve to introduce this volume because the essays that follow are all, in some sense, about bodies, and about the relationship of part to whole. Moreover, the essays themselves are fragments, parts. Any author faced with the possibility of assembling her recent essays for publication necessarily confronts a problem of parts and whole.

The introduction to a collection must speak of underlying themes and connections – must, that is, unite the fragments into something larger. In musing here briefly about these essays I shall inevitably, therefore, suggest that common patterns and concerns undergird them. But I also wish to assert that none of the *partes* here stands *pro toto*. I assert this not so much because these essays are only a partial view of the high Middle Ages — because they are not a survey of women's religious practices or of attitudes toward the body or of theological debates concerning eschatology and the human person — although that is true. Rather, I assert this because my understanding of the historian's task precludes wholeness. Historians, like the fishes of the sea, regurgitate fragments. Only supernatural power can reassemble fragments so completely that no particle of them is lost, or miraculously empower the part to *be* the whole.

The seven essays republished here were written between 1982 and 1989. They fall naturally into three groups. First, there are three occasional pieces, written at the request of conference organizers or journal editors, and addressing directly a major theoretical position in a field outside history. Second, there are three essays in women's history, all of which treat women's piety not in isolation but in such a way as to reformulate also our understanding of men's religious practices and beliefs. Third, there is a long essay on religious conceptions of the body, substantially rewritten for this volume and drawn from two independently published pieces. The seven essays are, as I shall explain, closely related.

The three methodological pieces all use major twentieth-century intellectual figures as means to better understand late medieval religion. None has as its aim an attack on the thinker, an application of the thinker's ideas, or a general evaluation of the thinker's place in his discipline. I have tried to understand each thinker fairly and fully, but basically I have used their works as I use other theoretical material in other essays — not as a key but as one tool among many. The later essays in the volume make essentially similar reference to theory: the seventh, for example, uses contemporary philosophy of mind to raise new questions about medieval philosophical debate; the fifth is stimulated by, yet in certain ways disagrees with, recent feminist writing in the field of religion. All the essays in the volume, therefore, arise fundamentally from medieval material, not from contemporary theoretical perspectives. Behind whatever smooth surface they may present to the modern reader lies the hard grappling with texts – reading them, dating them, ascribing them – that is the ordinary work of the medievalist.

If I do not adopt the method or the conclusions of any of the theorists I consider, there are nonetheless several general points that might be made about my use of disciplines outside history. Victor Turner, Max Weber and Leo Steinberg – the subjects of the first three essays – provide fundamental stimuli to historians. Turner (and Clifford Geertz, with whom his approach is allied) challenges historians to consider how symbols function to give cohesion to community, yet how, given their many facets, they cannot be reduced to function. Weber and Troeltsch suggest to students of religion that they must pay more attention to the forms of association characteristic of certain basic religious impulses, such as asceticism or mysticism. Steinberg has made it abundantly clear to both his fellow art historians and to students of literature that an artistic object is not an illustration of a written text but is itself a text in its own right. My discussion of Turner implies a fairly standard critique of functionalism; my criticism of Weber suggests that he in some ways reduces religion to sociology; my examination of Steinberg argues that he sometimes violates his own understanding of the relationship of art object and text. But the three essays also surely suggest how much historians have to learn from recourse to the disciplines of anthropology, sociology and art history, all of which provide interpretations of the nature and context of human creativity.

Moreover, each of the three essays makes its point by adducing material concerning gender ignored by the theorist in question.

A consideration of texts written by women and rituals attractive to them leads to a critique of Turner's notions of liminality and reversal; attention to recent research on nuns, beguines, tertiaries and laywomen suggests not only that Weber's application of his ideal types to the period before the Protestant Reformation is faulty, but also that the types themselves should be reformulated in certain ways; Steinberg's reading of the significance of genitality and body in art is radically revised by my argument that medieval devotional writers and natural philosophers did not think as we modern folk do about biological sex and culturally constructed gender. When even the small bit we are able to retrieve about medieval women's experience is taken into account, each modern theorist appears less universal in conclusion and implication. The course of history seems more complex. Periodization must be revised, influences reassessed. Although modern historians such as Gertrude Himmelfarb have argued that consideration of gender and social status derails historians from their fundamental task of organizing narrative, diagnosing decisive events and assessing the nature and consequences of power, this does not seem to me to be so.[7] My essays would indeed suggest that generalizing from the experience of one gender is far more likely to reduce history writing — as well as art history, sociology and anthropology — to a monochromatic *longue durée*. This is a point to which I shall return.

In subject matter as well as method, these essays thus have much in common. The last four all address directly the subject of gender raised in the first three as an aspect of methodological critique. Several of the essays describe women's surprisingly "experiential" literary voices; all underline the somatic quality of women's piety. None treats women simply as dominated or repressed by men. All assume, with social scientists such as Pierre Bourdieu and Michel de Certeau, that marginal and disadvantaged groups in a society appropriate that society's dominant symbols and ideas in ways that revise and undercut them. But none of the essays ignores the cultural construction of categories such as "female," "heretic" or "saint"; and none denies the asymmetrical power relations between men and women or clergy and laity.

Each essay therefore acknowledges that – in the creation of ideas of "maleness" and "femaleness," "heroine" or "heretic" – those with greater access to means of communication and to raw power contribute in disproportionate ways. Female creativity must be facilitated by men; female saints are not canonized or revered unless they are in some way religiously useful to men; female rejection of family and fertility must be conceptualized by men as acceptance of other communal and generative possibilities. Each one of these essays – no matter how explicitly focused on women – thus deals with the men who permitted and aided female cultural expression and, by placing women's ways of writing and behaving alongside men's interpretation of them, makes the point that men's understanding of women's piety and of their own has certain specific characteristics not necessarily generalizable as "medieval religion." There is no such thing as *homo religiosus* and no such thing as "*the* medieval attitude toward women." Every one of these essays turns us back toward questions about men as well as women. The study of gender is a study of how roles and possibilities are conceptualized; it is a study of one hundred percent, not of only fifty-one percent, of the human race.[8]

Yet these essays are also about the creativity of women's voices and women's bodies. They discuss how some women manipulated the dominant tradition to free themselves from the burdens of fertility yet made female fertility a powerful symbol; how some women extricated themselves from family yet served society in the stinking streets of medieval towns; how some used Christian dichotomies of male/female, powerful/poor to facilitate their own *imitatio Christi*, yet undercut these dichotomies by subsuming all dichotomy into *humanitas*.

In their confidence in female creativity these essays are, in a sense, animated by hindsight. The Western tradition that has made possible in the twentieth century such powerful and effective female self-confidence and female anger has deep roots. Late medieval women spoke little of inequality and little of gender, yet there is a profound connection between their symbols and communities and the twentieth-century determination to speak of gender asymmetry and to study women. Modern social structure and religious sensibility do not descend directly from the convents, beguinages and female friendship groups of the later Middle Ages, although, as Hajnal has pointed out, late medieval institutions and demographic patterns make a place for the first time in history for the single woman.[9] The determination of medieval women writers to speak of themselves more as human than as female, while nonetheless also utilizing rich domestic and female imagery, has no direct connection with current feminism, although the late Middle Ages may be the first time in history when we have large enough numbers of women's voices to be sure we are hearing characteristically female concerns. Reformation and Counter Reformation reacted against as well as drew upon the female religious movement of the later Middle Ages. My point here is that our dissimilarity from women in the thirteenth and fourteenth centuries should not lead us to suggest, as some feminists have, that they were mere victims of patriarchy. This is so, first, because the dissimilarity is far from total. More importantly, it is so because no voice – past or present – is more than partially empowered or partially distinctive. We hear women of the past speaking exactly as (and only to the extent that) we hear ourselves. If we have confidence in the righteousness of our own rage and in the diagnosis of our own oppression, how can we deny the power of female communities and female visions that, different from our own, are nonetheless our heritage?[10] My essays are all undergirded by the conviction that we do hear creative female voices – not merely literary genres or male superegos – speaking from the past.[11] They are also, in their recognition of the partial, committed to the proposition that women in every age speak in a variety of accents.

In Chapters 6 and 7, my focus appears to shift away from gender. Yet, in fact, the last two essays move explicitly to the topic implicit in the earlier discussions: the cultural construction of body itself. In these essays, the body in which we are all either male or female is taken not merely as a biological given, understood by experiencing subjects; it is seen to be actually created as what it is – to behave as it does – because of the categories in which it is conceptualized. These two essays therefore make clear why gender must always be an aspect of the history of attitudes and behavior. They also, however, attend to a duality in the Western tradition more profound even than gender: a tension between body as locus of pain and limitation, and body as locus not merely of pleasure but of personhood itself.

Body as allegory for community has recently been studied by historians such as Natalie Davis, under the influence of the symbolic anthropology of Clifford Geertz;[12] body as culturally constructed has been explored by scholars and critics such as Michel Foucault, Peter Brown and Thomas Laqueur.[13] Such approaches are surely in the background of my own essays. But my point is in some ways an altogether simpler one. However we construct it and whatever it stands for to us, body is what we've got. Thus, all these essays circle back to a point made by the earliest article anthologized here – back, that is, to what Victor Turner calls the "orectic" (sensory) quality of symbols. All evidence for the doing of history opens out beyond itself to an intractible physicality. My final essay undercuts all the others even as it affirms them: what we study – what we can study – is culturally constructed. But we know we are more than culture. We are body. And, as body, we die. This is also a point to which I shall return.

These essays were not written with any thought of publication as a whole. Nor were they conceived in discipleship to any particular methodological dispensation. They were simply the work of a younger historian who found, as she grew older, that there was around her an increasing interest in the sort of issues she had always found fascinating.[14] But because the seven years during which the essays were written saw great changes in the historical enterprise in America, it is worth a few words to say how these essays relate to those changes.

In the seventies, medievalists still had a modest but important place in shaping the discipline of history. Although the great Marc Bloch, cofounder of the journal *Annales*, was long dead, some thought the so-called *Annales* paradigm remained dominant within the new social history.[15] Readers of the lively English journal *Past and Present* found articles by medievalists prominent in its pages. In my essay on Victor Turner, the earliest piece collected here, I could still write as if medievalists were in the forefront of the use of anthropological models, although by the seventies the most-often cited practitioners of such use were early modern historians, such as Natalie Davis, John Bossy and Keith Thomas, not medievalists. In the eighties, two changes occurred. The historical profession turned increasingly to explicit discussion of method, as the available methodologies proliferated; and, simultaneously, medieval historians departed from the fray.

In the past few years, literary theory has joined anthropology and quantitative methods as a challenge to what historians earlier in the twentieth century understood their task to be. Articulate scholars such as Jim Clifford, Gertrude Himmelfarb, Dominic LaCapra, Joan Scott, Lawrence Stone, John Toews and Judith Walkowitz have turned increasingly to writing about method. Every article in a recent issue of the *American Historical Review* is devoted to controversy – which sometimes degenerates into acrimonious and inattentive polemic – over what historians ought to be doing. Two large issues are at stake. They are not mutually exclusive; neither are they quite the same issue, although some recent polemic has asserted that they are. First, there is debate over how far the subject matter of history should shift away from great thinkers and powerful leaders, from war and philosophy, toward the marginal and dispossessed, toward daily life and folk wisdom. Second, there is debate over the nature of historical analysis: Can historians determine causes for events and ferret out the intention of actors and writers? Or do causation and intentionality remain impenetrable, because we, left with only texts from the past, can do no more than read those texts from our own twentieth-century perspective?[16]

Students of medieval literature have welcomed the new questions; literary specialists such as Stephen Nicols, Howard Bloch and Eugene Vance have charged ahead, waving the banners of Foucault, deconstruction and the "new historicism."[17] But, aside from a few mavericks among intellectual historians, Americans who study medieval history have folded their tents and slunk away. Absent from contemporary debates, they seem unaware of trends and novelties. No medievalist is referred to in the *American Historical Review* symposium or anthologized in Lynn Hunt's *New Cultural History*; no scandal or triumph of medieval scholarship is reported in the pages of Peter Novick's recent history of the historical profession in America: *That Noble Dream*.[18] Today there is war between the practitioners of new historical methods and the guardians of the old order. Some of the rhetoric is unattractive, to be sure – especially where the goal seems to be to exclude certain social groups from the practice of history – and some of the research done under the new dispensation is silly. (Silly scholarship has been done under the aegis of every dispensation.) But by and large the war is a rather cheerful, noisy one, in which the casualties (even among the professionals) are few. Some of the debate is stimulating and productive. But medievalists play no role.[19] It seems a shame to miss the fun.

Whatever else my seven essays do, they don't miss the fun. They engage subjects – such as sexuality, gender, the body and death – that are often seen as typical of the new history. They have been both criticized and praised by feminists. They have been anthologized as "the new social history," published under the rubric "the new historicism," and edited in the company of writers seen as representing a new approach to religion.

In fact, I have not aligned myself explicitly with any current dispensation. In all my work I have struggled first with medieval texts, and discovered only subsequently that my formulation of their significance has resonances with (although also differences from) such theoretical positions as postmodern feminism, deconstruction or poststructural symbolic anthropology. Nonetheless it would be churlish not to admit that what I am doing in this volume fits many of the prescriptions of the "new cultural history."[20] My approach is focused on texts; it comes to events obliquely, sure that we know them not in themselves but only as they are presented in some record or other from the past. My sense of subject matter is pluralistic. While I have not spent a great deal of time combing medieval records for information about groups and experiences simply because those groups and experiences are important in the modern world or neglected in the medieval, I have also not assumed that history has, by definition, a particular subject matter (for example, war or politics or

22

oppression) or that only the unique, the accomplished, the influential is historical. I have also implicitly rejected certain forms of intentionality without rejecting causal analysis or context. I have assumed we can know the context of texts, because we can find groups of texts written and preserved and read together. I have assumed we can and must determine both chronological order and social structure – surely two elements of what we mean in common parlance by "cause." But I have also assumed that – while we can see how one text borrows from another and how actors assert themselves to be guided, even forced, by texts – we can never know what an author or an actor "really meant."[21] We can only, from our own text-surrounded vantage point, read the texts in context (i.e., with other texts among which they belong both chronologically and by self-ascription). Our readings will change because we change, both as individuals and as a culture. No one of us will ever read more than partially, from more than a particular perspective. Indeed, it is exactly because we admit that we are particular individuals, at a particular historical moment, using and affirming our own standards, that we move with confidence to speak of the beautiful, the cogent, the intellectually courageous and the moral in past writings and events. We know that what significance or nobility we find is significant or admirable to a particular "us."[22] But we also learn from texts, and the events they describe and incite, because we find in them the ignoble, the insignificant, the self-contradictory and paradoxical. In the inconsistencies and ironies of texts – judged as such by our standards – we learn things the past did not understand about itself. If we are humble, we learn something as well about our own capacity for self-contradiction. As the philosopher Thomas Nagel has recently said: "Sometimes, in the philosophy of mind but also elsewhere, truth is not to be found by travelling as far away from one's personal perspective as possible."[23]

23

I thus agree with Lynn Hunt when she suggests, in a flash of humor all too rare in current polemic, that the mode of the new cultural history may be comic.[24] If tragedy tells a cogent story, with a moral and a hero, and undergirds our sense of the nobility of humanity, comedy tells many stories, achieves a conclusion only by coincidence and wild improbability, and undergirds our sense of human limitation, even our cynicism about our motives and self-awareness.[25] Comedy is about compromise. In comedy there is resolution for only a moment. Although the traditional comedy ends with a wedding, we all know there is, in reality, no "happily ever after."

Yet comedy is fun. Perhaps the practitioners of the "new cultural history" are beginning to teach us that history – exactly because it too is about compromises and partialities and improbabilities – is fun as well. What gives me pleasure in perusing recent issues of the *American Historical Review* is a clear sense that – despite occasional lapses of civility and fairness – the participants in the debate are enjoying themselves and invigorating the profession by even their most irresponsible assertions. The doing of history is chaotic and pluralistic as never before. It is not so much a war as a tournament. Surely it is time for medievalists to reenter the fray.

Yet I myself have turned to dark topics. These essays move from body as ecstasy to body as decay and fragmentation. Why then do I assert the comic mode? Why stress the pleasure of doing history and minimize the acrimony of those scholars who feel excluded and those who would exclude them, while simultaneously thrusting our noses into torture and putrefaction? Why concentrate on aspects of the body that are surely, in some sense, ahistorical and, in all senses, not much fun? There seems something perverse in entitling the introduction to a set of essays on oppression and death "history in the comic mode."

The answer is that the comic is not necessarily the pleasant, or at least it is the pleasant snatched from the horrible by artifice and with acute self-consciousness and humility.[26] In comedy, the happy ending is contrived. Thus, a comic stance toward doing history is aware of contrivance, of risk. It always admits that we may be wrong. A comic stance knows there is, in actuality, no ending (happy or otherwise) – that doing history is, for the historian, telling a story that could be told in another way. For this reason, a comic stance welcomes voices hithertofore left outside, not to absorb or mute them but to allow them to object and contradict. Its goal is the pluralistic, not the total. It embraces the partial as partial. And, in such historical writing as in the best comedy, the author is also a character. Authorial presence and authorial asides are therefore welcome; methodological musing – even polemic – is a part of, not a substitute for, doing history.

So I see my approach in these essays not as a new method but as a new voice or a new mode in history writing: the partial or provisional voice, the comic mode. I see the topic to which I have turned most recently in my research as comic too. The last essay below reproduces pictures, such as those of the *Hortus deliciarum*, in which animals regurgitate body parts for reassemblage at the general resurrection. It explores medieval debates over the resurrection of aborted fetuses and modern controversy over reanimation of corpses and the beaming of bodies to the planet Mars. Such pictures and texts are surely comic in the common sense meaning of the word as well as in the more literary meaning I have employed above. They evidence what Henri Bergson sees as crucial to the comic: a moral response to the "recalcitrance of matter."[27]

I find our human capacity to tell such stories, to hide horror from ourselves while allowing it to peek through, profoundly comforting. The very implausibility of the restoration of pared

25

fingernails and amputated limbs at the end of time underlines, for me, the despicableness of human beings, who in fact torture and mutilate their fellow human beings. Yet the implausible, even risible, doctrine of the resurrection of the body asserts that – if there is such a thing as redemption – it must redeem our experience of enduring and even inflicting such acts.[28] If there is meaning to the history we tell and the corruption (both moral and physical) we suffer, surely it is in (as well as in spite of) fragmentation. Bodily resurrection at the end of time is, in a technical sense, a comic – that is, a contrived and brave – happy ending.

Thus, I find a comic stance empowering both as a historian and as a human being. Why not take the notion of digested and regurgitated fragments as a metaphor of the historian's subject matter? And why not – whatever despair we may feel concerning resurrection and reassemblage – find comic relief in the human determination to assert wholeness in the face of inevitable decay and fragmentation?

I

Women's Stories, Women's Symbols:
A Critique of Victor Turner's
Theory of Liminality

Victor Turner's Theory

Before considering the usefulness of Victor Turner's "processual symbolic analysis" or "social drama approach" to my work as a historian of the religion of the western European Middle Ages,[1] I should begin by stating what I do *not* intend to do.[2] First, I do not intend to address the general relationship of history and anthropology as academic disciplines or methods. Much has, of course, been written on this topic. Traditional historians are fond of the cliché that anthropology seeks to delineate general laws, history to describe particular events. But the more venturesome in both fields have sought a marriage of the two disciplines. The anthropologist Evans-Pritchard repeatedly argued that good history *is* good anthropology and vice versa, and dubbed eminent medieval historians such as Marc Bloch and F.W. Maitland the best of anthropologists.[3] The British historian Keith Thomas wrote recently that in the history departments of the eighties the last vestiges of the innovations of the sixties may lie in the use of certain insights from cultural anthropology.[4] I cannot, on the basis of study of a single figure, launch a new theory of the relationship of the disciplines. But my sympathies have always lain with those in each camp who make use of the other. And it seems clear

27

to me that Victor Turner's own sense of what he is up to, taken very broadly, is appealing to any historian of religion. Turner's notion of the fundamental units of social reality as dramas builds temporality and change into all analysis;[5] Turner's sense of dominant symbols as multivocal requires that symbols and ritual be understood in their social context;[6] Turner's emphasis on the "orectic" (sensory) pole of meaning enables students of religion to talk of emotional, psychological and spiritual elements that psychohistory has tried, woefully unsuccessfully, I fear, to introduce into historical analysis.[7] Therefore, in concluding that certain of Turner's theories seriously misrepresent the complexity of religious experience, I shall *not* be suggesting that anthropology and history are incompatible. Rather, I shall be arguing both that some of Turner's generalizations violate the subtlety of his own methodological commitments and that Turner's theory of religion is inadequate because it is based implicitly on the Christianity of a particular class, gender and historical period.

Second, I do not intend to provide a critique of Turner's own application of his theory to the European Middle Ages, particularly in his well-known essays on Thomas Becket and Francis of Assisi.[8] It would be easy to show that, compared to the richness of Turner's analysis of Ndembu ritual, his sense of twelfth- and thirteenth-century symbols is thin. "Poverty" to Francis, the *imitatio Christi* or *via crucis* to Becket, become in Turner's own hands almost "signs" rather than "symbols"; they lose much of the multivocality they unquestionably have in their own historical context. For all Turner's effort to use a social drama analysis, his history of the Franciscan order sounds remarkably like the history of the institutionalization and, therefore, corruption of a dream that was the standard interpretation of Francis until recently.[9] His discussion of Becket does not advance much beyond the picture of radical conversion from one ideal to another, which has always

28

been seen as the crux of the matter – in legend and literature as well as in the work of historians.[10] It is not surprising that Turner uses Turner's model best when he knows the society under study most deeply. And indeed, one is struck by the fact that even in his most recent writings, the Ndembu examples are the most powerful – the clearest, most precise, most analytical and cogent – whereas the modern examples are often tossed in without the care or the elaboration necessary to make the analysis convincing.[11] But for me to suggest simply that Turner could sometimes do a Turnerian analysis better than he does would contribute nothing to a study of Turner's model.

What I want to do, therefore, is to apply to my own research in the later Middle Ages Turner's notion of social drama as underlying both narrative and ritual. I want to focus especially on two aspects of Turner's notion of social drama, namely his understanding of "dominant symbols" (particularly as elaborated in the *Forest of Symbols* [1967]) and his notion of the central place in what he calls "liminality" of images of status reversal or status elevation (particularly as elaborated in *The Ritual Process* [1969] and in subsequent works).[12] I understand Turner to be arguing at his most general (and he is frequently quite general) that human experience, at least a great part of the time, occurs in units Turner calls "social dramas" (a subset of what he calls "processual units") – namely, that it takes a four-stage form: breach between social elements, crisis, adjustment or redress, and, finally, either reintegration of the group or person or "element" into the social structure or recognition of irreparable breach.[13] This social drama, to Turner, underlies both narrative (that is, the way we tell our important stories) and ritual (that is, the way we behave when we perform or enact certain formal, prescribed patterns that not only express but also move us into and elaborate our shared values). It is in the third stage that we find what Turner calls, borrowing the idea from van Gennep, "liminality" – a moment of suspension of normal rules and roles, a crossing of boundaries and violating of norms, that enables us to understand those norms, even (or perhaps especially) where they conflict, and move on either to incorpoate or reject them.[14] In the specific form of social drama called ritual, we find that rituals of life-crisis (that is, change in life-status: for example, puberty or election as chief) often use images of inversion in the liminal stage (for example, the initiate becomes a "fool" or a "woman"). Calendrical rituals (that is, those that celebrate the recurring pattern of the year: for example, harvest rituals) often use images of status elevation (for example, children wear masks of adults or of monsters at Halloween). Especially central in the liminal stage of ritual are what Turner calls "dominant symbols" – symbols that "condense" and "unify" into a moment disparate *significata* and bring together two poles of meaning: normative and emotional. A dominant symbol (for example, the Ndembu milk tree) can, therefore, only be understood in the context in which it is experienced. There it has meaning that includes as much the sensory, natural and physiological facts to which it refers (for example, milk, food, nurture, nursing, breasts, etc.) as the disparate social values for which it may stand (for example – in the case of the milk tree – both tribal custom and matriliny, on the one hand, and, on the other, conflict between mother and daughter, men and women).[15] From such fine and multitextured analysis of symbol and story, Turner sometimes moves on – quite a bit less successfully – to general cultural critique, calling for the liminoid (that is, the liminal-like) in modern life and cautiously praising *communitas*, his term for that feeling of union with one's fellow human beings which in preindustrial societies was released in the liminal phase of ritual.[16]

There are some obvious problems with applying Turner's writings to historical research, not least among them the fact that

Turner does not have a complete and coherent theory to the extent that Geertz and Lévi-Strauss do. As I indicated above, all Turner's ideas involve in some way the insight that, in explaining human experience, one is explaining process or drama rather than structure, and that liminality or suspension of social and normative structures is a crucial moment in the process. But the very fact that periods of liminality provide escape from roles and critiques of structures (in a functionalist sense of "structure") indicates that Turner has in certain ways never left the functionalist anthropology in which he was trained. And Turner himself, however quick he may have been to provide commentary on modernity, has said repeatedly that for the industrialized world "liminality" is only a metaphor.[17] It is, therefore, not certain either how far Turner's insights fit together into a system or how many of Turner's own insights Turner himself thinks applicable to the European Middle Ages, a society between "primitive" and industrial. I do not, however, want either to create a single "Turner theory" or to criticize such a theory by doing an exegesis of Turner. Others can do that better than I – Turner himself among them. Rather, I want to apply what clearly *are* some of Turner's insights – his notions of narrative, of dominant symbol and of the imagery of reversal and elevation – to my work on later medieval piety. Since Turner himself has extrapolated from analysis of ritual in "primitive" societies to more general theories about symbols and stories, I feel free to test his ideas against the religious texts that are the major source for historians of the Middle Ages. I want to show how certain of Turner's ideas, especially his sensitive and subtle notion of dominant symbols, enable me to describe aspects of European religiosity for which scholars have long needed terms. But I also want to argue that there are places where Turner's notions fail to describe what I find in my research, that those places fit into a pattern, and that this

31

pattern suggests a fundamental limitation in the Turnerian idea of liminality, at least in the extended or metaphorical sense of Turner's later writings.

In evaluating Turner's social drama model and his theory of symbol, I want to concentrate on a major form of medieval narrative, the saint's life, and on a major Christian ritual or dominant symbol, the eucharist. I chose these initially because they seem to be the most obvious illustrations of Turner's ideas. Although many historians of religion and literature have pointed out that saints' lives as a genre are *not* chronologically or linearly arranged – the goal of the biographer being to depict the saint as static model – conversion *is* often the climax of the story that lies behind and generates the literary life.[18] And the eucharist is not only obviously a dominant symbol, condensing, unifying and polarizing meaning; it is also the central symbol in a clearly processual ritual, one that recapitulates what is certainly a social drama – the crucifixion – and one in which the moment of reception of sacred food was frequently accompanied by the extreme liminality of ecstasy or possession. Moreover, although the eucharist is not in any simple sense either a calendrical or life-crisis ritual, the imagery of this liminal moment is obviously imagery of reversal: omnipotent God becomes dying man; the receiving Christian gains eternal life by eating and becoming the moment of death.[19] But as I have explored more closely the relationship of Turner's models to these medieval stories and symbols, a curious fact has emerged. Turner's ideas describe the stories and symbols of men better than those of women. Women's stories insofar as they can be discerned behind the tales told by male biographers are in fact less processual than men's; they don't have turning points. And when women recount their own lives, the themes are less climax, conversion, reintegration and triumph, the liminality of reversal or elevation, than continuity. Moreover, women's images and symbols – which, according to Turner's model, should reflect either inversion (for example, poverty) insofar as women are superior (for example, of aristocratic status), or elevation (for example, maleness, military prowess) insofar as women *qua* women are inferior – do not quite do either. Rather, they continue or enhance in image (for example, bride, sick person) what the woman's ordinary experience is, so that one either has to see the woman's religious stance as permanently liminal or as never quite becoming so.

These observations suggest to me that Turner's theory of religion may be based, more than he is aware, on the particular form of Christianity (with its strong emphasis on world denial and inversion of images) that has characterized elites in the Western tradition – educated elites, aristocratic elites and male elites. We will, however, understand this only if we use the category of gender very carefully. For my examination of Turner in no way implies that he fails to look at women either in his theory or in his fieldwork (where surely his analysis of women's rituals has been both extensive and subtle).[20] In many places he suggests that women are liminal or that women, as marginals, generate *communitas*.[21] What I am suggesting is exactly that Turner looks *at* women; he stands with the dominant group (males) and sees women (both as symbol and as fact) as liminal to men. In this he is quite correct, of course, and the insight is a powerful one. But it is not the whole story. The historian or anthropologist needs to stand *with* women as well.[22] And when Turner attempts to stand with the inferior, he assumes symmetry – that is, he assumes that the inferior are exactly the reverse of the superior. If the superior in society generate images of lowliness in liminality, the inferior will generate images of power. To use Turner's own example, ghetto teenagers in Chicago have first and second vice presidents in their street gangs.[23] My research indicates that such things are very rare

and that the images generated by the inferior are usually not reversals or elevations at all. Thus, liminality itself – as fully elaborated by Turner – may be less a universal moment of meaning
needed by human beings as they move through social dramas than
an escape for those who bear the burdens and reap the benefits
of a high place in the social structure. As recent liberation theologians have pointed out, it is the powerful who express imitation
of Christ as (voluntary) poverty, (voluntary) nudity and (voluntary) weakness. But the involuntary poor usually express their
imitatio Christi not as wealth and exploitation but as struggle.[24]

Male and Female Stories

Let me now turn to the later Middle Ages to illustrate the strengths
and limitations of Turner's notion of liminality. First, then, the
stories and symbols of men.

Male lives from the twelfth to the fifteenth centuries – both as
lived and as told – may be nicely explicated as social dramas. As
one would expect for religious virtuosi, charismatic figures and
saints, the liminal phase usually issues in breach with previous
role and previous group – that is, in conversion. Images of reversal and inversion are dominant in the converted life, particularly
at moments of transition. If we take as an example one of the most
famous of all medieval biographies, Bonaventure's life of Francis,
we find that the story is not only told as a series of successful crises, breaches with former status and life, but also that Francis,
the wealthy merchant's son, adopts images of poverty, nudity,
weakness, even of femaleness, at key moments. At the two most
decisive breaches of a life filled with crisis – that is, when he
renounces his earthly father and when he dies – Francis takes off
all his clothes.[25] These two moments are each accompanied by
adoption of disease and suffering (in the first case, dwelling among
lepers; in the second, union with the crucifix in stigmata).[26] And

34

the moment of conversion is a moment of womanly fertility: Bonaventure tells us that Francis took off his clothes and his shoes, renounced his father, threw away his money, prayed to Mary, and like her gave birth to his first child (his first disciple).[27] When the pope first rejects and later accepts Francis, Francis tells the story of a poor woman (by implication himself) who bears children of the Holy Spirit;[28] three women meet Francis and address *him* as "Lady Poverty";[29] Bonaventure suggests that ministers are fathers and preachers, but Francis, who insisted on remaining layman rather than cleric, is a mother, laboring for her children by example — that is, by suffering birth pangs.[30] Francis is described as cradling all creation — from a rabbit to the baby Jesus — in his arms as a mother.[31] But Francis's renunciation of his earthly father is decisive; real change occurs. And, in Bonaventure's prose, the Francis who returns from being crucified in the stigmata is now a "knight," a captain of Christ's army, sealed (for all his lay status) by the seal of Christ the High Priest.[32] In death Francis is described as founder and leader, model and exemplar, and father of his friars.[33] The life is a drama. The story told of it is a drama. From the liminality of weakness, nudity and womanliness comes the leader and model who changes the religious life of the thirteenth century.

Not only are male lives social dramas; men themselves use images of reversal to express liminality. And chief among these images is woman — as fact and as symbol. As Simone Roisin has shown, recourse to and comfort by the Virgin is a more common theme in the visions of men than in those of women.[34] Men frequently describe not only themselves but even Christ and God as female and, as I have argued in *Jesus as Mother*, such descriptions are frequently part of their anxiety over administrative responsibilities. Abbots and novice masters in the throes of self-doubt about their leadership talk of themselves and their God as tender and maternal.[35] "Woman" was clearly outside medieval Euro-pean notions of social structure, as Georges Duby repeatedly emphasizes in his study of the "three orders" of society;[36] and male writers clearly saw the image of the "female" (virgin, bride or mother) as an image for the male self when it escaped those three orders. In a very common metaphor, the monk Guerric of Igny wrote of the advancing soul as the "mother of Christ."[37] Bernard of Clairvaux not only elaborated the notion of the soul as bride and of the religious leader as mother but even suggested that monks, who fled the world, were women, whereas bishops, who led the world, were men.[38] To Bonaventure, not only the soul but also the illumined mind is bride, daughter, friend, sis-ter and member of Christ.[39] Monks and friars, whose status as set-apart was what Turner calls institutionalized liminality, also spoke of themselves as "fools," "acrobats" and "children" – all images of reversal – and even in their clothing adopted the child's hood as a distinctive feature.[40] In a particularly vivid fourteenth-century example, Richard Rolle underlined his conversion and his rejec-tion of family by fashioning hermit's clothing for himself out of two of his sister's dresses.[41]

To the well-known fact that men described themselves as women in moments or statuses of liminality, we can add the less commonly observed fact that men had recourse to actual women as liminal. Hildegard of Bingen, Birgitta of Sweden, Catherine of Siena and Joan of Arc are only the most obvious examples of women whose visions, attained while they were in a state of rad-ical apartness (underlined by virginity or illness or low social status), were *for men* a means of escape from and reintegration into status and power.[42] Two important biographers of the early thirteenth century, Thomas of Cantimpré and James of Vitry, cre-ated, through a number of lives, the image of the holy woman as critique of, reproach to, and solution for male pride, ambition and irreligiosity.[43] The biographers of two Franciscan tertiaries, Angela of Foligno and Margaret of Cortona, see these women as "mothers" who have only "sons" — that is, the local friars for whom they provide healing, visions, advice, rebuke and comfort.[44] John Coakley in his study of fifteenth-century saints' lives points out that, in sharp contrast to male saints who often hold power and office in the world, all women saints from this period are known through the eyes of their male confessors and are depicted by these confessors as models of interiorized spirituality.[45] The woman is thus, to the man, a retreat from the world into inner, often mystical repose. What she says (and her rhetoric is sometimes strident) and what she is, is a criticism of male power and an alternative to it. Contact with her is, for the male, an escape from the world; after recourse to her he returns to that world girded with information and consolation. The male biographers of Christina of Markyate in the twelfth century, Juliana of Cornillon in the thirteenth, and Angela of Foligno in the fourteenth century stress explicitly that God chose to act through the weak vessel, the woman, as a condemnation of male religious failure, so that the last becomes the first, the first last.[46] Turner himself expresses this sense of woman as liminal for man in his recent work on pilgrimage when he refers repeatedly to the Virgin as expressing the affective, emotional side of human character, holding up to society that escape from and evaluation of status and wealth which those who possess power apparently need in order to survive psychologically.[47]

Moreover, in the Middle Ages as today, men tended to assume that reversal was symmetrical. In other words, men writing about women assumed that women went through sharp crises and conversions and that their liminal moments were accompanied by gender reversal (in this case, of course, elevation). The twelfth-century biographer of Christina of Markyate tells a highly dramatic story of Christina escaping from marriage disguised as a man.[48] And from the patristic period (even more than from the later Middle Ages) there survives a host of stories of women disguising themselves as men in order to flee the world and join monasteries.[49] The lives of such early thirteenth-century saints as Margaret of Ypres or Mary of Oignies — although noticeably lacking in any images of gender reversal — are, as told by their male biographers, tales of high romance. Margaret avoided an earthly suitor by "marrying" Christ, and Mary, married young, more or less escaped marriage through extraordinary self-torture and starvation. It is only by reading between the lines that we realize that circumstances and social norms denied to Mary the mendicant poverty she really wanted as *imitatio Christi* or that Margaret' sought in an unresolved pattern to become dependent on one male after another (uncle, lover, Dominican spiritual adviser, the other clergy of Ypres, finally Christ).[50] The stories are not exactly social dramas with crises, liminality, reintegration, although the male biographers shape them into the traditional medieval narrative form of situation, rupture, resolution.[51] Moreover, the male dress adopted in fact by such women as Joan of Arc, Margery Kempe, Dorothy of Montau and Christina of Markyate was less a religious symbol than a social mechanism. Joan of Arc wore it in order to be a warrior; Margery Kempe and Dorothy of Montau in order to go more safely on pilgrimage; Christina of Markyate in order to escape husband and family.[52] Although a powerful and sometimes threatening image to the *men* who encountered it, so much so that they perhaps saw female cross-dressing where none existed,[53] to women it was a means to change roles. In the later Middle Ages, it is male biographers who describe women as "virile" when they make religious progress. To men, women reverse images and "become men" in renouncing the world.[54] But medieval women do not describe themselves as men as a way of asserting either humility or spiritual prowess. Women either describe themselves as truly androgynous (that is, they use male and female images without a strong sense of a given set of personality characteristics going with the one or the other gender) or as female (bride, lover, mother). If we look at the relatively few women whose own writings survive, Gertrude of Helfta and the Flemish mystic Hadewijch are examples of the former; Mechtild of Magdeburg and Beatrice of Nazareth examples of the latter.[55]

The complex and powerful imagery in the writings by and about Catherine of Siena also illustrates this point. When Catherine's male biographer, Raymond of Capua, worried about the validity of her ecstatic experiences, he received from God a vision in which Catherine's face fused into or became a bearded male face, which Raymond understood to be Christ. Thus, the man needed the woman's visionary ability authenticated either by seeing her as male or by seeing a male Christ acting through her. But Raymond reported that God told Catherine herself that she need not adopt male disguise, as she had desired to do when she was a child; God, "who has created both sexes and all sorts of men," who can "create an angel as easily as an ant," would send her to preach and teach *as a woman* in order to shame immoral men. The woman in her own vision remains woman and the male dress once wished for (not, however, as image but as mechanism of actual role change) is not necessary.[56] In her *Dialogue*, Catherine's own images for herself are female; her Christ is androgynous – bridegroom but also mother.[57]

So, when we take our stand with male storytellers, whether their tales be of women or of men, we find social dramas everywhere, with liminal moments expressed in images of gender reversal. But when we stand with women and look at how their stories and their symbols really work, we find something different. The life of Beatrice of Ornacieux, for example, written by another

Carthusian nun, is an entirely static picture of extreme self-mortification and eucharistic frenzy.[58] There are dramatic elements certainly. At one moment Beatrice, locked in by her caretaker because
she has made herself ill by extreme asceticism during Lent, passes
through the locked door by putting a picture of the Virgin out
through a little window.[59] But there is no conversion, no breach
and reintegration. Beatrice's own self-image in her visions and her
biographer's images for her are female. Like dozens of other thirteenth-century women, Beatrice repeatedly receives the Christchild at the eucharist and cradles him as a mother; her central
images for her encounters with Christ in ecstasy are eating and illness or suffering.[60] To an astonishing extent, hers is a life in which
"nothing happens," at least if we expect to find a social drama.

Moreover, if we turn to what is one of the most fascinating
of all medieval texts, the autobiography of the English woman
Margery Kempe, written in the early fifteenth century, we find
constant change and excitement but no completed social drama.
There are dozens of occasions on which, we might say, Margery
strains desperately for liminality, strains for transition in status, for
conversion, for escape from her normal role as "married woman"
into the role, two hundred years old at least, of the *mulier sancta*.
As the book opens, her depression about her failed business venture into brewing and her guilt about sex and food culminate in
a vision in which Christ seems to substitute for her husband as
her true lover, the eucharist to substitute for fleshly meat as her
true food.[61] But the vision does not result in a conversion to
chastity and abstinence. Margery must obey her husband, who,
annoyed by her asceticism, says he will insist on the marriage debt
unless she gives up her fasting. Margery then reports a conversation with Christ in which Christ says that she may give up the
less important practice, fasting, in order to gain chastity. There
is thus the amusing suggestion that Christ and Margery together

have tricked the male, who has the power to grant to – and withold from – the woman her own conversion.[62] Such manipulating and maneuvering then are the pattern of Margery's life. Wandering on pilgrimage, she must take her husband along or find another male protector; desiring weekly communion, she must get permission from her bishop and her confessor.[63] When Christ comes to tell her she is pregnant, he comforts her: "I love wives also, and especially those wives who would live chaste if they might."[64] And once her husband permits her to live in chastity (although for long years she cannot escape the responsibility of caring for him physically), Christ admonishes her: "Daughter, if thou knewest how many wives there are in this world that would love me and serve me right well and duly if they might be free from their husbands as thou art from thine, thou wouldst see that thou wert right much beholden unto me."[65] The message is almost: "be grateful for the little liminality permitted to you." In her own vivid prose, Margery sees herself as mother to the baby Jesus and bride to the human Christ, carrying such images to heights of literalism by actually feeling Jesus's toes in her hands in bed and weeping profusely at the sight of any male baby.[66] In her own eyes, Margery achieves spiritual growth not by reversing what she is but by being more fully herself with Christ. It is not possible to see Margery's dominant symbols – virginity (which is also its opposite, sexuality) and eucharist (which is also its opposite, fasting) – as moving her through a crisis, redressing or consolidating a breach or a conflict of norms. This is because Margery, for all her fervor, her courage, her piety, her mystical gifts and her brilliant imagination, cannot write her own script.

Such constriction is what we generally find in women's stories, even when they are told by men. Juliana of Cornillon received a vision of the new liturgical feast of Corpus Christi and was ordered by Christ to have it established in the Church. For twenty years she did nothing. She finally dared to approach a powerful male and, with his help, the observance made limited headway; but her further efforts to support monastic as well as liturgical reform led to her exile, and she wandered indecisively from religious house to religious house until her death. Dorothy of Montau, a fourteenth-century precurser of Margery Kempe, took her husband and her daughter along on pilgrimage. Although used by her confessor as propaganda for eucharistic devotion, she had to fight that same confessor in her lifetime for access to the eucharist and, when dying, was denied the final reception she craved. Even the life of Christina of Markyate, so skillfully organized by medieval narrative convention into a series of exciting crises, is, when one reads between the lines, a story of very *un*decisive change. Christina hangs from nails behind tapestries and leaps from windows to avoid her husband's advances; but it is years before she can legally escape the marriage and then only because her husband desires to marry someone else.[67] Umiltà of Faenza (or Florence) was able to adopt chastity only when doctors persuaded her husband that he must practice continence to preserve his health.[68] When Clare of Assisi's sister Agnes tried to flee her family, she was beaten half to death by her kinsmen; and the author of the nuns' book of Unterlinden tells a similar but even more gruesome story.[69] Although Clare herself did manage to renounce her noble family, shedding her jewels and her hair, she was never able to live the full mendicant life she so desired. Her story is a complex one, but it seems that, fleeing family and a possible husband only to accept the leadership of brother Francis, she was led by Francis's rejection to accept enclosure, which she did not originally want. It was only two days before her death that her rule, with its insistence on poverty, was confirmed.[70] Indeed, in a recent quantitative study of saints' lives from 1000 to 1700, Weinstein and Bell have demonstrated that women's saintly vocations often grew slowly through childhood and into adolescence; a disproportionate percentage of women saints were certain of their commitment to virginity before age seven. Despite the fact that both chastity and marital status were more central themes in women's lives than in men's, male saints were far more likely to undergo abrupt adolescent conversions, involving renunciation of wealth, power, marriage and sexuality.[71]

The point I am making here is an obvious one. Women could not take off all their clothes and walk away from their fathers or husbands, as did Francis. Simple social facts meant that most women's dramas were incomplete. And there may be psychological reasons for women's images as well as social ones. Ramanujan, who has found a similar pattern in the lives of female Indian saints, has argued, using Nancy Chodorow's psychological research, that women are in general less likely to use images of gender reversal or to experience life-decisions as sharp ruptures because women, raised by women, mature into a continuous self whereas boys, also raised by women, *must* undergo one basic reversal (i.e., from wanting to "be" their mothers to acceptance of being fathers).[72]

The Eucharist as Symbol to Men and Women

If we turn from women's stories to women's symbols, we find that certain aspects of Turner's approach are extremely helpful. Although Western Christianity had few women's rituals, certain key Christian rituals and symbols were especially important in women's spirituality in the later Middle Ages. One of these was the eucharist. And if one applies to late medieval eucharistic devotion Turner's notion of "dominant symbol," much that was before neglected or obscure becomes clear. Turner's idea of symbols as polysemic or multivocal, as including in some real sense the physiological and natural processes to which they refer as well as normative and social structural abstractions, provides a welcome escape from the way in which the eucharist and its related devotions have usually been treated by liturgists, historians of theology and literary historians.

Such historians have frequently assumed that a devotion or an experience is "explained" once its literary ancestors or theological content are found: thus, Dorothy of Montau's quite physical pregnancy (swelling) with Christ before receiving the eucharist is explained by the biblical metaphor of the good soul as Christ's mother (Mark 3.35); Margery Kempe's cuddling with Christ in bed is simply a case of an uneducated woman taking literally metaphors from the Song of Songs.[73] Turner's sense of ritual as process or drama moves us beyond this old-style history of theology or literature with its search for sources toward the new "history of spirituality" – where "spirituality" really means "lived religion" – which has been proposed recently by scholars such as André Vauchez and Lester Little.[74]

When we turn to the eucharist in particular, Turner's notion of symbol as involving in some deep way a "likeness" between the orectic (the sensory) and the abstract or normative poles of meaning redirects our attention to the fact that the communion was *food*. People were eating God. The eucharist, albeit a recapitulation of Christ's execution, was not therefore a symbol of death but of life, birth and nursing. As I have argued elsewhere, it stood for Christ's humanness and therefore for ours.[75] By eating it and, in that eating, fusing with Christ's hideous physical suffering, the Christian not so much *escaped* as *became* the human. By "saturating," as Turner puts it, the fact of eating, the eucharist itself summed up the asceticism (denial of the body, especially through fasting) and the antidualism (joy in creation and in physicality), which were part of medieval Catholicism. Not merely a mechanism of social control, a way of requiring yearly confession and therefore submission to the supervision of local clergy, the eucharist was itself both intensely feared and intensely desired. As symbol, it encapsulated two themes in late medieval devotion: an audacious sense of closeness to the divine (Christians ate Jesus!) and a deep fear of the awfulness of God (if one ate without being worthy, one ate one's own destruction!). Moreover, processual analysis helps us to see that the liturgy surrounding the eucharist was a drama. Thus, we understand that when, in the thirteenth century, elevation of the host came to replace either consecration or reception of the elements as the climax of the ritual, the entire meaning was changed. God came to be taken in through the eyes rather than the mouth; he was thus taken in most fully where ecstatic, out-of-body experiences added a deeper level of "seeing" to bodily seeing.[76]

But if Turner's notion of dominant symbol is useful in deepening any historian's understanding of this central Christian ritual, certain problems arise in seeing *women's* relationship to the eucharist in particular as processual. Turner's model would predict that, for women (excluded in theory from Church office because of social and ontological inferiority), the eucharist would express status elevation.[77] To a limited extent, this is what we find. Women occasionally – although only very occasionally – feel empowered to act in a priestly capacity by their reception of the eucharist, or see themselves (or other women) in vision as priests.[78] Gertrude of Helfta, Angela of Foligno, and Lukardis of Oberweimar, among others, receive from Christ in the eucharist the power to preach, teach and criticize, to hear confessions and pronounce absolution, to administer the eucharist to others.[79] More frequently, women's visions criticize clerical incompetence or immorality. But the women, released into another role in vision and image, never, of course, actually become priests. And such visions, exactly as Turner's model would predict, serve as much to integrate the female ecstatic into basic Christian struc-

45

tures as to liberate her from them when they fail her. In some visions, recipient is elevated above celebrant, as when the host flies away from the corrupt priest into the mouth of the deserving nun or when Christ himself brings the cup to a woman who has been forbidden to receive it exactly because of her ecstatic possession.[80] But the very fact that the majority of visions that project women into power through reversed images actually occur in the context of the eucharist ultimately only integrates the woman more fully into clerically controlled structures. In order to have visions, she must attend the liturgy, controlled by exactly that clergy which her visions might seem to bypass or criticize.

There are thus elements of status elevation ritual in women's images. But the more thoroughly one explores women's experience the more unimportant images of reversal appear to be. Indeed, unlike teenage gangs with second vice presidents or Indian untouchables who mimic high caste structures,[81] women's religious life in the later Middle Ages is strikingly without structure. The beguines, the only movement created by women for women before the modern period, were a puzzle to contemporary male chroniclers, who sought (as modern historians have continued to do) a specific founder for the movement and a specific legal status or rule or form of life characteristic of it.[82] But that which characterized the beguines (women who simply lived chastely and unostentatiously in their own houses or in groups, praying and working with their hands) was exactly *lack* of leaders, rules, detailed prescriptions for the routine of the day or for self-regulation, *lack* of any overarching governmental structures. Moreover, many of the women saints of the later Middle Ages whose lives we know in detail cannot be located within any specific religious status. Although male orders fought to define themselves and each other in sometimes very uncharitable polemic,[83] women floated from institution to institution. Later claimed by

46

the various orders as Premonstratensians, Cistercians or Franciscans, a strikingly large number of the women saints of the thirteenth and fourteenth centuries cannot really be seen as affiliated
closely with any religious house or possessing any clear status.
They were simply women in the world (in their fathers', uncles'
or husbands' houses), being religious.[84] Historians have repeatedly
argued that women's failure to create or to join orders was owing
to male oppression. In their different ways, Grundmann, Greven,
Southern and Bolton all suggest that women were quasi-religious
because male orders and supervisors would not take them on or
because the Church was not prepared to allow women to create
their own structures.[85] It may be, however, that women's rather
"structureless" religion simply continued their ordinary lives
(whose ultimate status they usually did not control), just as the
economic activity of "holy women" – weaving, embroidery, care
of the sick and small children – continued women's ordinary
work. Recent research indicates that, in some instances, women
who could have chosen the more formal life of the convent chose
the quasi-religious status instead. The loosely organized beguines
were a desired alternative.[86] In any case, if women's communities (convents or beguinages) were institutionalized liminality in
Turner's sense, that liminality was imaged as continuity with, not
as reversal of, the women's ordinary experience.

Of course, if one starts by assuming Turner's notion of "anti-
structure," one may describe this "structureless" aspect of woman's
religious life by Turner's term *communitas*. But Turner's *communitas* is the antithesis to structure: the source for it, the release from
it, the critique of it. What I am describing here is not something
that "breaks into society through the interstices of structure" but
something both simpler and more central: a normal aspect of
women's lives.[87] If one looks *with* women rather than *at* women,
women's lives are not liminal *to* women – but neither, except in

47

a very partial way, are male roles or male experiences.[88]

Medieval women, like men, chose to speak of themselves as brides, mothers and sisters of Christ. But to women this was an accepting and continuing of what they were; to men, it was reversal. Indeed, all women's central images turn out to be continuities. Equally important for women, in eucharist and in ecstasy, were images of eating and images of illness – and both eating and illness were fundamentally expressions of the woman's physicality. Told by the theological and exegetical tradition that they represented the material, the physical, the appetitive and lustful whereas men represented soul or mind, women elaborated images of self that underlined natural processes. And in these images, the woman's physical "humanness" was "saved," given meaning by joining with the human-divine Christ. Illness, self-induced or God-given, was identification with the Crucifixion; eating was consuming and being consumed by the human body that was also God. We should not be misled by modern notions of illness or of brides as images of passivity. When the woman saw herself as bride or lover, the image was deeply active and fully sensual; when the woman sought illness as fact and as metaphor, it was a fully active fusing with the death agonies of Christ. Although each of these women's symbols is complex in ways I cannot elaborate here, none is in any obvious sense either elevation or reversal.[89]

Moreover, those women mystics, like Margaret Porete (burned in 1310 for the "Free Spirit" heresy – that is, antinomianism), who seem from the standpoint of the culture as a whole an extreme case of liminality or antistructure, are really not in their own context liminal at all.[90] It is true that Margaret (like Eckhart, whom Turner loves to cite) recommends bypassing all "works," all practices and disciplines, rules and formulas, to escape to an ultimate freedom, a sort of God beyond God.[91] But one questions whether, for women, such quietism and structurelessness (which in Margaret's case are intended to be permanent!) are moments of oneness with humankind achieved as an escape from the weight of social structure and human responsibility. Is it not rather a reflection in image of the woman's own experience of the irrelevance of structure, of continuing to strive without resolution, of going beyond only by becoming what one is most deeply?

My work on late medieval religiosity thus indicates that Turner's notion of liminality, in the expanded, "metaphorical" sense which he has used for nonprimitive societies, is applicable only to men. Only men's stories are full social dramas; only men's symbols are full reversals. Women are fully liminal only to men. I do not think the problem lies in the fact that later medieval Europe is a society that presented a far greater variety of roles and possibility of choice than the society of the Ndembu, for which Turner first began to formulate his processual anthropology. If this were so, I would not find both his specific and his general insights so useful for understanding male stories. Bonaventure's view of Francis and James of Vitry's view of Mary of Oignies seem well described and deeply penetrated when scrutinized through the lens of "liminality." The problem seems rather to be that the dichotomy of structure and chaos, from which liminality or *communitas* is a release, is a special issue for elites, for those who in a special sense *are* the structures. A model that focuses on this need for release as *the* ultimate sociopsychological need may best fit the experience of elites. Indeed, in the Western tradition, such a model may, however unwittingly, arise from a particular form of Christianity that has been that of the elites. The model of Jesus as poor, naked, defenseless, suffering, tender and womanly – which was particularly popular in the later Middle Ages – was an idea that especially appealed to the lower aristocracy and the new urban, merchant class.[92] As Herbert Grundmann pointed out many years ago, the Marxists were wrong to see medieval notions of the "poor of Christ" as the revolt of either the economically disadvantaged or of women; voluntary poverty *can* be a religious response *only* to those with some wealth to renounce.[93] But, as recent liberation theology reminds us, the "suffering servant" can be a more polysemic image than most Christians are aware. There are options beyond a claim to victory and kingship on the part of the oppressed, a release into poverty and suffering on the part of the advantaged.[94] To medieval women, at any rate, Christ on the cross was not victory or humility but "humanity." And in eating and loving that "humanness" one became more fully oneself. What women's images and stories expressed most fundamentally was neither reversal nor elevation but continuity.

I would object to any effort to make my description of women's images at a particular moment in the Western tradition either universalist or prescriptive. A good deal of what seems to me irresponsible theologizing about women has been done recently, based on a superficial understanding of the history of Christianity; and certain claims about women's need for female symbols or for affectivity or for the unstructured are among the most empty and ill-informed.[95] Indeed, they may succumb to something of the same stereotype of "the female" that is built into Turner's notion of women as liminal *for men.* But my description of how actual women's stories and symbols function in the later Middle Ages does raise doubts about Turner's notion of liminality as universalist and prescriptive. Perhaps, after all, "social drama" and van Gennep's concept of liminality are less generalizable than Turner supposed and speak less fully to the complexity of human experience.

These doubts, however, throw us back exactly to the implications of the very best of the work of the early Victor Turner.

Insofar as I am arguing that we must, at least some of the time, stand *with* those whom we study, Turner has already said it. If symbols are, in fact, multivocal, condensing and lived, we will understand them only when we look *with* as well as over and beyond the participants who use them, feeling as well as knowing their dramas in their own context. My critique of Turner's theory of liminality is thus one he might have given himself.

II

The Mysticism and Asceticism

of Medieval Women:

Some Comments on the Typologies of

Max Weber and Ernst Troeltsch

Sociologists and intellectual historians interested in the thought of Max Weber and Ernst Troeltsch have not paid much attention to their characterizations of late medieval religious women. Such neglect is understandable, for neither thinker was particularly interested in the piety of the thirteenth to fifteenth centuries, even in its male variety. My examination of female mysticism and asceticism in the light of Weberian typologies may thus seem an odd exercise.[1] To the Weber experts, I may appear to chide the master for lacking sympathies and information he could not have possessed seventy years ago. To medievalists, I may seem merely to describe the obvious or to resurrect outdated perceptions and biases. Nonetheless, the process of comparing early twentieth-century insights with late twentieth-century research has produced, I would argue, something of broader significance. Troeltsch and Weber can provide medievalists with tools for describing the nature and importance of female piety in the later Middle Ages. The effort to confront Weberian sociology with new material can suggest where certain of its classifying categories and developmental theories need to be reconsidered.

As I have looked at the religiosity of medieval women through Weberian lenses, two concepts have emerged as particularly important. Troeltsch's notion of the "free groups" that are, socio-logically speaking, characteristic of mysticism and Weber's idea of asceticism as methodical conduct are surprisingly useful ana-lytical categories for understanding the a-institutional quality of thirteenth-century female religious life and the busy, engaged piety of many thirteenth- and fourteenth-century women. From Mary of Oignies to Catherine of Siena and Joan of Arc, holy women saw themselves as acting – not merely as suffering – in *imitatio Christi*; indeed, in their own view, suffering *was* acting and vice versa. Scholarly attention to medieval women's extrava-gant and self-punishing asceticism has perhaps obscured this point, although it would not have done so if readers had studied carefully the best of recent research. In any case, the characteris-tics of female religiosity from the thirteenth to the fifteenth cen-tury are worth presenting again, for – in any assessment of the transition from medieval to Reformation Europe – they need to be taken far more seriously than historians have been accustomed to do. In considering Weber and Troeltsch in the light of current knowledge, I intend less to make the obvious point that socio-logical theory and historical research are mutually fructifying than to suggest a new way of formulating, I hope without anachronis-tic misrepresentation, the active nature of women's piety in the period from 1200 to about 1420.

I shall proceed from a consideration of what Weber and Troeltsch actually said about women and religion, through an investigation of the general applicability of their categories, to some insights about the nature and periodization of women's piety. To begin with Weber's offhand remarks about women is not to consider the great sociologist at his strongest or most engaged. But it is necessary to look at the little he did say before using his typologies in ways that did not occur to him.

Weber on Women

Weber talks about religious women in the Middle Ages in only two places: a section on "the religious equality of women among disprivileged strata" and a section on "the religious status of marriage and women" – both in *Economy and Society*.[2] He makes four points that strike a late twentieth-century reader as interesting, although none is of more than passing concern to Weber himself. First, he associates women's religiosity with the sentimental, the emotional and the hysterical.[3] Second, he views women as accorded a greater role (or greater equality) by the religion of the disprivileged. By implication then he treats women as *among* the disprivileged, as outsiders. Third, he associates women's religiosity, their "distinctly feminine emotionality," with the bourgeoisie or petite bourgeoisie.[4] Fourth, he points out that the equality of women before God does not necessarily mean equality of opportunity for them in cult. Moreover, the presence of female deities or female symbols or even female cult leaders (priestesses) is also not a guarantee either of equality of participation in cult or of social equality.

All of these points are of peripheral interest to Weber, but none is trivial, and none – either substantively or methodologically – is wrong (although we would formulate them somewhat differently today). I shall take them up in order.

First, women's emotionality. This is a matter about which we do well to be careful, for assertions about women's emotionality or sentimentality often simply reflect the sexual stereotypes common in the Western tradition.[5] Nonetheless, it is true that anthropologists have documented the greater prominence of ecstasy and possession in women's religiosity all over the world.[6] Recent work on late medieval piety would, if anything, go beyond Weber in emphasizing the highly emotional tone of women's spirituality. Scholars such as the Catholic Herbert Thurston and the non-

Catholic Rudolph Bell have provided much evidence of what psychiatrists call "conversion phenomena" (what we used to call "hysteria") in women's piety.[7] All but two documented cases of full and visible stigmata are female, for example, and women account for all but two or three cases of what Bell calls "holy anorexia" (a self-starvation which is a kind of psychosomatic manipulation).[8] The sentimentality of late medieval piety, too, so often associated with Francis of Assisi, is actually to a significant extent a creation of women. Women were particularly devoted to the Holy Family, Joseph as well as Mary.[9] It was a Low Country woman, Mary of Oignies, not Francis of Assisi, who invented the Christmas crèche (and, incidentally, is perhaps the first case of stigmata). There is some evidence (and more will probably accumulate as the research is done) that many of the new devotional objects of the fourteenth and fifteenth centuries that sentimentalize the baby Jesus or the Mother–Son relationship (e.g., the pietà and the liturgical cradle) were paid for by female patrons or communities of women.[10]

Second, women and the disprivileged. This involves two vexing questions: first, the substantive question of whether women are accorded a greater role in the religion of the disprivileged and are therefore attracted to it, and, second, the methodological question of whether women should be studied primarily as outsiders. I cannot explore this issue thoroughly here, but two observations are in order.

German scholars in Weber's day and since have put forward the argument that women were attracted in disproportionate numbers to the medieval heresies because these heresies gave greater scope for female participation.[11] This argument has stimulated much controversy, and the debate is still not over. But recent research seems to show that women *were* somewhat overrepresented in these groups in their early years (although not to the extent Koch has argued).[12] Thus, on the substantive issue, Weber was not incorrect to associate women with the marginalized and the heretical. Was he, however, correct to limit his treatment of women to this issue?

A focus on women as disprivileged has been characteristic of much recent feminist scholarship.[13] It is thus accurate to say that Weber's assumptions have continued into the eighties. But there is a problem with such assumptions. A focus on women as oppressed or as outsiders obscures the extent to which women – particularly in the late Middle Ages – were the actual creators of some of the distinctive features of mainstream Christian piety. On this point, a corrective to Weber's emphasis (and to that of some recent feminists) has existed since 15 years after Weber's death. It was Herbert Grundmann in the thirties who pointed out that, if women were overrepresented in heterodox movements, they were overrepresented in orthodox ones as well, and that the women (like the men) often came from the privileged classes.[14] It seems to me that today, in both Germany and America, the most creative and thoughtful scholarship on women in religion is based more on Grundmann's sense that women's piety was at the center of late medieval developments than on Weber's (and Bücher's and Koch's) sense of women as outsiders or disprivileged. But neither sense is wrong. And the two approaches need to be integrated more than has been done.[15]

Third, women's piety as bourgeois. Weber merely suggests this; and any such sweeping characterization is likely to need modification once we look more closely at the evidence. But there is a sense in which research has corroborated the generalization. Recent books on medieval saints,[16] the relatively large amount of work on the beguines,[17] and the few studies (which badly need to be supplemented) on Italian tertiaries[18] suggest that the piety we can see as distinctively female in the fourteenth and fifteenth centuries first appeared in the areas of the medieval urban revival: the thirteenth-century Low Countries, the late thirteenth- to early fourteenth-century Rhineland, and thirteenth-, fourteenth- and fifteenth-century Italy. Moreover, it was especially attractive to the daughters and wives of merchants and the lower nobility in towns.

One caveat is necessary. As the work of Suzanne Wemple has shown,[19] aristocratic women (both lay and cloistered) played a prominent role in religion in the early and central Middle Ages. Indeed, so important were convents of high-status women, sometimes ruled by powerful abbesses who ruled adjacent houses of clerics as well, that some scholars have actually seen a comparative decline of opportunities for women in the later Middle Ages.[20] Nonetheless, I would argue that the period in which women can clearly be documented to have been the creators of new forms of piety was the later Middle Ages and that this new piety emerged in a context that can be called bourgeois.

Fourth, equality before God and inequality in cult. Here, I would merely applaud the precision and common sense of Weber's passing remarks. A good deal of recent feminist scholarship in the United States and in France has assumed that the presence of female deities or prominent female symbols in a religion correlates with cultic opportunity for women or even with improved social conditions.[21] Yet the relationship between imagery, doctrine, opportunity in cult and social situation is far more complicated than such arguments imply. The late Middle Ages saw, for example, the end of quasi-clerical roles for women and the increased power of the (male) clergy in the church. At the same time, female figures and symbols became more prominent in piety (for example, the increased devotion to the Virgin, to Mary Magdalen, to Jesus as mother). Several recent comparisons of male and female visions and devotional practices suggest that in this period men were more devoted to female figures such as the Virgin and women more devoted to the human figure of Christ. And indeed, heretical movements such as the Guglielmites in Italy and the followers of Bloemardine in the Low Countries (which revered holy women, claimed female deities, or tried to create a female clergy) may, *as movements*, have been created by men.[22] As Weber knew very well, the gender of the deity or of leaders of cult does not determine the presence or absence of either religious or social opportunities for either gender.

So much then for what Weber said about medieval women. (And Troeltsch, who elaborated Weber's thought in so many ways, said nothing at all.) Weber's few remarks are not wrong. But they are, to a considerable extent, only the throwaway observations any knowledgeable person of his generation would have made, and they are too fragmentary to be of much scholarly use today. If, however, we start with current knowledge, we can ask questions about Weberian theory and medieval women on a very different level.

Religious Women in the Later Middle Ages

Before turning to a Weberian or Troeltschian analysis of women's piety, I shall quickly describe the phenomenon. The later Middle Ages, especially the period from the late-twelfth to the mid-fourteenth century, saw a significant proliferation of opportunities for women to participate in specialized religious roles or behaviors. The number of convents, especially convents loosely affiliated with the Cistercian order, increased greatly. What we call quasi-religious statuses appeared. In other words, large numbers of women – called beguines in the north, tertiaries in the south – undertook to lead holy lives of chastity, service and labor without withdrawing from the world physically, making permanent vows or founding complex organizations. The fact that women account for over half of those called as witnesses in the canonization proceedings of saints of both sexes suggests that female influence in popular piety was increasing.[23] Moreover, even lower-class women found a kind of temporary religious status through participation in pilgrimage, especially to local shrines.[24]

In the same period, the number of female saints – that is, of women canonized or revered for their piety – also greatly increased. Recent research has demonstrated that the proportion of women among those canonized rose from less than 10 percent in the eleventh century to about 28 percent in the fifteenth.[25] At the same time, male and female styles of sanctity diverged sharply. Those men canonized or venerated were almost exclusively clerics. By about 1320 women account for 71.5 percent of the layfolk who were canonized.[26] The model of conduct offered to the Catholic laity was thus increasingly female.

Recent studies, including an exceptionally good collection edited by Dinzelbacher and Bauer that appeared in 1985,[27] agree that women's spirituality shows consistent differences from men's. Mysticism was more prominent in women's religiosity and claims to sanctity; and paramystical phenomena (such as trances, levitations, stigmata, miraculous fasting) were far more common among women. The reputations of holy women were based, far more often than men's, on charismatic authority, especially visions. Women's devotion was characterized by penitential asceticism, especially self-inflicted suffering. (For example, during a period in which women account for only 17.5 percent of the saints, they are almost 53 percent of those whose reputations for sanctity were primarily based on patient bearing of illness.[28]) Women's religious writing was in general more affective than men's, and certain devotional emphases, especially devotion to Christ's humanity and to the eucharist, were more prominent in women's words and deeds.[29]

These then are the contours of the medieval "women's movement." What happens if we try to analyze that movement in the
categories of Weber and Troeltsch? I shall begin with Troeltsch's
tripartite typology of church, sect and mystic, because Troeltsch's
treatment of the later Middle Ages is much more extensive than
Weber's own.

"Church," "Sect" and "Mystic" in the
Writings of Troeltsch

If one takes Troeltsch's terms in their most literal sense, of course,
some medieval women were in the church and some were in sects.
Some in both institutions were mystics. We learn nothing useful
from saying this. We may, however, take Troeltsch's terms as referring to three religious mentalities and ask whether the distinctive characteristics of what I have called the women's religious
movement were churchly, sectarian or mystical. If we ask the
question this way, it seems clear that the distinctive piety of
beguines, tertiaries, laywomen and nuns was neither a churchly
nor a sectarian mentality, not even if one hypothesizes that certain austere monastic movements in the Middle Ages to which
women flocked in record numbers were an expression of a sectarian mentality. But neither do pious women fit neatly under
Troeltsch's category "mystic," where at first glance they appear
to belong. I shall take up these points in order.

Women's piety is clearly not a churchly mentality, above all because it refuses the sort of compromise with the world Troeltsch
sees as lying at the heart of the social teaching of medieval Christianity. The miracles and visions of female virtuosi often implicitly undercut the sacramental power of the clergy. While both
men and women received eucharistic miracles, men's miracles
underlined the magical powers of the clergy who consecrate,
whereas women's miracles emphasized the virtue of women who

receive and sometimes implied that priests were unnecessary.[30] There were also charismatic women (although not many) who explicitly challenged clerical (even occasionally divine) authority. Lidwina of Schiedam rejected the eucharistic wafer brought by a priest and insisted that she had her own, which came directly from Christ in a vision.[31] The Flemish poet Hadewijch insisted that God himself move four souls from hell to purgatory – something supposedly theologically impossible – and she said she succeeded in her request, although she later repented of her audacity.[32] I have elsewhere cited several late medieval theologians who urged the laity in general and women in particular to moderation of religious practice, and I have argued there that women's extravagant sense of both their own abasement and their religious power was in part a theologically based rejection of these male counsels of compromise with the world.[33] Pious women refused the advice that they moderate their fasts and austerities and reach God merely through clerical mediation.

In a certain sense then, these women (both heterodox and orthodox) reflected a sectarian mentality. By implication certainly they were a voluntary group of the elect, set in opposition to the world and rejecting sacraments and clergy. By implication also they felt the law of God to be an immediate and absolute command and rejected complex stages toward God and levels of mediation between earth and heaven. But, at the same time, such a description of them is inaccurate. For all the implicit bypassing of sacraments and clergy we sometimes find in their piety, they revered priests with an extraordinary obsequiousness. Catherine of Siena called the clergy "little christs" and Dorothy of Montau – probably the best documented holy woman of the fourteenth century – was so frantic for the sacrament that she fought with her confessor over her desire to receive or at least "see" it dozens of times a day.[34] Far from rejecting the doctrine of purgatory and the cult of saints, as Troeltsch argues sectarians must,[35] these women found in the idea of substituting their suffering for that of those in purgatory an answer to their deep desire to serve their fellow Christians.

Moreover, the piety of medieval women expressed itself in no characteristic institutional form. Or, to put it more accurately, its characteristic organization was anti-institutional or a-institutional.

No matter how far women carried their reverence for the clergy, they were in some sense excluded from the church. The church from the time of the Gregorian reform *was* the clergy, and the clergy was male. Nor did the women's movement take place predominantly within monasteries or express itself in monastic institutions as the institutions of choice. Although women did flock to the new monasticism, especially the Cistercians, many whose piety was virtually identical with that of Cistercian nuns chose to remain in the world as quasi-religious, pursuing a life of prayer and handicraft or social service in the homes of fathers, husbands or friends.[36] Moreover, there is no evidence that women created sects — radical groups of the holy set apart from society and characterized by moral rigorism and apocalyptic prophecy. When women joined the existing sects — Cathars, Waldensians, Lollards or Hussites — their basic motive was probably not so much rebellion against the church as expression of the same pious concerns they expressed in the orthodox monastic and mendicant orders. Thus, the basic characteristics of women's piety cut across the lines between lay and monastic, heterodox and orthodox, churchly and sectarian. Although women were found in all institutions — church, monastery and sect — their mystical, charismatic piety seemed to express itself most comfortably in amorphous groups, such as tertiary or beguine communities, or in friendship networks within religious houses.

The amorphous, a-institutional quality of women's groups has

63

sometimes been obscured in modern accounts. Both medieval men and modern scholars have strained to identify religious women with specific institutional forms. It was male chroniclers and observers who first described the beguines and tertiaries as identifiable movements or orders. It was males who wrote rules for them and (in the case of the beguines) invented male founders. It was clergy who attempted to suppress the beguines (in the early fourteenth century) and then later restored and supported them in a more monasticized (that is, institutionalized) form. But the women themselves do not seem to have wanted elaborate organization. They merely refused to marry (a very important "merely") or, if already married, insisted on celibacy. They thereby made a small space for themselves and set about "being Christian."[37] Earlier in this century, scholars often fought over which order could claim certain female saints as members. Recent research suggests that some of these women belonged to no order; they were simply laywomen being religious.[38] After repeated scholarly assertions about the differences between beguines and tertiaries, current work accepts that they may in fact have been virtually indistinguishable in their early years, mostly because neither group had a prescribed way of life or an institutional structure.[39] Although it is true that by the late fourteenth century beguines and tertiaries had become more like monastic groups and were thought of by contemporaries as closer to clergy than to laity, in the thirteenth century those women whom we call quasi-religious were in no sense an order, nor did they have identifying institutional characteristics.

The amorphous groups in which beguines, tertiaries and laywomen often found themselves are appropriately labeled "anti-institutional" or "a-institutional," because they lacked rules, complex structures, permanent vows, hierarchical leadership roles, endowments and so on. This anti-institutional or a-institutional aspect of women's piety seems to be "mystical" in Troeltsch's sense. For Troeltsch, mysticism "is simply the insistence upon a direct inward and present religious experience";[40] it is "the belief in the direct presence of Christ in the soul through the flowing in of the spirit of Christ in the miracle-working and direct revelation of God."[41] It is individualistic; therefore it is always a rebellion against or a bypassing of ecclesiastical structures. Despite its individualism, however, Troeltsch does not argue that it has no sociological characteristics or that it "achieves fellowship incidentally."[42] Because mystics too need other people,[43] mystics tend to form "freie christliche Gruppenbildungen um religiöse Virtuosen" – study groups or intimate personal circles.[44] On this point, Troeltsch is genuinely helpful to the medievalist. The small beguine or tertiary groups of the later Middle Ages (and even the circles of like-minded mystics found within monasteries) may fairly accurately be described as such free Christian communities of *virtuosi*.

Further examination of Troeltsch's discussion of mysticism, however, reveals fundamental problems. Troeltsch mentions as mystics almost no medieval figures who would today be recognized as such,[45] and he mentions no women at all. Such scholarly neglect of women's mysticism is part of a general prejudice against all religiosity with paramystical elements that has characterized both German- and English-language scholarship almost to the present day; it is not surprising in a church historian of the early twentieth century.[46] But the problems with Troeltsch's model go deeper. Not only does he assert that the only creative mysticism is Protestant (Catholic mysticism is merely a "compensation for ecclesiastical formalism"[47]); he also asserts that mysticism is by definition ahistorical and anti-incarnational. It rejects "Christ after the flesh."[48]

It is beyond the scope of this discussion to analyze all the problems implicit in such generalizations. But I must point out that their application to history results in the verdict that many figures ordinarily understood to be the greatest Western mystics – Catherine of Siena, Teresa of Avila, Tauler, John Gerson, Julian of Norwich, Catherine of Genoa – were not mystics at all. Moreover, such typology is totally misleading when applied to female mystics. As I and many others have argued over the past ten years, women's mysticism was more historical and incarnational – more fleshly and bodily, if you will – than ordinary Christian piety.[49] The eucharist as body, flesh, meat, was a central focus of female religiosity. Paramystical phenomena were common in female (and increasingly in male) piety in the fourteenth century exactly because the fundamental religious goal was seen to be union with the physical body Christ took on in the Incarnation and daily in the mass. It thus appears that, however helpful Troeltsch's observations about the sociological implications of mysticism may be, his definition of "mysticism" as a religious type is useless for the medieval historian. According to Troeltsch's model, medieval women, including women mystics, display neither churchly, sectarian nor mystical mentality.

Weberian Categories: "World-Fleeing" versus "Innerworldly," "Asceticism" versus "Mysticism"

Weber wrote much less about medieval religion than did Troeltsch. He showed less interest in and knowledge of its phenomenological and theological characteristics. Are his categories any more useful to historians of women? Can women's piety be fitted under Weber's dichotomies of asceticism and mysticism, "world-fleeing" and "innerworldly"?

In *Economy and Society* and in the "Intermediate Reflections," Weber elaborates two sets of crisscrossing dichotomies: "asceticism" versus "mysticism,"[50] and "innerworldly" versus "world-fleeing" [*ausserweltlich, weltablehnend* or *weltflüchtig*].[51] Although in both texts he stresses asceticism and mysticism as "polar concepts"[52] – one involving *action* by people who are God's instruments, the other involving *possession* of God by his vessels – he also asserts that "in practice" the contrast can disappear: "some combination of both forms of the quest for salvation may occur."[53] If mystics remain in the world, their behavior may look very like that of ascetics; if ascetics focus their attention on destroying "creatural wickedness," their conduct comes close to that of contemplatives fleeing society.[54]

It is clearly possible to construct four types by combining Weber's two sets of terms: innerworldly asceticism (Weber's example is ascetic Protestantism), world-fleeing asceticism (Weber's example is Christian monasticism), world-fleeing mysticism (Weber's example is the mysticism of India) and innerworldly mysticism (Weber's examples are Tauler and Lutheranism). But it may be that innerworldly versus world-fleeing is a more important category of historical analysis for Weber than asceticism versus mysticism. Certainly, what interests him most in both *Economy and Society* and the "Intermediate Reflections" is the consequences of the way in which religious figures or movements turn toward or away from the world. Certainly, also – for all his interpretation of Tauler as a mystic who "completes his day's work in the world" – Weber views no late medieval figure or movement (either ascetic or mystical) as truly world-affirming.[55]

If we try then to use Weber's notions of innerworldly versus world-fleeing, and of asceticism (action directed toward the goal of discipline) versus mysticism (possession of truth) – bearing in mind that the former dichotomy may be sharper and more consequential for Weber than the latter – do we discover anything new or useful about female religious movements?

Much recent scholarship would suggest that women's piety in

the Middle Ages can be usefully considered as a contrast between world-fleeing mysticism and world-rejecting asceticism, on the one hand, and innerworldly asceticism on the other. Among the recent studies of medieval saints, two look particularly at social context and give attention to describing women.[56] These studies agree in suggesting a contrast both in institutional structures and in the emphases of piety between the north and south of Europe. They argue that northern women (here they seem to mean primarily England, France and Germany) tended to be nuns or recluses and displayed a mystical, contemplative piety with strong elements of what Weber would call world-rejecting asceticism. In contrast, they see southern women (by which they mean north Italian) as typically tertiaries involved in active charity and social service (caring for the sick, distributing food and alms, etc.). This contrast between action and contemplation utilizes categories with which medieval theorists were at home[57] and seems close to Weber's contrast between innerworldly (asceticism) and world-fleeing (mysticism and asceticism).

My own study of holy women from these same regions suggests, however, that the north/south dichotomy is misleading. Recent work has unaccountably neglected the thirteenth-century Low Country women – beguines as well as nuns – who combined extravagant world-rejection and mystical yearning with quite busy and effective charitable activity in the world. (Indeed the Flemish woman Mary of Oignies was a mendicant – far closer to the Italian male Franciscan model than the Italian nun Clare, who so desired to follow the active mendicant life and was denied the opportunity.[58]) Thus, Low Country women, by combining the supposed northern and southern forms, raise doubts both about the north/south dichotomy and about the innerworldly–active/world-fleeing–contemplative dichotomy. And the more I study the lives of thirteenth- and fourteenth-century women, the more I find that, in the women's own self-understanding, there is in general no contrast between action in the world and contemplation (or discipline) that flees the world.

Lidwina of Schiedam languished paralyzed on her bed. Catherine of Siena withdrew for several years into her bedroom and starved herself to death. Lutgard of Aywières was so afraid of human contact that she asked to have her gift of healing touch taken away. These women (and many others) afflicted their bodies in world-denial and sought, in considerable frenzy, the ecstasy of mystical union. But they all served their neighbors quite actively – Lidwina by almost constant feeding of the poor; Catherine by miraculous cures, by berating the clergy and even by dabbling in papal politics; Lutgard by the very curing she rejected and by her long fasts which propitiated God for the depredations of heretics.[59] Most medieval holy women in fact practiced what late medieval theorists called the "mixed life."[60] They carried out both charity and a meditation that issued in mystical union. But what is more important is the fact that they understood the meaning of their lives to be such a profound combination of action and contemplation that the contrast between the categories vanishes. Alice of Schaerbeke, for example, said of the gruesome course of her own death from leprosy: "Dear sister, do not grieve [for me]; and do not think that I suffer for or expiate my own sins; I suffer rather for those who are already dead and in the place of penitence [i.e., purgatory] and for the sins of the world."[61] Catherine of Genoa – the great theorist of purgatory – argued that, because human suffering can join the pool of suffering that is purgatory and the pool of suffering that is Christ's eternal sacrifice, mysticism and asceticism and charity are all finally one act.[62] Ascetic suffering *is* both union – ecstatic, glorious, pleasurable union – with the suffering Christ and (because it can substitute for others' time in purgatory) service of one's fellows. The point here is not so much that these women (like Weber's Tauler) are mystics and ascetics *in* the world as that they understand themselves as both active and receptive, both world-fleeing and world-serving.

Thus, it seems to me that medieval women, in their life-styles and in their religious writing, fall exactly between – or, better, embody both sides of – the contrasts between ascetic and mystical, world-fleeing and innerworldly. Medieval women clearly were often ecstatics, resting in glorious experiential union with divinity. A majority of the fourteenth-century examples of extravagant mystical visions and of paramystical phenomena come from women's lives. Moreover, medieval women of course practiced what Weber calls world-rejecting asceticism. It is hard to see whipping oneself, hanging oneself, burning oneself, starving oneself, as anything else.[63] Thus, in Weber's terms, medieval women combined world-rejecting asceticism with world-fleeing mysticism. But, in the final analysis, women's piety was also innerworldly asceticism – that is, asceticism turned toward the world not just to accept it but to serve it and direct it to virtue as well.[64] Pious beguines, tertiaries and laywomen did hospital work, ran childcare centers, distributed to the poor money they earned by various crafts, harangued corrupt prelates, made peace in urban feuds, and counseled those in spiritual and physical distress.

Weber wrote:

Concentration upon the active pursuit of salvation may entail a formal withdrawal from the "world": from social and psychological ties with the family, from possession of worldly goods, and from political, economic, artistic and erotic activities.... This is "world-rejecting asceticism."

On the other hand, such concentration on activities leading to salvation may require participation within the world (or more precisely within the institutions of the world but in opposition to them)

on the basis of the individual's religious commitment and his quali-
fications as the elect instrument of God. This is "innerworldly
asceticism."[65]

The laywomen, tertiaries, beguines and occasionally even the nuns
found in medieval towns cannot be located within either pole of
this dichotomy. And the inapplicability of the concepts lies not
in the fact that the specific historical case partakes of aspects of
two types (something we should expect of any specific case), but
in two other considerations. First, there was something about the
way in which women were "in the world" that was more world-
serving (perhaps even world-affirming) than Weber's categories
suggest. Second, *being* a vessel, to a medieval person, meant being
active and serving in a way Weber's understanding of mysticism
seems almost to preclude.

Let me illustrate the characteristic female combination of
ascetic and mystic, innerworldly and otherworldly, with one final
story. The late thirteenth-century Flemish saint Ida of Louvain
was the daughter of a prosperous wine merchant. In her adolescent years Ida, who later became a Cistercian nun, insisted on
receiving nothing from her family except the roof over her head
and tried to support herself (and the poor who depended on her)
by handicraft and begging. Her hagiographer tells us that, one
day, when she was returning from Vespers, she was snatched into
ecstasy in the middle of the street and, in a vision, saw Mary carrying Jesus in her arms. She fell down "as if dead" and what the
biographer calls "a great wave of corpulence" invaded her body.
At this very moment, however, a poor man was asking Ida's father
for hospitality. The hospitality was denied and the beggar, mut-
tering imprecations against the family, then made his way past
Ida in the street. At this, Ida came back to herself, went to her
father, and insisted on alms for the beggar. Only after obtaining

her request did she retire to her room, where, we are told, she "dallied in spiritual delights for thirteen days." During this time she took physical food only once, when the bread lying beside her bed began to smell unnaturally sweet. Then she snatched it up and ate it "by divine purpose, that her body, which was taking no material bread, might be strengthened during these thirteen days."[66] This little story illustrates quite clearly the extent to which asceticism (both self-denying and charitable) combines with ecstatic mysticism in the lives of holy women.

Weber, like Troeltsch, overestimated the world-fleeing implications of medieval ecstasy and self-discipline. Nonetheless, I think it would not surprise him completely to find medieval female piety described as I have done. I say this for two reasons. First, Weber argues — and it is one of his major points about East/West differences — that all Western mysticism has elements of asceticism.[67] I think this is true. But late medieval women would be far better examples of his point than Eckhart and Tauler, the examples he gives. (Indeed, among males, Bernard of Clairvaux, who actually argued explicitly that the mystic must be a conduit [i.e., an instrument] as well as a vessel [i.e., a receptacle], would be a better example than those Weber chose.[68]) I have argued above that women's piety unites action and contemplation, not only in its intentionality but also in its nature. If I am right, medieval women would provide for Weber a better example than any he actually gives of the tendency of Western mysticism to veer in an ascetic direction.

Second, I find Weber's definition of asceticism far more satisfactory — that is, far truer to what seem to me to be the basic structures of piety — than the definition normally assumed by medievalists. Studies of medieval holy people by and large treat asceticism as self-punishment or self-denial based in some kind of practical dualism (that is, a sense of matter or body as evil).

Weber, in contrast, sees discipline and method (not dualism) as being at the heart of asceticism. Again, this appears to me to be correct for the Western tradition. One of the paradoxical poles at the heart of women's piety in the fourteenth century is systematic, disciplined, determined self-manipulation with the understanding that the result of such manipulation is both beneficial to neighbor and a path to God. This sort of asceticism comes closer to what Weber meant by asceticism than to the masochism or self-torture many modern scholars assume asceticism to be.[69]

Indeed, I would modify Weber's understanding and description of medieval asceticism in only one important respect – that is, by including more integrally the charitable activity so essential to late medieval women.[70] To a far greater extent than Weber realized, women's piety can be described as innerworldly asceticism – as discipline oriented toward the world. In Weber's understanding, innerworldly asceticism really describes only Protestantism, arguably only Puritanism. Weber's interest in economic history and in the economic effects of methodical conduct led him to characterize only conduct with certain economic consequences as truly innerworldly. But it seems to me that a slightly broader definition – a definition that did not focus so narrowly toward the result that innerworldly striving might have in an economic realm invariably controlled by males – would describe very well the striving of late medieval women. These women were often, as we have seen, *in* the world. They were busily, almost obsessively, driven toward activity for neighbor. David Herlihy and Sharon Farmer have argued that we have underestimated the extent to which women were attributed force and importance as moral teachers in the late medieval family, even in the public space of the town.[71] Moreover, these women sometimes had an almost quantitative, calculating sense of the results of their pious activity. Mechtild of Magdeburg and Hadewijch both counted the number of souls they were allotted to remove from purgatory.[72] Gertrude of Helfta thought God would remove from punishment exactly as many souls as the number of crumbs into which she chewed the eucharistic bread in her mouth.[73] Despite his sensitivity to the methodical aspects of medieval asceticism, Weber failed to notice the active, busy quality of women's piety (and lay piety generally), characterized as it was by almsgiving and service of neighbor. This is probably because he did not look enough at either the nature or the consequences of kinds of "busyness" other than economic.

It thus seems that women's piety must be described with both sides of all the Weberian and Troeltschian dichotomies if it is to be described accurately. Medieval women both rejected and embraced the world, both disciplined themselves to serve their neighbors and languished beyond all consciousness of others in the inexpressible joy of union with God. Women understood the suffering that lay at the core of their lives to *be* both mystical ecstasy and active, innerworldly service of their fellow human beings.[74]

Certain of the insights of Weber and Troeltsch are thus useful to historians of medieval women. In particular, Troeltsch's idea of the free groups that are, sociologically speaking, characteristic of mysticism provides a way of describing the a-institutional aspects of beguine and tertiary communities. And Weber's understanding of asceticism as methodical conduct moves us beyond notions of medieval women as masochistic and captures the quality of busy discipline found in female piety.

The fact that sociological observations from the early twentieth century prove useful in categorizing the findings of recent research is important to me less because it shows in a general way that the writings of Weber and Troeltsch can still be relevant than because it underlines aspects of medieval religious life that need badly to be emphasized. Neglect of the disciplined and methodical aspects of female piety and of the a-institutional character of its first hundred years has led to overemphasis on its contemplative, rigid and self-punishing aspects. Such overemphasis has led in turn to attacks – both feminist and non-feminist – on the religious life of women as masochistic and pathological.[75] It is ironic that Weber and Troeltsch, neither of whom had any real interest in women's religious experience, should provide analytical categories that enable us to sum up the women's perceptions of themselves more aptly than do the standard descriptions found in many late twentieth-century historical surveys.

As Michael Goodich, John Coakley, Karen Glente and Karen Scott have recently shown, male biographies of women between 1200 and 1400 stressed sensationalist and masochistic performance, whereas women writing about themselves or about other women stressed service and the details of ordinary life in the context of cloister or beguinage, private dwelling or civic community.[76] Standard accounts of late medieval religion have yet, however, to incorporate into their descriptions of female piety women's self-understanding. I would argue that the categories of Weber and Troeltsch capture, more successfully than recent descriptions by even such excellent historians as Richard Kieckhefer and Rudolph Bell, the methodical, busy and communal aspect of female spirituality, of which medieval women themselves were acutely conscious.

We must also conclude, however, that greater attention to women's piety (and to lay piety generally) would have forced Weber and Troeltsch to change their characterizations of the later Middle Ages. Had Troeltsch considered women, it would have been far harder for him to hold up Pietism as the only significant mystical movement in the history of the Christian church.

Had Weber and Troeltsch studied religious women they would each – in different ways, to be sure – have been forced to reconsider the notion of mysticism as a passive orientation toward an impersonal divine power and to pay more attention to the theme of incarnation in the history of Christianity. Had Weber looked more closely at the charitable activity of late medieval women and layfolk generally, it would have been harder for him to represent medieval asceticism and mysticism as primarily world-fleeing.

The attempt to use Weberian and Troeltschian categories to describe late medieval piety thus reveals certain problems in the categories themselves. Although it is self-evident that no ideal type can be overturned from a historical example,[77] analysis of a series of historical cases may indicate that a type is not in fact a type at all, but only one case writ large. With two of the terms considered above, this appears to be what has happened. Troeltsch's definition of mysticism and Weber's of innerworldly asceticism are, respectively, derived from single Protestant examples. If we take these definitions literally, we must conclude that late medieval women were neither mystics nor innerworldly ascetics. Yet most scholars would today agree that the thirteenth to fifteenth centuries (not the seventeenth) saw the flowering of Christian mysticism and that women were the majority of its practitioners. Recent work has also argued that service in the world – particularly service carried out by pious women who often resided in the homes of their parents or spouses – reached new heights in the towns of the later Middle Ages. I would thus suggest that the terms "mysticism" and "innerworldly" (as Weber and Troeltsch used them) need to be rethought to a certain extent. There is nothing wrong with understanding mysticism as experiential union with "the other," nor is there a problem in defining innerworldly asceticism as methodical religious conduct in the world. Indeed, as I have shown above, these definitions are perceptive and apposite. But assuming, as Weber and Troeltsch do, that these religious phenomena have certain consequences possible only in Protestantism obscures our vision of the development of Christianity.

My final conclusion therefore is to argue that sociologists who wish to understand the massive changes in religion, society and economic life in the sixteenth century need to take the later Middle Ages more seriously. We will not understand the background to the Reformation by projecting forward into the fifteenth century either the Church of the Gregorian reform or the ethics and theology of Thomas Aquinas.[78] The fourteenth and fifteenth centuries are a separate stage in the history of Christian ideas and institutions, and to understand it we must pay serious attention to female piety. In the twelfth and thirteenth centuries, women's piety was a special case of lay piety. Increasingly in the fourteenth century, lay piety *became* female piety and as such, of course, increasingly suspect. Thus, the religiosity of medieval women, ecstatic and self-denying, yet profoundly oriented toward service *in the world*, is a distinct socioreligious type that needs to be explored as background to the Reformation.

Women remained outsiders in the later Middle Ages. As Georges Duby has shown, the three orders of medieval society describe only men.[79] In the fourteenth century, women's mysticism was repeatedly criticized and sometimes persecuted. Women's asceticism was discouraged and their begging forbidden. Women's charitable activity in the world was made more difficult as time went on, and women's forms of religious life were pressured into monasticized arrangements not all women wanted. Yet, by the fifteenth century, as Lucien Febvre argued many years ago, a highly emotional, sentimental, frantically active yet mystical piety was characteristic of many layfolk in Europe.[80] This piety began, to some extent of course, with the Franciscans,[81] but it also originated with the thirteenth-century laywomen, beguines, nuns and tertiaries of the Low Countries, the Rhineland and Italy.

Against such piety, the sixteenth-century reformers reacted in violent ways. They found the sentimentality (even eroticism) of such mysticism offensive. They felt it denigrated the majesty of God. Yet their notion that every Christian is priest and that every Christian should serve his or her fellows in the world is an extension of the innerworldly asceticism of late medieval layfolk, especially women. Thus, there may be a sense in which the piety of Europe on the eve of the Reformation was, in Reinhard Bendix's general description of historical process, the "style of life of a distinct status group" (women) that eventually became "the dominant orientation" of Christianity.[82]

The Reformation both continued and rejected the female piety of the late Middle Ages.[83] What is certain is that the relationship needs to be studied.[84] If Max Weber could be given the evidence we now have, he might well produce both a new socio-religious type to characterize the medieval women's movement and a new developmental theory to relate late medieval piety to the Reformation. Perhaps the time is ripe for sociologists to attempt a new Weberian formulation, using and modifying the categories Weber and Troeltsch defined. But, even if such a sweeping task is absent (as it appears to be) from the agenda of contemporary sociology, historians of the Middle Ages and early modern period would do well to utilize (and themselves revise) Weberian insights in treating late medieval religiosity.

III

The Body of Christ in the

Later Middle Ages:

A Reply to Leo Steinberg

Steinberg's Argument

Most of us who inhabit the Western, post-Christian world are so accustomed to pictures of the Madonna and Child or of the Holy Family that we hardly notice the details.[1] When we encounter such images in museums, on posters or on Christmas cards, we tend to respond sentimentally if at all. We note whether the baby looks like a baby or not. We are pleased if the figures appear happy and affectionate. Perhaps we even feel gratitude for the somewhat banal support of an institution – the human family – that seems worn a little thin in the modern world. But we are not shocked. Recognizing that the Incarnation is a central Christian tenet, we feel no surprise that Christian artists throughout the Western tradition should have painted God as a male baby. It takes a jolt to make us look carefully at how such artists depict family and child. I want to begin this essay with just such a jolt: the impish painting made in 1926 by the surrealist painter Max Ernst, which shows the artist himself and two contemporary surrealist poets looking through the window at an unusual scene (Figure 3.1).

This picture of Mary spanking Jesus is, of course, "anti-theology." If Jesus needs spanking or if Mary spanks unjustly, something is badly wrong between the supposedly sinless mother and her supposedly sinless son. The picture brings home to us a profound truth. Not every aspect of family life is depicted in artistic renderings of the Holy Family. There are all sorts of homely scenes within which Jesus is not located, all sorts of childish actions that are not attributed to the baby God. Immediately we realize that there are complex reasons for what *is* depicted concerning the Holy Family. It is not enough to say, as historians have sometimes said, that scenes of the Holy Family were merely opportunities for artists who wanted to draw domestic interiors, to depict bodies naturalistically or to render in paint the affection of parents and children.[2] Pictures of the Holy Family are themselves theological statements. For example, the very large number of statues and paintings in medieval and Renaissance Europe that depict the so-called Anna Selbdritt – that is, Mary's mother Anne, Mary and Mary's baby Jesus – are not merely paintings or statues of grandmothers (Figure 3.2). It is true that such representations, which are particularly common in northern Europe, present a kind of female genealogy for Christ that perhaps reflects the importance of women in late medieval conceptions of family despite the development of primogeniture.[3] But the pictures also reflect the emergence in the late Middle Ages of the doctrine of the Immaculate Conception – the claim that Mary was born of her mother Anne without the taint of original sin.[4] The sinless baby in the lap of his sinless mother who herself sits in the lap or on the arm of her own female forebear emphasizes the purity and physicality of the flesh Christ takes from Mary and the flesh Mary takes from her own mother.

The realization that not all possible human actions or settings are attributed to Christ in paint or sculpture thus leads us to realize that there is theological significance to what *is* depicted.[5] It also leads us simply to look more carefully. And when we look, we find that more has in fact been painted – and for more com-

FIGURE 3.1. Max Ernst, *The Virgin Chastising the Christ Child before Three Witnesses: André Breton, Paul Eluard and the Painter* (1926). This twentieth-century depiction of the Madonna and Child shocks viewers into recognizing what is omitted in the medieval tradition of devotion to the human Christ.

plex reasons – than we have noticed before. This point is the one that Leo Steinberg has made in his tour de force, *The Sexuality of Christ in Renaissance Art and in Modern Oblivion* (1983).[6] Bringing together a number of pictures never before considered as a group, Steinberg has shocked conventional sensibilities by showing that late medieval and Renaissance artists made the penis of the infant or the adult Christ the focal point of their depictions.

Steinberg's book has been much criticized and much admired.[7] And, as will become clear, I share both the reservations and the admiration felt by his critics. But I do not intend here so much to contribute to the debate about his book as to use it as the starting point for further exploration of late medieval notions of the body of Christ, both in literature and in iconography. Sharing with Steinberg the conviction that medieval art has theological content, I wish to point out another set of paintings and to draw a very different conclusion. I wish to call attention to artistic depictions that suggest another sex for Christ's body – depictions that suggest that Christ's flesh was sometimes seen as female, as lactating and giving birth. I also wish to argue that, whereas Steinberg must extrapolate from medieval and Renaissance texts in order to conclude that theologians emphasized Christ's penis as sexual and his sexuality as a symbol of his humanity, we do not have to extrapolate at all in order to conclude that theologians saw the wound in Christ's side as a breast and emphasized his bleeding/lactating flesh as a symbol of the "humanation" of God. Theologians did not discuss Christ as a sexual male; they did discuss Jesus as mother. First, however, I must consider Steinberg's own argument a little more carefully.

Steinberg has clearly demonstrated that late medieval and Renaissance artists called attention to the genitals of the baby Jesus. In picture after picture, we find Mary, John, Anne and other saints uncovering, admiring, pointing to or even fondling the baby's

82

·FIGURE 3.2. *Anna Selbdritt* (sixteenth century; now in the Museum of the
Catherine Convent, Utrecht). In the later Middle Ages, devotional objects
such as this figure of Jesus' grandmother, Anne, holding the Virgin and Child,
stressed the female lineage of Christ.

penis. Although Steinberg's reading of a number of pictures of the adult Christ in which he sees an actual erection under the loincloth is questionable, he has been able to show that Christ's own hands (or even Mary's) cover or point to the genitals in a number of deposition scenes or pietàs.[8] He has also shown us, without perhaps realizing their full significance, pictures in which the artist calls attention both to Christ's penis and to his mother's breast[9] and pictures in which the blood flows from Christ's own breast into his crotch.[10]

Steinberg's brilliance and courage do not stop with discovery. He also interprets these pictures in a new way, placing them in the context of Renaissance theology, particularly the extraordinary devotion in the fifteenth and sixteenth centuries to the holy foreskin and to the feast of the circumcision.[11] Arguing that theologians from Augustine to the Renaissance increasingly stressed what they called the "humanation" of God in Christ, Steinberg shows that "humanation" meant "enfleshing," and that Renaissance sermons often emphasized the bleeding of Christ's penis at the circumcision as a special proof of his true – that is, his fleshly – humanity.[12] Thus, Steinberg suggests that artists intended the genitals of Christ, especially in those few pictures that he interprets as erections, as the ultimate symbol of what Christ shares with all of us. Christ was fully male in gender and sexuality, even to the involuntary movements of his penis, and as such he represents the salvation of the totality of what we as human beings are. Christ redeems not only our physiological differences as men and women; he redeems our sexual nature (if not our sexual acts) as well. It is a noble and consequential reading of medieval art and theology and one that several recent commentators have seen as true to essential Christian doctrine.[13]

Genitality and Sexuality

I will leave aside here some of the legitimate questions critics have raised about Steinberg, such as the question of how much of the artistic attention to genitals is simply naturalism, or doubts about what certain painted folds of drapery really conceal. Rather, I wish to discuss two points that are relevant to my own topic. First, are we entitled to associate genitality with sexuality in fifteenth- and sixteenth-century art? Did medieval people immediately think of erections and sexual activity when they saw penises (as modern people apparently do)? Or, to put it another way, is Steinberg right – matters of taste aside – to call his book "the sexuality" rather than "the genitals" of Christ? Second, are there medieval or Renaissance texts that suggest this association? Did theologians of the period themselves talk of the penis as a sign of sexual activity or as a sign of maleness and associate it, as such, with the humanity of Christ?

The first is the harder question. It is impossible to prove that medieval people did not assume what we assume when we look at pictures. And we clearly see breasts and penises as erotic. But let me at least suggest that we would do well to be cautious about projecting our ways of seeing onto the artists or the viewers of the past.

Twentieth-century readers and viewers tend to eroticize the body and to define themselves by the nature of their sexuality. But did medieval viewers? For several reasons, I think we should be cautious about assuming that they did. Medieval people do not, for instance, seem to have defined themselves by sexual orientation. Despite recent writing about "gay people" in the Middle Ages, it is questionable whether anyone had such a concept. To medieval theologians, lawyers and devotional writers, there were different kinds of sexual acts – between people of different sexes, between people of the same sex, between people and animals –

and all had some kind of taint attached. But there was no clear notion of being one or the other kind of sexual being.[14]

Nor did medieval people understand as erotic or sexual a number of bodily sensations which we interpret that way. When, for example, the medieval nuns Lukardis of Oberweimar and Margaret of Faenza breathed deeply into their sisters' mouths and felt sweet delight flooding their members, they did not blush to describe this as receiving God's grace or even as receiving the eucharist. Twentieth-century readers think immediately of lesbianism.[15] When Hadewijch, the Flemish poet, described herself as embracing Christ, feeling him penetrate deep within her and losing herself in an ecstasy from which she slowly and reluctantly returned, she thought of – she *experienced* – the love of God.[16] We modern readers think of sexual arousal or orgasm, as we do when we read the account of a twelfth-century monk, Rupert of Deutz, who climbed on the altar, embraced the crucifix, and felt Christ's tongue in his mouth.[17] When Catherine of Siena spoke of the foreskin of Christ as a wedding ring, she associated that piece of bleeding flesh with the eucharistic host and saw herself appropriating the pain of Christ.[18] It is we who suspect sexual yearnings in a medieval virgin who found sex the least of the world's temptations.

There is reason to think that medieval viewers saw bared breasts (at least in painting and sculpture) not primarily as sexual but as the food with which they were iconographically associated. Dozens of late medieval pictures of the lactating Virgin place her in a grape arbor or associate her feeding breasts with other forms of offering food.[19] There is also reason to think that medieval people saw Christ's penis not primarily as a sexual organ but as the object of circumcision and therefore as the wounded, bleeding flesh with which it was associated in painting and in text. When artists painted the blood from Christ's pierced breast running sideways across his groin into his crotch (in defiance of the laws of gravity), they were assimilating the later bleeding of the Cross to the earlier bleeding of the circumcised infant (Figure 3.3).[20] Since medieval physiological theory saw all bodily fluids as reducible to blood and saw bleeding basically as purging, bleeding was an obvious symbol for cleansing or expiation, and all Christ's bleedings were assimilated.[21]

I am not here denying that religious people saw a penis when they saw Christ's penis. Moreover, as I shall demonstrate below, they sometimes saw a breast (or a womb) when they saw Christ's side (see Figure 7.6). But they probably did not associate either penis or breast primarily with sexual activity. Rather, both their writing and their art suggest that they associated penis and side with pain and blood, and therefore, astonishing as it may be to us, with salvation. For example, Catherine of Siena wrote:

[Jesus] made of his blood a drink and his flesh a food for all those who wish it. There is no other means for man to be satisfied. He can appease his hunger and thirst only in this blood.... A man can possess the whole world and not be satisfied (for the world is less than man) until blood satisfies him, for only that blood is united to the divinity.... Eight days after his birth, Christ spilled a little of it in the circumcision, but it was not enough to cover man.... Then on the cross the lance...opened his heart. The Holy Spirit tells us to have recourse to the blood....

And then the soul becomes like a drunken man; the more he drinks, the more he wants to drink; the more it bears the cross, the more it wants to bear it. And the pains are its refreshment and the tears which it has shed for the memory of the blood are its drink. And the sighs are its food.[22]

None of this is to suggest that medieval writers were unaware of what modern interpreters see as erotic elements in affective spirituality. Mystical writers as diverse as Margaret Porete, Eckhart and John Gerson were suspicious generally of affectivity, in part because of its bodily pleasures.[23] And male theologians warned repeatedly that women's mystical strivings and visions might be merely sensual "ticklings."[24] Moreover, it may be that religious women were more likely than religious men to read as encounters with God bodily occurrences that we would attribute to sexual arousal.[25] For physiological reasons, a woman's erotic (particularly autoerotic) responses are different from a man's (and less obviously genital). Nonetheless, it seems clear both that bodily stirrings frequently accompanied love of God in the later Middle Ages and that what bothered or delighted medieval people about such stirrings was not their exact physiological location, in genitals or heart, mouth or bowels.[26] What worried medieval theorists was whether the sensations were inspired or demonic – that is, whether they were sent by God or by the devil. When John Gerson wrote his famous treatise on the testing of spirits, what he feared was not that lesbianism or eroticism was veiled in the cloister, but that nuns and laywomen, even monks and laymen, might be speaking of their visions with the tongue of Satan.[27]

The Relationship of Text to Image

The above analysis leads naturally to my second, less difficult point: the question of texts. Are there medieval and Renaissance texts that see Christ's penis as a special sign of "humanation" because the penis is a male or a sexual organ? The answer appears to be that there are not. Although medieval and Renaissance theologians discuss the circumcision in dozens of different ways and repeatedly stress the enfleshing of God at the moment of the Incarnation, Steinberg has been able to find no text that treats the cut and bleeding penis of the circumcised Christ as sexual,

FIGURE 3.3. Jean Malouel (?), *Pietà* or *Lamentation of the Holy Trinity* (ca. 1400). The blood from Christ's side, flowing into his crotch, associates the side-wound received in the Crucifixion with the earlier wound of the circumcision.

no text that treats circumcision either as the cutting off of Christ's sexual urges or as a sign that his penis was pure and not in need of disciplining. In fact, the only text Steinberg has found that suggests an association of the penis with the erotic or the sexual is one Renaissance sermon in which the word used for holding the penis before circumcising it might be translated as "fondle."[28] But surely this refers not to eroticism but simply to tenderness for a baby who is about to be hurt.

It is true that medieval and Renaissance texts increasingly and movingly emphasized the humanation of God as the salvation of us all. And by "humanation" they often meant enfleshing. But the emphasis on humanation appeared earlier in European spirituality than Steinberg notes and was associated with the full range of Christ's bodily members. Growing out of a twelfth-century concern for imitating the human Christ, the theme of humanation was present in a wide variety of saints' lives and devotional texts of the thirteenth and fourteenth centuries.[29] For example, Angela of Foligno supposedly said, in words that have probably been reworked by a scholastically educated redactor:

> [The soul in this present life knows] the lesser in the greater, and the greater in the lesser, for it discovers uncreated God and "humanated" God [*Deum humanatum*], that is divinity and humanity, in Christ, united and conjoined in one person.... And sometimes...the soul receives greater delight in the lesser.... For the soul is more conformed and adapted to the lesser which it sees in Christ, the incarnate God, than it is to that which it sees in Christ, the uncreated God; because the soul is a creature who is the life of the flesh and of all the members of its body. Thus it discovers both God "humanated" and God uncreated, Christ the creator and Christ the creature, and in that Christ it discovers soul with flesh and blood and with all the members of his most sacred body. And this is why, when the human

intellect discovers, sees and knows in this mystery Christ the man and Christ-God, ordainer of the mystery, this intellect feels delight and expands in him, because it sees God "humanated" and God uncreated conformed and made like itself – because, that is, the human soul sees the soul of Christ, his eyes, his flesh, and his body. But while it looks..., it should not forget also to turn to the higher..., the divine....[30]

In Angela's piety as in that of many other fourteenth-century saints, all Christ's members – eyes, breasts, lips and so on – were seen as testimony to his humanation, and the devout soul responded to this enfleshing with all its bodily capabilities. For example, the obscure French nun Marguerite of Oingt, who swooned with love over Christ's bleeding side, received a vision in which she flowered like a tree in spring when watered by Christ, and her verdant branches were labeled with the names of the five senses.[31] It is hard to imagine a more graphic illustration of the medieval conviction that those who love Christ should respond to all of his body with all of theirs.

By the fifteenth century, theological attention was focused on the body of Christ. But theologians did not usually emphasize Christ's humanity as physiologically male. The closest they came to such an emphasis was the well-known argument that limited priestly status to men because Christ was male physiologically.[32] But even such argument frequently referred as much to the social preeminence of males (i.e., the father's rule in the family) as to their supposed physical superiority.[33]

The major context in which Christ's maleness was theologically relevant was the circumcision. But sermons on the circumcision did not discuss Christ's sexuality or his gender. In the scores of texts we have on this topic, blood is what is emphasized – blood as covenant, in part, but primarily blood as suffering. What the texts say is that the circumcision foreshadows the Crucifixion. Thus, blood is redemptive because Christ's pain gives salvific significance to what we all share with him; and what we share is not a penis. It is not even sexuality. It is the fact that we can be hurt. We suffer. Steinberg may be right that one could extrapolate from medieval art and medieval texts to the notion that Christ's coming in male flesh is a sign of sexuality and therefore of humanness. There may even be a profound modern need for such theological argument. My point is simply that the argument as such is not made in medieval or Renaissance texts. Those who preached and wrote in the fifteenth century associated humanness with the fleshliness of all bodily members and found in suffering (rather than in sexual temptation) the core of what it is to be human.

It is clear that the body of Christ was depicted as male in late medieval art. It is far from clear, however, that artists emphasized Christ's penis *as a sign of his sexuality and therefore his humanity*. Moreover, there is both iconographic and textual evidence for the argument that late medieval people sometimes saw the body of Christ as female. There is thus better evidence for the assertion that the late Middle Ages found gender reversal at the heart of Christian art and Christian worship than there is for the thesis that Renaissance artists emphasized the sexuality of Jesus. If we as modern people find Steinberg's argument more titillating and Steinberg's illustrations more fascinating than those I will consider now, this may suggest merely that there is a modern tendency to find sex more interesting than feeding, suffering or salvation. It may also suggest that, pace Huizinga, twentieth-century readers and viewers are far more literal-minded in interpreting symbols than were the artists, exegetes and devotional writers of the fifteenth and sixteenth centuries.[34]

The Body of Christ as Female in Medieval Texts

Medieval texts and medieval art saw the Church as the body of Christ. And *ecclesia* was, of course, feminine, as a noun and as an allegorical personification. Thus, Church was depicted in medieval art as a woman – sometimes as Christ's bride, sometimes as a nursing mother (Figures 3.4 and 3.5).[35]

To depict Church as a woman who is Christ's bride or as the mother of all Christians is not, of course, to make Christ's physical body female. But medieval texts went further. *Ecclesia* was identified in texts as Christ's body, not merely his spouse, and such identification led in a number of passages to discussions of Jesus as mother. The connection was clearly the notion that teachers and authorities should be nurturing; therefore Church, and Church's leaders, and Church's head himself were mothers. For example, Bernard of Clairvaux commented on Song of Songs 1.1–2 ("For your breasts are better than wine, smelling sweet of the best ointments") in a way that makes clear not only the medieval tendency to associate breasts with food (rather than sex) but also the medieval tendency to assimilate Church as Christ's spouse with Church as Christ's body. Bernard said explicitly that Christ's bride is the Church who nurses us, and that the bride-Church nurses from Christ who is also therefore a mother, and that this motherly body is all of us.[36] Following Bernard, William of St. Thierry wrote, addressing Christ:

> ...it is your breasts, O eternal Wisdom, that nourish the holy infancy of your little ones....[37]
>
> It was not the least of the chief reasons for your Incarnation that your babes in the church who still needed your milk rather than solid food...might find in you a form not unfamiliar to themselves.[38]

In this twelfth-century text, Christ's body is treated as female, as

93

FIGURE 3.4. From Honorius Augustodunensis's Commentary on the Song of Songs, Cod. lat. 4550, fol. 4, Bayerische Staatsbibliothek, Munich (twelfth century). The female allegorical figure *Humanitas* is here saved and subsumed by the bride, *Sponsa*, whom Christ, the Bridegroom, marries. *Sponsa* is often understood to symbolize both Church and Mary.

FIGURE 3.5. Giovanni Pisano (d. 1314), *Ecclesia lactans* standing over the Cardinal Virtues, detail from a pulpit in the Cathedral, Pisa. The Church was frequently depicted by medieval writers and artists as a lactating mother.

subsuming Church, and as accessible to humans of both sexes exactly in its femaleness. Similarly, the fourteenth-century theologian, mystic and ecclesiastical activist Catherine of Siena assimilated Christ and Charity (a female personification), stressed the humanation of Christ, and associated that humanation with motherhood:

> We cannot nourish others unless we nourish ourselves at the breasts of divine charity.... We must do as a little child does who wants milk. It takes the breast of its mother, applies its mouth, and by means of the flesh it draws milk. We must do the same if we would be nourished. We must attach ourselves to that breast of Christ crucified, which is the source of charity, and by means of that flesh we draw milk. The means is Christ's humanity which suffered pain, and we cannot without pain get that milk that comes from charity.[39]

One might argue, of course, that such texts are merely elaborate similes — statements that saving is like mothering or that instructing is like nurturing. Therefore, Christ's activity is like Church's activity and mother's activity, and nothing more is meant. But in the *Showings* of the greatest female theologian Julian of Norwich, as several scholars have recently pointed out, the use of the Jesus-as-mother motif is clearly more than simile.[40] It expresses a theological truth that is, Julian holds, better said in female than in male images. Julian comments explicitly that holy Church is our mother because she cares for and nurtures us and that Mary the Virgin is even more our mother because she bears Christ. But Christ is mother most of all.

> For in the same time that God joined himself to our body in the maiden's womb, he took our soul, which is sensual, and in taking it, having enclosed us all in himself, he united it to our substance.

96

In this union he was perfect man, for Christ, having joined in himself every man who will be saved, is perfect man.

So our Lady is our mother, in whom we are all enclosed and born
of her in Christ, for she who is mother of our Savior is mother of all
who are saved in our Savior; and our Savior is our true mother, in
whom we are endlessly born and out of whom we shall never come.[41]

To Julian, mothering means not only loving and feeding; it also
means creating and saving. The physiological role of the mother,
whose uterine lining provides the stuff of the fetus (according to
medieval medical theory) and whose blood becomes breast milk,
clearly underlies Julian's sense that, if gender is to be used of God
at all, Christ is mother more than father when it is a matter of
talking of the Incarnation.[42]

Such an identification of Christ's saving role with giving birth
as well as feeding is found in a number of fourteenth-century
texts, such as the following meditation by Marguerite of Oingt:

My sweet Lord...are you not my mother and more than my mother?... For when the hour of your delivery came you were placed on
the hard bed of the cross...and your nerves and all your veins were
broken. And truly it is no surprise that your veins burst when in one
day you gave birth to the whole world.[43]

The same theme is clearly suggested in miniatures that show
Church emerging from the side of Christ (Figure 3.6). In the moralized Bibles of the thirteenth and fourteenth centuries, artists
frequently drew parallels between the birth of Eve from Adam's
side and the birth of the Church from Christ's body.[44]

Late medieval theologians never forgot that Christ's person was
soul as well as body. Christ was not merely flesh. For example, a
writer as effusive (and as orthodox) as Catherine of Siena stressed

97

both the unity of Christ's person and the union of divine with human. Discussing the eucharist, Catherine attributed the following admonition to God:

> The person of the incarnate Word was penetrated and kneaded into one dough with the light of my Godhead....
>
> I have said that this body of his [that is, Christ's] is a sun. Therefore you would not be given the body without being given the blood as well; nor either the body or the blood without the soul of this Word; nor the soul or body without the divinity of me, God eternal. For the one cannot be separated from the other – just as the divine nature can nevermore be separated from the human nature, not by death or by any other thing past or present or future. So it is the whole divine being that you receive in that most gracious sacrament under that whiteness of bread.[45]

But despite issuing repeated warnings that souls must "also turn to the higher...the divine," theologians and devotional writers frequently stressed Christ's humanity (conceived of as Christ's fleshliness) and associated it with the female. Three very different strands fed into this complex association of feminine and flesh.

First, theologians drew on the long-standing analogy "spirit is to flesh as male is to female," familiar in exegesis from patristic days.[46] This dichotomy led both to Hildegard of Bingen's statement that "man represents the divinity of the Son of God and woman his humanity" and to the vision in which Elizabeth of Schönau saw Christ's humanity appear before her as a female virgin sitting on the sun.[47] It is also reflected both in the fact that Hildegard's vision of *imago mulieris* under the cross links the figure with *humanitas* as well as with *ecclesia*, and in the miniatures and texts from the later Middle Ages that show Christ marrying *humanitas* as a man marries a woman.[48]

FIGURE 3.6. Detail from a French Moralized Bible, MS 270b, fol. 6r, Bodleian Library, Oxford (ca. 1240). Using the inversion so common in medieval religious imagery, artists depicted Christ as a mother giving birth to Church on the cross, and drew a parallel to the birth of Eve from Adam's side.

Medieval writers also drew on a second strand that associated flesh and female: ancient physiological theory. This theory included two different accounts of conception.[49] According to Aristotelian theory, the mother provided the matter of the fetus and the father its life or spirit or form. Aristotelian theory clearly linked woman with the unformed physical stuff of which the fully human is made. According to Galen, two seeds (from mother and father) were necessary for conception. Galenic theory associated both male and female with the physiological stuff. But even according to Galen, the mother was the oven or vessel in which the fetus cooked, and her body fed the growing child, providing its matter as it matured. Moreover, all ancient biologists thought that the mother's blood fed the child in the womb and then, transmuted into breast milk, fed the baby outside the womb as well. Thus, blood was the basic bodily fluid and female blood was the fundamental support of human life.

Ancient theory also held that the shedding of blood purged or cleansed those who shed it. Indeed, bleeding was held to be necessary for the washing away of superfluity, so much so that physiologists spoke of males as menstruating and recommended bleeding with leeches when they did not do so. Thus, medical theory not only associated female bodies with flesh and blood; it also saw bleeding as feeding and as the purging away of excess.[50] Such medical conceptions of blood led naturally to the association of Christ's bleeding on the cross, which purges our sin in the Atonement and feeds our souls in the eucharist, with female bleeding and feeding.

A third strand of medieval ideas also linked flesh, especially Christ's flesh, with woman. This strand was the doctrine of the Virgin Birth and the emerging notion of the Immaculate Conception.[51] Whatever the respective roles of male and female in ordinary conception, Christ's body had to come from Mary

because Christ had no human father. Since theologians increasingly stressed Mary's humanity as sinless from her conception,
they were able to suggest that just as the Logos (the divinity of
Christ separate from that of God) preexisted the Incarnation, so
the humanity of Christ also preexisted the Incarnation in the sinless humanity of Mary. Such arguments could, of course, be carried to dubious theological lengths, but a thinker such as Mechtild
of Magdeburg began to make them.[52] And the entirely orthodox
idea of Mary as the flesh of Christ was suggested by William
Durandus's commentary on the mass and by the prayers of Francis
of Assisi, Suso and others, who spoke of Mary as the tabernacle,
the vessel, the container, the robe, the clothing of Christ.[53] The
notion is clearly depicted in those eucharistic tabernacles that
Mary surmounts as if she were the container,[54] and in the so-called
Vierges ouvrantes – late medieval devotional objects in which a
statue of Mary nursing her baby opens to show God inside.[55] As
Carol Purtle and Barbara Lane have demonstrated, such a concept
is also reflected in the late medieval Marian paintings in which
Mary takes on priestly characteristics. Mary is priest because it
is she who offers to ordinary mortals the saving flesh of God,
which comes most regularly and predictably in the mass.[56]

Thus, many medieval assumptions linked woman and flesh and
the body of God. Not only was Christ enfleshed with flesh from
a woman; his own flesh did womanly things: it bled, it bled food
and it gave birth. Moreover, in certain bizarre events of the late
Middle Ages, there is further support for the argument that bleeding food and giving life through flesh were seen as particularly
female activities. I allude here to the blood miracles of the thirteenth, fourteenth and fifteenth centuries.

As scholars such as James Marrow and Lionel Rothkrug have
recently shown, blood became an increasingly powerful symbol in
late medieval art and devotion.[57] But blood in this period became

more than symbol. It literally appeared, on walls and wafers, hands and faces. Blood miracles proliferated. And they took place primarily in the bodies and the experiences of women.[58] The two most astonishing new miracles of the later Middle Ages are the miracle of the bleeding host, in which consecrated eucharistic wafers turn into bleeding flesh, and the miracle of stigmata, in which the bodies of ordinary people suddenly receive and display the various wounds of Christ. Not only are almost all late medieval stigmatics women; visions and transformation miracles of the bleeding host (like all eucharistic miracles) were received mostly by women as well.[59] Stigmatic women clearly saw themselves as imitating Christ's bleeding flesh both as it hung on the cross and as it was consecrated in the wafer. Indeed, stigmata sometimes appeared as a result of taking communion.[60] Thus, it was women's bodies almost exclusively that bled as Christ bled, and this blood not only purged the woman of her sin but also saved her fellow Christians by substituting for the expiation they owed in purgatory.[61] Holy women imitated Christ in their bodies; and Christ's similar bleeding and feeding body was understood as analogous to theirs.

Iconographic Evidence

It is clear then from the many texts I have quoted that medieval writers spoke of Jesus as a mother who lactates and gives birth. They called the wound in Christ's side a breast. They saw the flesh of God as a clothing taken from Mary's flesh. Moreover, there is iconographic support for the textual tradition of Jesus as mother. When we look at late medieval painting, we find that the bleeding Christ is treated as the feeder of humankind. The wound of Christ and the breast of Mary are clearly parallel in picture after picture.

The lactating Virgin is, of course, one of the most common iconographic themes in all of Christian art. Mary's breast is linked with other kinds of feeding – with milk soup and with the grape that is a eucharistic symbol.[62] In late medieval and Counter Reformation art, Mary feeds adult males as well, especially Bernard of Clairvaux, whose lactation is depicted in dozens of paintings.[63] Mary also feeds ordinary Christians. In a number of pictures, she directs her breast toward the viewer, while the baby turns aside, thus suggesting that we share the baby's need for sustenance and that Mary offers to us the blessed food.[64]

Mary's feeding is sometimes explicitly seen as eucharistic. For example, several art historians have pointed out that van Eyck's Lucca Madonna presents Mary as the altar on which Christ sits.[65] Vessels to the right of the painting reinforce the suggestion that the artist is depicting the mass. Both baby and breast are the eucharist, presented to us. The two foods are assimilated. We the viewers are offered the bread and wine that are God. Similarly, art historians have also linked Robert Campin's Madonna and Child before a Firescreen with the eucharist (Figure 3.7). Once again, in this painting, Mary not only offers her breast; she also presents her baby, as if he were bread fresh from the oven. Mary is assimilated to Christ and celebrant.[66] Thus, we should not be surprised to find paintings that depict Mary as priest,[67] or representations of the Mystical Mill in which Mary as the miller (i.e., celebrant) pours in the flour while Christ emerges below as bread fed to the assembled prelates, who become recipients (Figure 3.8).[68]

All of these pictures are of Mary increasingly assimilated to Christ. But there are also medieval paintings that assimilate Christ to Mary. Over and over again in the fourteenth and fifteenth centuries we find representations of Christ as the one who feeds and bleeds. Squirting blood from wounds often placed high in the side, Christ fills cups for his followers just as Mary feeds her baby. Christ's body, like woman's, is depicted as food (Figure 3.9). In two very different fifteenth-century paintings, for example,

FIGURE 3.7. Robert Campin (d. 1444), *Madonna and Child before a Firescreen*.
Late medieval art emphasized Mary both as provider of food to her son
Jesus and as provider of Jesus-as-food to all Christians. The Virgin here offers
both her baby and her breast to the viewer.

FIGURE 3.8. Retable of the Mystical Mill, central panel (ca. 1440). In this Swabian painting of the eucharist, ordinary religious roles are reversed. Mary, with the assistance of the four evangelists, serves as miller or celebrant, while the assembled prelates kneel humbly below to receive the food of God.

Christ's wound is treated almost as if it were a nipple and pro-
duces in one case the wafer, in another case the blood of the
eucharist (Figures 3.10 and 3.11).[69]

In medieval experience, as in modern, it was women's bodies,
not men's, that fed with fluid from the breast. Medieval people
clearly found this fact symbolically useful, as recurrent representations of nursing Charity or of the lactating Virtues (Figures 3.5
and 3.12) attest.[70] It thus seems possible to argue that a picture
such as Quirizio of Murano's *The Savior* (Figure 3.10), which treats
Christ as a body that provides food from the breast, is an evocation (if not a depiction) of the traditional notion of Jesus as
mother. The texts on the picture (borrowed from the Song of
Songs) underline the emphasis on eating Christ's body, for they
read: "Come to me, dearly beloved friends, and eat my flesh,"
"Come to me, most beloved, in the cellar of wine and inebriate
yourself with my blood."

A number of fourteenth-, fifteenth- and sixteenth-century
paintings make the association of Christ's wound and Mary's breast
quite clear (see, for example, Figure 3.13). The parallel is more
than visual: texts on the pictures make the point explicitly. In a
painting of 1508 by Hans Holbein the Elder, for example, the
words above Christ read: "Father, see my red wounds, help men
in their need, through my bitter death." And above Mary: "Lord,
sheath thy sword that thou hast drawn, and see my breast, where
the Son has sucked."[71]

Such pictures are known to art historians as the "double intercession." They are usually glossed as an association of two sacri-
fices: Christ's bleeding and dying for us on the cross, Mary's
suffering for her baby and therefore for all sinners. But I would
like to suggest that the parallel is not merely between two sacri-
fices; it is also between two feedings. I argue this partly because,
as we have seen, Mary's breast and Jesus' wound, when treated

FIGURE 3.9. Studio of Friedrich Herlin, *Christ with Ears of Wheat and Grape Vine* (1469). In this striking illustration of the medieval conception of Christ as food, a stalk of wheat and a grapevine grow from the wounds in the Savior's feet.

independently, are seen as supplying food (Figures 3.7, 3.9, 3.10, 3.11). I also suggest such an interpretation because artists themselves sometimes indicate that it is really Mary's breast *as lactating* that is in question. In an early sixteenth-century triptych from the Low Countries, for example, not only is Mary's breast parallel to Jesus' bleeding wound (a wound which is recapitulated in the bleeding heart above), but Mary's breast is also explicitly associated with lactation through the presence at her side of Bernard of Clairvaux, who, according to legend, nursed from her (Figure 3.14).[72]

The Mixing of Genders in Religious Images and Scientific Discussion

It thus seems that medieval writers and occasionally even artists represented God's body with both feminine and masculine characteristics – something modern thinkers rarely attempt and only with considerable awkwardness and embarrassment. For all their application of male/female contrasts to organize life symbolically, medieval thinkers used gender imagery more fluidly and less literally than we do. Projecting back onto medieval symbols modern physiological theory or post-Enlightenment contrasts of nature and culture, we have tended to read medieval dichotomies too absolutely.[73] Medieval thinkers and artists, however, saw not just the body of Christ but all bodies as both male and female.

Careful reading of the theological and scientific traditions I discussed above makes it clear that theologians and natural philosophers assumed considerable mixing of the genders. From the patristic period on, those who saw the female as representing flesh while the male represented spirit wrote of real people as both. To say this is not to deny that men were seen as superior in rationality and strength. Clearly they were. But existing, particular human beings were understood as having both womanly and virile characteristics.[74] Moreover, we must never forget the emphasis on reversal that lay at the heart of the Christian tradition. According to Christ and to Paul, the first shall be last and the meek shall inherit the earth.[75] Thus, not only did devotional writers mix gender images in describing actual men and women; they also used female images to attribute an inferiority that would – exactly because it was inferior – be made superior by God. For example, male devotional writers such as Bernard, Eckhart and Gerson spoke of male mystics as fecund mothers or weak women.[76] And women mystics were even more likely to cut the terms "male" and "female" loose entirely from the social or physiological dichotomies they usually represented, speaking of mothers as administering harsh discipline or of a father God with souls in his womb.[77]

This mixing of the genders was also apparent in the scientific tradition, where in one sense it was not even clear that there *were* two sexes. Medieval natural philosophy held – as Thomas Laqueur has pointed out – that men and women are really a superior and inferior version of the same physiology. Woman's reproductive system was just man's turned inside out.[78]

Ancient biology, especially in its Aristotelian form, made the male body paradigmatic. The male was the form or quiddity of what we are as humans; what was particularly womanly was the unformed-ness, the stuff-ness or physicality, of our humanness. Such a notion identified woman with breaches in boundaries, with lack of shape or definition, with openings and exudings and spillings forth.[79] But this conception also, we should note, put men and women on a continuum. All human beings were form and matter. Women were merely less of what men were more. We can see this assumption at work in medieval discussions of specific physiological processes. For example, all human exudings – menstruation, sweating, lactation, emission of semen and

FIGURE 3.10. Quirizio of Murano (fl. 1460–1478), *The Savior*. This stunning fifteenth-century evocation of the theme of Jesus-as-mother shows a sweet-faced Christ offering the wound in his side with the lifting gesture so often used by the Virgin in offering her breast (see Figure 3.7). Angels carry banners bearing those phrases from the Song of Songs that were traditionally interpreted as referring to the eucharist. A nun of the order of Poor Clares kneels to receive the host.

FIGURE 3.11. A northwest German master, *Christ and Charity* (ca. 1470). This picture of the Eucharistic Man of Sorrows with Charity possibly depicts a vision received by Gertrude of Helfta. Although the female figure here is allegorical, both this painting and Figure 3.10 illustrate the medieval tendency to associate Christ's feeding with female recipients.

FIGURE 3.12. Fountain of the Virtues, Nürnberg. In this sixteenth-century fountain, all seven allegorical figures lactate as a symbol of the fertility of virtue; several also provide food in other ways.

FIGURE 3.13. In the style of Konrad Witz, *Man of Sorrows and Mary Intercede with God the Father* (ca. 1450). Pleading with God the Father on behalf of sinners, Mary lifts up her breast and Christ exposes his wound.

so on – were seen as bleedings; and all bleedings – lactation, menstruation, nosebleeds, hemorrhoidal bleeding and so on – were taken to be analogous. Indeed, in the case of bleeding, the physiological process, which was understood to be common to male and female bodies, functioned better (or at least more regularly) in women. Medieval writers, for example, urged men to apply leeches to their ankles when they failed to "menstruate" – that is, to purge their bodies by periodic bleeding.

Thus, to a medical writer, men's and women's bodies often did the same things. A medieval theologian, whose assumptions about the body were formed at least partly by this medical tradition, might therefore see the blood Christ shed in the circumcision and on the cross as analogous to menstrual blood or to breast milk – an analogy that seems to us, with our modern theories of glands and hormones, very farfetched. Such medieval ideas made it easy for writers and artists to fuse or interchange the genders and therefore to use both genders symbolically to talk about self and God. As mystics and theologians in the thirteenth, fourteenth and fifteenth centuries increasingly emphasized the human body of Christ, that body could be seen both as the paradigmatic male body of Aristotelian physiological theory and as the womanly, nurturing flesh that Christ's holy mother received immaculately from her female forebear.

The analysis above suggests that there is little textual support for Steinberg's argument that the artistic focus of Renaissance painters on Christ's penis was a theological statement about sexuality. There is, however, much textual and iconographic support for the argument that the flesh of Christ was seen by fifteenth-century people as both male and female. Thus, Steinberg is not wrong to argue that artists gave a new prominence to the body of Christ.

FIGURE 3.14. Goswyn van der Weyden, *Triptych of Antonius Tsgrooten* (1507). Christ offers his wound to God the Father; Mary, in a parallel gesture, offers her breast. The symbolic significance of breast as food is underlined by the presence next to her of Saint Bernard of Clairvaux, to whom (according to a popular medieval legend) she gave milk.

He has merely failed to explain the range of that bodiliness in its full complexity. To writers, painters and sculptors of the fourteenth and fifteenth centuries not only the penis, but also the eyes and breasts, even the toes, of Christ engendered extravagant emotional response.[80] Devotion poured out to Christ our brother, Christ our mother, Christ our bridegroom and Christ our friend.

Nonetheless, my examination of late medieval concepts of Christ agrees in certain ways with Steinberg's emphasis. I am arguing here *with* rather than *against* Steinberg that things are seldom what they seem, at least if the seeming is based on unexamined modern attitudes. Medieval symbols were far more complex – polysemic as anthropologists say – than modern people are aware. They were, as Steinberg tells us, rooted in theology and piety. Moreover, we can unquestionably learn from their complexity, as Steinberg has also suggested. Rather than mapping back onto medieval paintings modern dichotomies, we might find in medieval art and literature some suggestion of a symbolic richness our own lives and rituals seem to lack.

As my discussion above demonstrates, medieval artists and devotional writers did not either equate body with sexuality or reject body as evil.[81] There was a misogynist clerical tradition, to be sure.[82] But medieval piety did not dismiss flesh – even female flesh – as polluting. Rather, it saw flesh as fertile and vulnerable; and it saw enfleshing – the enfleshing of God and of us all – as the occasion for salvation.

We should therefore be wary of any modern appeals to medieval traditions that oppose male to female or equate flesh with sexuality. We should also understand that there is little basis in late medieval art or devotion for treating body as entrapment rather than opportunity, suffering as evil to be eschewed rather than promise to be redeemed. My argument then is not titillating antiquarianism. It is rather a challenge to us to think more deeply about what our basic symbols mean. There may be warrant in the Christian tradition for equating the penis with maleness and maleness with humanity, but I would argue that medieval theology at least as explicitly equates the breast with femaleness and femaleness both with the humanity of Christ and with the humanity of us all. There may be warrant in the Christian tradition for seeing the resurrection as triumph over body, but I would suggest that medieval piety (at least in the fourteenth and fifteenth centuries) speaks far more urgently of life coming from death, of significance located in body, of pain and suffering as the opportunity – even the cause – of salvation.[83] A better understanding of the medieval past might thus enable modern people to give to age-old symbols new meanings that would be in fact medieval. If we want to express the significance of Jesus in both male and female images, if we want to turn from seeing body as sexual to seeing body as generative, if we want to find symbols that give dignity and meaning to the suffering we cannot eliminate and yet fear so acutely, we can find support for doing so in the art and theology of the later Middle Ages.

IV

Women Mystics and Eucharistic

Devotion in the Thirteenth Century

Early in the thirteenth century, the hagiographer James of Vitry described thus the eucharistic piety of the beguine, Mary of Oignies:

> The holy bread strengthened her heart; the holy wine inebriated her, rejoicing her mind; the holy body fattened her; the vitalizing blood purified her by washing. And she could not bear to abstain from such solace for long. For it was the same to her to live as to eat the body of Christ, and this it was to die, to be separated from the sacrament by having for a long time to abstain.... Indeed she felt all delectation and all savor of sweetness in receiving it, not just within her soul but even in her mouth.... Sometimes she happily accepted her Lord under the appearance of a child, sometimes as a taste of honey, sometimes as a sweet smell, and sometimes in the pure and gorgeously embellished marriage bed of the heart. And when she was not able to bear any longer her thirst for the vivifying blood, sometimes after the mass was over, she would remain for a long time contemplating the empty chalice on the altar.[1]

By the next generation of Low Country beguines, we find such eucharistic fervor expressed in women's own words. The poet,

Hadewijch, writing probably in the early to mid-1220s, spoke of a vision at mass in which Christ came from the altar "in the form and clothing of a man. . . ."

> Then he gave himself to me in the shape of the sacrament, in its outward form, as the custom is; and then he gave me to drink from the chalice. . . . After that he came himself to me, took me entirely in his arms, and pressed me to him; and all my members felt his in full felicity, in accordance with the desire of my heart and my humanity. So I was outwardly satisfied and fully transported. And then, for a short while, I had the strength to bear this; but soon, after a short time, I lost that manly beauty outwardly in the sight of his form. I saw him completely come to nought and so fade and all at once dissolve that I could no longer recognize or perceive him outside me, and I could no longer distinguish him within me. Then it was to me as if we were one without difference.[2]

Throughout her poems – the first great literature in the Flemish language – runs the theme of love as eating and being eaten.[3]

Half a century later, at the other end of Europe, Margaret of Cortona – a peasant woman who had lived nine years with a lover to whom she bore a son and had then spent three long years in penance before being accepted as a Franciscan tertiary – felt a similar craving for the eucharist. In one of her many visions, Christ appeared on the cross saying that, if he could cry in heaven, he would cry that day over the corruption of preachers and prelates. "If you have perfect love," he said to Margaret, "you will not just cling to the breasts of my consolation but will weep with my pains." And Christ gave Margaret the privilege of daily communion, although her own anxiety frequently kept her from availing herself of the opportunity.[4]

At about the same time, in yet another part of Europe, the

Cistercian nun, Lukardis of Oberweimar, was visited by a fellow nun named Agnes, whose eyesight was failing and who was denied frequent communion through what Lukardis's biographer calls "the laziness of her superiors." Agnes had heard a voice telling her: "Believe, daughter, and you shall eat. And let no one put away from you the consolation of suffering for me.... Hasten to Lukardis, your sister, and join yourself thus to her so that your mouth can receive breath from hers." So Agnes hastened to Lukardis, who blew into her mouth. And, the biographer tells us,

> in that moment, [Agnes] felt in her mouth as if she had the sacrament of the host given to her by the hand of a priest. Through this, she afterwards asserted, a great savor of the sweetness of divine grace penetrated her...so that, her inner eye being illumined..., she saw openly many miraculous things worked within her sister by God. And among many other things she saw celebrated in the heart of the handmaiden of Christ the delicious banquet of God.... There, if it is permitted to say it, she knew the holy Trinity in unity of essence as if it celebrated mass.... And each [sister] saw herself in the other as if in a mirror and knew there marvelous things in the light of divine understanding.[5]

In such stories and quotations, which I could multiply by the dozens, we see reflected the most prominent, characteristically female concern in thirteenth-century religiosity: devotion to the eucharist.

The attention which thirteenth-century women paid to the eucharist has been noticed before.[6] But scholars have tended to correlate eucharistic concern either with order (particularly the Cistercians or the Dominicans), or with region (particularly the Low Countries or southern Germany), or with type of religious life (particularly nuns or recluses). If one reads widely in thirteenth-century saints' lives and spiritual treatises, however, it is glaringly obvious that laywomen, recluses, tertiaries, beguines, nuns of all orders and those women (especially common in the early thirteenth century) who wandered from one type of life to another were inspired, compelled, comforted and troubled by the eucharist to an extent found in only a few male writers of the period. In this essay I want not only to illustrate the importance of women in the development of this aspect of thirteenth-century piety, but also to explain why women's religiosity expressed itself in eucharistic devotion.

Devotion to the Eucharist: A Female Concern

The centrality of the eucharist to women and of women in the propagation of eucharistic devotion is easy to demonstrate. Women were especially prominent in the creation and spread of special devotions, such as the feast of Corpus Christi (revealed to Juliana of Cornillon and established as a result of her efforts and those of Eva of St. Martin)[7] or the devotion to the Sacred Heart (found especially in the Flemish saint, Lutgard of Aywières, and the many visions of the nuns of the Saxon monastery of Helfta).[8] Some thirteenth-century women (e.g., Ida of Nivelles and the Viennese beguine Agnes Blannbekin) made vocational decisions or changed orders out of desire to receive the eucharist more frequently.[9] Stories of people racing from church to church to attend as many masses as possible were usually told of women – for example, Hedwig of Silesia.[10] Moreover, female visions and miracles make up such a large proportion of the total number of eucharistic miracles known from the thirteenth century that the eucharistic miracle almost seems a female genre (and this despite the fact that women were less than a quarter of thirteenth-century saints).

If one uses Peter Browe's categories of eucharistic miracles, at least eight types are almost exclusively female, whereas only two types are exclusively or primarily male, and both are limited to priests.[11] Almost exclusively female are: miracles in which the recipient becomes a crystal filled with light, miracles in which the recipient distinguishes consecrated and unconsecrated hosts, miracles in which worthy and unworthy recipients and celebrants are distinguished, and miracles in which the eucharist has a special effect on the senses (smelling sweet, filling the mouth with honey, announcing its presence when hidden, etc.). Predominantly but not exclusively female are miracles in which the host or chalice changes into a beautiful baby – miracles that sometimes have highly erotic overtones for both men and women. Most striking of all, there is only one male example of the common story of the saint who lives predominantly or entirely on the eucharist. There are very few male examples of the various distribution miracles, whereby the eucharist is brought by doves or angels or soars by itself through the air; and these are mostly told of males of low status – lay brothers or altar boys. And there appears to be extant only one male example of the miracle in which Christ himself becomes the priest and offers himself as food – an act sometimes accomplished with frightening literalism, as when he tears off flesh from the palm of his hand for Adelheid of Katharinental.

Even in accounts by male authors written for male audiences, we find the eucharist and the attendant theme of the humanity of Christ associated especially with women. For example, Caesarius of Heisterbach, writing in the early thirteenth century for male novices and drawing on his own male world, in general told overwhelmingly male stories. On dying, he gives 54 stories about men, 8 about women; on the punishment of the dead, 47 male stories and 8 female; and on such topics as lust and gluttony, we find similar ratios. But we find as many cases of nuns receiving the infant Jesus in visions as of monks, more than half as many appearances of the crucifix to women as to men, and in Caesarius's section on the eucharist, where he turns from celebrant to recipient, we find an almost equal number of eucharistic miracles occurring to women and men.[12] Although male theologians in the thirteenth and fourteenth centuries wrote much on the eucharist and certain formal theological considerations of the sacrament were (like all scholastic theology) exclusively male genres, it is striking how many important treatises on the eucharist or on the closely connected theme of the humanity of Christ were addressed by men to women (for example, the works of Ruysbroeck, Richard Rolle and Henry Suso) and how many of the preachers who were important in elaborating eucharistic piety preached most often to women (for example, Guiard of Laon and Tauler).[13] It is also striking how many of the earliest texts recommending frequent communion are directed to women, since very little medieval theological injunction was so directed.[14]

With the predictable and fascinating exception of the "heretic" Margaret Porete, all thirteenth-century women who wrote at length on spiritual matters emphasize the eucharist. The eucharist is important in female saints' lives from all regions and orders; in many, the eucharist and the closely associated theme of fasting (i.e., abstaining from non-eucharistic food) provides a leitmotif that is both the major literary device tying the story together and the underlying psychological theme of the woman's life. In addition to those lives (like that of Clare of Assisi) in which eucharistic piety is one among several themes,[15] there are at least eight female lives from the Low Countries,[16] at least four from the north of Italy,[17] and dozens of vignettes from German-speaking areas[18] in which desire for the eucharist is a central theme, fasting is a major form of asceticism, and metaphors of eating, tasting, drinking, nursing – woven in part from the Song of Songs and from the Gospel of John – are central images for union with God. Two examples will suffice. In the life of Margaret of Ypres, eucharistic visions coincide with major psychological changes. A laywoman in Dominican circles who first communicated at the age of five, Margaret found in her confessor, Siger of Lille, a psychological substitute for the young man with whom she fell passionately in love at 18 (and also perhaps for the father she lost in childhood and for the curate-uncle who died in her eighteenth year). Later, unable to bear Siger's absence from the city, Margaret sought other clerics, but their support and sympathy were minimal. Finally, however, Christ came to replace all other males whom she loved and relied on – and he came in the eucharist. In the life of Ida of Louvain, dominated thematically and psychologically by the eucharist more than is any other thirteenth-century life, detestation of earthly food arose from conflict over values in her adolescent years with her wine-merchant father. (His vocation is surely no accident!) In her frenzy of self-mortification and craving for the eucharist, the girl received stigmata, which later disappeared. Ida once became frenetic over the hand of a priest holding the eucharist, stormed the altar of an empty church in an effort to wrench open a pyx, slipped (either bodily or in a vision) into the ranks of nuns while yet a novice in order to receive the eucharist, and received from the Holy See itself permission for daily communion.

Thus, the importance of the eucharist to women, in their own eyes and in the eyes of their male supporters, advisers and detractors, can be established easily. In order to understand it, however, we must look more closely at two other aspects of women's piety which their eucharistic devotion epitomized: ecstasy and *imitatio Christi*.

Eucharist and Ecstasy
To thirteenth-century women, the mass and the reception or adoration of the eucharist were closely connected with mystical

union or ecstasy, which was frequently accompanied by paramystical phenomena. To some extent, reception of Christ's body and blood was a substitute for ecstasy – a union that anyone, properly prepared by confession or contrition, could achieve. To receive was to become Christ – by eating, by devouring and being devoured. No "special effects" were necessary. In the eucharist Christ was available to the beginner as well as to the spiritually trained. This is what the German beguine Mechtild of Magdeburg means when she says:

> Yet I, least of all souls,
> Take Him in my hand,
> Eat Him and drink Him,
> And do with Him what I will!
> Why then should I trouble myself
> As to what the angels experience?[19]

Simply to eat Christ is enough; it *is* to achieve union.

For many holy women, however, the eating and the ecstasy fused; paramystical phenomena were expected. The biographer of Douceline of Marseilles, for example, tells us that the saint went into ecstasy every time she communicated. So automatic was the experience that the countess of Provence, who wanted to observe a real ecstatic, tried to manipulate Douceline into receiving communion alongside her so she could see the accompanying trance; and Douceline had to sneak off to church on the eve of feast days in order to escape the crowds that went so far as to scale the grillwork to observe her.[20] By the early fourteenth century, Agnes Blannbekin thought everyone would experience the taste of the honeycomb upon receiving the host, and Christina Ebner was puzzled by the presence at Engelthal of a nun who did *not* have visions and ecstasies.[21]

The circumstances of the celebration of the mass make such expectations understandable. Despite the efforts of canonists to establish a minimum of yearly communion and to urge more frequent reception, thirteenth-century theologians, basing themselves especially on Augustine, viewed frequent communion with ambivalence. Familiarity might breed contempt. Abstaining out of awe was equal to receiving with confidence and joy. Albert the Great, for example, argued that monthly communion was "frequent" and particularly opposed daily communion for women because of their "levity."[22] In an atmosphere where confessors and religious superiors controlled access to the eucharist and stressed scrupulous and awe-filled preparation, recipients naturally approached the altar in a spiritually and psychologically heightened state.

A number of changes in practice also contributed to the emergence of a spirituality in which eucharistic visions were expected. From the early twelfth century, the unleavened host began to be stamped with pictures of Christ rather than with simple crosses or monograms as before, and from the early thirteenth century, this host was elevated after the consecration;[23] some visions of Christ in the host can therefore be explained naturalistically. Furthermore, the canon of the mass was said silently, while those attending engaged in their individual, personal devotions. Communion was not closely connected with consecration and was frequently administered after mass. By the mid-thirteenth century the cup received in most religious orders and by the laity was the ablution cup, not the chalice, and many of the uneducated must not have understood whether or not it really contained Christ's blood. A new enthusiasm for "seeing" the host at the moment of consecration led to the practice of ringing bells to herald the elevation and, in the early fourteenth century, to displaying the consecrated host in a monstrance for reverencing.[24] All this contributed to a spirituality in which devotion and reception were separated, in which the mass was as much the occasion for inner mystical eating as for real reception of the awesome sacrament.

It is not surprising therefore that, in women's visions, the women themselves sometimes do not know whether they receive actually or mystically. Nor is it surprising that, in orders where communion was infrequent (as with Franciscan nuns or tertiaries), ecstasies come at the moment of elevation rather than of reception of the host. Eucharistic miracles could even involve knowing whether "Christ" (i.e., the consecrated host) was present on the altar, or being oneself transported, when there was no service, into the tabernacle to taste Christ.[25]

Indeed, ecstatic experiences and mystical feeding were often not merely the result of reception of communion, but a substitute for it, particularly in cases where confessors or superiors denied the woman access to the elements. Alice of Schaerbeke, denied the cup because of leprosy, was reassured by Christ in impeccable thirteenth-century theology that she received both body and blood in the host;[26] but it was far more common for Christ to provide the desired communion in a vision than to reassure the woman about its absence. When Lutgard of Aywières was required to omit frequent communion by her abbess, God saw to it that the benefit was restored.[27] When little Imelda Lambertini was denied communion because she was too young, the host flew down from heaven and hovered over her, and the priest was forced to give her the eucharist.[28] When Ida of Léau's Cistercian superiors passed legislation denying access to the cup to any nun who went out of her senses, Christ provided Ida with communion.[29] Stories of Christ as a priest bringing the host or the chalice to sick women are very common. The nuns' book of Töss describes a nun, too sick to swallow the eucharist, to whom a tablecloth descended in a vision with Christ's body on a platter; and finally a right hand appeared from heaven and gave her "our Lord" "just as if she received him from the altar."[30] Sometimes (for example, at Helfta) such visions were accompanied by exhortations to the recipients to hasten to actual confession and communion when they were able.[31] But sometimes (as in the case of Ida of Louvain or Lukardis of Oberweimar) the woman who was stricken with fainting fits, paralysis or nosebleeds at mass and experienced a "filling" by Christ, accompanied by sensations of chewing and sweetness on the tongue, *preferred* the mystical communion and had no desire afterward to receive the actual elements.[32]

Eucharistic Devotion and the Humanity of Christ

The eucharist was, however, more than an occasion for ecstasy. It was also a moment of encounter with that *humanitas Christi* which was such a prominent theme of women's spirituality. For thirteenth-century women this humanity was, above all, Christ's physicality, his corporality, his being-in-the-body-ness; Christ's humanity was Christ's body and blood.

Both in a eucharistic context and outside it, the humanity of Christ was often described as "being eaten."[33] To popular twelfth-century metaphors for union (often ultimately of Neoplatonic origin) – metaphors of light, of darkness, of wine diffused in water – women added the insistent image and experience of flesh taken into flesh. Lutgard of Aywières rejected an earthly suitor, calling him "thou food of death"; she later nursed from the breast of Christ so that afterward her own saliva was sweet to the taste, and she received Christ as a lamb who stood on her shoulders and sucked from her mouth.[34] Angela of Foligno nursed from Christ and saw him place the heads of her "sons" (the friars) into the wound in his side.[35] Anna Vorchtlin of Engelthal exclaimed, upon receiving a vision of the baby Jesus: "If I had you, I would eat you up, I love you so much!" Mechtild of Magdeburg spoke of mystical union as "eating God."[36] And Ida of Louvain was able to eat Christ almost at will by reciting John 1.14. For, whenever she spoke the words *Verbum caro factum est* – which she inserted into the Hours whenever possible – she tasted the Word on her tongue and felt flesh in her mouth; when she chewed it, it was like honey, "not [her biographer tells us] a phantasm but like any other kind of food."[37] This example makes clear to the modern reader how insistently Christ's humanity was thought of as flesh, as food (*corpus, caro, carnis*), eaten in the eucharist, a substitute for the meat many women denied themselves in long fasts. Moreover, the incorporation of self into Christ or of Christ into self was so much a matter of flesh swallowing flesh that women who were not able to eat still received and digested Christ's physicality. For example, when the host was placed on the breast of the dying Juliana Falconieri it simply sank into her body and disappeared.[38]

The humanity of Christ with which women joined in the eucharist was the physical Jesus of the manger and of Calvary. Women from all walks of life saw in the host and the chalice Christ the baby, Christ the bridegroom, Christ the tortured body on the cross. The nuns of Helfta, Töss and Engelthal, the Franciscan tertiary Angela of Foligno, the Carthusian Beatrice of Ornacieux and the beguine Mary of Oignies saw Christ as a baby in the host.[39] Agnes of Montepulciano and Margaret of Faenza became so intoxicated with the pleasure of holding the baby that they refused to give him up.[40] Ida of Louvain bathed him and played with him.[41] Tiedala of Nivelles could not rest until her spiritual friend, a monk of Villers, also received the baby at his breast.[42] Lukardis of Oberweimar, Lutgard of Aywières, Margaret of Ypres, Ida of Louvain and Marguerite of Oingt received Christ as a beautiful young man; Angela of Foligno and Adelheid Langmann married him in the eucharist.[43] (To Adelheid, he gave the host as pledge instead of a wedding ring!) Most prominent, however, was the Christ of the cross. No religious woman failed to experience Christ as wounded, bleeding and dying. Women's efforts to imitate this Christ involved *becoming* the crucified, not just patterning themselves after or expanding their compassion toward, but *fusing with*, the body on the cross. Both in fact and in imagery the *imitatio*, the fusion, was achieved in two ways: through asceticism and through eroticism.

Thirteenth-century women joined with the crucifix through physical suffering, both involuntary and voluntary − that is, through illness and through self-mortification. Ernst Benz has pointed out the special prominence of illness as a theme in women's visions and, if anything, he has underestimated its significance.[44] But the most important thing to note is that there is no sharp line between illness induced by the eucharist and illness cured by the eucharist, nor between illness and self-torture or mutilation. We see this particularly in the case of stigmata, where it is sometimes not only impossible to tell whether the wounds are inner or outer, but also impossible to tell how far the appearance is miraculous and how far it is self-induced. Horrible pain, twisting of the body, bleeding − whether inflicted by God or by oneself − were not an effort to destroy the body, *not* a punishment of physicality, not primarily an effort to shear away a source of lust, not even primarily an identification with the martyrs (although this was a subsidiary theme). Illness and asceticism were rather *imitatio Christi*, an effort to plumb the depths of Christ's humanity at the moment of his most insistent and terrifying humanness − the moment of his dying.

Mary of Oignies, in a frenzied vision of the crucifix, cut off pieces of her own flesh and buried them in the ground to keep the secret of what she had done.[45] Lukardis of Oberweimar drove the middle finger of each hand, hard as a nail, through the palm of the opposite hand, until the room rang with the sound of the hammering; and stigmata "miraculously" (says her biographer) appeared.[46] Beatrice of Ornacieux thrust a nail completely through her hands and only clear water flowed from the wound.[47] Mary of Oignies refused prayers for relief of illness; Gertrude of Helfta embraced her illness as a source of grace; Beatrice of Nazareth, who desired the torments of illness, was healed almost against her wishes; Margaret of Ypres so desired to join with Christ's suffering that she prayed for her illness to last beyond the grave.[48] Illness and asceticism are common themes in the *Nonnenbücher*, where, for example, the nuns expose themselves to bitter cold or pray to be afflicted with leprosy.[49] Even religious women who were not ill desired to identify with Christ through loneliness and persecution (for example, Mechtild of Magdeburg and Hadewijch).[50] Angela of Foligno, whose asceticism was less intense than that of some of the northern nuns, drank the scabs from lepers' wounds and found them "as sweet as communion."[51] Common ascetic practices included thrusting nettles into one's breasts, wearing hair shirts, binding one's flesh tightly with twisted ropes, enduring extreme sleep and food deprivation, performing thousands of genuflexions and praying barefoot in winter. Among the more bizarre manifestations were rolling in broken glass,[52] jumping into ovens, hanging oneself from a gibbet,[53] and praying while standing on one's head (skirts clinging, miraculously and modestly, around one's ankles).[54] The author of the nuns' book of Unterlinden, in the Alsace, wrote:

> In Advent and Lent, all the sisters, coming into the chapter house after Matins, or in some other suitable place, hack at themselves cruelly, hostilely lacerating their bodies until the blood flows, with all kinds of whips, so that the sound reverberates all over the monastery and rises to the ears of the Lord of hosts sweeter than all melody....

And she called the results of such discipline *stigmata*.[55]

Not only do illness and self-mortification fuse with each other as each fuses with the experience of the cross; suffering and ecstasy also fuse. In one of the most touching of all thirteenth-century lives, an anonymous biographer describes Alice of Schaerbeke:

> And a little after this,...as she surpassed in virtues what could be expected from the number of her years, God wished to purge her within...because she was his spouse.... And so that she would be free to rest with God alone and dally in the cubicle of her mind as in a bridal chamber and be inebriated with the sweetness of his odor..., he gave her an incurable disease, leprosy. And the first night when she was sequestered from the convent because of the fear of contagion, she was afflicted with such sadness her heart was wounded.... [So she cried and prayed at God's feet].... And when she had learned from what she experienced to take refuge in the most secure harbor of God, she ran to Christ's breasts and wounds, in every tribulation or anguish, every depression or dryness, like a little child drinking from its mother's breasts, and by that liquid she felt her members restored.[56]

Thus, the most feared of all diseases becomes a bridal bed, wounds are the source of a mother's milk; the physicality into which the woman sinks is unspeakable suffering and unspeakable joy.[57]

Physical union with Christ is thus described not only in images of disease and torment but also in images of marriage and sexual consummation; it sometimes culminates in what appears to be orgasm – as in Hadewijch's beautiful vision quoted above.[58] Although scholars have, of course, suggested that such reactions are sublimated sexual desire, it seems inappropriate to speak of "sublimation." In the eucharist and in ecstasy, a male Christ was handled and loved; sexual feelings were, as certain contemporary commentators (like David of Augsburg) clearly realized, not so much translated into another medium as simply set free.[59]

Asceticism and eroticism sometimes fused so completely that it is hard to know under which category to place a mystic like Ida of Louvain, who went mad from desire for the eucharist and had to be put in chains, or Beatrice of Nazareth, who consulted a spiritual adviser to find out whether God would sanction her effort to drive herself literally "crazy" as a way of "following" him.[60] We misunderstand the power of the erotic, nuptial mysticism of Low Country figures like Hadewijch and Beatrice of Nazareth if we project onto their image of lover seeking Lover stereotyped notions of brides as passive and submissive. Their search for Christ took them through a frenzy they called insanity (*orewoet* in Flemish, *aestus* or *insania amoris* in Latin).

Erotic imagery is unimportant in some women's writing. And nuptial language is often most elaborate in *male* biographers, who may have had their own reasons for describing women they admired and loved in erotic metaphors. But the image of bride or lover was clearly a central metaphor for the woman mystic's union with Christ's humanity. In the twelfth century, Hildegard of Bingen actually dressed her nuns as brides when they went forward to receive communion.[61] And Hadewijch and Mechtild of Magdeburg, women given voice by the emergence of the vernaculars, found in secular love poetry the vocabulary and the pulsating rhythms to speak of the highest of all loves.

Ecstasy and the Power of the Recipient
Women's devotion to the body and blood of Christ was thus an affirmation of the religious significance of physicality and emotionality. The eucharist was, to medieval women, a moment at which they were released into ecstatic union; it was also a

moment at which the God with whom they joined was supremely human because supremely vulnerable and fleshly. But why were these aspects of the eucharist so central to female piety? Why did ecstasy and *humanitas Christi* matter so much to women?

Part of the answer seems to be that women's ecstasy or possession served as an alternative to the authority of priestly office. From the time of the Gregorian reform of the late eleventh century, theology and spirituality increasingly stressed priesthood and preaching as the way of imitating Christ. By the thirteenth century the priest, momentarily divinized by the Christ whom he held in his hands at the consecration, and the friar, imitating the life of Jesus in poverty, begging, penance and preaching, were the admired male roles. Increasingly prohibited from even minor "clerical" tasks (such as veiling nuns or touching altar vessels) and never permitted full evangelical poverty or wandering, women emerged – in their own eyes and in the eyes of their male advisers – as what I have elsewhere called a "prophetic" or "charismatic" alternative.[62] Thus, the eucharist and the paramystical phenomena that often accompanied it were substitutes for priesthood in two complementary senses. First, eucharistic ecstasy was a means by which women claimed "clerical" power for themselves, or bypassed the power of males, or criticized male abuse of priestly authority. Second, ecstasy was a means of endowing women's nonclerical status – their status as lay recipients – with special spiritual significance.

In the visions that women received at mass, they sometimes acquired metaphorical priesthood. I have discussed elsewhere the fact that women's visions sometimes gave them general authorization to prophesy and teach and hear confessions.[63] What should be noted here is that eucharistic visions occasionally projected women, in metaphor and vision, into access to the altar, even into the role of celebrant – things strictly forbidden to them. For example, a woman who had loved Juliana of Cornillon very much in her life saw her after death at mass, assisting the priest.[64] Angela of Foligno, feeling that the celebrant was unworthy, had a vision of Christ bleeding on the cross and angels said to her: "Oh you who are pleasing to God, behold, he has been administered to you...in order that you may administer and present him to others."[65] Benevenuta of Bojano saw the Virgin administering the chalice in a vision.[66] And, in addition to the infrequent visions in which women actually see themselves or other women as priests or acolytes, there are hundreds of visions in which Christ himself gives the chalice or the host to a nun or beguine or laywoman who is unable to receive, either because of illness or because the clergy prevent it.[67]

Moreover, criticism of corrupt clergy was – in the eyes of both women and men – the special role of religious women; and female eucharistic miracles were a favorite vehicle for this. Margaret of Cortona, Mary of Oignies and Ida of Louvain, among others, knew miraculously when celebrants were unworthy, particularly unchaste.[68] Mechtild of Magdeburg, who did not scruple to hurl abusive epithets at local canons and friars, saw visions in which hell and the lower circles of purgatory were populated entirely by men (with the important exception of princesses – presumably, to Mechtild, the only powerful and therefore dangerous female role).[69] Although the function of pointing out uncomfortable truths to society was sometimes seen as possession by demons rather than an inspiration by Christ, all agreed that – whether demonic or divine – such criticism was particularly female.[70]

But women's ecstatic eucharistic devotion was not merely a bypassing or criticizing of priests, nor was it primarily a claim to charismatic authority that competed with or substituted for priesthood. Women's devotion to the mass and the eucharistic elements was also an endowing of their role as "nonpriests" with a new spiritual importance. In a recent study of canonization, André Vauchez has shown that women were 50 percent of the laity canonized in the thirteenth century and 71.4 percent after 1305. By the later Middle Ages, the male saint was usually a cleric or a friar; the ideal layperson was female.[71] As representative laity, women were quintessentially recipients. It is thus not surprising that almost all thirteenth-century eucharistic miracles of recipients are female miracles. And it is significant that the occasional male who receives directly from Christ or angels or doves — that is, whose act of *receiving* is given special recognition — is not a priest, but a layman. Both men and women seem to have seen the religious roles of men and women as different. Women's eucharistic devotion was the devotion of those who receive *rather than* consecrate, those who are lay *rather than* clergy, those whose closeness to God and whose authorization to serve others come through intimacy and direct inspiration *rather than* through office or worldly power.

There is no question that this aspect of thirteenth-century religious women was particularly stressed by men, that it was men in particular who saw women as an alternative to and a criticism of wealth, power and office. Woman, both as symbol and as fact, was "liminal" to man in the technical sense given the term by Victor Turner.[72] In her visions and her devotions, woman — particularly the mystical bride of Christ — was the point where the powerful male found a reversal and a critique of exactly those things about which he felt greatest ambivalence. In saints' lives from the twelfth to the fifteenth century, women receive striking political visions for the assistance of men. Hildegard of Bingen, Elizabeth of Schönau, Mary of Oignies, Lutgard of Aywières, Elizabeth of Hungary, Catherine of Siena, Birgitta of Sweden and Joan of Arc are the most obvious examples. But less well-known figures, like Christina of Markyate in the twelfth century,

Mechtild of Magdeburg, Douceline of Marseilles and Margaret of Faenza in the thirteenth, also advised counts and kings on politics and war.[73] Thirteenth-century heretical groups such as the Guglielmites in Italy, who tried to set up a female church may, as heresies, have been male creations.[74] The offering of comfort and spiritual advice to powerful males, burdened and tempted by responsibility for the world, is a theme in many lives of women mystics written by their confessors and supporters. James of Vitry and Thomas of Cantimpré speak of the women whose stories they chronicle as "mothers" to clerics and actually see them as "preaching" *through* inspiring men. The biographers of Angela of Foligno and Margaret of Cortona see them as spiritual mothers who have only "sons" (the Franciscan friars).

But if certain aspects of woman's role as alternative and recipient are male emphases, there are also ways in which women viewed themselves as recipients. Thirteenth-century women clearly saw themselves as "not priests." Both Juliana of Cornillon and Mechtild of Magdeburg, inspired by God to lead and to criticize, suggested that he should send clerics instead; they both, however, came to accept their prophetic and visionary role as an alternative.[75] Gertrude of Helfta, tougher in her self-image, envied priests their ability to handle God but pointed out that it might be more dangerous than useful to their own spiritual state.[76] Already in the twelfth century, the theologian Hildegard of Bingen explained the different and fully complementary contributions of men and women both to human reproduction and to worship.[77]

Moreover, women saw receiving as serving. As the doctrine of "vicarious communion" – that is, the notion that one person could receive communion for another – was developed in the thirteenth century, monasteries of women were especially attracted to it. Although male theologians expressed the doctrine in clerical form, arguing that the priest is the "mouth" of the Church, women asserted the possibility of offering up *their* communions for others. A beguine in Strasbourg in 1317 argued that the communion of a layperson would profit as much for the redemption of a departed soul as the mass of a priest.[78] In a final and peculiar extrapolation of this notion of service, Alice of Schaerbeke was assured by Christ that her suffering, including her suffering at the *loss* of communion, released souls from purgatory.[79]

Women's visions sometimes even elevated the status of recipient above that of priest. Juliana of Cornillon advised a priest to be a recipient.[80] Agnes Blannbekin saw the eucharist depart from a corrupt priest and fly into her own mouth.[81] Ida of Louvain, who had been criticized by the chaplain to her convent, miraculously received the host while he celebrated, unaware of her presence. Moreover, on the following day she again miraculously received the sacrament during a mass at which "no one was usually admitted to receive the host with the exception only of the minister who celebrated."[82] In this case the alliance of Christ and recipient not only bypassed but also directly challenged the authority of the priest and the monastic discipline.

The Psychological and Social Context

Eucharistic ecstasy was not, however, merely a response to the clericalization of the Church, to a pattern of religiosity in which holy men were clerics and holy laypeople were women. Women's devotion to the body and blood of Christ was also a response to their social and psychological experience.

A few decades ago, female mysticism was frequently seen as an expression of psychological deprivation or outright pathology.[83] I have no interest in reducing the phenomena I have been describing to abnormal (or even normal) psychology. But one element, which is specifically relevant to eucharistic devotion, must be mentioned. There are clearly, in some medieval women, behavior patterns that parallel what modern psychologists call "anorexia nervosa" – an inability to tolerate food, which leads to self-starvation (usually in adolescent girls) and which has in our own day been given powerful spiritual significance in the life and writings of Simone Weil.[84] Anorexia nervosa typically involves insomnia, hyperactivity, grossly distorted sense perception and suppression of menstruation. Anorectics focus obsessively on food, which is, to them, a symbol both of physicality and of control. Obsession with food – either through binge eating or through intense fasting – is often triggered by the nagging awareness of corporality evidenced by the onset of menstruation. Refusal to eat is a way of asserting power over a body that appears to have slipped away from control into painful or embarrassing excretions, and over a family or a society that is rushing the girl headlong into an adult female role she does not choose – one that promises less freedom than did childhood. Although one should not say that medieval women suffered from anorexia nervosa (or, for that matter, from hysteria or depression – since any such syndrome must be part of a particular culture and should not per se be transferred across cultures), medieval women do show striking parallels to the modern syndrome – parallels that suggest psychological and social reasons for the fact that eating and not-eating are more central images in women's lives than in men's.

All medieval miracles of surviving on the eucharist alone are female miracles (with one exception). Most are told of adolescent girls.[85] In addition, fasting is a more common practice among female ascetics, and visions and miracles having to do with food are also more common among women. Miracles in which special sensations (especially sweet taste) accompany the eucharist are almost exclusively female; so are miracles in which consecrated and unconsecrated hosts are distinguished.[86] And there is no question that, in some female mystics, disgust at all non-eucharistic food becomes an involuntary physiological reaction. The vomiting out of unconsecrated hosts, for example, was sometimes part of a general revulsion at food, especially meat. Moreover, refusal to eat ordinary food was often accompanied, as it is in modern anorectics, by frenetic attention to feeding others. Women saints, who fasted themselves, frequently multiplied loaves and fishes for their adherents.

Such reactions to food are found especially in religious women who experienced puberty in the world and whose conflict with family over vocation was intense. Mary of Oignies, married at fourteen, moved immediately to extreme fasting. The memory of having eaten a bit of meat after an illness precipitated the vision during which she cut off her own flesh with a knife.[87] Ida of Louvain's adolescent conflict with her father led to bodily mortification and stigmata.[88] Christina *Mirabilis*, a laywoman of origins so humble she had nothing to renounce for God except food, fled into the desert in adolescence to fast; but (says her biographer) "no matter how subtle her body," she still needed some nourishment, so God filled her "dry virgin breasts" with milk and she nursed herself.[89] Juliana of Cornillon as a young child was forbidden by her nurse to fast as much as she liked; later in life she found it very difficult to eat and literally could not swallow what she chewed until after Vespers.[90] A century later, Catherine of Siena, after protracted conflict over vocation with her family, became unable to eat anything except the eucharist. Ordered by Christ to join her family at table and taste something, she afterward rammed twigs down her throat to bring up the food she could not bear in her stomach.[91]

For such cases it is easy to give psychosocial explanations. It is not surprising that women, who often could not control the disposition of their own bodies against the wishes of family or religious advisers, voluntarily or involuntarily punished those bodies at moments of life-crisis. Nor is it surprising that, since women were usually not able to renounce property (either because, like Christina *Mirabilis*, they possessed none to renounce or because medieval mores did not permit even religious women to beg), they chose to renounce food, the one pleasure they not only fully controlled but were also chiefly responsible *by role* for preparing for all of society.[92] As in modern anorexia, "control" was a basic issue to medieval women who adopted relentless fasting as a kind of self-definition.

But if food was sometimes a symbol of self and of the world, invoked at moments of decision or conflict, the fasting and nausea of medieval women were not simply world rejection, nor were they simply control of self substituted for control of circumstance. Angela of Foligno, desiring to punish herself for hypocritical piety, wanted to parade through the streets with rotting fish and meat tied around her neck; she described herself as tempted by the devil to give up eating entirely. Later, she came to see these reactions as pathological and found the eucharist to taste like especially delicious meat.[93] Thus, not-eating was complemented by holy eating. Food was filth; it was also God. The woman's revulsion at her own body, even when it took what appeared to her and her contemporaries to be bizarre forms, was given a theological significance more complex than dualism. The peasant saint Alpaïs of Cudot did not, after all, die of "anorexia." She survived for forty years on the eucharist and became a living proof of the efficacy of the sacrament.[94] The point of even the oddest of these stories was ultimately not rejection of the physical and bodily, but a finding of the truly physical, the truly nourishing, the truly fleshly, in the humanity of Christ, chewed and swallowed in the eucharist. Even here, physicality was not so much rooted out or suppressed as embraced and redeemed *at that point* where

it intersected with the divine. So, in addition to the psychological and social explanations I have just given, there are theological
and religious reasons for women's spirituality.

Opposition to Dualism and Imitatio Christi

If we look at the thirteenth-century theological context, it is clear
that women's concern with matter, with physicality, with imitation of the human Christ, must be located against the background of the war against heresy. Controversy over the eucharist
reemerged after centuries of silence in the late eleventh century;
and twelfth-century theologians themselves (for example, Hildegard of Bingen) saw denial of the eucharist as one of heresy's major
threats.[95] Modern scholars have frequently argued that the central theological purpose behind the proliferating eucharistic miracles was support for the doctrine of transubstantiation. Recent
historians have also suggested that thirteenth-century eucharistic
devotion was part of the general effort of theology and spirituality to propose an alternative to Cathar dualism.[96] We can see such
motives reflected, for example, in the writings of James of Vitry
and Thomas of Cantimpré, who held up women saints, with their
concentration on Christ's body and blood, as a counter to the
Cathar view that the physical world is the creation of an evil
God.[97] The cardinal legate who helped Juliana of Cornillon propa-
gate the feast of Corpus Christi supported it explicitly as a weapon
against dualism.[98] Furthermore, it seems clear that confessors
urged women toward eucharistic piety in an effort to keep their
devotional life not only orthodox but also firmly under ecclesiastical control.

We must, however, look beyond any conscious effort to prop-
agandize against the Cathars if we are to understand the extent
to which thirteenth-century spirituality is a response to the threat
of dualism. Indeed, it is possible to argue that the theme of the

143

positive religious significance of physicality runs throughout thirteenth-century theology. For example, the piety of the mendicants – the Church's army of preachers against dualist heresy – was permeated by attention to the fact of physicality, both in a newly intense asceticism and in an interpretation of all creation as the footprints of God. Moreover, one of the most important of thirteenth-century philosophical formulations, Thomas Aquinas's statement of the hylomorphic composition of the human person, is a new effort to come to terms with matter. Most fundamentally, that doctrine says that what the person *is* – the existing substance *homo* – is form and matter, soul and body. To Aquinas, the person is his or her body, not just a soul using a body; and the resurrection of the body becomes, for the first time, not merely theologically but also philosophically necessary. Usually not directly in touch with abstract theological or philosophical speculation, women nonetheless evidenced in their visions this general antidualist stance. The author of the nuns' book of Unterlinden commented that *homo* (our humanness) really includes all creatures. Marguerite of Oingt saw Christ's humanity as a clear mirror in which is reflected all the beauty of creation. Gherardesca of Pisa worshiped God's glory in a piece of straw.[99] Mechtild of Hackeborn saw a vision of the celebrating priest in which his vestments were covered with every twig and hair of the flora and fauna of the universe. And as she looked in surprise she saw that "the smallest details of creation are reflected in the Holy Trinity by means of the humanity of Christ, because it is from the same earth that produced them that Christ drew his humanity."[100]

In fact, eucharistic practice as reflected in art and architecture underlines the extent to which reverence for the host was reverence for the divine *in the material*. Not only did the thirteenth century see the growth of the practice of reserving the host in pyxes or tabernacles; the eucharist was also sometimes reserved in a reliquary, mobile tabernacles were modeled on reliquaries, and pyxes were sometimes displayed alongside reliquaries. The practice of burning candles or lamps before the host was borrowed from the manner in which relics were revered. Thus, the host was clearly treated as a relic of Christ; tabernacles were thrones or tombs for Christ's body. And it is interesting to note that our earliest evidence for visits to the reserved host seen as a relic of Christ, a fragment of his physicality, comes from an English rule for female recluses and from the life of Mary of Oignies.[101]

Changes in the twelfth-century notion of *imitatio* also lie behind women's eucharistic devotion. Scholars have stressed that the twelfth-century search for the *vita apostolica* was a search for perfect poverty; somewhere in the course of the century (in a by-no-means unidirectional development), the apostolic life came to mean preaching. What scholars have failed to underline, however, is the extent to which imitation – of the martyrs, of the apostles and of Christ – became more and more literal.[102] Thus, by the late twelfth century, *imitatio* had moved far beyond the Cistercian notion of affective meditation. Whereas Bernard of Clairvaux taught that we identify with Christ by extending our compassion to his humanity through pitying the suffering humanity of our neighbors, Francis and Mary of Oignies *became* Christ on the cross while a seraph looked on.[103] Indeed some male descriptions of holy women explicitly stress that *imitatio* is fact, not memory or imagination. We are told, for example, that Margaret of Cortona and Lukardis of Oberweimar became one with the Crucifixion *rather than* simply remembering or pitying Christ's suffering.[104] Margaret of Ypres's extreme self-flagellation as a means of joining with Christ was called a *recordatio* (remembrance); but in such a passage the very meaning of the word "remember" has changed.[105] Beatrice of Nazareth, more theologically sophisticated than many of her fellow women mystics, spoke of the three grades of moving toward Christ: turning toward grace; growing in the memory of Christ's passion; and, finally, inhering in Jesus.[106]

This sense of *imitatio* as *becoming* or *being* lies in the background of women's eucharistic devotion. The eucharist is an especially appropriate vehicle for the effort to become Christ because the eucharist *is* Christ. The fact of transubstantiation is crucial. One *becomes* Christ's crucified body in *eating* Christ's crucified body. Thus, reception of the eucharist leads so naturally to stigmata, visibly or inwardly, that contemporaries hardly worried about how to account for their appearance. *Imitatio* is incorporation of flesh into flesh. Both priest and recipient are literally pregnant with Christ. The metaphor of the good soul as Christ's mother, which had a long lineage, became in the thirteenth century more than metaphor.[107] Caesarius of Heisterbach described a priest who swelled up at the consecration, pregnant with Christ. Ida of Louvain swelled with the eucharist. By the fourteenth century, Dorothy of Montau repeatedly experienced mystical pregnancy and was almost required by her confessor to exhibit it as part of her preparation for communion.[108]

Women and Physicality in the Theological Tradition

Concern with the literal following of Jesus, with the problem and the opportunity of physicality, was thus a basic theme in thirteenth-century religiosity. But it was reflected and espoused especially intensely in women's lives and in women's writing. For this, there are specific theological reasons. To put it simply, the weight of the Western tradition had long told women that physicality was particularly their problem.

Some modern commentators have made much of the fact that certain patristic figures argued that woman *qua* woman was not created in God's image, although woman *qua* human being was.[109]

This is a complex point – and certainly in thirteenth-century legal and theological writing it was often interpreted as referring to woman's social role (namely, her subordination to man in the family) more than to her anatomical nature or biological role.[110] But in any case it was not absorbed by late medieval women (even married women) as a prohibition of their approach to God, their imitation of Christ. Their writing is full of references to being created in God's image and likeness.[111]

Women were also told that, allegorically speaking, woman was to man what matter is to spirit – that is, that they symbolized the physical, lustful, material, appetitive part of human nature, whereas man symbolized the spiritual or mental. The roots of this idea were multiple, scientific as well as theological; and it did unquestionably influence women writers. The first great woman theologian, Hildegard of Bingen, knew the tradition, and indeed argued against some of its implications.[112] Women do not, however, seem to have drawn from such teaching a debilitating sense of female incapacity. Most of the references to womanly weakness in thirteenth-century spiritual writing come from the pens of male biographers. These biographers occasionally compliment women saints on their "virility."[113] But women writers by and large either ignore their own sex, using mixed-gender imagery for the self (as did Gertrude the Great and Hadewijch),[114] or embrace their femaleness as a sign of closeness to Christ. Where they do refer to female weakness, the reference is often, as Peter Dronke has argued, an ironic comment on male failure to achieve even the level of virtue of "weak women."[115] If anything, women drew from the traditional notion of the female as physical a special emphasis on their own redemption by a Christ who was supremely physical because supremely human. They sometimes even extrapolated from this to the notion that, in Christ, divinity is to humanity as male is to female.[116]

As I have explained elsewhere, such an idea did not imply that the human Christ was a body without a soul (a clearly heretical Christological position), nor did it deny Christ's divinity.[117] But as spirituality in general came increasingly to stress Christ's humanity as manifested in his physicality, women – who were the special symbol of the physical – suggested that that physical, tangible humanity might be symbolized or understood as female. And the doctrine of the Virgin Birth contributed to this. One could argue that all of Christ's humanity had to come from Mary because Christ had no human father. So in some sense Mary could be seen as adding humanity to the Logos. This is in fact exactly what Hildegard of Bingen and Mechtild of Magdeburg do argue. Hildegard describes that which is redeemed by Christ – the physicality that comes from Mary – as feminine; and this is enhanced by her sense that Christ's body is also *ecclesia*, which is equally feminine. In a eucharistic vision, Hildegard saw woman (*muliebris imago*) receiving from Christ, hanging on the cross, a dowry of his blood, while a voice said: "Eat and drink the body and blood of my Son to abolish the prevarication of Eve and receive your true inheritance." Although the priesthood is, to Hildegard, both revered and essential, the priest enters this eucharistic vision only after Holy Church; and the image of both sinful *and saved* humanity is the image of woman.[118] A century later, Mechtild of Magdeburg argued that the Incarnation joined the Logos (the preexistent Son of God) with a pure humanity, created along with Adam but preserved as pure in Mary after the fall. Thus, Mary became a kind of preexistent humanity of Christ.[119] Such a notion is reinforced even in iconography, where we find that Mary has a place of honor on eucharistic tabernacles. For Mary, the source of Christ's physicality and his humanity, is in some sense the reliquary or chest that houses Christ's body.[120] To Hildegard of Bingen as to Marguerite of Oingt, she was explicitly the *tunica humanitatis*, the clothing of humanity which God put on in the Incarnation.[121]

Mary was, of course, important in women's spirituality. Particularly in southern European saints' lives, the theme of *imitatio Mariae Virginis* is strong. The biographer of Douceline of Marseilles, for example, actually sees Douceline as imitating the poverty of Mary, whereas her beloved Francis imitated the poverty of Christ directly.[122] But the reverence for Mary that we find in thirteenth-century women mystics is less a reverence for a "representative woman" than a reverence for the bearer and conduit of the Incarnation. The ultimate identification was with Christ as human. Some women saints swoon with Mary before the cross;[123] *all* women saints swoon on the cross with Christ himself.

Thus, women theologians took from the theological and scientific tradition a notion that male is to female as soul is to matter and elaborated it in their own way as an identification with the human Christ in his physicality. Modern claims that medieval women were alienated from a male Christ (i.e., a God not of their gender) quite miss the point; these women saw themselves less in terms of gender than in terms of matter. Modern claims that women were deprived of a sense of self-worth or forced into denial of their sexuality by the traditional association of woman with the physical also miss the point: these women found physicality, as they understood it, redeemed and expressed by a human God. Contrary to what some recent interpretations have asserted,[124] thirteenth-century women seem to have concluded from their physicality an intense conviction of their *ability* to imitate Christ without role or gender inversion. To soar toward Christ as lover and bride, to sink into the stench and torment of the Crucifixion, to eat God, was for the woman only to give religious significance to what she already was. So, female devotion to the eucharist — and to the dying or the infant or the bride-

149

groom Christ – expresses a special confidence in the Incarnation. If the Incarnation meant that the whole human person was capable of redemption, then what woman was seen as being – even in the most misogynist form of the Christian tradition – was caught up into God in Christ. And if the agony of the Crucifixion was less sacrifice or victory than the redemption of that which is human (matter joined to form), then the Crucifixion could be imaged as death or as eating or as orgasm (all especially human – bodily – experiences). Women mystics seem to have felt that they *qua* women were not only *also* but even *especially* saved in the Incarnation.

V

"...And Woman His Humanity":

Female Imagery in the Religious

Writing of the Later Middle Ages

The misogyny of the later Middle Ages is well known. Not merely a defensive reaction on the part of men who were in fact socially, economically and politically dominant, it was fully articulated in theological, philosophical and scientific theory that was centuries old.[1] *Male* and *female* were contrasted and asymmetrically valued as intellect/body, active/passive, rational/irrational, reason/emotion, self-control/lust, judgment/mercy and order/disorder. In the devotional writing of the later Middle Ages, they were even contrasted in the image of God – Father or Bridegroom – and soul (*anima*) – child or bride. Although noble women managed property while their husbands were away on crusades and middle-class women ran businesses and formed guilds in towns, there was little positive discussion of the role of mother or wife.[2] When devotional writers mentioned marriage and motherhood, it was by and large to warn against the horrors that accompanied them; when secular literature commented on women's roles, it was chiefly to romanticize adultery by aristocratic ladies or to mock the sexual appetites of peasant or middle-class wives and girls. Even the folk rituals of town and countryside suggested an identification of woman with the disorderly.[3] And as sex ratios and life expectancies altered in favor of women, the size of dowries went steadily up; the birth of a daughter sometimes seemed an extraordinary piece of ill luck.

Historians, whether they have found such misogyny titillating or horrifying, have in general assumed that medieval women internalized it. Much recent interpretation of later medieval religion, for example, has seen misogyny as a causal factor not only in the persecution of women as witches, heretics or eccentric mystics, but also in women's own religious behavior. Such interpretation has argued that women – seeing themselves as "lust" or "emotionality" or "disorder" – castigated their flesh for its fleshly desires and were sometimes driven to hysteria by the notion that they remained sexual by definition, even if their bodies were anesthetized by self-abnegation.[4] Assuming that women's religiosity was fundamentally shaped by the misogyny their clerical advisers so often articulated, historians have suggested that chastity was the central religious issue for women and that Mary, God's ever-virgin mother, was the dominant symbol. Behind such suggestions lies an even more basic assumption – that is, that the image of woman in the later Middle Ages is primarily an aspect of, and an influence on, the history of women.

But, if we look carefully at what medieval religious people wrote, how they worshiped, and how they behaved, their notions about gender seem vastly more complex than recent attention to the misogynist tradition would suggest. In the period from the twelfth to the fifteenth century, in contrast to the early Middle Ages, positive female figures and feminine metaphors took a significant place in spirituality alongside both positive male figures and misogynist images of women. Devotion to the Virgin and to women saints increased; the proportion of women among the newly canonized rose sharply; heretical movements occasionally claimed female clergy or a female god; female erotic experience, childbirth and marriage became major metaphors for spiritual advance, for service of neighbor and for union with the divine.[5]

Such ideas and images were not, however, created by or especially attractive to women. As Simone Roisin has demonstrated,
the Virgin Mary appeared more often to men than to women in
northern European visions.[6] The recent quantitative study of 864
saints by Weinstein and Bell establishes conclusively that devotion to the human Christ was a "female" theme in a way devotion
to Mary was not.[7] Moreover, the fullest elaboration of the notion
that Mary is a model for women or the notion that women are
models for each other was found in biographies written by men
(for example, those of Clare of Assisi and Columba of Rieti).
Where we can compare the biographer's perspective with that of
the subject (as we can in the case of Clare), we find that the
woman herself tended to ignore the female model to discuss
instead the imitation of Christ.[8] The idea of Jesus as mother was
first elaborated by male devotional writers. In addition, women
writers had no monopoly on homey, domestic metaphors. Christ
or the soul as seamstress, washerwoman or serving maid appeared
in the writings of, for example, Marguerite of Oingt, the Helfta
nuns, Henry Suso, Richard Rolle and the monk of Farne.[9]

There was, in the later Middle Ages, no clear association of
ordinary women and men with saints of their own sex. Some
female saints performed miracles predominantly for women, but
so did some male saints.[10] Some shrines dedicated to male saints
had predominantly female clientele and vice versa.[11] Since wom-
en's visits to shrines were frequently on behalf of sick children,
they quite naturally responded to the particular curative powers
of the saint (for sore throats, eye disease and so on) rather than
to his or her gender. Indeed, certain male religious leaders and
writers (Richard Rolle, Henry Suso and John Tauler, for example) acquired circles of female followers, and certain religious
women had mostly male followers. Sometimes, when their adher-

ents were of both sexes, women in their exhortations focused on those whom they described as "sons."[12]

Women did not, moreover, develop a religious subculture motivated by the need to counter the stereotype of woman as fleshly, weak, irrational and disorderly. Throughout the period, women's religiosity overlapped in characteristics with men's. For both sexes, asceticism, mysticism, evangelism, eucharistic piety and devotion to the human Christ increased.[13]

Women's spirituality did have distinctive emphases. Penitential asceticism was more prominent in women's religiosity, particularly in the form of food deprivation, self-inflicted suffering and an interpretation of illness as religious experience. The religious authority and significance of holy women for others in the society (both male and female) lay more centrally in their charismatic, especially their prophetic, gifts, whereas male saints often owed their power to ecclesiastical or even secular office.[14] The life pattern of holy women showed less adolescent crisis and more childhood vocation than that of men. Those women whose biographies are recorded are frequently said to have found their vocation before the age of seven or, much later, in widowhood, whereas adolescent conversion is the predominant pattern for males. Of 646 male saints studied by Weinstein and Bell, 357 (or 55 percent) converted as teenagers and only 96 (or 15 percent) as children; of 172 female saints, 55 (or 31 percent) converted as children and 58 (or 34 percent) as adolescents.[15] As I have argued elsewhere, women's stories are less frequently told as stories of crisis and change, regardless of the sex of the narrator, and women writers seem less interested in stories of conversion than in stories of constant and courageous suffering.[16] But there is still little reason to feel that these distinctive themes of women's religiosity were primarily an effort by women to counter the notion that they were lustful and weak. The immediate religious motive was, as it was for men, desire to imitate Jesus.

In fact, religious women paid surprisingly little attention to their supposed incapacity. Although told by the theological tradition that, *qua* women, they were not created in God's image, women writers ignored the warning. Creation in the image of God and return to his likeness were reiterated and significant themes in their spirituality.[17] For example, when Douceline of Marseilles asked herself, "What is the soul?" she answered confidently, "It is the mirror of divine majesty; in it God has put his seal." The nun Mechtild of Hackeborn saw herself in a vision, resting on Christ's breast and receiving the "word and works of his holy humanity" from his own hands. "Incorporated in Christ and liquefied in divine love," she then received "the imprint of resemblance [to God] like a seal in wax." On another occasion, she was reassured by a vision that the married are not further from Christ than virgins because the "Word is made flesh."[18] Becoming one with God in mystical union was a more frequent aspect of women's devotional life than of men's in the thirteenth and fourteenth centuries. Francis of Assisi received the marks of Christ's Passion from a seraph, but such gifts came more frequently to women. In the later thirteenth century the nun Lukardis of Oberweimar appeared to a monk in a vision as Christ on the cross, with two thieves – one male and one female – crucified on either side.[19] The religious history of the later Middle Ages, characterized by the appearance of new quasi-religious roles for women and for the married, does not support the argument that women shaped their self-conception either in conformity with or in opposition to the misogynist image of Eve, symbol of female sinfulness and sexuality.

Both men and women were aware of the misogynist tradition, to be sure. Its interwoven and mutually reinforcing notions of woman's physiological, ontological and functional inferiority shaped the male and the female sense of self. Hildegard of Bingen used, and argued against, the idea that woman is to man as flesh is to spirit; she supported the denial of ordination to women, arguing that woman's role as bride of Christ (that is, mystic) was complementary to the priesthood.[20] Many of the Italian tertiaries or northern beguines, who remained in the world and were dominated not only by male confessors but by male adherents as well, spoke sometimes of women as weak and urged women and men to "virility."[21] Women visionaries occasionally expressed resentment, wonder or fear at the male monopoly of clerical authority. Male biographers enjoyed pointing out the weakness – moral and physical – of their female subjects, particularly in order to castigate male readers who, by their own failure and worldliness, allowed the "inferior sex" to reach greater heights of spiritual achievement.[22]

Asymmetrical valuing of the genders and some association of male with spiritual and rational, female with fleshly and irrational, were seldom completely absent from medieval gender imagery. But if we take our stand with male and female religious writers respectively, and chart the differences in their use of gender-related notions, we find not only that men and women use the image of woman differently, but that it is not simply misogyny in either usage. Moreover, we find that it is a more articulated, self-conscious notion in men's religiosity than in women's. Women say less about gender, make less use of dichotomous gender images, speak less of gender reversal, and place more emphasis on interior motivation and continuity of self. Men use more dichotomous images, are more concerned to define "the female" as both positive and negative, and speak more often of reversal and conversion. A careful and comparative reading of texts by male and female authors from the twelfth to the fifteenth century thus suggests that it is men who develop conceptions of gender, whereas women develop conceptions of humanity. My purpose in this essay is, first, to demonstrate that this is so and, second, to suggest some reasons why.

To demonstrate the difference in male and female perspectives, I shall explore a variety of female images in late medieval spiritual writing, taking care to locate the particular images in the clusters of other images among which they appear. So as not to prejudice my conclusions by my initial choice of texts, I shall compare those male and female writers who are, on the surface, most similar. After all, to compare the university-trained Thomas Aquinas or Meister Eckhart with a virtually illiterate Italian nun or tertiary would reveal differences in educational background and philosophical sources so vast that differences owing to gender or social experience could never be determined. Not only do I limit myself to comparable genres by male and female authors (vision collections, saints' lives and devotional texts); I also limit myself to those male writers whose spirituality is most "affective" – that is, to those male writers who, in style of religious life and in style of devotion, come closest to the piety of twelfth-, thirteenth- and fourteenth-century women. I concentrate here therefore on men such as Bernard of Clairvaux, Francis of Assisi, Richard Rolle and Henry Suso, whose spirituality has been called "emotional," "lyrical" and "nuptial," and on men such as Thomas of Cantimpré, James of Vitry and John Tauler, who cultivated and were influenced by female followers. If these men give to images drawn from gender a significantly different meaning from that given by women writers, the difference is likely to stem at least in part from the gender of the author.[23] Let me begin, then, with a topic I have treated before: maternal images for the deity.[24]

Female Images of God
When we look at medieval devotional writing, we note at once that God is described in both masculine and feminine terms. To

the traditional and dominant description of God as Father and Christ as Son, central to the Christian belief in a personal God, devotional and occasionally even theological writers added the idea of the motherhood of Christ (and more occasionally of the Holy Spirit). In general, the image of the motherhood of Christ expressed three aspects of Christian belief about Christ's role in the economy of salvation. First, Christ's sacrificial death on the cross, which generated redemption, was described as a mother giving birth; second, Christ's love for the soul was seen as the unquestioning pity and tenderness of a mother for her child; third, Christ's feeding of the soul with himself (his body and blood) in the eucharist was described as a mother nursing her baby. In general also we can say that, between the twelfth and the fourteenth century, the use of these images became "darker"; suffering was increasingly stressed. Death on the cross as birthpangs, and feeding with the blood from Christ's wound, tended to replace images of conception, gestation and lactation when Christ's motherhood was elaborated in prayer, sermon and vision. Within this broad pattern, in which both theology and chronology help to account for the specific use of images, we find that men and women differ in their use of the idea of Christ's motherhood. The difference is not merely that *mother* has one set of connotations to women and another to men; it is also that, in male and female writing, *mother* occurs among a different group of images.

To male writers (such as Bernard of Clairvaux, Aelred of Rievaulx, the monk of Farne, Francis of Assisi and Henry Suso), *mothering* meant not only nurturing but also an affectivity that was needed to complement authority. Aelred of Rievaulx, describing the crucifix (a new devotional object in twelfth-century monasteries), emphasized motherhood as union, tenderness, nurture and nourishment: "On your altar let it be enough for you to have a representation of our Savior hanging on the cross; that will bring before your mind his Passion for you to imitate, his outspread arms will invite you to embrace him, his naked breasts will feed you with the milk of sweetness to console you."[25] Two hundred years later, the anonymous monk of Farne wrote in a similar vein, although the food was now blood rather than milk:

> Little ones... run and throw themselves in their mothers' arms.... Christ our Lord does the same with men. He stretches out his hands to embrace us, bows down his head to kiss us, and opens his side to give us suck; and though it is blood he offers us to suck we believe that it is health-giving and *sweeter than honey and the honey-comb* (Psalms 18.11).[26]

Repeatedly in such texts, mothering meant security, compassion, nurture, whereas fathering or fatherhood meant authority, instruction and discipline. Guerric of Igny wrote in a sermon for Saints Peter and Paul's Day (and it is significant that the context in which the image occurs is a discussion of the authority of apostles and preachers):

> The Bridegroom [Christ]... has breasts, lest he should be lacking any one of all duties and titles of loving kindness. He is a father in virtue of natural creation... and also in virtue of the authority with which he instructs. He is a mother, too, in the mildness of his affection, and a nurse.[27]

Christ's affectivity as a complement to authority was often connected by male writers with their own roles as abbots or preachers. Commenting on Song of Songs 1.1-2, the Cistercian abbot Bernard of Clairvaux associated nursing with Christ the Bridegroom, but moved swiftly to the issue of clerical or monastic authority:

She [the bride, i.e., the soul] would seem to say to the bridegroom [Christ]: "What wonder if I presume to ask you for this favor since your breasts have given me such overwhelming joy?"... When she said, then, "Your breasts are better than wine," she meant: "The richness of grace that flows from your breasts contributes far more to my spiritual progress than the biting reprimands of superiors.".... [H]ow many [superiors] there are today who reveal their lack of the requisite capabilities.... They display an insatiable passion for gain.... Neither the peril of souls nor their salvation gives them any concern. They are certainly devoid of the maternal instinct.... There is no pretense about a true mother; the breasts she displays are full for the taking. She knows how to *rejoice with those who rejoice*, and to be sad with those who sorrow [Romans 12.15], pressing the milk of encouragement without intermission from the breast of joyful sympathy, the milk of consolation from the breast of compassion.[28]

Moreover, Bernard applied such analysis explicitly to himself. To a delinquent monk he wrote:

And I have said this, my son... to help you as a loving father... I begot you in religion by word and example. I nourished you with milk.... You too were torn from my breast, cut from my womb. My heart cannot forget you.[29]

Male writers thus linked their own "motherhood" (i.e., nurturing) with that of Christ and explored, through these images, their own ambivalence about the exercise of authority and, at a deeper level, about the growing power of the clergy.

In contrast, women writers (such as Marguerite of Oingt, Hadewijch, the nuns of Helfta and Catherine of Siena) did not associate mothering so exclusively with nurturing and affectivity, nor did they use *mother* and *father* as paired and contradictory descriptions. To Mechtild of Hackeborn, for example, Christ as spouse and father is both merciful and judgmental, tender and severe.[30] Gertrude of Helfta uses mixed-gender imagery to describe God, Jesus, Mary and John the Evangelist as emperors, queens, soldiers, fathers, mothers, nurses and friends. To Gertrude, Christ's fatherhood includes loving, cuddling, feeding from his breast and teaching the baby soul its letters; Christ's motherhood includes protecting the soul during a storm at sea, clothing it with fine dresses, punishing it, denying it jewels and ornaments, refusing it affection so that it learns patience, and frightening it with ugly faces or masks.[31] Not only are characteristics we would call affective and merciful, on the one hand, judgmental and authoritarian, on the other, distributed randomly between father and mother, but the sets are not usually discussed together or as complements to each other. In the letters and visions of Hadewijch, for example, motherhood (usually her own spiritual motherhood) means disciplining as well as loving. In only one letter does Hadewijch identify maternal with loving and paternal with discipline, speak of the two as complements, and apply the description to Christ. The wording of this particular text, unlike others, turns out to be borrowed from William of St. Thierry, a twelfth-century monk and abbot deeply influenced by Bernard of Clairvaux.[32]

Women writers did not ordinarily use the image of Jesus as mother in a context that associated it with their own leadership roles or with leadership in general – either as critique or as complement. Women writers simply projected themselves into the role of child vis-à-vis mother Jesus, whereas men sometimes drew an analogy between God's motherhood and their own. Moreover, in women's visions and writing, the image does not seem to refer primarily to women's social roles. If any male/female contrast is implied, it is one of biological roles – a contrast between beget-

161

ting and conceiving, perhaps, but not one between authority and love. By and large, women seem to move from images of lactation or giving birth directly to theological matters, such as eucharist and redemption. The idea of Christ's motherhood becomes either a way of referring to the fact that Christians eat and drink Jesus or a metaphor for Christ's suffering on the cross, which gives birth to the world.

Lutgard of Aywières, for example, had visions of nursing from Christ's side, which occurred at crucial points in her own life.[33] Angela of Foligno and Catherine of Siena were nursed by Christ, and Angela saw him place the heads of her spiritual sons in his wound to drink.[34] Aldobrandesca of Siena tasted a drop of blood from Christ's side and, in memory of this, had a picture of the Virgin Mary painted, holding Christ in her arms and drinking from his wound.[35] Marguerite of Oingt spoke thus of mother Jesus:

> My sweet Lord, I gave up for you my father and my mother and my brothers and all the wealth of the world.... You know, my sweet Lord, that if I had a thousand worlds and could bend them all to my will, I would give them all up for you... for you are the life of my soul. Nor do I have father or mother besides you nor do I wish to have. For are you not my mother and more than my mother? The mother who bore me labored in delivering me for one day or one night but you, my sweet and lovely Lord, labored for me for more than thirty years. Ah, my sweet and lovely Lord, with what love you labored for me and bore me through your whole life. But when the time approached for you to be delivered, your labor pains were so great that your holy sweat was like great drops of blood that came out from your body and fell on the earth.... Ah! Sweet Lord Jesus Christ, who ever saw a mother suffer such a birth! For when the hour of your delivery came you were placed on the hard bed of the cross... and your nerves and all your veins were broken. And truly

it is no surprise that your veins burst when in one day you gave birth to the whole world.[36]

Although fourteenth-century male writers such as Richard Rolle and the monk of Farne also emphasized the Crucifixion as birthing more than did twelfth-century male writers, the fullest development of a theology of motherhood as creation and redemption is by an English anchoress of the late fourteenth century, Julian of Norwich, in whose hands it became a solution to the problem of evil. Unlike earlier women, Julian saw motherhood as the completion of fatherhood, but her theological position went well beyond all earlier formulations, male and female. To Julian, God's motherhood, expressed in Christ, is not merely love and mercy, not merely redemption through the sacrifice of the cross, but a taking on of our physical humanity in the Incarnation, as a mother gives herself to the fetus she bears:

I saw and understood that the high might of the Trinity is our Father, and the deep wisdom of the Trinity is our Mother, and the great love of the Trinity is our Lord; and all these we have in nature and in our substantial creation. And furthermore I saw that the second person, who is our Mother, substantially the same beloved person, has now become our mother sensually because we are double by God's creating, that is to say substantial and sensual. Our substance is the higher part, which we have in our Father, God almighty; and the second person of the Trinity is our Mother in nature in our substantial creation, in whom we are founded and rooted, and he is our Mother of mercy in taking our sensuality. And so our Mother is working on us in various ways, in whom our parts are kept undivided; for in our Mother Christ we profit and increase, and in mercy he reforms and restores us, and by the power of his Passion, his death and his Resurrection he unites us to our substance. So our Mother

163

works in mercy on all his beloved children who are docile and obedient to him.[37]

Moreover, Julian sees discipline, judgment and wisdom as part of mothering. Elsewhere, she writes:

> The mother can give her child to suck of her milk, but our precious Mother Jesus can feed us with himself, and does, most courteously and most tenderly, with the blessed sacrament, which is the precious food of true life. . . . The mother can lay her child tenderly to breast, but our tender Mother Jesus can lead us easily into his blessed breast through his sweet open side, and show us there a part of the godhead. . . . And always as the child grows in age and in stature, [the mother] acts differently, but she does not change her love. And when it is even older, she allows it to be chastised to destroy its faults, so as to make the child receive virtues and grace.[38]

Use of the theme of mother Jesus in late medieval writing is clearly conditioned by the tenets of Christian theology, by recognition of male/female biological differences, and by the misogynist definition of women as weak. Within these constraints, however, men and women used the image in complex and different ways. Men were more apt to pair mothering with fathering. They saw motherhood as a social role and a set of personal characteristics (especially tenderness and emotionality), contrasted to male authority and power. Women were less likely to pair motherhood with fatherhood or to define motherhood as a given set of personal characteristics. To them, mothering was associated most clearly with eating and feeding, and with *passio* (suffering, which was in some sense childbirth). This difference in use of the theme of mother Jesus takes on deeper significance when we move from gender-related images of God to gender-related images of the soul. For the dominant religious image of the self in the late Middle Ages was female; the soul was woman or bride (or sometimes child). Not surprisingly, this image expressed very different meanings in the hands of male and female authors.

Images of the Soul

When male writers used female images of the soul, they sometimes simply slipped into the metaphor in order to express the "childlike" or "womanly" dependence of the good Christian on a powerful, "fatherly" God. But they also expressed something more complicated: conversion or renunciation. When describing the self, as when describing God, male writers made more frequent use than did women writers of male/female as a contrasting pair. Moreover, men often called attention to their adoption of the opposite gender as self-description. In other words, men saw male and female as contrasting sets of values or behaviors and used gender reversal as an image of their exchange of ordinary (male) for extraordinary (female) status.

Sometimes men used *woman* as a term of opprobrium and accused themselves (as did Helinand of Froidmont) of being weak – even menstruating – women.[39] More frequently, however, their description of themselves as "weak women" expressed something positive: their desire to reject the world, to become the meek who inherit the earth. Bernard of Clairvaux wrote that monks were women, whereas bishops were men.[40] In the words of his male biographer, Francis of Assisi not only married Lady Poverty, he *was* Lady Poverty.[41] In the biographies and writing of some male religious leaders (often those whose own mothers deeply influenced their lives), we find not just elaboration of the notion of the soul as bride; we also find consistent avoidance of male imagery for the self.[42] Henry Suso, for example, when offered the role of knight in a vision, debated with himself over

165

the appropriateness of the image. But he happily adopted as self-description the image of a maiden picking roses, a baby being nursed or a mother nursing, and he explicitly identified himself with his own mother's religiosity.[43]

Indeed male appropriation of the notion of woman as weak sometimes became a claim to superior lowliness. Women, whose lives were in fact characterized by more virulent asceticism than men's and who might have been presumed to need such asceticism to purge their greater physicality, were advised by Suso and Abelard, among others, that theirs should be the way of moderation.[44] When male writers took femaleness as an image to describe their renunciation of the world, they sometimes said explicitly that women were too weak to be women. They sometimes implied that their own role reversal – that is, their appropriation of or choice for lowliness – was a superior "femaleness" to the femaleness of women, which was not chosen. Suso, for example, occasionally suggested that the tears and suffering of real women were whining, whereas men's austerities were imitation of Christ.[45]

Thus, to men, woman was a marked category, an exception to the generalization *homo*, a reversal of ordinary condition. "To become woman" was an obvious image of renunciation and conversion. Moreover, as I have argued elsewhere, male writers assumed that women would undergo reversals too.[46] Male biographers not only labeled women as weak far more frequently than women described themselves in such terms, they also told women's stories as stories of radical conversion and urged women to become virile, masculine, in rising to God. Late medieval men, like those of the patristic period, were titillated and made anxious by stories (some of which they clearly fabricated) of women masquerading as men in order to enter monasteries.[47] Male biographers (who also, somewhat inconsistently, advised women to choose female models) felt that saintly women must be elevated or authenticated by male qualities. For example, when Raymond of Capua worried about the authenticity of Catherine of Siena's visions, he received a vision from God in which Catherine's face changed into the face of a bearded man. (Raymond understood the bearded man to be Christ.)[48]

But women themselves did not, by and large, see woman as a marked category, nor did they worry about themselves as exceptions or special cases of the general category "humanity." Women did not assume that their religious progress involved "becoming male." Women, of course, described themselves in female images. Moreover, religious women – whether nuns, beguines, tertiaries or laywomen without ostensible affiliation to any order – adopted practices (such as fasting, chastity, white garments, uncontrolled weeping) that distinguished them from those in worldly roles. But female writers often seem, by *woman*, to have meant human being. And conversion or reversal was a less central theme in women's spirituality than in men's.

Women sheltered by special religious status, especially those raised in convents, rarely spoke of female weakness as a bar to theological expression or religious practice. Gertrude of Helfta and Mechtild of Hackeborn, for example, did not speak of themselves as weak. And Julian of Norwich eliminated her one reference to woman's intellectual inferiority between the first and second recensions of her famous *Showings*.[49] Even ordinary housewives could be forthright and fierce in defending their religious inspiration. Margery Kempe's spirited assertion of her right to point out clerical failings is well known:

> Then the Archbishop said to her: "I am evil informed of thee. I hear it is said that thou art a right wicked woman."
>
> And she answered back: "I also hear it said that ye are a wicked

man. And if ye be as wicked as men say, ye shall never come to Heaven, unless ye amend whilst ye be here."

"Ah! Sir," said the clerks, "here wot we well that she hath a devil within her, for she speaketh of the Gospel."

As quickly as possible, a great clerk brought forth a book and laid Saint Paul, for his part, against her, that no woman should preach.

She answering thereto said: "I preach not, sir; I come into no pulpit. I use but communication and good words, and that I will do while I live."[50]

Female authors who discuss woman as a social category – a gender contrasted to and weaker than maleness – are usually women such as Mechtild of Magdeburg, Catherine of Siena and Angela of Foligno, who remained in the world, experienced lengthy struggle with family over vocation, and had predominantly male followers.[51]

When describing self, as when describing God, women tended to fuse male and female images more than did men. It is true that women described their souls as female, and such imagery sometimes enabled them to release highly erotic energy toward God. Margery Kempe, for example, cuddled with Christ in bed and clearly saw herself as a woman responding to a male Jesus.[52] Marguerite of Oingt wrote thus of her meditation on the Crucifixion:

And when I see that the evil crowd has left, I approach and take out the nails and then I carry him on my shoulders down from the cross and put him between the arms of my heart.... And in the evening, when I go to bed, I in spirit put him in my bed and I kiss his tender hands and his feet so cruelly pierced for my sins. And I lean over that glorious side pierced for me.[53]

Hadewijch, in a eucharistic vision of great beauty, described mystical union with images that evoke female orgasm.[54]

But, as even these examples make clear, women did not have a strong sense of binary opposites grouped around the male/female contrast. They did not associate specific personality characteristics or roles — such as authority, rationality, nurture, emotion — with one or the other sex. Although they made use of the conventions of vernacular love poetry to write of themselves as brides, they also slipped easily into male imagery where no reversal or even gender-specific meaning was implied. Hadewijch saw the soul sometimes as a knight seeking his lady, sometimes as a bride reaching her lover. To Julian of Norwich, the soul that is saved and cared for by mother God is a genderless "child." (The pronoun *it* rather than he or she is used in the Middle English.)

A sharply defined sense of the male as superior was unimportant in women's writings and visions. Although women in the early Church sometimes had visions in which they acquired spiritual maleness, this motif drops out of late medieval visions.[55] In the later Middle Ages, women such as Joan of Arc cross-dressed in order to change social roles, but not (or at least not primarily) to gain spiritual advantage. Tengswich of Andernach tells us that Hildegard dressed her nuns for mass as brides.[56] Despite God's revelation to Raymond of Capua that a male authority lay behind Catherine's visions, Catherine herself received a different message. She had thought since childhood that she ought to put on male attire in order to entitle her to the role of preacher and prophet. But God sent a revelation that he "who has created both sexes and all sorts of men..., who can create an angel as easily as an ant," would send her to preach and teach as a *woman* in order to shame immoral men.[57] Although women who influenced or directed men sometimes urged those men to be virile rather than womanly, I know of only a few cases where a woman urged a woman to maleness.[58] Indeed, women such as Margery Kempe, Lutgard of Aywières, Ida of Louvain or Agnes of Montepulciano, who received visions of Jesus as bridegroom or as suckling child, were implicitly responding to their own gender as a positive route to union with God.[59]

The issue of actual and metaphorical cross-dressing is worth pursuing a little further. Natalie Davis has demonstrated the prevalence of role inversion generally in the calendrical rituals of medieval and early modern peasants and townspeople; in such festivals and carnivals – by definition infrequent and unusual events – men aped women as children aped the powerful, providing an expression of and escape valve for psychological discomfort and social discontent. But, as Vern Bullough has shown, cross-dressing by males (outside a ritual context) was extremely rare in the Middle Ages because such acts represented decline in status.[60] Actual cross-dressing by laywomen, even by women who gave it some religious significance, was fairly common. Joan of Arc was unusual in donning male clothes to lead an army, but a number of cases are recorded of women who put on male clothing to travel – especially on pilgrimage – or to run away from home.[61] Their cross-dressing was a mechanism to aid in role change or a real disguise to gain the physical protection offered by superior status. In short, cross-dressing and role reversal were more common among women than men and less disturbing to them. Such inversions (both women masquerading as men and men cross-dressing or reversing gender) were far more disturbing possibilities, and thus more heightened and powerful symbols, to men. It does not seem surprising, therefore, that religious men spoke of their renunciation of the world as adopting another gender, as the cross-dressing they seldom in fact did. On the other hand, women, who more commonly put on male dress in the world in order to accomplish certain goals (occasionally even religious goals), did not in the safety of the cloister or anchor-hold use "acquiring maleness" as a symbol or metaphor with spiritual content.

The male writer who saw his soul as a bride of God or his religious role as womanly submission and humility was conscious of using an image of reversal. He sought reversal because reversal and renunciation were at the heart of a religion whose dominant symbol is the cross – life achieved through death. When a woman writer (often but not always a virgin) spoke of herself as either a bride or a knight, each image was in a sense a reversal. But neither was as highly charged as the notion of the male as bride or woman, for neither expressed renunciation. Because women were women, they could not embrace the female as a symbol of renunciation. Because society was male-dominated, they could not embrace the male as a symbol of renunciation. To become male was elevation, not renunciation, and elevation was a less significant reversal given the values at the core of medieval Christianity. Thus, women did not in their writings play with male and female oppositions; they did not tell their own stories or the stories of other women as reversals or conversions. They did, however, explore and play in very complicated ways with what femaleness meant in the theological tradition – that is, physicality.

Women's Concern with Physicality

From Hildegard of Bingen and Elizabeth of Schönau to Catherine of Siena and Julian of Norwich, women theologians in the later Middle Ages saw woman as the symbol of humanity, where humanity was understood as physicality. To Hildegard of Bingen, Christ's humanity was to Christ's divinity as woman is to man, and *mulier* represented humankind, fallen in Eve, restored in *ecclesia* and Maria. Hildegard wrote explicitly in the *Liber divinorum operum* the words I have taken as the theme of this essay: "Man...

signifies the divinity of the Son of God and woman his humanity."[62] Moreover, to Mechtild of Magdeburg and Catherine of Siena, Mary was the source and container of Christ's physicality; the flesh Christ put on was in some sense female, because it was his mother's.[63] And to Julian of Norwich, God was mother exactly in that our humanity with its full sensuality was not merely loved and saved, but even given being by and from him.

Thus, *female* was not to women writers primarily paired with *male* as contrasting image. The one woman theologian (Hildegard of Bingen) who did discuss the two genders directly, stressed complementarity.[64] The woman writer's sense of herself as female was less a sense of herself as evil or as not-male than a sense of herself as physical. And women saw the humanity-physicality that linked them to Christ as in continuity with, rather than in contrast to, their own ordinary experience of physical and social vulnerability.

Women, of course, sought to leave the world, as did men; and they marked themselves off from their worldly sisters by renouncing such things as jewels, cosmetics, soft beds, gaiety, food, husbands, lovers, children and parents. But they spoke of their union with Christ in images that continued ordinary female roles (bride, child, mother) and stereotypical female behavior (vulnerability, illness, bleeding). Thus, women reached God not by reversing what they were but by sinking more fully into it. In fact and in image, suffering (both self-inflicted and involuntary) and food (both eucharist and fasting) were women's most characteristic ways of attaining God. For example, not only was blood (blood as food) Catherine of Siena's most frequent image; her most frequent description of loving one's neighbor was "eating souls on the table of the cross," and her most characteristic practice was fasting. Although her male biographer described a vision in which she married Christ with a golden ring, Catherine herself referred to a ring of skin. The context of her letters makes it clear that she saw herself as married with Christ's foreskin – a graphic indication of the centrality for her of humanness as physicality.[65]

Late medieval spirituality abounds in examples of women emphasizing their physicality in order to join with Christ. Ida of Louvain in the thirteenth century and Dorothy of Montau in the fourteenth experienced mystical pregnancy as a preparation for or a result of the eucharist.[66] The vast majority of stigmatics were women, and the reception of stigmata (bearing the marks of Christ's physical body in one's own physicality) was frequently the result of communion – of eating physical elements that literally *were* the similarly marked body of Christ.[67] It is against this background that we must place the little-noticed fact that eating is a far more central image to late medieval women than to men. Hadewijch wrote, of encounter with God:

> In the anguish of the repose of the madness of love, ...
> The heart of each devours the other's heart. ...
> As he who is Love itself showed us
> When he gave us himself to eat ...
> ... love's most intimate union
> Is through eating, tasting, and seeing interiorly.
> He eats us; we think we eat him,
> And we do eat him, of that we can be certain.
> But because he remains so undevoured ...
> Each of us remains uneaten by him. ...
> As soon as Love thus touches the soul,
> She eats its flesh and drinks its blood.[68]

While penitential asceticism and devotion to the human Christ are found in male lives also, they are more prominent themes in women's religiosity. Indeed, patient bearing of debilitating illness was a major factor in female reputations for sanctity.[69] Mary of Oignies and Villana de' Botti refused prayers for relief of sickness; Gertrude of Helfta welcomed headaches. Dauphine of Puimichel even suggested that if people knew how useful diseases were for self-discipline, they would purchase them in the market-place.[70] Julian of Norwich asked for and received the grace of literal *imitatio Christi*, of dying with Jesus in anguish that became unspeakable joy. She wrote:

> This revelation was made to a simple, unlettered creature, living in this mortal flesh, the year of our Lord one thousand, three hundred and seventy-three, on the thirteenth day of May; and before this the creature had desired three graces by the gift of God. The first was recollection of the Passion. The second was bodily sickness. The third was to have, of God's gift, three wounds....
>
> And when I was thirty and a half years old, God sent me a bodily sickness in which I lay for three days and three nights, and on the third night I received all the rites of Holy Church, and did not expect to live until day....
>
> After this the upper part of my body began to die, until I could scarcely feel anything. My greatest pain was my shortness of breath and the ebbing of my life. Then truly I believed that I was at the point of death. And suddenly at that moment all my pain was taken from me, and I was as sound, particularly in the upper part of my body, as ever I was before. I was astonished by this sudden change, for it seemed to me that it was by God's secret doing and not natural....
>
> Then suddenly it came into my mind that I ought to wish for the second wound as a gift and a grace from our Lord, that my body might be full of recollection and feeling of his blessed Passion, as I had prayed before, for I wished that his pains might be my pains, with compassion which would lead to longing for God....
>
> And at this, suddenly I saw the red blood running down from

under the crown, hot and flowing freely and copiously, a living stream, just as it was at the time when the crown of thorns was pressed on his blessed head. I perceived, truly and powerfully, that it was he who just so, both God and man, himself suffered for me, who showed it to me without any intermediary.

And in the same revelation, suddenly the Trinity filled my heart full of the greatest joy.... And I said: Blessed be the Lord! This I said with a reverent intention and in a loud voice, and I was greatly astonished by this wonder and marvel, that he who is so to be revered and feared would be so familiar with a sinful creature living in this wretched flesh.[71]

Conclusions and Explanations

Medieval men and women looked at and used gender-related notions very differently. Male writers saw the genders as dichotomous. They stressed male as power, judgment, discipline and reason, female as weakness, mercy, lust and unreason. They applied female images to themselves to express world denial, and the world they renounced was predominantly the world of wealth and power. Women writers used imagery more fluidly. Personal and social characteristics were more often shared by the two genders in women's writings. The female was a less marked category; it was more often simply a symbol of an almost genderless self. When women did give the female content taken from the traditional idea of asymmetrical genders, they saw it as physical and bodily. And this physicality was seen as useful in joining with a human Christ. Women's religiosity was less characterized by conversion and inversion; their sense of self and of Christ as physical stressed continuity between their social and biological experience, on the one hand, and the experience of encounter with God, on the other.

Why then do men and women use gender imagery so differently in the religious writing of the later Middle Ages? The reasons undoubtedly lie in part in the nature of medieval society. For example, men renounced power and wealth, whereas women renounced food, because these were aspects of experience that the two sexes respectively controlled.[72] But men's renunciations were more radical breaks with previous life, whereas women's fasting and illness in certain ways enhanced their sense of being bodies and being vulnerable. For this contrast, there are social reasons also. As I pointed out above, men frequently changed roles as adolescents; women who took on specialized religious roles often found their vocations in childhood. Thus, men underwent conversions and inverted previous roles more frequently than did women. This was undoubtedly because medieval men had greater ability than women to determine the shape of their lives. For example, Mary of Oignies and Clare of Assisi, wishing to renounce property, were virtually forced to retain income and servants; women such as Margaret of Cortona, Umiliana Cerchi and Angela of Foligno had to wait for the death of husbands or lovers before espousing chastity.[73] As Weinstein and Bell note:

> Men may have been slower to recognize a call to the holy life, but once called they progressed steadily to ever higher plateaus of heroic virtue. Women were inspired earlier, but their quest for spiritual perfection was less regular. Not only did they encounter obstacles in the form of angry parents and a distrusting world, but they were more likely to judge themselves harshly, to condemn their own backsliding.[74]

Indeed there may be psychological as well as social reasons for the differing male and female patterns. In any society where child rearing is done predominantly by women, young men are forced to undergo more fundamental reversals in self-conception than women, who grow up to be "like" the mother who is their first love. One need not invoke ideas as complicated and problematic as the Oedipus complex to suggest that, since male maturation involved breaking with mother and mother's world, medieval males were more used than females to seeing self as defined by conversion, reversal and renunciation.[75] Moreover, as Weinstein and Bell point out, male saints tended to see sin as a response to an external stimulus. By contrast, in the lives of female saints, sin "usually appears to arise from the depths of woman herself."[76] Such evidence suggests that women had a greater sense of interior motivation and of continuity of self, although the evidence may merely show that male biographers were more likely to blame male sins on forces outside men's control.

Such explanations relate the differing perceptions characteristic of men and women to their differing social and psychological experiences. And there is an even simpler – and equally convincing – explanation that relates male and female perspectives to women's experience of constricted opportunities. It may be that, in any patriarchal society, men will stress gender differences because such an emphasis consolidates their advantage. Women, on the other hand, unable to propose their experience as dominant and unwilling to accept it as exceptional, will quite naturally couch their perceptions in terms of "humanity."[77]

Such an explanation does not, however, quite capture the meaning of humanity to religious women. To them, humanity was, as Mechtild of Hackeborn said, the "Word made flesh." Behind medieval women's concern with physicality lay the doctrine of the Incarnation. To understand male and female perspectives fully, we must thus turn to the religious context of behavior and ideas.

In the dominant theological tradition inherited by the later Middle Ages, *male* and *female* were contrasted and asymmetrically valued as soul and body. Such values suggested that men were like God in a sense women could never achieve, that women ought to sluff off femaleness in rising to meet the divine. In early Christianity we find some use of imagery that suggests that both men and women felt this way about gender, and writing by men in the later Middle Ages sometimes implied that women's spiritual advance was advance toward maleness – that is, toward rationality and self-control.[78] Women in the late Middle Ages seem, however, to have partially abandoned this concept; and, for men as well, the notion of woman's irrationality and disorder became in some ways positive – an image of mercy and meekness.

The positive image of woman in the later Middle Ages must be understood against the background of the fierce world-denial that characterized the period. As social and religious roles proliferated with bewildering rapidity in the twelfth century, the rhetoric of reversal and renunciation grew more strident. Since religious conversion meant the reversal of all earthly values, men enthusiastically adopted images of themselves as women – that is, powerless, poor, irrational, without influence or authority. If God was male and the soul was other than God, woman was a natural image both for what God redeemed and for what the powerful, successful male became when he renounced the world. In revering female saints, worshiping the Virgin Mary, attracting female followers, holding up saintly women as a reproach to worldly prelates, and describing themselves as women and fools, medieval men were in one sense ignoring the negative side of the earlier medieval image of woman. But in another sense, asymmetry was implicit in the very notion of reversal.

Such gender images were, in any case, as problematic to religious women as the notion of woman as lust. If reversal and renunciation were the heart of religious dedication, women, who were already inferior, did not have much to offer. Moreover, nei-

178

ther maleness nor femaleness could serve for them as an image of renunciation.

Women thus asserted and embraced their humanity. They asserted it because traditional dichotomous images of woman and man opposed humanity–physicality–woman to divinity–rationality–man. Women stressed their humanity and Jesus' because tradition had accustomed them to associate humanity with the female. But humanity is not, in the final analysis, a gender-related image. Humanity is genderless. To medieval women humanity was, most basically, not femaleness, but physicality, the flesh of the "Word made flesh." It was the ultimate negative – the otherness from God that the God-man redeemed by taking it into himself. Images of male and female alike were insipid and unimportant in the blinding light of the ultimate asymmetry between God and creation.

If religious women spoke less frequently in gender terms than did religious men, it is because they understood that "man...signifies the divinity of the Son of God and woman his humanity." And they understood that both equations were metaphorical. But, given the ultimate dichotomy of God and creation, the first was only metaphorical. Man was not divinity. The second was in some sense, however, literally true.

VI

The Female Body and Religious

Practice in the Later Middle Ages

One night in the early fifteenth century, as she prayed to the Virgin Mary, the Franciscan reformer Colette of Corbie received a vision of Christ. The Christ who came to Colette was neither the sweet-faced bridegroom nor the adorable baby familiar to us from medieval paintings and illuminations. Christ appeared to Colette as a dish completely filled with "carved-up flesh like that of a child," while the voice of God warned her that it was human sin that minced his son into such tiny pieces.[1]

A hundred years earlier, in the Rhineland, a Dominican friend of the nun Lukardis of Oberweimar received a vision of the Crucifixion. Yet, the figures he saw were not the executed bodies of Christ and two thieves common both in art and in visionary experience. Rather, the friar saw his friend Lukardis and two others nailed to crosses, and the voice of God informed him that it was Lukardis who was to be identified with Christ because she suffered most.[2]

These visions startle the modern reader. Conditioned by classic accounts such as Johan Huizinga's and recent popularizations such as Barbara Tuchman's to see the late Middle Ages as violent in its daily practice, morbid, graphic and literal-minded in its images, we are nonetheless surprised to find Christ depicted as chopped meat or to read of a crucified body as female.[3] The images seem, if not disgusting, at least distasteful. Boundaries appear to be violated here – boundaries between spiritual and physical, male and female, self and matter. There is something profoundly alien to modern sensibilities about the role of body in medieval piety.[4]

It is not my purpose in this essay to explore our modern discomfort with such boundary crossing, but rather to provide a context for understanding the ease with which medieval people mixed categories. Nonetheless, we do well to begin by recognizing the essential strangeness of medieval religious experience. The recent outpouring of work on the history of the body, especially the female body, has largely equated body with sexuality and understood discipline or control of body as the rejection of sex or of woman.[5] We must wipe away such assumptions before we come to medieval source material. Medieval images of the body have less to do with sexuality than with fertility and decay.[6] Control, discipline, even torture of the flesh is, in medieval devotion, not so much the rejection of physicality as the elevation of it – a horrible yet delicious elevation – into a means of access to the divine.[7]

In the discussion that follows, I wish first to illustrate the new religious significance body acquired in the period from 1200 to 1500 and second to argue that female spirituality in the same period was especially somatic – so much so that the emergence of certain bizarre miracles characteristic of women may actually mark a turning point in the history of the body in the West. Then I wish to explain briefly the ecclesiastical and social setting of women's somatic and visionary piety before turning to an exploration of its context in two sets of medieval assumptions – assumptions about male/female and assumptions about soul/body. The final two sections of the essay discuss these assumptions at length in order to show that the very dualisms modern commentators have emphasized so much were far from absolute in the late Middle Ages. Not only did theology, natural philosophy and folk tradition mingle male and female in their understanding of human character and human physiology, theological and psychological discussion also sometimes mingled body and soul. The spirituality of medieval women owed its intense bodily quality in part to the association of the female with the fleshly made by philosophers and theologians alike. But its somatic quality also derived from the fact that by the thirteenth century the prevalent concept of person was of a psychosomatic unity, the orthodox position in eschatology required resurrection of body as well as soul at the end of time, and the philosophical, medical and folk understandings of body saw men and women as variations on a single physiological structure. Compared to other periods of Christian history and other world religions, medieval spirituality – especially female spirituality – was peculiarly bodily; this was so not only because medieval assumptions associated female with flesh but also because theology and natural philosophy saw persons as, in some real sense, body as well as soul.

The Body in Late Medieval Piety

One aspect of the medieval enthusiasm for body as means of religious access remains prominent in modern Catholic Europe: the cult of relics. From the early Middle Ages down into modern times, pieces of dead holy people have been revered as the loci of the sacred. Medieval relics were jealously guarded, feared, fought for and sometimes even stolen from fellow Christians.[8] According to at least some learned and some popular opinion, relics were far more than mere aids to pious memory; they were the saints themselves, living already with God in the incorrupt and glorified bodies more ordinary mortals would attain only at the end of time.[9]

The cult of relics was only one of the ways in which late medieval piety emphasized body as the locus of the sacred. The graphic physical processes of living people were revered as well. Holy people spit or blew into the mouths of others to effect cures or convey grace.[10] The ill clamored for the bathwater of would-be saints to drink or bathe in and preferred it if these would-be saints themselves washed seldom and therefore left skin and lice floating in the water.[11] Following Francis of Assisi, who kissed lepers, several Italian saints ate pus or lice from poor or sick bodies, thus incorporating in themselves the illness and misfortune of others.[12] Holy virgins in the Low Countries lactated miraculously and cured their adherents with the breast milk they exuded.[13]

Medieval people, moreover, manipulated their own bodies for religious goals. Both male and female saints regularly engaged in what modern people call self-torture – jumping into ovens or icy ponds, driving knives, nails or nettles into their flesh, whipping or hanging themselves in elaborate pantomimes of Christ's Crucifixion.[14] Understood sometimes as chastening of sexual urges or as punishment for sin, such acts were more frequently described as union with the body of Jesus. Henry Suso, for example, said of ascetic practices:

> If suffering brought with it no other gain than that by our griefs and pains we grow in likeness to Christ, our prototype, it would still be a priceless benefit.... Even if God should choose to give the same eternal reward to those who suffer and to those who do not, we should nevertheless prefer afflictions as our earthly portion in order to resemble our leader.[15]

The ecstatic, even erotic, overtones of such union are often quite clear. Starving her body into submission, the Italian tertiary Angela of Foligno spoke of encounter with Jesus as "love and

184

inestimable satiety, which, although it satiated, generated at the same time insatiable hunger, so that all her members were unstrung...."[16]

Pious folk in the later Middle Ages also gave extraordinary religious significance to the body of God. Not only did they believe that the bread on the altar became Christ at the moment of consecration; they also experienced miracles in which the bread turned into bloody flesh on the paten or in the mouth of the recipient.[17] Increasingly, therefore, eucharistic reception became symbolic cannibalism: devotees consumed and thus incorporated (as they are understood to do in other cannibal cultures, such as the Iroquois or Aztec) the power of the tortured god.[18] Moreover, pious practice came to revere the consecrated wafer as a physical remnant (or relic) of Christ — the only such relic that could exist on earth, Christ's body having been assumed into heaven. As the cult of the eucharistic host developed in the late twelfth century, consecrated wafers were reserved in reliquaries and honored with the sort of candles and lamps that burned before the relics of the saints.[19] Such an understanding of the host as relic is clearly illustrated by the story of Bishop Hugh of Lincoln, who chewed off a bit from the bone of Mary Magdalen preserved at Fécamp and defended himself to her outraged supporters by claiming that if he could touch Christ's body in the mass he could certainly chew the Magdalen's arm.[20]

Specific members of Christ's body were revered by the devout in ways that astonish and sometimes offend us. As Leo Steinberg has demonstrated, artists in the fifteenth century often called attention to the penis of the infant or the adult Christ.[21] And the cult of the holy foreskin was popular in the later Middle Ages. Although the hagiographer Raymond of Capua and the artists of early modern Europe depict Catherine of Siena as marrying Christ with a ring of gold and precious stones, Catherine herself says she married him with his circumcised flesh.[22] Birgitta of Sweden received a revelation from God saying where Christ's foreskin was preserved on earth; and the Viennese beguine Agnes Blannbekin received the foreskin in her mouth in a vision and found it to taste as sweet as honey.[23]

The Female Body and Female Experience

Behavior in which bodiliness provides access to the sacred seems to have increased dramatically in frequency in the twelfth century and to have been more characteristic of women than of men. Although both men and women manipulated their bodies from the outside, so to speak, by flagellation and other forms of self-inflicted suffering, cases of psychosomatic manipulation (or manipulation from within) are almost exclusively female. I refer here to a number of phenomena that are sometimes called "paramystical" by modern scholars of religion and "hysterical" or "conversion phenomena" by modern psychologists.

Trances, levitations, catatonic seizures or other forms of bodily rigidity, miraculous elongation or enlargement of parts of the body, swellings of sweet mucus in the throat (sometimes known as the "globus hystericus") and ecstatic nosebleeds are seldom if at all reported of male saints, but are quite common in the *vitae* of thirteenth- and fourteenth-century women. The inability to eat anything except the eucharistic host (which Rudolph Bell calls "holy anorexia") is reported only of women for most of the Middle Ages.[24] Although a few stories of fasting girls are told from Carolingian Europe, reports that see self-starvation as a manifestation of sanctity begin to proliferate about 1200. These reports often include claims to other forms of miraculous bodily closure as well: women who do not eat are reputed neither to excrete nor to menstruate.

Despite the fame of Francis of Assisi's stigmata, he and the modern figure Padre Pio are the only males in history who have claimed all five visible wounds. There are, however, dozens of such claims for late medieval women. Francis, who died in 1226, may indeed have been the first case (although even this is uncertain); but stigmata rapidly became a female miracle, and only for women did the stigmatic wounds bleed periodically.[25] Miraculous lactation was, of course, female behavior, and it appears to have originated in the Low Countries in the early thirteenth century. Other kinds of holy exuding – particularly the exuding of sweet-smelling oil after death – seem more characteristic of women as well.[26] Bodily swelling understood as "mystical pregnancy" was usually (although not always) a female claim.[27] The most bizarre cases of pictures etched on hearts and discovered during preparation for burial are told of women.[28] Indeed, if we look outside the religious sphere, we find that writings by rather matter-of-fact fourteenth-century surgeons express an odd combination of reverence and almost prurient curiosity about what is contained inside women – that is, their "secrets."[29]

Although a number of blood prodigies are attributed to the bodies of male saints, female bodies provide a disproportionate percentage of the wonder-working relics in late medieval Europe.[30] As Claude Carozzi has argued, we can sometimes, in hagiographical accounts, see a woman turning into a relic even before her own death.[31] Moreover, incorruptibility, either of the whole cadaver or of a part, seems a virtual requirement for female sanctity by the early modern period. According to Thurston, incorruptibility (that is, remaining lifelike and supple for long years after death) has been claimed for all six of the female saints added to the universal Roman calendar between 1400 and 1900 (although it is mentioned for fewer than half of the male saints).[32] In short, women's bodies were more apt than men's to display unusual changes, closures, openings or exudings; such changes were either more common or much more frequently reported after 1200; religious significance was attached to such changes when they seemed to parallel either events in Christ's life or in the mass.

Another kind of bodily experience – illness or recurrent pain – was also more apt to be given religious significance in women's lives than in men's. In their statistical study of saints, Weinstein and Bell have pointed out that, although women were fewer than one in five of those canonized or revered as saints between 1000 and 1700, they were over half of those in whose lives patient suffering of illness was the major element of sanctity.[33] Ernst Benz, Richard Kieckhefer and Elizabeth Petroff have also pointed out the prominence of illness – as theme and as fact – in women's spirituality.[34] Some visionary women (such as Julian of Norwich) prayed for disease as a gift from God; some (such as Lidwina of Schiedam) at first desired to be cured. But, whatever the cause of disease or the saint's initial reaction to it, many medieval women – for example, Serafina of San Gimignano, Villana de' Botti, Margaret of Ypres, Dorothy of Montau, Gertrude of Helfta and Alpaïs of Cudot – made physical and mental anguish an opportunity for their own salvation and that of others.[35] Hagiographers fairly frequently described their female subjects as impelled to bodily frenzy by God's presence: Beatrice of Nazareth, for example, wondered whether it would be desirable to drive herself insane out of love for God.[36] The leper Alice of Schaerbeke explained that illness could be offered for the redemption of one's neighbor.[37] By 1500 there are extant women's *vitae*, such as Catherine of Genoa's, in which much of the account is devoted to physiological changes in the saint's dying body.

It is true that medieval writers, like modern ones, frequently saw disease as a condition to be avoided.[38] Indeed, cures of illness were the most common miracles performed by saints. But it is also true that sickness and suffering were sometimes seen by medieval people as conditions "to be endured" rather than "cured." Alpaïs of Cudot, for example, clearly indicated such an attitude when she saw the devil appear in a vision as a doctor. To Alpaïs, as to Elsbeth Achler and Catherine of Siena, the offer of cure was a temptation.[39] Indeed, a nun of the monastery of Töss composed a poem in which Christ said to her: "The sicker you are, the dearer you are to me."[40]

There is reason to believe that conditions that both we and medieval people would see as "illnesses" were given different meanings depending on whether they occurred in male or female bodies. Illness was more likely to be described as something "to be endured" when it happened to women. For example, in a ninth-century account of the posthumous miracles of Walburga, a man and a woman suffering from what we would term an "eating disorder" both present themselves before the saint's relics. The man is cured of his loathing for food when he is offered a chalice by three nuns; the woman, however, turns from voracious hunger to inability to eat – a condition of which she is not "cured." Rather, she is miraculously sustained for three years without eating.[41]

Statistics tell the same story. Pierre-André Sigal, in his recent study of miracles in eleventh- and twelfth-century France, finds that females account for only between 18 and 42 percent of recipients of miraculous cures. (The percentage varies with the disease cured.) Females are an even smaller percentage of the miraculous cures of children and adolescents, and of the cures that take place at shrines rather than at a distance. These facts cannot be accounted for by sex ratios in the population or by disproportionate percentages of men among those falling ill. Rather, they clearly indicate, as Sigal argues, that the society found it more valuable to cure one sex than the other. They also suggest that

endurance of a condition of illness without supernatural amelio-
ration was considered more appropriate to women, whether the
endurance was a prelude to sanctity or not.[42]

The tendency of women to somatize religious experience and
to give positive significance to bodily occurrences is related to
what is generally recognized to be a more experiential quality in
their mystical writing.[43] Male writers too, of course, use extremely
physical and physiological language to speak of encounter with
God. Indeed, the *locus classicus* for descriptions of eating God or
being eaten by him is Bernard of Clairvaux's sermons on the Song
of Songs, later graphically echoed in John Tauler's sermons for
Corpus Christi.[44] But men's writing often lacks the immediacy
of women's; the male voice is impersonal. It is striking to note
that, however fulsome or startling their imagery, men write of
"*the* mystical experience," giving a general description that may
be used as a theory or yardstick, whereas women write of "*my*
mystical experience," speaking directly of something that may
have occurred to them alone.[45] This is true even when, as in
the case of Hildegard of Bingen or Julian of Norwich, a highly
sophisticated theology is elaborated over many years as a gloss on
visionary experiences.

Women regularly speak of tasting God, of kissing him deeply,
of going into his heart or entrails, of being covered by his blood.
Their descriptions of themselves or of other women often, from
a modern point of view, hopelessly blur the line between spiritual or psychological, on the one hand, and bodily or even sexual,
on the other. Lidwina of Schiedam and Gertrude of Delft, for
example, felt such maternal desire for the Christchild that milk
flowed from their breasts; Beatrice of Nazareth experienced a joy
in Christ that contorted her face and wracked her with hysterical laughter; Lukardis of Oberweimar and Margaret of Faenza
kissed their spiritual sisters with open mouths and grace flowed

from one to the other with an ardor that left both women shaken. The thirteenth-century poet and mystic Hadewijch spoke of Christ penetrating her until she lost herself in the ecstasy of love.[46] Watching sisters sometimes saw the bodies of mystical women elongate or levitate or swoon in ecstatic trances; but the visionary women themselves often did not bother to make clear where the events happened — whether in body, heart or soul, whether in the eye of the mind or before the eyes of the body. Indeed, in the books of women's Revelations, which are really a new literary genre by the fourteenth century, the point is not to provide proof that one woman or a group of women received charismatic gifts, so much as to communicate and share a piety in which spiritual-somatic experiences lie at the center.[47] Devotional books from the later Middle Ages, especially those composed for nuns, offer pictures of the ecstasy and the suffering of *imitatio Christi*, not as illustrations of texts, but as inducements and reflections of spiritual delights themselves (Figure 6.1).[48]

It would be wrong to draw an absolute contrast between male and female piety. Medieval men also saw visions, and their hagiographers described their affective experiences of God.[49] But those men (such as Bernard of Clairvaux, Francis of Assisi, Suso, Ruysbroeck or Richard Rolle) whose religiosity was most experiential and visionary often understood themselves in feminine images and learned their pious practices from women.[50] Moreover, whether they denigrated, admired or used the experiences of mystical women, men such as Albert the Great, Eckhart and Gerson spoke explicitly of somatic and visionary experiences as peculiarly female. David of Augsburg ridiculed them as "erotic ticklings." John Tauler wrote more sympathetically, but even he made it clear that he was a bit suspicious of such piety.[51]

Thus, if we speak phenomenologically, it seems clear that when "the other" breaks through into the lives of individuals, it often throws men into profound stillness. Male mystics write repeatedly of being at a core or ground or inner point (as Eckhart or Walter Hilton put it).[52] Women, on the other hand, are "switched on" by "the other," heightened into an affectivity or sensuality that goes beyond both the senses and our words for describing them. Even those female mystics, such as Hadewijch and Margaret Porete, who distrust or reject affectivity, speak with intimate knowledge of that which they wish to transmute or transcend.[53]

Women's sense that Christ is body, received and perceived by body, is vividly reflected in a little-known text, to which I have called attention in another essay. The text describes a vision given to the French nun, Marguerite of Oingt. In this vision, Marguerite saw herself as a withered tree, which suddenly flowered when inundated by a great river of water (representing Christ). She then saw, written on the flowering branches of her self, the names of the five senses: sight, hearing, taste, smell and touch. It is hard to imagine a more pointed way of indicating that the effect of experiencing Christ is to "turn on," so to speak, the bodily senses of the receiving mystic.[54]

The Italian mystic Angela of Foligno expresses the same awareness when she says that "the soul is more conformed and adapted to the lesser which it sees in Christ the incarnate God, than it is to that which it sees in Christ the uncreated God; because the soul is a creature who is the life of the flesh and of all the members of its body."[55] To Angela, the encounter with the body of Christ into which grace lifts her is beyond ordinary affectivity, for it is a transport simultaneously of pain and of delight. Even filtered through the screen provided by her confessor-redactor, the exuberance of Angela's enthusiasm contrasts sharply with the moderation and hesitation of a Tauler or an Eckhart. She says:

FIGURE 6.1. The Rothschild Canticles, MS 404, fol. 66, Beinecke Library, Yale University (early fourteenth century). This miniature of Soul receiving her Lover in the mystical marriage bed not only depicts but also evokes the ecstasy of mystical union.

> Once, when I was at Vespers and was contemplating the Crucifix,... suddenly my soul was lifted into love, and all the members of my body felt a very great joy. And I saw and felt that Christ, within me, embraced my soul with that arm by which he was crucified... and I felt such great security that I could not doubt it was God.... So I rejoice when I see that hand which he holds out with the signs of the nails, saying to me: "Behold what I bore for you."[56]

> Now I can feel no sadness at the Passion... for all my joy is in that suffering God-Man. And it seems to my soul that it enters within that wound in the side of Christ and walks there with delight....[57]

In such piety, body is not so much a hindrance to the soul's ascent as the opportunity for it. Body is the instrument upon which the mystic rings changes of pain and of delight. It is from body – whether whipped into frenzy by the ascetic herself or gratified with an ecstasy given by God – that sweet melodies and aromas rise to the very throne of heaven.[58]

Thus, as many recent scholars have argued, the spiritualities of male and female mystics were different, and this difference has something to do with body.[59] Women were more apt to somatize religious experience and to write in intense bodily metaphors; women mystics were more likely than men to receive graphically physical visions of God; both men and women were inclined to attribute to women and encourage in them intense asceticisms and ecstasies. Moreover, the most bizarre bodily occurrences associated with women (e.g., stigmata, incorruptibility of the cadaver in death, mystical lactations and pregnancies, catatonic trances, ecstatic nosebleeds, miraculous anorexia, eating and drinking pus, visions of bleeding hosts) either first appear in the twelfth and thirteenth centuries or increase significantly in frequency at that time. These facts suggest – hard as it is for sober

194

modern historians to countenance such arguments – that the body itself may actually have a history. The body, and in particular the female body, seems to have begun to behave in new ways at a particular moment in the European past.[60] The question is: Why is this so?

The Ecclesiastical and Social Context

Many explanations can be proposed for the bodily quality of female spirituality in the later Middle Ages. I have written elsewhere about the importance of charismatic authorization for women at a time when clerical control increased in the Church, and it is customary now for scholars to emphasize women's mysticism as a form of female empowerment.[61] Since the Gregorian reform of the late eleventh century, priest and layperson had been sharply separated in status and form of life; clerical dignity had become ever more elevated and awesome. Thus, one might argue that women *had* to stress the experience of Christ and manifest it outwardly in their flesh, because they did not have clerical office as an authorization for speaking. This argument must also recognize that the clergy themselves encouraged such female behavior both because female asceticism, eucharistic devotion and mystical trances brought women more closely under the supervision of spiritual directors and because women's visions functioned for males, too, as means of learning the will of God. Moreover, theologians and prelates found women's experiential piety useful in the thirteenth-century fight against heresy. The increased emphasis on bodily miracles and indeed the appearance of new miracles of bodily transformation came at exactly the time of the campaign against Cathar dualism. Women whose bodies became one with the crucified man on the cross in stigmata, and visions in which the consecrated wafer suddenly turned into bleeding meat, were powerful evidence against the Cathar assertion that matter and flesh could not be the creations of a good God. Some of the earliest supporters of this bodily aspect of women's piety, James of Vitry and Thomas of Cantimpré, held it up explicitly as a reproach to the dualists.[62]

In addition, we must not forget the educational context. At least since the work of Grundmann in the thirties, we have been aware of how much women's writing was shaped both by their lack of formal theological training and by the availability of the new vernacular languages with their characteristic literary genres.[63] In other words, part of the reason for the more open, experiential style of women's writings is the fact that women usually wrote not in the formal scholastic Latin taught in universities, but in the vernaculars – that is, in the languages they grew up speaking. The major literary genres available in these languages were various kinds of love poetry and romantic stories: the vocabulary provided by such genres was therefore a vocabulary of feelings. A comparison of two women from much the same milieu, Mechtild of Hackeborn and Mechtild of Magdeburg, shows clearly that the one who wrote in Latin wrote more impersonally and to a much greater extent under the influence of the liturgy, whereas the vernacular poet wrote more experientially, with a greater sense both of personal vulnerability and of an immediate and special relationship to God.[64] Furthermore, women's works, especially their accounts of visions, were often dictated (that is, spoken) rather than penned – a fact that is clearly one of the explanations for women's more discursive, conversational, aggregative, tentative, empathetic and self-reflective style. As Elizabeth Petroff has recently pointed out, the prose of a female writer such as Julian of Norwich, which tends to circle around its point, evoking a state of being, displays exactly those traits Walter Ong has seen as characteristic of oral thought and expression.[65]

Social context also sheds light on the nature of women's piety.

As David Herlihy and others have argued, devotional attitudes sometimes compensated for personal deprivation or provided escape from oppression. Little girls who lacked loving families sometimes found a mother in Mary and a father in Saint Joseph or in God; unhappy wives found a tender and considerate bridegroom in Jesus.[66] For example, the handicapped Margaret of Città di Castello, abandoned as a baby by her parents, was especially fond of children and saw visions of the Holy Family, including Joseph, at the elevation of the host. After death, Margaret was found to have three precious stones in her heart; on one of them, a picture of herself and Joseph was etched.[67] As a six-year-old child, watching by the body of her dead mother, the French saint Jane Mary of Maillé received a vision of Mary. Angela of Foligno found, in a quasi-religious role, welcome escape from the burdens of both husband and children; Margery Kempe was quite explicit about substituting Christ for her unsatisfactory husband.[68]

Secular society expected women to be intimately involved in caring for the bodies of others (especially the young, the sick and the dying). Women assisted in childbirth, prepared corpses for burial, carried out ritual mourning for the dead. Despite the professionalization of medical care in the later Middle Ages, which led to male control of certain healing procedures, women retained the right and the obligation to nurse the aged, the young and the ill, and especially to provide what little obstetrical and gynecological care there was.[69] The theologian Hildegard of Bingen was deeply interested in women's diseases, sexual reproduction and gynecology, and wrote on medical and pharmacological matters.[70] Several of the most famous female saints of the Middle Ages (for example, Elizabeth of Hungary, Angela of Foligno and Catherine of Siena) were especially identified with care of the sick in the eyes of their contemporaries.

To some extent, women simply took these ordinary nurturing

roles over into their most profound religious experiences (and found that Mary and the Christchild appreciated their services more than did the whining children, disgruntled husbands and embittered beggars of more mundane situations). The somatic quality of visionary experience was thus, in part, a continuation of women's somatic social responsibility. Not only did female mystics kiss, bathe and suckle babies in visions and grieve with Mary as she received her son's dead body for burial; they actually acted out maternal and nuptial roles in the liturgy, decorating life-sized statues of the Christchild for the Christmas crèche or dressing in bridal garb when going to receive their bridegroom in the eucharist. Anyone who has stood before the lovely beguine cradle on display in the Metropolitan Museum in New York (Figure 6.2) and realized that it is a liturgical object must have thought, at least for a moment: "Why these nuns and beguines were just little girls, playing with dolls!"[71]

Indeed, devotional objects such as the pietà or Anna Selbdritt (see Figure 3.2) came increasingly in the fourteenth and fifteenth centuries to reflect and sanctify women's domestic and biological experience. As Jeffrey Hamburger has recently pointed out, Gertrude of Helfta's vision of the pregnant Virgin not only suggests her own interest in maternity, but perhaps also indicates that she was familiar with statues, such as the Visitation group from the nuns' house of Katharinental (Figure 6.3), that represent the life-bearing womb as a crystal similar to a reliquary. Gertrude wrote that she saw:

> the immaculate womb of the glorious virgin, as transparent as the purest crystal, through which her internal organs, penetrated and filled with divinity, shone brightly.... Indeed, one saw the little blossoming boy, the only Son of the highest Father, nurse avidly in delight at the heart of His virgin mother.[72]

FIGURE 6.2. Liturgical cradle from the Grand Beguinage in Louvain (fifteenth century). Cribs such as this, in which figures of the Christchild were placed, were especially popular in convents and beguinages in the later Middle Ages.

Iconographic motifs such as the Visitation, the Anna Selbdritt and the Holy Kinship (which depict Jesus' extended family as predominantly female) and stories of the childhoods of Jesus and Mary clearly responded to women's interests; these legends and devotional objects were popular with female readers and viewers, secular as well as religious.[73]

In addition to social, ecclesiastical and even artistic influences, it is possible that there is a biological element in women's predisposition to certain kinds of bodily experiences. The fact that, in many cultures, women seem more given to spirit possession and more apt to somatize their inner emotional or spiritual states suggests a physiological explanation. In cultures as different as medieval Europe, medieval China and modern America, self-mutilation and self-starvation seem to be more characteristic of women than of men.[74] But we should be cautious about espousing biological explanations too hastily. Biology and culture are almost impossible to distinguish in these matters, because men and women differ from each other consistently across societies in their social and psychological as well as their physiological experiences. The various cultures in which women are more inclined than men to fast, to mutilate themselves, to experience the gift of tongues and to somatize spiritual states are all societies that associate the female with self-sacrifice and service.

Intellectual Traditions: Dualism and Misogyny

Basic assumptions about body and about gender provide another context against which we must place the new miracles of bodily transformation and the graphic physiological visions of the later Middle Ages. There were intellectual traditions that conditioned women *and men* to certain expectations of women's bodies. Medieval thinkers associated *body* with *woman*; they therefore expected women's expressiveness to be more physical and

FIGURE 6.3. Visitation Group from Katharinental (thirteenth century). Devotional objects such as this depiction of Mary's meeting with Elizabeth were especially popular in women's religious houses. The figure not only emphasizes the importance of Jesus' female relatives but also displays a fascination with the process of pregnancy itself. The womb is a transparent crystal.

physiological than men's. They also associated body with God, through the doctrine of the Incarnation, and eschewed sharp soul/body dichotomies more than did either patristic theologians or those of the early modern period. They could therefore give to the bodily experiences of members of both sexes a deeply spiritual significance.

It may appear odd to emphasize the bodiliness of God, or the bodiliness of women as a means of approaching God, in a discussion of the Middle Ages. Standard accounts of the period are much more inclined to emphasize its misogyny and dualism. And there is no denying these aspects of medieval attitudes. The practical dualism of medieval Christianity is well known. As Jacques Le Goff has pointed out, twelfth- and thirteenth-century literature presented the body not merely as dust but as rottenness, a garment masking the food of worms (Figure 6.4).[75] Ascetic theologians often wrote of spirit and flesh warring with each other. Both in Latin and in the emerging vernaculars, the genre of the debate between body and soul became popular. In one Latin version, so well known it survives in at least 132 manuscripts, Soul describes herself as a noble creature blackened by Flesh, which must be overcome by hunger, thirst and beatings.[76] Indeed, chastity for men and virginity for women were almost preconditions for sanctity. Even in the later Middle Ages, when some married saints were added to the calendar, rejection of actual conjugal sex was taken as a major sign of the saint's growth toward holiness.[77]

It is also clear that theological, scientific and folk traditions associated women with body, lust, weakness and irrationality, men with spirit or reason or strength.[78] Patristic exegetes, for example, argued that woman (or Eve) represents the appetites, man (or Adam) represents soul or intellect.[79] As Weinstein and Bell have pointed out, hagiographers were inclined to see female sin as bodily or sexual, as arising from within the woman's body,

FIGURE 6.4. *A Disputacion Betwyx the Body and Wormes*, MS Add. 37049, fol. 32v, The British Library, London. This depiction of the female body as food for worms is a drawing of a popular type of medieval funerary sculpture known as the transi tomb. Such sculptures contrasted the putrefaction all could expect in the grave with the pleasures and privileges of the world. In the fifteenth-century dialogue from which this illustration is taken, however, the worms do not have the last word. After suffering a decay that parallels Christ's agony on the cross, Body triumphs in the resurrection. Because the female was especially associated with the physical, the poet depicts Body as female and stresses her descent from Eve.

whereas male sinners were depicted as tempted from without – often indeed as tempted by the proffered bodiliness of women.[80] In James of Voragine's *Golden Legend*, a collection of saints' lives retold for use by thirteenth-century preachers in edifying sermons, the major achievement of holy women is dying in defense of their virginity. Defense of chastity is an extremely infrequent theme in the male lives James tells. Resurrection from the dead is, however, a fairly common motif in accounts of holy men, and these men are raised in order to complete tasks or make reparation for deeds done on earth. This pattern suggests that women's lives can be complete only when death has assured perpetual virginity. In contrast, male lives are complete when virtue is won, evil defeated or restitution made. Whereas an early demise is advisable for women, assuring that their weak bodies can no longer be tempted or violated, death itself may be temporarily suspended to give men time to assert themselves and finish the job of winning salvation.[81]

As these examples demonstrate, medieval writers did associate body and flesh with woman, and they did sometimes draw from this dualist and misogynist conclusions. But, as I have argued elsewhere, the impact of medieval conceptions of woman and of body was more complex than scholars have realized, because the concepts themselves were more complex. Medieval men and women did not take the equation of woman with body merely as the basis for misogyny. They also extrapolated from it to an association of woman with the body or the humanity of Christ. Indeed, they often went so far as to treat Christ's flesh as female, at least in certain of its salvific functions, especially its bleeding and nurturing. This fact helps us to understand why it was women more than men who imitated Christ bodily, especially in stigmata.

Moreover, if we look closely at the various traditions that associated woman with body or flesh, we find that neither medieval gender contrasts nor medieval notions of soul and body were as dichotomous as we have been led to think by projecting modern contrasts back onto them.[82] Thus, I would like to argue that we must consider not just the dichotomy but also the mixing or fusing of the genders implicit in medieval assumptions. Only in this way will we understand how mystical women could see themselves and be seen by men as especially apt to imitate and fuse with the male body of Christ. We must also consider the ways in which treatments of body and soul, particularly in the period after 1200, tended to mix rather than separate the two components of person. Such background is necessary in order to comprehend how medieval people of both sexes could see the holy manifest in that same flesh which lured humans into lust and greed during their lives and, after death, putrefied in the grave.

Medieval traditions concerning male/female and body/soul are complex enough that I need to take them up separately and in some detail.

"Woman is to Man as Body is to Soul"

As all medievalists are by now aware, the body of Christ was sometimes depicted as female in medieval devotional texts – partly, of course, because ecclesia, Christ's body, was a female personification, partly because the tender, nurturing aspect of God's care for souls was regularly described as motherly. Both male and female mystics called Jesus "mother" in his eucharistic feeding of Christians with liquid exuded from his breast and in his bleeding on the cross which gave birth to our hope of eternal life.[83] Anselm of Canterbury, in the late eleventh century, wrote of Jesus as a loving mother, reviving dead souls at his breast; in the twelfth century, the Cistercian Guerric of Igny spoke of nursing from and hiding in the side of Christ. In the thirteenth century, Margaret of Oingt described Jesus' pain on the cross as birthpangs; the fourteenth-century English mystic Julian of Norwich spoke of creation as a maternal act because God, in taking on our humanity in the Incarnation, gives himself to us as a mother gives herself to the fetus she bears.[84]

Iconography illustrates the same theme. In the moralized Bibles of the thirteenth and fourteenth centuries, artists depicted Church being born from Christ's side, as Eve is born of Adam (Figure 3.6).[85] Miniatures and panel paintings showed Christ exuding wine or blood into chalices or even into hungry mouths and drew visual parallels between his wound and Mary's breast offered to suckle sinners (Figures 6.5, 6.6, 6.7 and also 3.9, 3.11, 3.13).[86] We know that such traditions lie behind sixteenth-century depictions of Christ feeding Catherine of Siena from his side, because the various versions of Catherine's *vita* speak of Christ nursing her at his breast (Figure 6.8).[87] The motif of "Jesus as mother" may also help explain the unusual northern Renaissance paintings by Jan Gossaert that depict the infant Christ with engorged breasts[88] (Figure 6.9).

There were several separate strands on which medieval mystics drew in identifying woman with flesh and Christ's flesh with the female. Although it is easiest to cite these strands from treatises on theology, natural philosophy and medicine, recent work by French and Italian anthropologists and historians of medicine makes it abundantly clear that we have to do here not merely with learned ideas, but with assumptions widespread in the culture.[89] I have written about these elsewhere, but it seems advisable to repeat some of the material in order to make my argument clear.[90]

The first set of roots is theological. Medieval interpreters of the Bible regularly taught that "spirit is to flesh as male is to female" – that is, that the dichotomy male/female can serve as a symbol for the dichotomies strong/weak, rational/irrational, soul/body. This use of pairs of symbols led Hildegard of Bingen

FIGURE 6.5. Jacob Cornelisz, *The Man of Sorrows* (ca. 1510). Medieval artists emphasized Christ's saving blood both as suffering and as food.

FIGURE 6.6. *The Intercession of Christ and the Virgin* (ca. 1402). In the so-called Double Intercession, Mary and Jesus plead with God the Father; the parallelism of wound and breast is clearly underlined.

FIGURE 6.7. *Mass of St. Gregory* (end of the fifteenth century), altarpiece from the parish church of Villoldo, Spain. According to a popular medieval legend, Christ appeared to Pope Gregory the Great and filled a chalice with his blood, thus demonstrating his true presence in the eucharist. In a departure from the standard iconography of the miracle, this Spanish altarpiece draws an explicit visual parallel between the feeding Christ and his lactating mother.

209

to see the male as symbol of Christ's divinity, the female as symbol of his humanity. Hildegard's association of women with Christ's humanity underlay her reiterated position that women were appropriately denied the priesthood because they had another way of joining with Christ. As Christ's brides in mystical union, women were the body of Christ, not merely his representatives. The analogy "male is to female as divinity is to humanity" also underlay Elizabeth of Schönau's vision – confusing even to its recipient – in which a female virgin, representing Christ's human- ity, appeared sitting on the sun (his divinity). The analogy is reflected in the many medieval texts which say that Christ mar- ried human nature as a man marries a woman, and it lies behind miniatures that depict not only *ecclesia*, but also *humanitas* as female (Figure 3.4).

Such an association of Christ's humanity with the female and the fleshly was also supported by the theological doctrine of the Virgin Birth and the emerging notions of the Immaculate Concep- tion and Bodily Assumption. Because Christ had no human father, his body came entirely from Mary and was therefore closely associated with female flesh. As Thomas Aquinas put it:

> According to Aristotle, the male semen does not play the role of "matter" in the conception of animals. It is rather prime agent, so to speak, while the female alone supplies the matter. So even if male semen were lacking in Christ's conception it does not follow that the necessary matter was missing.
>
> It is not given to the blessed Virgin to be father of Christ but mother.... So it is to be held that in the actual conception of Christ, the blessed Virgin did not actively effect anything in the conceiving, but ministered the matter only. But she actively effected something before the conception by preparing the matter to be apt for conception.

FIGURE 6.8. M. Fiorini after F. Vanni, Saint Catherine of Siena; from the
Legenda Maior (1597). Saint Catherine of Siena drinks pus from the infected
breast of an ill woman and then receives Christ's side to suck.

Associating the flesh of Christ with Mary in another way, Bonaventure wrote:

> Indeed she [Mary] is raised above the hierarchy of the perfect [in
> heaven].... And thus it can be said that she is there corporeally, for
> she has a special sort of perfection in the celestial city.... The soul
> of Christ is not from her soul – since soul does not come by trans-
> mission [from the parents] – but his body is from her body. There-
> fore she will not be there [in heaven] in the mode of perfection
> unless she is there corporeally.[91]

Since some theologians increasingly stressed Mary's humanity as sinless from her conception, they were able to suggest that
just as the Logos (the divinity of Christ separate from that of God)
preexisted the Incarnation, so the humanity of Christ also preexisted the Incarnation in the sinless humanity of Mary. Such arguments could, as I have noted elsewhere, be carried to questionable
lengths. But orthodox prayers and mass commentaries from the
period also speak of Mary as the humanity of Christ, especially
its bodily component or flesh. Catherine of Siena said that Christ's
flesh was Mary's, sealed like hot wax by the Holy Spirit; Francis
of Assisi called Mary Christ's robe or tabernacle. The notion is
clearly depicted in eucharistic tabernacles which Mary surmounts
as if she *were* the container, in monstrances made in her image
(Figure 6.10), and in the so-called opening Virgins – small statues of *Maria lactans* which open to show the Trinity inside (Figure 6.11). The concept is also reflected in those late medieval
paintings in which Mary wears priestly vestments (Figure 6.12).
Such images of Mary as priest have nothing to do with claiming
sacerdotal functions for ordinary women. Mary is priest because
it is she who offers to ordinary mortals the saving flesh of God,
just as the celebrant does in the mass.[92]

FIGURE 6.9. Jan Gossaert, *Madonna and Child* (1527). A puzzling picture, which exists in at least four versions, depicts the infant Christ with engorged breasts.

Scientific ideas – especially theories of conception or generation – were another set of roots for the medieval tendency to associate flesh with female, and God's body with woman's body.[93] According to the Aristotelian theory of conception, held by some medieval scientists and theologians, the mother provides the matter of the fetus and the father its form or life or spirit. This theory clearly associates woman with the unformed physical stuff of which the fully human is made. According to the competing theory of conception available at the time – Galen's theory – two seeds were necessary, one from the father and one from the mother. This theory in a sense associates both father and mother with the physiological stuff. But, even according to Galen, the mother is the oven or vessel in which the fetus cooks, and her body feeds the growing child, providing its stuff as it matures.[94] Moreover, Giles of Rome in the thirteenth century, who rejected the Galenic theory as mediated by Avicenna and turned to Aristotle, argued against Galen that if woman provided both the menstrual matter and seed, then she might impregnate herself and the male would have no role at all. Such an argument shows not only the tendency to associate matter with woman, but also a fear that this threatens the importance of the male contribution to life.[95]

Physiological theory associated matter, food and flesh with female in another sense. All medieval biologists thought the mother's blood fed the child in the womb and then, transmuted into breast milk, fed the baby outside the womb.[96] For example, a fourteenth-century surgeon wrote that milk is blood "twice cooked."[97] One of the Arab texts most frequently used by Western doctors argued: "Since the infant has just been nourished from menstrual blood [in the womb], it needs nurture whose nature is closest to menstrual blood, and the matter that has this quality is milk, because milk is formed from menstrual blood."[98]

Thus, blood was the basic body fluid and female blood was the fundamental support of human life. Medical theory also held that the shedding of blood purged or cleansed those who shed it.[99] Indeed, bleeding was held to be necessary for the washing away of superfluity, so much so that physiologists sometimes spoke of males as "menstruating" (presumably they meant hemorrhoidal bleeding) and recommended bleeding with leeches if they did not do so. Such medical conceptions of blood could lead to the association of Christ's bleeding on the cross – which purges our sin in the Atonement and feeds our souls in the eucharist – with female bleeding and feeding.

The sets of medieval assumptions just described associated female and flesh and the body of God. Not only was Christ enfleshed with flesh from a woman; his own flesh did womanly things: it bled food and gave birth to new life. If certain key moments in the life of Christ were described by devotional writers as "female," it is no wonder that women's physiological processes were given religious significance. Such processes were especially open to religious interpretation when they were not just ordinary, but also extraordinary – that is, when they were continuations of normal physiology, yet miracles as well (as in the cases of virgin lactation or periodic stigmatic bleeding). Not surprisingly, women strove to experience such bodily moments, which recapitulated events in the life of Christ. And, not surprisingly, men (for whom such experiences were not in any sense "ordinary") both revered these women and suspected them of fraud or collusion with the devil.[100]

The analysis I have just given seems, however, to beg an important question. For the human Christ was, after all, male. And, as we all know from the many medieval discussions of women's incapacity for the priesthood, the inferior female body was in certain contexts and by certain theologians prohibited from rep-

FIGURE 6.10. Monstrance from the cloister of Weyarn, Bavaria (1652). This monstrance, in which the consecrated wafer is held by the body of Mary, underlines the relationship of Mary's flesh to Christ's.

FIGURE 6.11. *Vierge ouvrante*, Middle Rhine (late thirteenth or early fourteenth century). This small nursing Madonna opens to show the Holy Trinity
inside. (The body has been broken off the crucifix.) For medieval Christians,
such devotional objects depicted the idea that Mary is the tabernacle that
houses God.

resenting God.[101] How then did it happen that medieval women came more frequently than medieval men to literal, bodily *imitatio Christi*, both in stigmata and in other forms of miraculous sufferings and exudings?

The answer lies in part in the fact that – for all their application of male/female contrasts to organize life symbolically – medieval thinkers used gender imagery fluidly, not literally. As I have explained in Chapter 3, above, many factors encouraged theologians, devotional writers and natural philosophers to mix and fuse the genders. The emphasis on reversal that lay at the heart of the Christian tradition led male devotional writers to describe themselves as "maternal" or "womanly" or subject to "female weakness." The description "woman" or "weak woman" attributed an inferiority that would – exactly because it was inferior – be made superior by God.[102] For example, male mystics such as Bernard of Clairvaux, Bonaventure, Eckhart and John Gerson spoke of devout men as fecund mothers or weak women. Male hagiographers sometimes complimented saintly women by describing them as "virile."[103] Exactly because reversal was less symbolically fruitful to women, they were less likely to employ inverted images. As Peter Dronke and Barbara Newman have argued, they sometimes used "poor little woman" as an ironic self-description in order to underline their special standing before God.[104] But they, too, sometimes adopted male roles (such as knight) in self-description, particularly when they utilized courtly love poetry to describe the mystical quest. And they tended to use words such as "fatherly" or "maternal" or "human" in ways that minimized what we would today call gender stereotyping.[105]

In the scientific tradition, mixing of the sexes was even more apparent. As Thomas Laqueur and Marie-Christine Pouchelle have recently pointed out, medieval natural philosophers argued that

FIGURE 6.12. *The Priesthood of the Virgin*, French panel painting commissioned
for the Cathedral of Amiens (ca. 1437). Mary was occasionally depicted in
sacerdotal robes. She was seen as a priest both because she offered the
Christchild to God in the Presentation in the Temple and because she gave
him to the faithful as their source of salvation.

men and women are really a superior and inferior version of the same physiology. Woman's reproductive system was just man's turned inside out. For example, the fourteenth-century surgeons Henri de Mondeville and Guy de Chauliac said: "The apparatus of generation in women is like the apparatus of generation in men, except that it is reversed"; "the womb is like a penis reversed or put inside." In the sixteenth century, Ambrose Paré even suggested that women could turn into men if, owing to an accident, their internal organs were suddenly pushed outward.[106]

Medieval scientific ideas, especially in their Aristotelian version, made the male body paradigmatic. It was the form or pattern or definition of what we are as humans; what was particularly womanly was the unformedness or physicality of our humanness. Such a notion identified woman with breaches in boundaries, with lack of shape or definition, with openings and exudings and spillings forth.[107] But this conception also made men and women versions of the same thing. Men and women had the same sex organs; men's were just better arranged. These assumptions made the boundary between the sexes extremely permeable.

Permeability or interchangeability of the sexes is seen in a number of aspects of physiological theory. For example, all human exudings — menstruation, sweating, lactation, emission of semen and so on — were seen as bleedings; and all bleedings — lactation, menstruation, nosebleeds, hemorrhoidal bleeding and so on — were taken to be analogous. Thus, it was not farfetched for a medical writer to refer to a man menstruating or lactating, or to a woman emitting seed.[108]

Because biological sex seemed so labile, the question of how to account for the observed sharpness of sexual difference — that is, for the fact that persons are distinctly male or female in gross anatomy — puzzled medieval writers. In discussions of generation, for example, natural philosophers held that the sex of the fetus resulted either from a combination of parts from both parents, or from the stronger or weaker impact of male seed on the menstruum, or from location of the fetus on the right or left side of the womb. Such explanations seem to put male and female along a continuum and leave it totally unclear why there are not at least as many hermaphrodites (midpoints on the spectrum) as there are males or females (endpoints on the spectrum).[109] Perhaps because of this uncertainty, the nature and cause of hermaphroditism, as of other embryological anomalies, was much discussed.[110]

Moreover, tales of pregnant men were fairly common in folklore and miracle stories from the twelfth to fifteenth centuries. These tales hardly suggest that doctors or ordinary folk actually thought males could become pregnant. Their purpose was either to ridicule the clergy (the pregnant male was often a cleric) or to warn against the dangers of unacceptable positions in sexual intercourse. Nonetheless, the popularity of the satiric notion that woman-on-top sex might drive the seed down into the man, impregnating him, suggests that those telling the tale have no good explanation why such things in fact do not happen.[111]

Medieval assumptions about maleness and femaleness associated body – particularly in its fleshly, oozing, unformed physicality – with woman. But such assumptions saw the physiological structure of the body as paradigmatically male. Thus, medieval thinkers put actual men and women on a continuum and saw their bodies as functioning in essentially similar ways. Such ideas perhaps suggested to writers and artists that they might mix or interchange the genders, thereby making it easier than it would otherwise have been to use both sexes symbolically to talk about self and God.[112]

Female *imitatio Christi* mingled the genders in its most profound metaphors and its most profound experiences. Women could fuse with Christ's body because they *were* in some sense body, yet women never forgot the maleness of Christ. Indeed, exactly because maleness was humanly superior, the God who especially redeemed and loved the lowly stooped to marry *female* flesh. Hildegard of Bingen saw *ecclesia* as both Christ's bride and Christ's body. Julian of Norwich, who forged the most sophisticated theology of the motherhood of God, never ceased to refer to "Christ our mother" with the male pronoun. Some mystics, such as Hadewijch and Angela of Foligno, met Christ erotically as female to his maleness; others, such as Catherine of Siena or Margery Kempe, met him maternally, nursing him in their arms. But women mystics often simply became the flesh of Christ, because their flesh could do what his could do: bleed, feed, die and give life to others.[113]

The Body/Soul Relationship and the Significance of Body
Before concluding this examination of the religious significance of the female body, one conceptual boundary remains to be considered – that between body and soul. For the theological writing of the thirteenth and fourteenth centuries came to treat the relationship between body and soul as much tighter and more integral than it had earlier been understood to be. It seems reasonable to suppose that the extraordinary importance given to body, especially female body, in thirteenth- to fifteenth-century religion, and what appear to be the historical beginnings of certain somatic events (such as stigmata or miraculous lactation), owe something to the fact that theorists in the high Middle Ages did not see body primarily as the enemy of soul, the container of soul, or the servant of soul; rather they saw the person as a psychosomatic unity, as body and soul together.

Received wisdom has held that pious folk in the Middle Ages were practical dualists who hated and attacked the body.[114] Moreover, some feminist analysis has recently claimed that the Thomis-

222

tic-Aristotelian association of form/matter with male/female laid the basis for modern theories of sex polarity and male supremacy, and for a certain denigration of the bodily or experiential as well.[115] There is truth in all this, of course. But when one reads medieval discussions, one is struck less by the polarities and dichotomies than by the muddle theologians and natural philosophers made of them, either by inserting entities between body and soul or by obscuring their differences. Those who wrote about body in the thirteenth and fourteenth centuries were in fact concerned to bridge the gap between material and spiritual and to give to body positive significance. Nor should we be surprised to find this so in a religion whose central tenet was the incarnation – the enfleshing – of its God.[116]

No scholastic theologian and no mystic (male or female) denied that the distinction between body and soul was in a technical philosophical sense a real distinction. None rejected the Pauline idea that flesh (which, to Paul, means "sin" more than "body") is a weight pulling spirit down.[117] Nonetheless, theological speculation in the period of high scholasticism modified considerably the traditional Platonic notion that the person is a soul, making use of a body.[118] A concept of person as soul *and* body (or, in modern parlance, a psychosomatic unity) undergirds scholastic discussions of such topics as bodily resurrection, miracles, embryology, asceticism, Christology and the Immaculate Conception. Indeed, it is because medieval thinkers felt it necessary to tie body and soul together, to bridge the gap between them while allowing body to retain a reality and significance of its own, that their writings in these areas are so extraordinarily difficult to understand. But, despite the obscurity of their theoretical writings, these theologians were in no way isolated from pious practice. They preached about miracles or trained others to preach; they inquired into accusations of heresy, claims for canonization and disputes over relics; they sometimes even supervised convents or advised others who did so. It thus seems likely that their attitudes toward body shaped and reflected the environment within which holy women found it easy to experience bizarre bodily miracles and people of both sexes admired them.

The thirteenth and fourteenth centuries saw a proliferation of treatises and quodlibetal questions concerning various aspects of body.[119] (Quodlibetal disputations were debates by university students and masters on freely chosen rather than set topics; they are therefore an excellent index to which issues excited contemporary interest.) There was, for example, much discussion of the resurrection of the body;[120] and this fundamental tenet of Christian belief was treated not so much as a manifestation of divine power (as it had been in the patristic period), but as a consequence of human nature. Certain scholastic theologians even questioned whether bodily resurrection after the Last Judgment might be natural – that is, not a gift of divine grace, but an implication of the fact that God created human nature as a body/soul unity.[121] Most theorists answered that resurrection was supernatural. But in several papal and conciliar pronouncements Christians were required to hold that damned as well as saved rise bodily, nevermore to suffer corruption;[122] and moralists repeatedly explained this doctrine by arguing that body sinned or gained merit alongside soul and must therefore also receive reward or punishment eternally.[123] Such arguments imply that persons *are* in some sense their bodies, not merely souls temporarily inhabiting matter. As is well known, heretics of the twelfth to fourteenth centuries were castigated for holding the obverse opinion.[124] What most bothered orthodox polemicists about heretical opinions was not the moral argument (i.e., the idea that flesh drags spirit down) but the ontological-cosmological one (i.e., the idea that matter and body cannot be included in the human).[125]

FIGURE 6.13. *Last Judgment*, Cologne (ca. 1425). In the high Middle Ages, the standard depiction of the Last Judgment showed the dead rising naked from the earth at the sound of the trumpet. In this version from the Rhineland, the blessed are led through the doorway of paradise, clothed with the garments of salvation, while demons drive the damned into the fiery mouth of hell.

225

Scholastic treatises often combined theological with scientific (i.e., natural philosophical) interests. The attention devoted to Mary's virgin conception of Christ, and the significantly larger amount of attention devoted to Mary's own Immaculate Conception and her Bodily Assumption, suggest that religious writers were fascinated by those Christian doctrines that forced an examination of bodily processes.[126] Some even considered explicitly the physiological effects of religious practice. Albert the Great, for example, asked whether cessation of eating and of menstruation in holy women was damaging to their health.[127] A number of the major theologians of the thirteenth century (for example, Albert the Great, Giles of Rome, Richard of Middleton) wrote both on embryology and on the resurrection of the body and explicitly stated that there was a connection between the topics, for both bore on the question of the nature and identity of the human person.[128] A quick perusal of Book II, Chapters 56 to 90, of the *Summa contra Gentiles* convinces the reader that Aquinas assumed that questions of psychology, embryology and eschatology must be solved together. Moreover, a large section of Aquinas's long discussion of miracles in his *On the Power of God* is concerned with whether demons or angels can make use of physical human bodies and, if so, exactly how they might do it. Since this kind of miracle did not loom large among those actually reported in Aquinas's day, one is tempted to attribute his interest in the question to the general fascination he and his contemporaries felt with the body/soul nexus.[129] Hagiographers, too, combined an interest in bodily miracles with exploration of medical lore, especially embryology. For example, Thomas of Cantimpré, the hagiographer who showed the greatest interest in collecting somatic miracles, especially female ones,[130] wrote on gynecology as well.[131]

In theological treatments of psychology and embryology we

see a tendency to confuse the body/soul boundary. Thirteenth-to fifteenth-century explorations into psychology used the Aristotelian conception of soul — that is, the idea that soul is the principle of life. According to such theory, plants and animals as well as humans have souls. This idea made it difficult for those who wrote about the biological process of conception to say at what point the fetus was ensouled with the rational soul given by God or, indeed, whether it had one or several souls as it developed. Moreover, under the influence of Avicenna, theologians and natural philosophers tried to work out a theory of "spirits" or "powers" located between soul and body as a sort of rarefied instrument to connect the two. Such discussions drew a sharper line between levels of soul than between soul and body.[132]

One of the reasons for the obscuring of the body/soul boundary in these treatments lay in Aristotle's theory itself, which actually worked less well to explain embryological development than the Galenic two-seed theory preferred by doctors.[133] As part of their general adoption of Aristotelian philosophy, theologians were drawn to the idea that the father provides the form for the fetus and the mother the matter (or menstrual material), but the concept proved difficult to use in detail. How does the father's seed, which is material, carry form or vital spirit? It is hard to follow Giles of Rome's explanation, in the *De formatione corporis humani in utero*, of how the father's body concocts a seed with vital spirits, which in some sense engenders spirits in the menstrual matter, which in turn form organs. But one thing is clear: the line between soul and body, form and matter, disappears in a complex apparatus that obscures the transition point from one to the other.[134]

In discussions of eschatology from the same period, we find the human person treated as a similarly tight and integral union of soul and body. Indeed, the doctrine of the resurrection of the body seemed to require a theory of the person in which body was integral. Accounts of the history of philosophy have long seen it as one of Aquinas's greatest achievements to utilize the Aristotelian form/matter dichotomy as a way of explaining that bodily resurrection after the Last Judgment is philosophically necessary.[135] According to Aquinas's use of hylomorphic analysis, the soul as a substantial form survives the death of the body, but the full person does not exist until body (matter) is restored to its form at the end of time: "anima...non est totus homo et anima mea non est ego."[136]

What historians of philosophy have not fully realized, however, is that Aquinas is not alone in emphasizing body. His conservative opponents also gave positive significance to physicality. Many theologians in the second half of the thirteenth century debated whether material continuity was necessary for bodily resurrection. Did God have to reassemble in the resurrected body the same bits of matter that had before been animated by a particular soul? They also debated whether the human person was to be explained by a plurality of forms or by a single form.[137] These debates are too complex to explain fully here,[138] but what is important for my purposes is that both conservative theologians and those who followed Aquinas wanted to make body integral to person. Aquinas made body philosophically necessary but in some sense telescoped body into form by holding both that soul is enough to account for individual continuity and that soul is the *forma corporeitatis*.[139] (In other words, it is soul that accounts for the "whatness" of body. Thus, any matter which soul informs at the end of time will be *its* body.)[140] Those who opposed Thomas, following an older, Platonic tradition, struggled to give body a greater substantial reality by positing a separate *forma corporeitatis* and arguing for material continuity in the resurrection. But to them, too, the union of body and soul is necessary for personhood –

and for happiness. Bonaventure, for example, asserted that the Virgin Mary must have been assumed bodily into heaven, for, without her body, she would be troubled by its lack and therefore unable to enjoy perfect happiness. "The person is not the soul; it is a composite," he wrote; "thus...[Mary] must be [in heaven] as a composite...; otherwise she would not be there in perfect joy."[141]

Indeed, one can argue that those who differed from Aquinas, following a more Platonic, Augustinian or Franciscan tradition, gave even more importance to body than did the Thomists.[142] Henry of Ghent, for example, held to the theory of a separate *forma corporeitatis* so that the gifts of the glorified body could be understood as real changes *of that body*, not merely as a consequence of change in the soul.[143] In general, Franciscan thinkers were as adamant as Dominicans in emphasizing the yearning of soul and body for each other after death.[144]

Discussions of eschatology emphasized the fascination and value of body in other ways as well, sometimes even obscuring differences between body and soul. In some of their more adventuresome explorations of the future life, theologians elevated aspects of body into the spiritual realm. They wondered, for example, whether the blessed in their glorified bodies would truly taste and smell, as well as see, the pleasures of heaven.[145] At other moments in theological discussion, soul seems almost to spill over into body. The gifts (*dotes*) of subtlety, impassibility, clarity and agility that characterize the bodies of the saved were understood to be a flowing over of the beatific vision – perhaps even a way in which soul expresses itself as body.[146]

A number of the issues theologians raised enabled them to explore the nature of bodiliness at its very boundaries. For example, they debated whether we can open and close our eyes in the glorified body, how old we will be in heaven, whether we will rise in two sexes, whether the wounds of the martyrs will still be present in the glorified body, and how the damned in their restored bodies (which are incorruptible but not impassible) can cry without losing any bodily matter through the dissolution of tears.[147] In such discussion, jejune though it has seemed to most modern commentators, a very profound conception of body is adumbrated – one in which both innate and acquired physical differences between persons, including biological sex and even the marks of human suffering, *are* the person for eternity. Theologians agreed that human beings rise in two sexes and with the traces not only of martyrdom, but of other particularities as well.[148] Although defects will be repaired in glory and woman's sex can, in Aristotelian terms, be seen as a defect, theologians nonetheless asserted that, for reasons they could not fully explain, God's creation was more perfect in two sexes than in one.[149] What is temporary or temporal, according to this view, is not physical distinctiveness or gender, but the change we call corruption (or decay or dissolution) of material being.[150] This conception of body as integral to person – indeed of body as being the conveyor of personal specificity – helps us understand how relics could in this culture be treated as if they *were* the saints.[151]

Moreover, the idea that body as well as soul is rewarded (or punished) at the end of time – an idea reflected not just in theology, but also in the literary genre of the debate between body and soul – seemed to give significance to physical rewards that might come *before* death or the Last Judgment. The catatonic trances and miraculous fasting of living holy women, like the incorrupt bodies they sometimes displayed beyond the grave, could easily be understood as having achieved in advance the final incorruption and impassibility of the glorified body in heaven. Indeed, Christ was understood to have assumed all general defects of body in the Incarnation because, as Aquinas said, "we know human nature only as it is subject to defect," and all particular defects are caused by the general defects of corruption and passibility.[152] Thus, even the ugliness of disease and suffering can be not only lifted up into the curative pangs of purgatory, but also transmuted, through Christ's wondrous yet fully human body, into the beauty of heaven. (Presumably stigmatics will still bear their marks before the throne of God, although the wounds will no longer bleed periodically.[153])

By the 1330s the faithful were required to believe that the beatific vision could come to the blessed before the end of time; and theologians held, although in different ways, that the gifts of the glorified body were in some sense a consequence of the soul's vision of God.[154] Indeed, some theologians argued that a special miracle had been necessary to block the manifestation of God's glory in the human body of his son Jesus; the body Jesus displayed at the Transfiguration was, they held, his normal body, manifesting the beatific vision he constantly possessed.[155] Theologians were, of course, cautious about stating that any specific person had actually received the beatific vision in this life; and, in general, the new interest in the doctrine of purgatory and in blessedness received by the soul *before* it rejoined the body lessened theological emphasis on bodily resurrection. But the notion that the beatific vision could spill over into bodily manifestations, such as beauty or agility, probably encouraged the extravagant claims of hagiographers, who described their holy subjects as rosy and beautiful despite flagellation and self-starvation, excruciating disease and death itself.[156] Aquinas wrote that the martyrs were enabled to bear up under pain exactly because the beatific vision flows over naturally into the body.[157] Both artistic representation and hagiographical story depicted saintly heroes and heroines as unaffected psychologically (and often even physiologically) by graphic and remarkable tortures (Figures 6.14, 6.15).[158]

FIGURE 6.14. Swiss School, *The Martyrdom of St. Agatha* (1473). Modern viewers are often surprised both at the sadism of medieval depictions of martyrdom and at the serenity with which the saints are shown to face torture and execution. Theologians argued that the martyrs' vision of God protected them from feeling pain, fear or humiliation. In this depiction of a particularly hideous torture, the saint seems almost smug in her imperviousness to discomfort.

232

FIGURE 6.15. The Master of the Holy Kinship (fl. 1480–1520), *Sebastian Altar*, middle wing: *The Martyrdom of St. Sebastian*, Cologne. Neither triumph over suffering nor graphic tortures with sexual overtones were limited to female saints. Like Saint Agatha in Figure 6.14, Saint Sebastian does not appear to feel the pain inflicted on him.

The widely shared assumption that bodies not only reflect the glory their souls receive in God's presence, but are also the place where persons are rewarded or punished in their specificity underlies the many hagiographical stories and *exempla* from this period in which incorruption or other miraculous marks touch only part of a body. Caesarius of Heisterbach, for example, told of a master who copied many books; after death, his right hand was found undecayed although the rest of his body had turned to dust.[159] In another tale from Caesarius's collection, a pious man who said his prayers as he walked returned after death in a vision with the words *Ave Maria* written on his boots; God, says Caesarius, puts "the mark of glory most of all on those members by which it is earned."[160] Given the tremendous emphasis on female virginity as an avenue to sanctity, it is hardly surprising that the bodies of many female saints were found wholly intact years after burial.[161] As Caesarius might have put it, God marked their unviolated bodies with permanent inviolability.

It is, moreover, hardly surprising that, as the doctrine of purgatory was elaborated, the experiences of souls there were imaged as bodily events, even though theologians taught that souls in this state subsisted without their bodies. Bodily metaphors for spiritual states are used in many societies. But more seems to be involved in these Christian ideas than mere convenience of metaphor. In technical theology as in popular miracle stories, pain was understood to be the experience of a psychosomatic unit. Aquinas said, about the suffering of Christ's soul: "soul and body are one being. So when body is disturbed by some corporeal suffering, soul is of necessity disturbed indirectly as a result (*per accidens*)...."[162] More generally in the culture the reverse was assumed as well: when soul is disturbed, body is disturbed. Pain and imperviousness to it happen to a personal entity that is body and soul together.[163] So many forces in the religious life of the period conspired to suggest that persons are their bodies that preachers found it almost impossible to speak of immortal souls without clothing them in their quite particular flesh. The many tales of temporary resurrections of the dead, of corpses bleeding to accuse their murderers or sitting up to reverence the eucharist, of cadavers growing or smelling sweet or even exuding food after death, point to a widespread cultural assumption that person is body as well as soul, body integrally bound with soul.[164]

About the topics I have discussed above, much more could be said. But I have explained and explored enough to make it quite clear that the extraordinary bodily quality of women's piety between 1200 and 1500 must be understood in the context of attitudes toward woman and toward body peculiar to the later Middle Ages. Because preachers, confessors and spiritual directors assumed the person to be a psychosomatic unity, they not only read unusual bodily events as expressions of soul but also expected body itself to offer a means of access to the divine. Because they worshiped a God who became incarnate and died for the sins of others, they viewed all bodily events – the hideous wounds of martyrs or stigmatics as well as the rosy-faced beauty of virgins – as possible manifestations of grace. Because they associated the female with the fleshly, they expected somatic expressions to characterize women's spirituality.

Two caveats are necessary. We must never forget the pain and frustration, the isolation and feelings of helplessness, that accompanied the quest of religious women. For all her charismatic empowerment, woman was inferior to man in the Middle Ages; her voice was often silenced, even more frequently ignored. Not every use of the phrase "weak woman" by a female writer was ironic; women clearly internalized the negative value placed on them by the culture in which they lived. Moreover, for all its expressiveness and lability, body was inferior to soul. The locus of fertility and of mystical encounter, it was also the locus of temptation and decomposition. Whereas soul was immortal, body rose again only after decay and as a result of the grace of Christ's resurrection. Body was not always a friend or a tool or a gateway to heaven. Nonetheless, one of the most striking characteristics of this period in Western religious history is the extent to which female bodily experience was understood to be union with God.

The thirteenth-century Flemish saint Christina *Mirabilis*, whose body lactated and levitated in mystical encounter, supposedly spoke of her own asceticism in a little dialogue that has many literary antecedents:

> Then wailing bitterly she began to beat her breast and her body.... "O miserable and wretched body! How long will you torment me...? Why do you delay me from seeing the face of Christ? When will you abandon me so that my soul can return freely to its Creator?"... Then, taking the part of the body, she would say... "O miserable soul! Why are you tormenting me in this way? What is keeping you in me and what is it that you love in me? Why do you not allow me to return to the earth from where I was taken and why do you not let me be at rest until I am restored to you on the Last Day of Judgment?"... She would then rest a little in silence.... Then, taking her feet with both hands, she would kiss the soles of her feet with greatest affection and would say, "O most beloved body! Why have I beaten you? Why have I reviled you? Did you not obey me in every good deed I undertook to do with God's help? You have endured the torment and hardships most generously and most patiently which the spirit placed on you.... Now, O best and sweetest body,... is an end of your hardship, now you will rest in the dust and will sleep for a little and then, at last, when the trumpet blows, you will

rise again purified of all corruptibility and you will be joined in eternal happiness with the soul you have had as a companion in the present sadness."[165]

Christina's words express much of what a thirteenth-century woman and her hagiographer assumed about female body. Source of temptation and torment, body is also a beloved companion and helpmeet; delay and hindrance on earth, it is essential to the person herself and will be perfected and glorified in heaven.

Christina's words can be supplemented by a later and more gruesome dialogue, which is nonetheless descended from the genre in which Thomas of Cantimpré, her hagiographer, wrote. In the fifteenth-century *Disputacion Betwyx the Body and Wormes*, the anonymous author modifies the traditional debate between Body and Soul to dramatize death and decay.[166] Here, a female body, so misled about the significance of flesh that she actually boasts of her descent from Eve, is forced to hear the message of Worms, who will strip the body of its stinking flesh, scouring the bones (Figure 6.4). Nonetheless, the poem does not end with the feast of Worms nor with the triumph of devils carrying Body off to hell. The poet argues for victory over death, not by denying the horrors of decay, but by identifying corruption with the suffering of Christ on the cross.[167] As Christina says in Thomas's quite similar account: Body itself will rise again. Welcoming the "kys" of Worms and agreeing to "dwell to gedyr" with them in "luf" until Judgment Day as "neghbors" and "frendes," Body arms herself with "gode sufferaunce" and anticipates the coming "blis of heuen" through the "mene and mediacione" of "our blissed Lord, our verry patrone."[168]

In such a dialogue, the modern reader glimpses the startling significance attributed to body, and especially female body, in the later Middle Ages. Clothing of decay and potential food for worms, female flesh was also an integral component of female person. Created and redeemed by God, it was a means of encounter with him. Healed and elevated by grace, it was destined for glory at the Last Judgment. And in that Judgment it rose as female. Although medieval theologians did not fully understand why, they were convinced that God's creation was more perfect in two sexes than in one.

VII

Material Continuity, Personal Survival and the Resurrection of the Body: A Scholastic Discussion in Its Medieval and Modern Contexts

To twentieth-century non-Christians and Christians alike, no tenet of Christianity has seemed more improbable – indeed, incredible – than the doctrine of the resurrection of the body.[1] Easter sermons in both mainline Protestant and Catholic churches tend to allegorize the doctrine as a parable of the rebirth of the soul or draw on I Corinthians 15 to emphasize the radical change "body" must undergo when, "sown corruptible," it rises "incorruptible." Nonetheless, Christian preachers and theologians from Tertullian to the seventeenth-century divines asserted that God will reassemble the decayed and fragmented corpses of human beings at the end of time and grant to them eternal life and incorruptibility. In this essay I wish to take seriously, rather than explain away, the medieval discussion of bodily resurrection. In doing so, I shall reinterpret a moment in the history of medieval philosophy and locate that moment in its context in religious practice. I shall also suggest that not only the basic concerns of the medieval discussion, but even the materialistic details are relevant to modern problems in ways present-day preachers, believers and skeptics have not understood.

The Medieval Discussion of Bodily Resurrection

Through the doctrinal controversies of the second to fifth centuries C.E., the resurrection of the body was firmly established as an element of the Christian faith.[2] Medieval councils confirmed this. The Fourth Lateran Council in 1215 required Cathars and other heretics to assent to the proposition that "all rise again with their own individual bodies, that is, the bodies which they now wear..."; and the Second Council of Lyon in 1274 reaffirmed the requirement.[3] Conservative theologians charged with curtailing the more dangerous speculations of the university teachers of their day included among the propositions they condemned in 1277 the idea "that the corrupted body does not return one and the same, that is, does not rise numerically the same."[4] If one argues, as scholars have recently done, that patristic and medieval polemics against heresy were less a quarrel with a clearly existent "other," than a process by which Christians defined themselves through creation of the "other," then one must say that theologians accorded importance, in eschatology, to the doctrine of resurrection not because it was under attack, but because they themselves chose to do so.[5]

In certain ways, eschatology sat uncomfortably among other tenets of scholastic theology. Consideration of "last things" was tacked on at the end of Peter Lombard's basic textbook, the *Four Books of Sentences*, coming rather incongruously after the discussion of marriage. Thus, some later commentators (for example, Giles of Rome) never reached the issue when they composed their Sentence commentaries. Some twelfth-century theologians (for example, Robert of Melun) never considered "final things"; others (for example, Honorius Augustodunensis) raised such issues but in ways that suggest that they did not find the doctrine of bodily resurrection completely compatible with other theological tenets.[6] Thomas Aquinas did not treat eschatology in detail in the *Summa theologiae*; and modern theologians must turn to the *Supplementum* (put together by a disciple) or to his early Sentence commentary for a statement of his position. Almost all twelfth- and thirteenth-century theologians warned their readers that questions about what the resurrected body would be like might lead to idle, or even heterodox, speculation. As Jacques Le Goff and others have recently reminded us, discussions of bodily resurrection became less frequent as elaboration of the doctrine of purgatory and disputes over the beatific vision increasingly directed the attention of schoolmen and preachers to the state of the soul in the period between death and Last Judgment.[7]

Nonetheless, theologians of the high Middle Ages neither abandoned the doctrine nor ceased to discuss it. Several (for example, Albert the Great and Giles of Rome) wrote treatises about it.[8] Moreover, it came up again and again in quodlibetal disputes;[9] and it provided the occasion for debating certain key philosophical issues raised by Aristotle, the most important being – as we shall see – the question of the unicity or plurality of forms.

What modern readers find most disturbing about medieval discussions is their extreme literalism and materialism. In order to illustrate these characteristics, I shall give a brief summary of the last section of Peter Lombard's *Sentences*, which determined the course of debate for hundreds of years. Although an overall principle of organization is difficult to discern in Peter's treatment, his emphasis is clear. He chose to consider final things in a way that gives pride of place to questions of the material reassemblage or reconstitution of the body.[10]

Beginning with the admonition (borrowed from Augustine) that not all questions can be answered, Peter devoted distinction (that is, section) 43 of his fourth book to a discussion of the sound of the last trumpet, concentrating on the question of whether those alive at that moment must die before being raised. In distinction 44, he turned to such questions as the following: What age, height and sex will we have in the resurrected body? Will all matter that has passed through the body at any point be resurrected? Must bits of matter return to the particular members (fingernails or hair, for example) where they once resided? Will the bodies of the damned as well as the saved rise with their defects repaired? Are aborted fetuses resurrected? How can the bodies of the damned burn without being consumed? Will demons (although incorporeal) suffer from corporeal fire in hell? Distinction 45, after considering where souls reside between death and resurrection and asserting (without explaining) that the blessed will experience an increase of joy in bodily resurrection, turns to lengthy consideration of the usefulness of prayers for the dead. Distinctions 46 and 47 explore in detail God's justice, especially the punishment of the damned. Distinctions 48 and 49 discuss specific questions concerning what we might call the topography and demography of blessedness: Where exactly will Christ descend as judge? Of what quality will light be after the Last Judgment? Will all the elect shine with the same glory, see with the same clarity, and rejoice with the same joy? Distinction 50 returns to details of the condition of the damned and, after considering the question of how the finger of Lazarus (Luke 16.22–26) could touch the tongue of the rich man when both (having died) were without body, repeats Augustine's warning that certain answers cannot be discovered.

As even such brief summary makes clear, the Last Judgment is primarily, to the Lombard, a matter of punishment and reward of exactly the same material stuff that constituted the body during life. The discussion, although almost pictorial in its vividness, is highly unoriginal, mostly borrowed in fact from Augustine's *City of God* and *Enchiridion*, with bits from Gregory, Julian of Toledo,

Jerome, Hugh of St. Victor, Honorius Augustodunensis and the school of Anselm of Laon thrown in. Nonetheless, Peter Lombard appears to have chosen from among the available authorities in such a way as to underline the corporeal experience of the resurrected body.

The Lombard was not alone among twelfth-century theologians in emphasizing the materialism of the risen body. Hugh of St. Victor wondered whether we shall be able to open and close our eyes after the resurrection.[11] Honorius (and Herrad of Hohenbourg who borrowed his discussion) queried what color we will be in heaven and whether we will wear clothes.[12] Guibert of Nogent fulminated against the cults of the tooth of Christ and of the holy foreskin because they implied that Christ had not risen in total bodily perfection and that our resurrection might therefore be defective as well.[13] Several theologians debated whether food taken in by the body during its lifetime would become part of that body and rise at the end.[14]

Such discussion continued throughout the thirteenth century. Schoolmen queried whether the gift of *subtilitas* received by the glorified body meant that that body could be in the same place at the same time as another body. The conclusion that it could be was, of course, suggested by gospel stories of Christ passing through closed doors after his resurrection.[15] Theologians also asked whether we will smell sweet odors or touch other bodies in heaven. Will we eat or taste? The latter question was an extraordinarily difficult one; the indignities of digestion could hardly be ascribed to a glorified body endowed with *impassibilitas*, yet the resurrected Christ had, according to Luke 24.42–43, eaten boiled fish and honeycomb with his disciples.[16]

The question of cannibalism and the resurrection, debated at least since the second century and engaged in new ways in the thirteenth, has seemed to modern commentators the most extravagant and offensive of such materialistic considerations. If human remains were eaten by other human beings, in which person would the common matter rise? By the time of Thomas Aquinas the discussion had become remarkably elaborate. A consensus had developed that digested food does become "of the substance of human nature" and rise at the end of time. Thus, eaten human remains will be resurrected in the person to whom they first belonged; the missing matter will be made up in the second person from the nonhuman stuff he or she has eaten. But what (hypothesized Aquinas) about the case of a man who ate only human embryos who generated a child who ate only human embryos? If eaten matter rises in the one who possessed it first, this child will not rise at all. All its matter will rise elsewhere: either in the embryos its father ate (from which its core of human nature, passed on in the semen, was formed) or in the embryos it ate. Although the cannibalism question had been considered seriously at least since the second century, the issue did not remain the same. To the early Fathers such questions were challenges raised by the enemies of Christianity, against whom one asserted, in answer, the absolute power of God to supplement missing matter in any way He chose. Aquinas, in contrast, insisted on tracking the bits of matter as far as possible through the processes of digestion, assimilation and reproduction before resorting (as he also had finally to do) to divine power to make up the difference.[17]

The Modern Debate over Personal Identity and Survival

Medieval debates about the resurrection of foreskins or eaten embryos have baffled modern historians and theologians.[18] Deeply embarrassed by such materialism and literalism, they have occasionally cited the debates in order to shock or titillate their colleagues,[19] or have, like Renaissance polemicists, used them to illustrate and condemn scholastic obscurantism. Most frequently, however, scholars have expressed their bewilderment and frustration with medieval arguments by trying to sweep away the offensive details while salvaging something of importance.[20] Twentieth-century treatments of the resurrection usually assert that, while particular aspects of the scholastic debate may be jejune or scientifically outdated, basic questions were at stake.[21]

At first glance, this approach seems promising. The distasteful details of medieval discussion can indeed be stripped away to reveal perennial questions. The doctrine of bodily resurrection does involve fundamental issues of survival and identity still moot in philosophical circles. Nonetheless, further consideration of this tactic suggests that it is misguided. We will not understand either medieval positions or their relevance for modern theological discussion if we strip away the materialist detail. The details of the medieval discussion are exactly the point. I can explain this more clearly if I turn for a moment to modern philosophical discussion.

When we consider current discussions of personal identity and survival, we find that they, too, involve lengthy consideration of cases even their investigators admit to be bizarre. The two most common examples used in philosophical discussions over the past two or three decades are "teletransportation" (the mode of travel used in the TV series *Star Trek*, whereby a person's body pattern is beamed through space in order to rematerialize on another planet) and the operation that we may alternatively call a brain or body transplant.[22] (How we label it, of course, turns out to make a good deal of difference in what we think happens.) One of the most gripping and accessible recent explorations of questions of survival is John Perry's *Dialogue on Personal Identity and Immortality*, which purports to be a deathbed conversation with a philosophy teacher from a small Midwestern college who has refused a body transplant operation after a motorcycle accident because she claims "she" will not survive if her brain occupies a new body.[23] Another such accessible exploration is Robert Nozick's discussion in *Philosophical Explanations* of audience reaction to the film *Invasion of the Body Snatchers*. Nozick points out that viewers see the pods which reproduce and replace the former bodies of characters (but without their emotions), not as murderers of the old selves, but as continuers of them which alter *them* in some fundamental and sinister way.[24]

Brain transplants, interstellar beaming of a body pattern, pods generated by invaders from outer space – speculation about such cases is perhaps no less odd than speculation about the resurrection of Christ's foreskin, about the "teletransportation" of glorified bodies or about the fate of eaten embryos. And the oddness has been noticed. The philosopher J.L. Austin has described discourse in his own discipline as the "constant and obsessive repetition of the same small range of jejune examples."[25] Nancy Struever has said of Bernard Williams' *Problems of the Self* (one of the very best of recent books on the survival question): "[It is] in many ways a wise book, but it is stuffed, literally stuffed, with bizarre examples: there are split personalities, amoebalike fissions of the body, nuclear fusions of minds, brain transfusions – a monstrous zoo seems to be the proper arena of discovery."[26]

Yet, odd though these examples are, they cannot simply be discarded while we seek the perennial questions that lie behind them. This is so for three reasons. First, the examples used in philosophical investigation are sometimes the most time-bound elements of the debate.[27] They may also be the place where popular assumptions and academic discourse touch each other most closely and most specifically. Thus, the historian of contemporary issues may find, in the particular illustrations chosen, the most telling information about historical context. Second, the bizarre examples are part of the discussion; often they bear the weight of the argument. For example, it is only by careful consideration of the case of teletransportation that we learn whether the philosopher using the example thinks personal identity depends on transported molecules or only on a transferred pattern or form. Third, it is in the examples that we see that current philosophical discussion clings, almost in spite of itself, to the issue of material continuity. It is therefore in the examples more clearly than in the articulated positions that we see the essential similarity of medieval and modern discussion.

Medieval and modern theories of survival are not the same, to be sure. All medieval thinkers held a soul–body dualism; few modern thinkers do. But recent philosophical discussion, unlike that of the late nineteenth and early twentieth century but like that of the Middle Ages, seems to find it almost impossible to envision personal survival without material continuity. It is the examples chosen by philosophers that make this clear.

By and large, in modern discussions, "soul" has been discarded. Even those, such as Richard Swinburne, who retain a dualist (that is, a body-and-soul) position seem to hold what Swinburne calls "soft dualism" – that is, a position which argues that soul is not reducible to body but does not survive without it.[28] Recent anthologies on the survival question put together for undergraduates represent the "soul position" with the same old article from the fifties – an article that cites psychic research done in the thirties or earlier.[29] Apparently, two theories are viable today: one a version of the memory theory that goes back to John Locke ("I am my continuous stream of memory");[30] the other a theory of material continuity ("I am my body" or – and this is clearly a very different sort of material continuity – "I am a particular part of my body: my brain").[31] While no one thinks that a self is only a body, recent discussion seems to find it difficult to account for identity without some sort of physical continuity.

247

What is characteristic of both sides in the current discussion is their fascination with the body and with transfer of body parts. Today's philosophers wonder, for example, why we tend to assume that "we" survive if our body is replaced little by little in organ transplants, but not if our entire body is replaced at once. They hypothesize experiments in which we are told that the body we occupy will wake tomorrow devoid of memory and then be subjected to intense pain; they ask whether, under these circumstances, we are afraid for ourselves and conclude that, since we do feel fear, we must assume in some sense that the body is our "self." Drawing on science fiction, they imagine cases in which a body pattern is beamed to another planet and rematerialized, while the original body is left behind; which of the resultant entities (they ask) is the self? In contrast, the sort of evidence that fascinated people at the turn of the century and that could be adduced today (evidence from parapsychological research, for example, or from the near-death experiences documented by E. Kübler-Ross) seldom finds its way into philosophical debate. Whatever money there is to be made in "new age" products or Scientology, indications that disembodied spirits survive death arouse little philosophical interest. Even elaborators of the memory theory either content themselves with answering the difficulties in Locke's formulation pointed out by Joseph Butler in the eighteenth century,[32] or, in fact, expend much energy discussing brain transplants and DNA extractions – that is, material continuity – as a way of explaining or questioning continuity of consciousness. Some recent theorists (Derek Parfit and Robert Nozick, for example) hold that there are a number of hypothetical cases in which I cannot decide whether "I" survive or not. But this latter group of thinkers tends also to devote extensive attention to cases having to do with bodily continuity.[33]

Thus, the most commonly examined and apparently pertinent examples in current philosophical discussion of identity and survival have to do with the place of body. And are these examples really so outré or jejune? I think we can say so only in a rather special sense of the word outré, for these cases are familiar. They are the stuff of popular culture – of TV shows and movies. of articles in the *New York Review of Books* and letters to Ann Landers. Oliver Sacks's superb popularization of research on mind, *The Man Who Mistook His Wife for a Hat*, has become not only a best-seller but also an opera.[34] The products of yellow journalism sold in supermarkets feature stories of organ recipients who feel invaded by the persons whose body parts they receive; and responsible medical sociologists take seriously the problems raised by such feelings. The sensationalist plot of a novel published in early 1989, *Broken-Hearted*, revolves around the case of a woman who falls in love with the recipient of her late husband's heart.[35] Many recent movies and TV programs deal with identity and survival, not through stories of ghosts and parapsychic phenomena nor through high-minded tales of heredity and morality, but through fantasies of body exchange and rejuvenation: *The Brain, All of Me, Maxie, Like Father Like Son, The Man With Two Brains, Heaven Can Wait, Chances Are*, the remake of *The Fly, Max Headroom* and so on.[36]

What is significant about the attitudes revealed in today's newpaper stories and movies is the underlying assumption that in some way the body is the self. Renée Fox and Judith Swazey's research on the sociological and psychological context of transplants has turned up repeated cases of persons who are convinced that identity is in some way transferred with organs.[37] They report the following remark, made by the father of a boy heart donor to the father of the young girl who received the organ: "We've always wanted a little girl, so now we're going to have her and share her with you."[38] Crammond's study of kidney recip-

249

ients reports a donor's reaction to the recipient's decision to return to work: "He's being unfair to himself and to me.... After all, it's my kidney.... That's me in there."[39] In the winter of 1987–1988, Los Angeles was shocked by stories of a cryonics group that froze heads with the hope of thawing them later and cloning bodies to accompany them. Accusations were made that the group had actually murdered an elderly woman by turning off life-support systems at the optimum moment for severing and freezing her head. Cryonics adherents claimed, however, that thawing the head now to ascertain whether murder had in fact been committed would murder the woman for all eternity by denying her hope of revival. To such a sect, bodily survival *is* resurrection.[40]

The sensationalist headline from November, 1988, reproduced in Figure 7.1 makes a similar assumption. What is striking here is not the assertion of some sort of immortality but the claim that the soul is in fact physical, that it is *a body*. It is physical continuation of a tiny, weighable fragment of the person that constitutes life after death.

Moreover, none of the repetitive and by no means consistently entertaining movies I list above suggests that the occupation of a body by another personality is simply the substitution of one person for another. Such a plot would imply that the memory/personality *is* the person. Rather, there is, in these fantasies, something disturbing about the new conjunction of mind and body exactly because characters in the film (and presumably the audience) see the body that continues as in some sense the person, who is invaded and threatened by another set of characteristics and memories. In the eighties remake of *The Fly*, for example, the man whose genes are spliced with those of a fly continues in a sense to "be himself" because his genes continue, even after he has also in a sense "become a fly" because he has the body of a fly.[41]

FIGURE 7.1. Cover, *Weekly World News*, November 1, 1988. A modern argument for survival after death emphasizes material continuity.

In their fascination with the bodily aspects of survival and identity, contemporary philosophers are just like the rest of us. Indeed, many of their most bizarre hypothetical cases come from mass culture. The now famous essay on survival by John Perry, for example, is based not only on John Locke and Bernard Williams, but also on a popular novel from 1972 about a brain transplant.[42] Moreover, the particular way in which the question of immortality and survival is posed in philosophical investigations, no less than in fiction, yellow journalism and film, has been precipitated by recent technological developments, with their attendant legal and moral complications – namely, artificial intelligence, organ transplants, brain surgery. Much current philosophical debate takes its departure from the Sperry experiments on epileptics, which offer evidence that the two hemispheres of the brain can exist separately; duplication of individuals through brain fission may be technologically feasible.[43]

One can therefore argue that the general human issues on which the philosophical problem of survival bears (the mind/body problem, the nature of identity, etc.) have not changed much recently. Nor do such general questions seem much closer to philosophical solution. What is in fact most time-bound – and therefore most instructive to us about ourselves – is the precise nature of the outré and jejune examples that apparently fascinate us, moviegoers and philosophers alike. It is the examples to which the philosophers continually refer, rather than their abstract positions, that tell us how far we go toward assuming that material continuity is crucial for personal survival. It is in the examples also that we see reflected the extent to which popular culture has moved away from concern with mind/body dichotomies and turned instead to issues of integrity versus corruption or partition.

Debates of the Medieval Schoolroom in the Context of the History of Philosophy

I wish now to offer a similar analysis of the seemingly outrageous and offensive schoolroom examples of the Middle Ages. Even a brief look at modern philosophy should weaken our resistance to taking seriously such medieval questions as the resurrection of hermaphrodites or of eaten embryos. This modern discussion reminds us, first, that we, too, explore the issue of personal survival through bizarre examples; second, that the examples we use to think with often come from popular culture and exactly for this reason express our deepest hopes and fears; third, that the cases currently under investigation – teletransportation and body or brain transplants – also treat survival and identity as matters involving body continuity or corruption. If the medieval question "Will my discarded fingernails rise again?" seems to us an odd one, we do well to admit the similar oddness of such modern questions as "if Caroline Bynum's brain were transplanted into the body of, for example, Lawrence Stone, who would the resulting person be?"

My thesis about the twelfth- and thirteenth-century theology of the body is twofold and, in both its parts, revisionist. First, much of the debate about the resurrection of the body and about the relation of body and soul revolved not around a soul/body contrast (although the soul and body were, of course, seen as distinct entities in a way they are not by most modern philosophers), but around the issue of bodily continuity. Questions of risen embryos, foreskins and fingernails, of the subtlety of glorified flesh, of how and whether God makes whole the amputee or the fat man, are questions about the reassemblage of physical parts. Scholastic theologians worried *not* about whether body was crucial to human nature, but about how part related to whole – that is, how bits could and would be reintegrated after scattering and decay. The crucial question to which discussion of the resurrected body returned again and again was not "Is body necessary to personhood?" Medieval theologians were so certain it was they sometimes argued that resurrection was "natural." Peter of Capua suggested, for example, that it was a consequence not of divine grace but of the structure of human nature that body returned to soul after the Last Judgment.[44] The crucial theological question was rather: What accounts for the identity of earthly and risen body? What of "me" must rise in order for the risen body to be "me"? Only by considering the specific examples debated by schoolmen can we see the extent to which, between 1100 and 1320, they were really debating how far material continuity is necessary for identity.

Second, I wish to argue that this issue of bodily continuity (of how identity lasts through corruption and reassemblage) was manifested *as an issue* not merely in the bizarre limiting cases considered by scholastic theologians, but also in pious practice: in the cult of saints and relics, in changes in legal, medical and burial procedures in precisely this period, in the kinds of miracle stories that were popular with preachers and audiences. Thus, I see a connection between actual Church practice and the debates of ivory tower intellectuals; and this connection is easiest to find not in the general philosophical issues such scholars considered, but in the strangest of their specific examples.

The story of philosophical discourse in the twelfth and thirteenth centuries is not, of course, usually told as a story in which issues of material continuity, or of part and whole, figure very prominently. The interpretation most of us have learned from the great Catholic historians of philosophy in this century is rather a story of Plato and Aristotle and of theories of soul.[45] It argues that twelfth-century thought was characterized, philosophically speaking, by Platonic dualism — that is, by the view (found especially in Hugh of St. Victor and Robert of Melun) that the person is the soul, to which body is attached as tool, garment or prison. Modern scholars have thus seen the twelfth-century insistence on bodily resurrection as a somewhat incongruous theological intrusion into a philosophical position that requires escape from body for human perfection.[46] According to this interpretation, the thirteenth-century adoption of Aristotle's definition of the soul as the form of the body (freed from Chalcidius's argument that a form could not be substantial) was a philosophical and theological triumph, undergirding with satisfactory theory for the first time a biblical view of the person as human rather than spiritual. Thomas Aquinas's theory of the human being as a hylomorphic (form/matter) union of soul and body is thus read as a victory over dualism, holding as it does that "the soul . . . is not the whole person, and I am not my soul."[47] The distrust and, in certain key areas, outright condemnation of Aquinas's ideas in the 1270s and 1280s are seen in this interpretation to stem from suspicion that, exactly in their close union of soul and body, such ideas might threaten the immortality of the soul and lend support to the hated teaching of Averroism.

Only a few perceptive Catholic philosophers read the story a different way.[48] They argue that what Aquinas's teaching actually threatens is *body*, since, in denying the plurality of forms, Aquinas must assert that the soul (our only form) is the form of our bodiliness, too, reducing what is left over to mere primary matter or potency.[49] Although, of course, the body we have at the moment is formed and therefore existing "second matter," *what it is* is, so to speak, packed into the soul.[50]

If we follow up the insight of those Catholic scholars who have seen Aquinas's formulation as threatening body, the history of philosophy looks different. We can then see in the many thirteenth- and fourteenth-century positions that rejected certain details of Aquinas – theories often called Platonic or Augustinian or Franciscan – an effort to retain both a sense of matter as a real entity teeming with shadowy, potential forms (called in the early part of the period "seminal reasons") and a sense of body, too, as a real entity alongside form, however inextricably the two are bound at the resurrection. It is patently not true (however much passing remarks about "Platonic dualism" may suggest it) that twelfth-, thirteenth- and fourteenth-century thinkers who attributed some independent substantial reality to matter and/or body were inclined to see such entities as unreal or (in a simple, categorical sense) evil.[51] Rather, they agreed with the poet Bernard Sylvestris, who expressed a conception of matter as pregnant, yearning stuff, filled with potential. "Matter," he wrote "the oldest thing [in creation], wishes to be born again and in this new beginning to be encompassed in forms."[52]

Indeed, as historians have sometimes noticed, to their puzzlement, it was those with the sharpest sense of body/soul conflict and the most ferocious ascetic practices (for example, Bernard of Clairvaux, Francis of Assisi or Angela of Foligno) who had the clearest and most passionate awareness of the potential of body to reveal the divine.[53] Bernard of Clairvaux spoke thus of the joys of bodily resurrection:

> Do not be surprised if the glorified body seems to give the spirit something, for it was a real help when man was sick and mortal. How true that text is which says that all things turn to the good of those who love God (Romans 8.28). The sick, dead and resurrected body is a help to the soul who loves God; the first for the fruits of penance, the second for repose, and the third for consummation. Truly the soul does not want to be perfected, without that from whose good services it feels it has benefited...in every way.... Listen to the bridegroom in the Canticle inviting us to this triple progress:

"Eat, friends, and drink; be inebriated, dearest ones." He calls to those working in the body to eat; he invites those who have set aside their bodies to drink; and he impels those who have resumed their bodies to inebriate themselves, calling them his dearest ones, as if they were filled with charity.... It is right to call them dearest who are drunk with love....[54]

Expressing a similar notion that body is necessary both for personhood and for eternal bliss, Bonaventure wrote, in a sermon on the Assumption of the Virgin Mary:

> Her happiness would not be complete unless she [Mary] were there personally [i.e., bodily assumed into heaven]. The person is not the soul; it is a composite. Thus it is established that she must be there as a composite, that is, of soul and body. Otherwise she would not be there [in heaven] in perfect joy; for (as Augustine says) the minds of the saints [before their resurrections] are hindered, because of their natural inclination for their bodies, from being totally borne into God.[55]

Henry of Ghent criticized Aquinas's doctrine of the unicity of form because he thought it made the gifts or dowries (*dotes*) of the body merely the consequence of the soul's blessedness. Henry himself held to the theory of a separate *forma corporeitatis* so that the gifts of the glorified body could be understood as real changes *in that body*, not merely as consequences of changes in the soul.[56] Richard of Middleton, like Bonaventure, actually saw the soul's yearning for the body as a motive for the saints in heaven. The blessed around the throne of God pray all the harder for us sinners, he asserted, because these blessed will receive again their own deeply desired flesh only when the number of the elect is filled up and the Judgment comes.[57]

257

It thus seems to me that a distrust of the strict hylomorphic theory of man and of the doctrine of the unicity of form was endemic in thirteenth-century debate because of a strong pull toward body as substantial – a pull reflected in the theory of resurrection that stressed numerical identity as material continuity. In other words, it was the more conservative, more Augustinian-Platonic thinkers (not the followers of Aquinas) who made body "real" in a commonsense way; and their ideas fit the needs of the pious to experience body as a separate entity that was the locus both of temptation and of encounter with the divine. But even those who departed from theories of material continuity were uncomfortable with, and inconsistent in, their departure. The philosophically elegant new identity theory implied by Aquinas and Giles of Rome and finally articulated by Peter of Auvergne, John of Paris and Durandus of St. Pourçain – a theory that obviated any need to consider material continuity – never caught on.[58] Not only were certain of its consequences explicitly condemned; it was not fully used by its creators, who continued to speak of the resurrected body as reassembled by God from its own tiny bits of dust scattered throughout the universe.

This last point needs further explanation. In the course of patristic discussion, theologians had come to see identity as the heart of resurrection.[59] As John of Damascus said (and scholastic theologians quoted him repeatedly): it is not *re-surrectio* unless the same human being rises again.[60] But what does it mean for a person to be "the same"? In the twelfth century, some felt that only the continuation of exactly the same matter qualified as sameness.[61] Indeed, some thinkers held that nutrition and growth were in a natural sense impossible, because food could never change substance and become flesh.[62] Hence, to Hugh of St. Victor, for example, any growth was a miracle: the growth of Eve from a rib of Adam or of a child from the seed of its father was likened to the miracle of the loaves and the fishes.[63] By the early thirteenth century most thinkers held that each person possessed a *caro radicalis* (a core of flesh) formed both from the matter passed on by parent or parents to child and from the matter that comes from food.[64] It was this *caro radicalis* that God reassembled after the Last Judgment. Thus, as William of Auxerre argued in the early thirteenth century, summing up previous teaching, there must be material identity for numerical identity: the ashes of Paul must rise as the body of Paul. If matter is somehow lacking, the power of God must make up the deficit by miracle.[65]

This insistence on material continuity raised, as I explained above, a host of problems. If, for example, all our matter comes back (and, on this point, theologians found Luke 21.18 – "Not a hair of your head shall perish" – very troubling), will not the fingernails of those who died as adults be too long in heaven? And, on the other hand, where will the matter come from for those who died in the womb? To these problems, the theory of form as identity, adumbrated by Aquinas and articulated by John of Paris and Durandus, was an elegant solution. Since only substances exist, matter does not exist apart from form: prime matter is potency. When the human being dies, therefore, one cannot say that its body or its matter waits to be reassembled, for *its* body or matter does not exist at all. When the human being is resurrected, the body that is matter to its form (which is also its form of bodiliness because it is its only form) will by definition be its body. The cadaver that exists after we die, like the body that exists before, is second matter – formed matter – but the cadaver is informed not by the form of the soul but by the form of the corpse. Thus, says Durandus, we may not say that God can make the body of Peter out of the body of Paul, because this is nonsense; if it is the body of Paul it is the body of Paul.[66] But God can make the body of Peter out of dust that was once the body of Paul.[67] And he need take no more or less dust than necessary to make a perfect human body.

This theory could have swept away, as sheer foolishness, the questions of fingernails, foreskins and aborted fetuses over which theologians had puzzled since Tertullian and Augustine. But it did not do so. Instead, its own proponents for the most part failed to use it in their discussions of resurrection. For example, Eustachius of Arras, who appears to understand the argument, in fact held that God created the glorified body from the same dust that body contained earlier.[68] Giles of Rome worried about how matter from several bodies could be understood to be in one resurrected body and devoted much attention to questions about the resurrection of eaten food and flesh – matters in which he would presumably have had no interest if he had gone over completely to a formal theory of identity.[69] Aquinas, who articulated a purely formal theory, pulled back from it in a famous and much debated passage of the *Summa contra Gentiles*, asserting merely the conventional position that people do not have to receive all their previous matter in the resurrection; God can make up the difference.[70] Indeed, in the discussion of eaten embryos, which would not come up if identity were only formal, Aquinas not only made material continuity the principle of identity, he also tipped the scales toward matter in a second way, violating the Aristotelian theory (which he elsewhere adopted) that the father provides form, the mother matter, in conception.[71] Something held the theologians back from using their own philosophy when they came to discussing problems of piety or of physics or of biology.

~ There appears to have been concern generally in the 1270s that the teachings of Aristotle as interpreted by the Arab commentators might lead not only to denial of the immortality of the soul, but also to denial of the resurrection of the body. Proposition 13, condemned in 1270, stated that "God cannot give immortality or incorruptibility to a corruptible or mortal thing."[72] Propositions condemned in 1277 included not only the idea that the same body, numerically speaking, does not return,[73] but also other positions in which the issue of bodily identity is implicated: for example, "that God cannot give perpetuity to a mutable and corruptible thing," "that man, through the process of nutrition, can become another numerically and individually," "that one should not take care for the burying of the dead," and "that death is the end of all terrors" (namely, that there is no eternal punishment of the damned).[74] Moreover, certain consequences of the new identity theory and of the connected theory of the unicity of form were also condemned. Controversy erupted in the 1270s over the implication that, if the cadaver is not the body, then Christ's body did not lie in the tomb for the three days between Crucifixion and Resurrection. Not all the events in the course of the debate are clear; but the record shows that the argument that a dead body is just a body equivocally (that is, that the word "body" in the two phrases "dead body" and "living body" is merely a homonym) was condemned at Oxford in 1277. The doctrine of the unicity of form was also condemned in England in March, 1277.[75] As Elizabeth Brown has recently shown, controversy over the unicity of form erupted again in Paris in 1285–1286, and questions about the implications of the doctrine for relic cult were explicitly raised.[76]

We must not make too much of the condemnations. Some were later revoked. And it is important to note that Durandus's identity theory was *not* condemned in the early fourteenth century when other aspects of his teaching were extracted from his Sentence commentary for censure.[77] What is informative for our purposes is the context of the discussion. Theologians themselves related abstruse considerations of the nature of body and person to such practical matters as burial customs and the veneration of saints.

Since the early days of the twelfth century, schoolmen had seen that the status of Christ's body in the tomb had implications for the cult of the dead. Sentence collections tended to insert entries on prayers for the departed among *quaestiones* concerning Christ's body in the *triduum*, the nature of resurrected bodies generally, or the problem of how food was assimilated in the Garden of Eden.[78] In the later thirteenth century, some charged explicitly that the notion of the equivocality of body threatened the cult of saints. Henry of Ghent argued that the Thomistic position might be heretical, since, in denying continuity of form (the *forma corporeitatis*) between living body and cadaver, it suggested that the relic was not really the saint.[79] John of Paris had to defend himself against critics who maintained that the unicity of form removed all justification for relic cult. In his reply, John not only argued, as theologians had since Augustine, that relics were to be honored because they bring before our memories the life and suffering of the saints. He also held – in what almost amounts to a concession to material continuity – that the "first matter" (which does not quite mean mere potency) in relic and living saint is the same and is glorified in the body.[80] We find a similar inconsistency in Aquinas himself when we look at *Summa theologiae*, pt. 3a, q. 25, art. 6: "Should we worship the relics of the saints?" Beginning with a quotation from Augustine to the effect that bodies are dearly loved garments, temples of the Holy Spirit, aids to memory, and tools for the working of miracles, Aquinas points out that "a dead body is not of the same species as a living body." It is thus to be worshiped only for the sake of the soul that was once united to it. But then Aquinas, contradicting at least the pure formulation of his own identity theory, concludes: "The dead body of a saint is not identical to that

262

which the saint held during life, on account of its difference of form — *viz.*, the soul; but it is the same by identity of matter, which is destined to be reunited to its form."[81] Not merely a mnemonic device, the body in the tomb is the body that will be joined to the saint in heaven.

Thus, in the late thirteenth century, when the new categories of Aristotelian hylomorphism seemed to make material continuity irrelevant, theorists nonetheless discussed survival and resurrection as if identity of matter — or, to put it another way, univocality of "body" — were necessary. The texts I have just cited suggest that the adherence of theologians to material continuity was owing in part to pious practice. Intellectuals were aware that relic cult implied material continuity; the ordinary folk for whom they (or their pupils) crafted sermons behaved as if the bodies were the saints. And medieval intellectuals apparently preferred philosophical inconsistency to scandalizing the faithful.[82]

Moreover, intellectuals sometimes even promoted veneration of holy bodies. Nor did they see such veneration merely as an aid to memory: it was veneration of the saints themselves. Preaching in the mid-twelfth century, Peter the Venerable, for example, was careful to emphasize that the souls of the saints are around the throne of heaven while their bodies are in churches for reverencing by the faithful; the saints are divided by death into two parts. But Peter nonetheless also spoke as if pieces of dead holy people are already touched by the glory they will attain at the end of time.[83] The "*bodies* of the saints," said Peter, "live" with God. Exhorting his monks on the occasion of a martyr's feastday, Peter argued:

> The divine dignity divides his martyr into equal parts, so that he may retain his soul for himself among the mass of the blessed and give, with marvelous largesse, the relics of his sacred body to be vener-

ated by the faithful still living in the flesh. But suppose someone says: "what does it profit us to honor a lifeless body; what does it profit us to frequent with hymns and praise bones lacking in sense?" Let this kind of thinking be far from the hearts of the faithful.... God, the creator of spiritual and corporeal things,...established the human creature and, in an excellent operation, joined it together from rational spirit and flesh..., one person of man conjoined from [two] diverse substances. And glorifying the unity of the wonderful conjoining with felicity appropriate to the proper nature of each [of the diverse substances], he bestowed justice on the soul and incorruptibility on the body.... Therefore we know the spirits of the just will in the meanwhile live happily in the eternal life which we expect through faith, which he promises who is faithful in his words, and we anticipate for them a future resurrection in their bodies with immortality and in every sense incorruptibility. For this reason we do not debase as inanimate, despise as insensate, or trample under foot like the cadavers of dumb beasts the bodies of those who in this life cultivated justice; rather we venerate them as temples of the Lord, revere them as palaces of divinity, hoard them as pearls suitable for the crown of the eternal king, and, with the greatest devotion of which we are capable, preserve them as vessels of resurrection to be joined again to the blessed souls....

Behold whose bodies you venerate, brothers, in whose ashes you exalt, for whose bones you prepare golden sepulchres. They are sons of God, equal to angels, sons of the resurrection. Hence you should receive them reverently as sons of God, extoll them as equal to the angels with suitable praises, and expect that they will rise in their own flesh as sons of the resurrection. And in this hope I have confidence more certainly than in any human thing that you ought not to feel contempt for the bones of the present martyrs as if they were dry bones but should honor them now full of life as if they were in their future incorruption.... Flesh flowers from dryness and youth is remade from old age, and if you do not yet see this in your martyr it is supported by sacred authorities; do not despair of the future. Having therefore, dearest brothers, the author of the old law and the new grace, Jesus Christ, who promises to his servants the resurrection of the flesh and the glorification of human substance totally, first through the saints of old and afterwards through himself, and demonstrates [this resurrection] in his own body, we ought to reverence with due honor the body of this blessed martyr as about to be resurrected, as it will be clothed in immortal glory, although we see it as dead....

I say that the bodies of the saints live with God.... And that they live with God innumerable miracles everywhere on earth demonstrate, which miracles are frequently experienced by those who come to venerate their sepulchres with devout minds.... Isaiah says: "Your bones shall flourish [germinabunt] like an herb." Therefore because the bones of the present martyr shall flower like an herb, rising to eternal life, because the corruptible shall put on the incorruptible and the mortal the immortal, because this body of a just man snatched up to meet Christ shall always remain with him, who will not, with full affection, bring to be honored in this life what he believes will be elevated in the future glory....

Eighty years later, Caesarius of Heisterbach wrote: "Although the souls of the saints always look upon the divine face, nevertheless they have respect to their bodies, and when they see us devoted to them, they are much pleased."[84]

Bodily Partition and Bodily Incorruption in Medieval Culture

It therefore seems clear that contemporaries were aware of certain connections between the oddest cases debated by theologians and the behavior of ordinary folk. Burial practices, prayers for the

dead and relic cult were sometimes the explicit context for theological debate; theological distinctions sometimes informed sermons composed for church dedications or saints' days.[85] I want
to argue, however, that the connection between the outré examples of scholastic debate and the concerns of the pious existed at
a deeper level as well. The assumption that material continuity
is crucial to identity is an assumption that runs throughout medieval culture; therefore, the theme of part and whole also runs
deep. When we look at the way in which ordinary thirteenth-
century people behaved, we find there, too, a concern with
material continuity and thus with the corruption, partition and
reintegration of bodies.

The assumption that the material body we occupy in this life
is integral to person and that the event we call death is not a radical break was reflected in legend, folktale and even "science."
Many stories that circulated in the later Middle Ages implied that
the body was in some sense alive after death. Moralists told of
temporary resurrections; hagiographers described dead saints who
sat up momentarily to revere the crucifix or eucharistic host;
medical writers spoke of cadavers that continued to move or grow
while on the embalming table or in the tomb; folk wisdom held
that corpses would bleed to accuse their murderers; holy bodies,
especially holy female bodies, were sometimes said to exude oil
or even milk that cured the sick.[86] Down into the seventeenth
century, learned treatises were written by doctors on the *life*
of the body after death — a phenomenon that seemed proved to
some by the apparent growth of fingernails and hair observed in
corpses.[87] The claim that all or part of a saint remained incorrupt after burial was an important miracle for proving sanctity,
particularly the sanctity of women.[88] Indeed, in what appears to
have some parallels to modern cryonics, alchemists and physicians
in the thirteenth century experimented with ways of returning

the body to its pristine state before the fall, convinced that they might thus free it, more or less indefinitely, from decay.[89] Although the development of the doctrine of purgatory and increased discussion of the nature of the soul's condition between death and Last Judgment forced theologians to make it clear that the body is restored and glorified only at the end of time, preachers and teachers sometimes suggested that the ability of the martyrs to withstand pain or corruption was owing to an assimilation of their bodies on earth to the glorified bodies of heaven (see Figures 6.14 and 6.15).[90]

Since the patristic period, theologians had asserted that God could reassemble — even recreate — any body. Neither the jaws of wild beasts nor the swords and flames of executioners could deny resurrection to the martyrs. The fourth-century church historian Eusebius reported that the Romans burned and scattered the bodies of the martyrs of Lyons in order to dash Christian hopes of resurrection.[91] But Christian apologists such as Minucius Felix delighted in claiming such repressive measures to be useless because divine power can renew even pulverized dust.[92] In the early third century, Tertullian hurled in the teeth of heretics and anti-Christian polemicists his confidence that the God who had created the universe could surely reassemble the bodies he had made:

> But that you may not suppose that it is merely those bodies which are consigned to the tombs whose resurrection is foretold, you have it declared in Scripture: "And I will command the fishes of the sea and they shall cast up the bones which they have devoured...." (Enoch 61.5) You will ask, Will then the fishes and other animals and carnivorous birds be raised again in order that they may vomit up what they have consumed...? Certainly not. But the beasts and fishes are mentioned...in relation to the restoration of flesh and

267

blood, in order the more emphatically to express the resurrection of such bodies as have even been devoured....

If God raises not men entire, He raises not the dead. For what dead man is entire, although he dies entire? Who is without hurt, that is without life? What body is uninjured, when it is dead, when it is cold, when it is ghastly, when it is stiff, when it is a corpse?... Thus, for a dead man to be raised again, amounts to nothing short of his being restored to his entire condition.... God is quite able to remake what He once made.... Thus our flesh shall remain even after the resurrection – so far indeed susceptible of suffering, as it is the flesh, and the same flesh too; but at the same time impassible, inasmuch as it has been liberated by the Lord for the very end and purpose of being no longer capable of enduring suffering.[93]

Despite such confidence in divine power, however, the early Christians continued to feel intense concern for proper burial, and writers such as Tertullian and Augustine reassured them that their concern was appropriate and devout.[94] Ordinary believers in the second and third centuries often went to extraordinary lengths to collect and reassemble the dismembered pieces of the martyrs for burial. Eusebius reports that they grieved when they could not return the mutilated pieces of their heroes and heroines to the earth.[95] Moreover, his accounts of martyrdom are accounts not only of personal courage, but also of victory over fragmentation. Speaking of a certain Sanctus, tortured on several occasions, Eusebius writes:

For when the wicked after some days again tortured the martyr they thought that they might overcome him now that his body was swollen and inflamed if they applied the same tortures, ... Yet not only did nothing of this kind happen, but, beyond all human expectations, he raised himself up and his body was straightened in the subsequent tortures, and he regained his former appearance and the use of his limbs, so that through the grace of Christ the second torturing became not torment but cure.[96]

Medieval readers loved stories such as Eusebius's and retold them with gusto. In the retelling, horrors became more horrible, even as triumph over pain, decay and fragmentation became more impressive and more improbable.[97] The pious in the thirteenth century, more frequently than in the third, spoke and behaved as if division of the cadaver were a deep threat to person.

The Parisian theologian Gervase of Mt.-St.-Eloi, for example, called even division for the purposes of burial *ad sanctos* a "horrible and inhuman" [*atrocitatem et inhumanitatem*] practice. Gervase admitted that divine power could gather scattered parts, but insisted that it was better to bury bodies intact so they were ready for the sound of the trumpet.[98] Gervase's contemporary, Godfrey of Fountains asserted division to be against reason, nature and desire.[99] In 1299, Pope Boniface VIII legislated against the nobility's practice of dividing bodies for burial and included a prohibition of embalming and boiling bodies (and in certain circumstances moving and reburying them).[100] Fulminating against division as monstrous and detestable, the pope gave no philosophical or theological justification for the condemnation, but simply required burial close to the place of death until the body turned by slow and natural process into dust.[101] Roger Bacon, who probably influenced Boniface and the Italian curia on these matters, argued that putrefaction is simply an "accident" of aging, treatable by proper medical precautions. Because Christ had promised bodily integrity to all at the Last Judgment, persons here below should prepare themselves for it, said Bacon, by striving for moral and physical intactness.[102]

Folktale and vernacular hagiography also expressed revulsion at bodily partition. Saints frequently effected miracles of healing or of temporary resurrection of corpses, but they sometimes simply reassembled cadavers without bothering to reanimate them. In an Old French life of Saint Barbara, for example, a decapitated head asks a priest for communion and is reunited with its body through the power of the saint (although both parts remain lifeless).[103] The popular story of a leg transplant performed by the physician saints Cosmas and Damian changes in its late medieval retelling to emphasize not only the grafting of a black leg onto a sick white man but also the attaching of the gangrenous white leg onto the corpse of the Moor from whom the original graft was taken.[104] Such tales surely suggest that the intact condition of the body, even after death, had deep significance.

Despite worries about fragmentation, however, division of the body was widely and enthusiastically practiced in the thirteenth century. The culture of ancient Rome had possessed strong taboos against moving or dividing corpses – taboos that were overcome in the Christian cult of relics only over the course of hundreds of years.[105] But by 1300 the practice was widespread of dividing not only the bodies of the saints to provide relics, but also the bodies of the nobility to enable them to be buried in several places near several saints.[106] Boniface's *Detestande feritatis* of 1299, which forbade this practice, was not enforced in the early fourteenth century; and, in 1351, Clement VI decreed that French rulers would no longer need any special exemption for division of the body. By the fifteenth century some popes had their own bodies eviscerated before burial.[107] Indeed, immediately after Boniface's death, opponents charged that he was a heretic because his concern for the fate of cadavers proved, they said, that he did not believe in resurrection.[108]

The early thirteenth century saw the first examples of autopsy to determine cause of death in legal cases; the first official dissections were carried out in medical schools in the years around 1300, for purposes of teaching as well as diagnosis.[109] By the fourteenth century bodies of putative saints were often opened not only for embalming, but also to collect evidence of remarkable austerities or bodily prodigies (such as miraculous fasting, or the "wound of love" in the heart).[110] The same period witnessed the revival of torture as a judicial practice and a significant increase in the use of mutilation and dismemberment to punish capital crimes.[111]

Even artists fragmented the body. Liturgical and artistic treatment of relics came increasingly to underline the fact that they are body parts. In the twelfth and early thirteenth centuries, fragments of saints were mostly housed in beautiful caskets, which diverted attention from their exact nature (Figure 7.2). Canonists and theologians debated whether there could be private property in relics, and whether wearing them as talismans or displaying them "naked" was acceptably devout. By the fourteenth century, however, holy bones were owned and worn by the pious as private devotional objects; they were often exhibited in reliquaries that mimicked their shape (for example, head, arm, or bust reliquaries) or in crystal containers that clearly revealed that they were bits of bodies (Figures 7.3, 7.4). In a remarkable picture from Cologne about 1500, which depicts the faithful gathering the fragments of Saint Ursula and her 11,000 virgin companions for burial, the scattered body parts (with their neatly rounded-off edges) seem already to have become the reliquary busts or arm reliquaries in which the faithful will venerate them (Figure 7.5).[112] Depictions of the sufferings associated with the Crucifixion – known as the *arma Christi* and the Five Wounds – came in the later Middle Ages to show Christ's body itself in parts, "put on display [as Sixten Ringbom has said] for the pious beholder to watch with myopic closeness" (Figures 7.6, 7.7).[113]

Artistic or actual, the practice of bodily partition was fraught with ambivalence, controversy and profound inconsistency. As late as the twelfth century, even north of the Alps – the area most enthusiastic about partition of bodies for burial *ad sanctos* – some felt that the gift of body parts was a dubious honor. The English chronicler, Roger of Wendover, tells us that Richard I's grant of his entrails to the Abbey of Charroux in Poitou was taken as a sign of disdain.[114] Some theologians in Paris in the 1280s argued that division of the cadaver was heinous cooperation with the forces of putrefaction because it severed a corpse that still retained its integrity and shape.[115] Although procedures for boiling the body and burying the viscera separately had been developed as early as the tenth century and were (as we have seen) enthusiastically adopted by certain noble families, a number of fourteenth-century wills still directed executors not to divide the body for burial.[116]

Prurient horror often accompanied the division of bodies for scientific or political purposes. The first medical dissections were touched, as Marie-Christine Pouchelle has brilliantly demonstrated, by an extraordinary sense of the mystery of the closed body, particularly the female body, and of the audacity required to open it.[117] Stories such as the legend of Nero's autopsy of his own mother expressed disgust at prying into the body in order to attain medical knowledge (Figure 7.8). Surgery – because it severed flesh – was viewed with ambivalence. The preferred method of curing was adjustment of fluids and humors inside the body, which was understood as a balanced system; physicians, who did not cut or cauterize, had higher status than surgeons, who were in certain ways assimilated to barbers, a social rank below them. So highly charged was bodily partition that torturers were forbidden to effect it; they were permitted to squeeze and twist and stretch in excruciating ways, but not to sever or divide. Chronicle accounts of the use of dismemberment in capital cases

FIGURE 7.2. Reliquary Casket, Limoges (ca. 1180). Medieval reliquaries were often gorgeous containers whose form and decoration diverted attention from the precise nature of the fragments contained within.

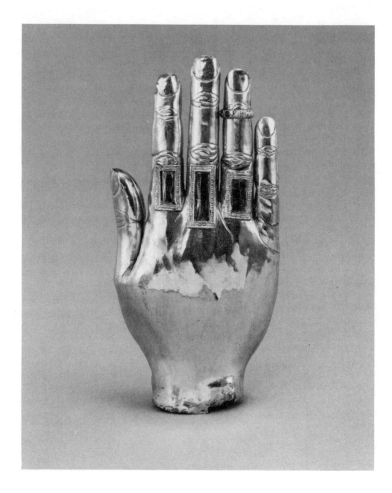

FIGURE 7.3. Flemish Hand Reliquary (thirteenth century). In the later Middle Ages, reliquaries came increasingly to underline the nature of the body parts contained inside. This hand reliquary, with crystal windows through which the finger bones may be seen, displays the precise anatomical nature of the relics. The gold sheathing suggests, however, that the fingers already possess something of the incorruptibility of heaven.

274

FIGURE 7.4. Reliquary monstrance of Saint Francis, Limoges (ca. 1228). Reliquaries sometimes displayed actual bits of holy body to the viewer. In such displays, the bits were surrounded with precious crystal.

make it clear both that it was reserved for only the most repulsive crimes and that the populace was expected to be able to read the nature of the offense from the precise way in which the criminal's body was cut apart and the pieces displayed. Drawing and quartering, or burning (that is, reduction to the smallest possible particles: ashes), were punishments reserved for treason, witchcraft and heresy, particularly when practiced by those of lower social status or inferior gender.[118] R.I. Moore and Saul Brody have convincingly suggested that the scapegoating of lepers about 1300 was owing not only to increased incidence of the disease, but also to conceptualizing of it as living decay and fragmentation. It was because parts broke off the leper's body, because it fragmented and putrefied and became insensate while alive, in other words because it was living death, that it was used as a common metaphor for sin.[119]

Even the saints sometimes opposed their own fragmentation, although without it the central cultic practice of relic veneration could not have existed at all. Moreover, when fragmented, the saints frequently remained incorrupt in their parts.[120] Caesarius of Heisterbach's *Dialogue on Miracles*, from the early thirteenth century, contains a number of stories of relics resisting division.[121] Robert Grosseteste may have forbidden division of his corpse on his deathbed.[122] The holy woman Mary of Oignies, who in a sense fragmented herself while alive by pulling out a large hunk of her hair to use as a device to cure the sick, castigated the prior of Oignies for "cruelly" extracting the teeth of a holy cadaver. After her own death Mary supposedly clenched her teeth when the same prior tried to extract them as relics; when he humbly asked her pardon, however, she shook out a few teeth from her jaw for his use.[123]

Thus, the years around 1300 saw a paradoxical attitude toward partition and mutilation of bodies. On the one hand, there was a

FIGURE 7.5. Master of the Ursula Legend, *The Burial of Ursula and Her Companions*, Cologne (ca. 1500). The story of Saint Ursula and her 11,000 virgin companions, martyred for the faith, was extremely popular in the high Middle Ages, especially in the area of Cologne, where supposed relics of the women were dug up with great frequency. This picture of the burial of Ursula illustrates the medieval concern with reassembling bodies for burial. The carefully collected body fragments, with their neatly rounded edges, already look a good deal like the reliquaries in which they will be preserved.

277

FIGURE 7.6. Cologne Master, *Altarpiece with Cycle of the Life of Christ*, central panel: *Arma Christi* (ca. 1340–1370). In this typical depiction of the instruments used to torture Christ at the Passion, the side-wound is presented as an independent body part. (It is displayed just under Christ's outstretched right arm.) The sexual overtones modern viewers find in such depictions may have been apparent also to medieval viewers, who frequently spoke of entering into Christ's side as into a womb.

FIGURE 7.7. Daniel Mauch, Buxheim Altar, outer panel: *Arma Christi with the Five Wounds* (ca. 1500). In this depiction of the Five Wounds received by Christ on the cross, the Savior's body disappears entirely, to be replaced by bleeding fragments.

279

new enthusiasm about dividing bodies for purposes of science, politics and piety. Division could be generative. Because the person was in some sense his or her body, the multiplication of holy body parts seemed pregnant with possibility. The heart of a king or the finger of a virgin made the earth where he or she was buried fertile with saintly or royal power. The greater the number of parts and places in which noble or holy figures resided after death, the greater the number of prayers they received or evoked and the more far-flung their presence.

On the other hand, the cultural assumption that material continuity is crucial to person made fragmentation horrifying as well as generative and didactic. Theologians therefore opposed cremation and partition; physicians tried to preserve corpses forever from crumbling and putrefaction. Displaying the bloody fragments of the executed was a way of underlining their eternal damnation. In the severed quarters of a traitor displayed on castle walls, the person who broke the integrity of community was himself presented broken.[124] Even those reliquaries that flamboyantly announced that fragments were fragments surrounded the precious bits with permanent substances: jewels, crystal and gold. Devotional pictures of Christ's wounds underlined the horror of the Crucifixion by representing Christ himself as fragmented by our sins, but in such paintings *pars* clearly stands *pro toto*; each fragment of Christ's body – like each fragment of the eucharistic bread – is the whole of God.

Altarpieces and miniatures even depicted the general resurrection as a victory over fragmentation. In the eleventh to early thirteenth centuries, artists in the West drew on the iconographic program of the Byzantine Last Judgment to present the regurgitation of body fragments at the end of time (Figures 7.9, 7.10).[125] Although theology stressed that saved and damned alike rise entire and intact at the Last Judgment, the Byzantine iconographic pro-

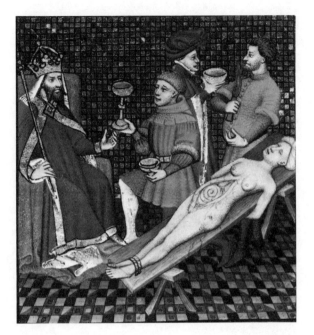

FIGURE 7.8. Nero's Autopsy of his Mother, from a fifteenth-century French translation of Boccaccio's *The Fates of Illustrious Men*, MS Fr. 5139, fol. 290v, Bibliothèque de l'Arsenal, Paris. In the later Middle Ages, dissection of the cadaver was viewed with horror. The story that the emperor Nero had performed an autopsy on his own mother was taken as proof of his depravity.

FIGURE 7.9. Herrad of Hohenbourg, *Hortus deliciarum*, fol. 251r (ca. 1176–1196; tracings made in the nineteenth century from a destroyed manuscript). This massive encyclopedia illustrates the Last Judgment with motifs drawn from Byzantine art. At the sound of the trumpet, bodies rise from tombs and body parts are regurgitated from the craws of birds and beasts; the saved appear before God not as an indistinguishable mass of humanity, but marked with the specific characteristics of their religious statuses.

FIGURE 7.10. *Last Judgment* (late eleventh century [?]; now in the Vatican).
The band of Latin inscription decorating this panel painting identifies the
figures emerging from sarcophagi in zone four as the artists Nicolas and John;
it states that they rise "from the dust of the earth." The regurgitated parts,
labeled by the inscription "devoured members," are here drawn so schemati-
cally that they appear to be bones and skulls rather than the enfleshed body
fragments usual in such Last Judgments.

283

gram makes complex visual use of the theme of part and whole by showing the potentially reassembled (i.e., regurgitated body parts) in the center of a vast, detailed and partially narrative representation, while the damned appear at the bottom right in fragments and the saved are whole and beautiful around the throne of God.[126] The rhythm of the composition associates fragmentation with evil, reassemblage with improvement, wholeness with good (Figure 7.11).[127] So powerful did Western artists find these themes that "Byzantine Last Judgments" crop up as far afield as Iceland.[128] Manuscript illuminations in the Rhineland occasionally separate the motif of reassemblage out from the total iconographic program in ways that emphasize the moment of the last trumpet as a process of reconstitution and revivification (Figure 7.12).[129]

Western artists depicted resurrection as reassemblage quite apart from their use of Byzantine motifs. The most common representation of "last things" showed men and women reborn already whole from the earth; it focused more on judgment than on rebirth (Figure 6.13). But, from the ninth to the sixteenth centuries, the resurrection of the dead was also depicted explicitly as the triumph of whole over part: the gathering together of bones, the reclothing of skeletons, the restoring of exactly those bits of matter scattered at death to the four winds. An eighth-century Anglo-Saxon ivory, for example, shows bodies at various stages of resuscitation: lying, still wrapped in grave clothes; sitting or standing, entangled in their shrouds; fully alive again, their souls depicted as doves flying in at the mouth (Figure 7.13).[130] The ninth-century Trier Apocalypse shows body parts given up by the sea (Figure 7.14).[131] The miniature (Figure 7.15) accompanying Vision 12, Book 3, of the *Scivias* of Hildegard of Bingen shows more graphically even than Hildegard's words that scattered pieces of human beings leap together when the trumpet sounds. Below the shining blessed, on Christ's right hand, are the bones from which they rise. Apparently detached human heads roll in the blasts of the four winds. Even Renaissance artists, although they subordinate the moment of resurrection to depictions of heaven and hell, continue occasionally to emphasize resurrection as reassemblage. In the famous Brizio chapel at Orvieto, the Umbrian artist Signorelli represented resurrection as the reclothing of bones with muscle and skin (Figure 7.16). Jean Bellegambe — in an early sixteenth-century altarpiece possibly from Douai, now in Berlin — depicted angels gathering bones and reassembling bodies at the Last Judgment (Figure 7.17).[132] The angel in the background of the picture, collecting body fragments, bears striking resemblance to the gatherers of relics in the Ursula painting (Figure 7.5). The angel in the foreground, who fits bodies carefully together, works both with fragments clothed in flesh and with an arm that is still bare bone.

Indeed, in pious practice and in literature no less than in art, part sometimes becomes whole without reassemblage. Claims that holy bodies do not decay, and especially that parts of holy bodies are incorrupt or intact, represent a widespread concern to cross or deny the part/whole boundary by asserting the part to *be* the whole. In thirteenth- and fourteenth-century saints' lives, synecdoche is more than a figure of speech; metonymy becomes miracle. Not only is incorruption of body evidence for sanctity;[133] the saint is fully present in his or her every part. For example, Mary of Oignies's finger healed others after death just as Mary's physical presence and ministrations had healed in life. Hagiographers regularly spoke of fragments as "whole," of mutilated flesh as "intact"; indeed, such descriptions were frequently the focal point of their stories.

As many recent scholars have pointed out, both the vernacular saints' tales of the high Middle Ages, which contain significant folkloric elements, and the new collections of legends made

FIGURE 7.11. *Last Judgment*, the Cathedral, Torcello (eleventh century). The great mosaic on the west wall of the Cathedral at Torcello, near Venice, is the best-known example of the so-called Byzantine Last Judgment. It is a powerful depiction of the idea that salvation is wholeness, damnation is decay and partition. The triumph of whole over part is illustrated here not only in the lovely pictures of animals, carrion birds and fishes regurgitating fragments for resurrection, but also in the structure of the entire composition. In the top zone, the blessed rise whole from the tomb, while below them the saints in paradise shimmer in glory. At the bottom right, the deadly sins are represented by worm-eaten skulls (the envious), decapitated heads with large ornamented ears (the avaricious) and fragmented body parts (the indolent). Thus, despite the orthodox doctrine that all rise intact for judgment, the damned are represented in a state of fragmentation that is a symbolic expression of their sins. Heaven is associated with wholeness, hell with partition; redemption is regurgitation and reassemblage.

287

FIGURE 7.12. Resurrection of the Dead, from a Psalter from Bamberg-Eichstätt, MS 1833, fol. 109v, Stiftsbibliothek, Melk (ca. 1255). In this thirteenth-century German miniature of the resurrection, salvation is clearly represented as a triumph over fragmentation and decay. A corpse rises in its shroud, disentangles itself, and receives the garment of salvation, while other corpses receive their missing parts from the beasts who have devoured them.

FIGURE 7.13. (left) Ivory (eighth century; now in the Victoria and Albert Museum). An Anglo-Saxon ivory depicts the dead at the moment of resurrection in various stages of reanimation.

FIGURE 7.14. (right) The Trier Apocalypse, MS 31, fol. 67r, Stadtbibliothek, Trier (ninth century). This depiction of the resurrection, found in more than one early manuscript of the Apocalypse, perhaps derives from earlier models; it is, however, unconnected to the so-called Byzantine Last Judgment. The parts are clearly represented as given up by the sea. The presence, in this particular version, of three hands suggests that more than one body is being reassembled.

for the use of mendicant preachers agree in their archaizing tendency. Looking to distant events in Christian history and choosing heroines or heroes singularly unsuitable for pious imitation, hagiographers filled their pages with stories of martyrdom and mutilation.[134] The "best-seller" among such works was James of Voragine's *Golden Legend*, at least as popular in the later Middle Ages as the Bible itself.[135] A brief analysis of James's use of language will serve as my final example of the medieval capacity simultaneously to abhor, deny and delight in bodily partition.

Recent studies of James have underlined the brutality of his accounts and his obsession with martyrdom, especially with torture and bodily division.[136] Of the 153 chapters of the *Golden Legend* devoted to saints' days, at least 75 have dismemberment as a central motif.[137] Nonetheless, the point of such tales is not the presence, but the absence of suffering; there are only one or two references in all James's accounts of the early martyrs to the fact that mutilation might hurt.[138] So extravagant, indeed, is the denial of fragmentation, that, as several modern students of hagiography have pointed out, it is hard to say why James finally allows one among a series of lengthy tortures to dispatch his hero or heroine; in any case the actual death is often singularly anticlimactic.[139] What is underlined repeatedly is the reassembling of the fragmented body for burial or the victory of intactness over division. For example, the story of Saint Margaret, bound on the rack, beaten with sharp instruments until her bones were laid bare, burned with torches and plunged into water, describes her body as remaining "unscathed."[140] Burned on the pyre, Saint Theodore renders up his soul, but his body is "unharmed by the fire [*ab igne illaesum*]" and perfumes the air with sweet odor. The wife of Saint Adrian journeys a long distance to join her husband's severed hand with his other remains, which have been preserved, by a miraculous rainfall, from burning. Left by the emperor Diocletian to wolves

FIGURE 7.15. Hildegard of Bingen, *Scivias*, book 3, vision 12, MS 1, Wiesbaden, Hessische Landesbibliothek (ca. 1165; manuscript lost in 1945). The miniature that accompanies the last vision in Hildegard of Bingen's *Scivias* graphically depicts the scattered pieces of human beings that come together when the trumpet sounds for the Last Judgment.

FIGURE 7.16. Signorelli, *The Last Judgment*, detail: *Resurrection of the Dead*,
S. Brizio Chapel, Orvieto Cathedral (1499–1504). Although late medieval
artists and poets turned increasing attention to the adventures of the soul in
purgatory, interest in the resurrection of the fleshly, human body did not
abate. This is a famous Renaissance depiction of resurrection as the enfleshing
of skeletons.

FIGURE 7.17. Jean Bellegambe (d. 1553), *Last Judgment* (Douai [?]; now in the Bode Museum, Berlin). This northern European altarpiece from the early sixteenth century shows angels gathering bones and reassembling bodies at the resurrection.

and dogs, the bodies of two martyrs survive "intact [*intacta*]" until the faithful can collect them for burial.[141] James (or a later interpolator) describes as "unharmed" and "unhurt" Sophia's three daughters, who were fried in a skillet, had their breasts torn off, were stretched on the rack and finally beheaded. In contrast, the emperor Hadrian, who presided over the torture of the three young girls, is said to have "withered away, filled with rottenness [*totus putrefactus*]."[142] Whether or not fragmentation or diminution is characterized as significant (or even in fact as occurring) depends not on what happens to the body physically but on the moral standing of the person to whom the bodily events pertain.

The fact of bodily division is often, in the *Golden Legend*, denied by exactly the account that chronicles it. The words attributed to the martyr James the Dismembered, as he loses his toes, are typical:

> Go, third toe, to thy companions, and as the grain of wheat bears much fruit, so shalt thou rest with thy fellows unto the last day.... Be comforted, little toe, because great and small shall have the same resurrection. A hair of the head shall not perish, and how much less shalt thou, the least of all, be separated from thy fellows?[143]

The message, with its explicit echoes of the Luke 21.18 and I Corinthians 15.42–44, is clear.[144] Dismemberment is horrible, to be sure; and even more horrifying is rottenness or decay. But in the end none of this is horrible at all. Beheaded and mutilated saints are "whole" and "unharmed." Severed toes are the seeds from which glorified bodies will spring. God's promise is that division shall finally be overcome, that ultimately there is no scattering.[145] As one of the more conservative theologians might have said: Material continuity *is* identity; body is univocal; the whole will rise and every part is in a sense the whole.

Anthropologists tell us that all cultures deal, in ritual and symbol, with putrefaction; all cultures strain to mask and deny the horror of the period between "first death" (the departure of breath or life) and "second death" or mineralization (the reduction of the cadaver to the hard remains — that is, teeth and bones).[146] And certainly we can see an effort both to deny — and to give meaning to — the process of decay in thirteenth-century miracles of effluvia and closure, of partition and incorruption. Miracles of holy exuding make oil, milk and blood, whether from cadavers or from the living, curative and therefore generative of life;[147] miracles of extravagant fasting in life and of incorruptibility in the grave assert living bodies to be changeless and cadavers to be without decay. Moreover, theological debates about the survival of hair and fingernails in the resurrection grapple directly with the fragmentation and change we fear in the tomb. Crystal or gold reliquaries that associate body bits with permanence, paintings in which body parts are assimilated to reliquaries or statues, stories in which torture does not divide and body cannot really be scattered because no fragment can ever be lost — such images hide the process of putrefaction, equate bones with body and part with whole, and treat body as the permanent locus of the person.

These medieval attitudes, practices and images have roots hundreds of years old; they may indeed — as anthropologists suggest — reflect cultural constants as old as civilization itself.[148] Their immediate context is not, however, age-old attitudes, but thirteenth-century changes. The later thirteenth century saw a new enthusiasm for bodily partition — for scientific, political and cultic reasons — coupled with new efforts to limit, prohibit and deny it. It is hardly surprising therefore that, in the last decades of the century, as debate erupted over the proper treatment of the cadaver, theologians not only experimented with new theories of personal identity, but also strove to retain a conception of person to which body, in the commonsense understanding of body, was integral.[149] Nor is it surprising that religious art and literature both detailed the process of reassemblage of parts into whole and, underlining the nature of part *as part*, asserted it to *be* the whole.

Enthusiastic recourse to bodily partition at the very heart of a religion that denied, on the ontological level, that partition occurred at all; prurient fascination with torture and division in a culture that not only articulated opposition to these practices, but also found innumerable euphemisms for them – these aspects of the thirteenth century are profoundly contradictory. Yet, underneath them all lies a deep conviction that the person *is* his or her body. The entire context of thirteenth-century life thus helps us to understand how contemporaries viewed the theological doctrine of bodily resurrection and why they debated it as they did. Resurrection was asserted by theologians and believed by ordinary Christians both because bodily fragmentation was not really a threat and because it was!

My discussion has ranged far afield from the scholastic debates with which it began. But I doubt whether, for all its range, it has succeeded in quelling the doubts and disagreeable sensations such material usually arouses in a modern audience. Some of the philosophical details may still seem far from clear. The theological details and hagiographical stories may remain distasteful. Even the historical conclusions may have no little capacity to shock, in view of the clichés about the spiritualism and dualism of the Middle Ages purveyed in college textbooks. Nonetheless, I hope I have compelled even outraged readers to recognize that the oddest medieval concerns are no more bizarre than modern ones.

Moreover, the opinions of twelfth- and thirteenth-century school-men and of late twentieth-century philosophers and medical sociologists have more in common than simply their respective oddity. In their debates about fetuses and fingernails as in their popular preaching and legends, medieval people expressed the understanding that body is essential to person and material con-tinuity to body. A significant group among modern intellectuals does not disagree. It is clear both that questions of survival and identity are not, even today, solved, and that they can be solved only through the sort of specific body puzzles medieval theolo-gians delighted in raising.

In a world where we are faced with decisions about heart (and possibly even brain) transplants, about the uses of artifical intel-ligence, about the care of Alzheimer's patients and severely birth-damaged infants, we are forced to confront as never before the question: "Am I my body?" Issues of part and whole, of life pro-longation and putrefaction, scream out at us from the headlines of the *National Enquirer* as we stand in supermarket checkout lines. We are no closer to definitive answers than were the medi-eval theologians who considered the resurrection of umbilical cords and fingernails. But, like them, we seem unwilling to jet-tison the conviction that material continuity is necessary for per-sonal survival. Perhaps then, perusal of the *New York Review of Books*, the *New York Times* science page or the *National Enquirer* – or an evening with *Star Trek* or *Max Headroom* or even *General Hos-pital* – suggests that we should feel greater respect than we have hitherto evidenced for the sophistication of medieval theologians.

Photo Credits:

Notes

In Praise of Fragments

  1. Guibert of Nogent, *De pignoribus*, in J.P. Migne (ed.), *Patrologiae cursus completus: series latina*, 221 vols. (Paris, 1841–1864) [hereafter PL], vol. 156, cols. 607–80. On Guibert, see Klaus Guth, *Guibert von Nogent und die hochmittelalterliĉhe Kritik an der Reliquienverehrung*, Studien und Mitteilungen zur Geschichte des Benediktiner-Ordens und seiner Zweige, Supplement 21 (Ottobeuren, 1970); Marie-Danielle Mireux, "Guibert de Nogent et la critique du culte des reliques," in *La Piété populaire au moyen âge*, Actes du 99ᵉ Congrès National des Sociétés Savantes Besançon 1954: Section de philologie et d'histoire jusqu'à 1610, vol. 1 (Paris: Bibliothèque Nationale, 1977), pp. 293–301; and John F. Benton (ed.), *Self and Society in Medieval France: The Memoirs of Abbot Guibert of Nogent* (New York: Harper Torchbooks, 1970), introduction, pp. 26–31.

  2. For arguments against moving and dividing bodies, see *De pignoribus*, bk. 1, PL 156, cols. 611–30; for Guibert's fascination with gruesome details of torture, see bk. 4, ch. 1, cols. 668–69; on synecdoche, see bk. 2, ch. 2, cols. 632–34. See also Caroline W. Bynum, "Bodily Miracles and the Resurrection of the Body in the High Middle Ages," in Thomas Kselman (ed.), *Belief in History* (Notre Dame: University of Notre Dame Press, 1990), nn. 68–73.

  3. Herrad of Hohenbourg, *Hortus deliciarum*, chs. 850–52, 855, 887, 1090, and plate 141; see *Hortus deliciarum: Reconstruction*, ed. Rosalie Green *et al.* (London and Leiden: Warburg Institute/University of London and Brill, 1979),

pp. 423–35, 447, 481. And see Otto Gillen, *Ikonographische Studien zum Hortus Deliciarum der Herrad von Landsberg* (Berlin: Deutscher Kunstverlag, 1931).

4. See B. Brenk, "Die Anfänge der Byzantinischen Weltgerichtsdarstellung," *Byzantinische Zeitschrift* 57 (1964), pp. 106–26, and *Tradition und Neuerung in der christlichen Kunst des ersten Jahrtausends: Studien zur Geschichte des Weltgerichtsbildes*, Wiener Byzantinische Studien 3 (Vienna: Hermann Böhlau, 1966). See also Chapter 7, below, nn. 125–28.

5. J. Rott, "L'Ancienne bibliothèque de Strasbourg, détruite en 1870: les catalogues qui en subsistent," *Refugium animae bibliotheca: Mélanges offerts à Albert Kolb* (Wiesbaden: Guido Pressler, 1969), pp. 426–42, and "Source et grandes lignes de l'histoire des bibliothèques publiques de Strasbourg détruites en 1870," *Cahiers alsaciens d'archéologie, d'art et d'histoire* 15 (1971), pp. 145–80.

6. See Chapter 7, below; and Piero Camporesi, *The Incorruptible Flesh: Bodily Mutation and Mortification in Religion and Folklore*, trans. T. Croft-Murray and H. Elsom (Cambridge: Cambridge University Press, 1988).

7. See n. 16, below.

8. See Natalie Z. Davis, "Women's History in Transition," *Feminist Studies* 3 (1976), pp. 83–103; and Joan Wallach Scott, *Gender and the Politics of History* (New York: Columbia University Press, 1988), especially pp. 15–50. I made this argument in a somewhat different form in "The Complexity of Symbols," in C. Bynum, S. Harrell and P. Richman (eds.), *Gender and Religion: On the Complexity of Symbols* (Boston: Beacon Press, 1986), pp. 1–20.

9. J. Hajnal, "European Marriage Patterns in Perspective," in D. Glass and D. Eversley (eds.), *Population in History: Essays in Historical Demography* (London: Arnold, 1965), pp. 101–43.

10. See nn. 21 and 22 below.

11. On this question, particularly as concerns medieval texts, see Peter Dinzelbacher, "Zur Interpretation erlebnismystischer Texte des Mittelalters," *Zeitschrift für deutsches Altertum und deutsche Literatur* 117 (1988), pp. 1–23; and Ursula Peters, "Frauenliteratur im Mittelalter? Überlegungen zur Trobairitzpoesie, zur Frauenmystik and zur feministischen Literaturbetrachtung," *Germanisch-Romanische Monatschrift* N.F. 38 (1988), pp. 35–56.

12. For example, Alan E. Bernstein, "Political Anatomy," *University Publishing* (Winter, 1978), pp. 8-9; Natalie Z. Davis, "The Sacred and the Body Social in Sixteenth-Century Lyon," *Past and Present* 90 (February, 1981), pp. 40-70; Charles Zika, "Hosts, Processions and Pilgrimages: Controlling the Sacred in Fifteenth-Century Germany," *Past and Present* 118 (February, 1988), pp. 25-64; and Jacques Le Goff, "Head or Heart? The Political Use of Body Metaphor in the Middle Ages," *Zone* 5: *Fragments for a History of the Human Body*, Part 3 (New York: Urzone, 1989), pp. 13-26.

13. Michel Foucault, *The History of Sexuality*, trans. Robert Hurley, 3 vols. (New York: Pantheon, 1978ff.); Catherine Gallagher and Thomas Laqueur (eds.), *The Making of the Modern Body: Sexuality and Society in the Nineteenth Century* (Berkeley: University of California Press, 1987); and Peter Brown, *The Body and Society: Men, Women and Sexual Renunciation in Early Christianity* (New York: Columbia University Press, 1988). See also Francis Barker, *The Tremulous Private Body: Essays on Subjection* (London: Methuen, 1984); Camporesi, *Incorruptible Flesh*; and *Zone* 3-5: *Fragments for a History of the Human Body*, Parts 1-3, ed. Michel Feher, Ramona Naddaff and Nadia Tazi (New York: Urzone, 1989).

14. The essays reprinted below have occasionally been rewritten in order to remove repetition of either substance or citation; such rewriting may obscure the fact that Chapters 1, 4 and 5 were written before there was much scholarly attention to gender in the field of medieval studies. It is therefore important to point out that the collection *Gender and Religion* in which Chapter 5 appeared was one of the first efforts by any scholar to formulate a theoretical statement of what it means to take gender – that is, the cultural construction of maleness and femaleness – and not merely women's experience, into account. From the perspective of 1989, some of the ideas in my early articles may, however, need reformulating. I have tried to suggest how this might be done in an occasional addendum to the notes; such addenda are in brackets. Readers should also note that citations that appear in brackets are to a recent scholarship that has not been incorporated into the text. I have found it impossible to remove all inconsistencies of citation between articles. Chapters 1 and 5 were written for an audience of nonspecialists and made use of English translations; the other chap-

ters adhered to the standard scholarly practice of citing original sources unless a recent English translation was actually quoted in the text.

15. See Traian Stroianovich, *French Historical Method: The Annales Paradigm* (Ithaca: Cornell University Press, 1976), and, for a discussion of some applications of the *Annales* method in medieval studies, see Susan Stuard, "Fashion's Captives: Medieval Women in French Historiography," in S.M. Stuard (ed.), *Women in Medieval History and Historiography* (Philadelphia: University of Pennsylvania Press, 1987), pp. 59–80. The *Annales* school retains influence in France, if not as a paradigm at least as an approach that emphasizes the history of daily life and of *mentalités*; see Georges Duby (ed.), *A History of Private Life*, vol. 2: *Revelations of the Medieval World*, trans. A. Goldhammer (Cambridge, MA: Harvard University Press, 1988); and the articles by Jean-Claude Schmitt and Jacques Le Goff in *Zone* 4 and 5: *Fragments* 2, pp. 128–47 and 3, pp. 13–26 respectively.

16. See the articles by David Harlan, David Hollinger, Allan Megill, Theodore Hamerow, Gertrude Himmelfarb, Lawrence Levine, Joan Scott and John Toews in *The American Historical Review* 94.3 (June, 1989); Gertrude Himmelfarb, *The New History and the Old: Critical Essays and Reappraisals* (Cambridge, MA: Harvard University Press, 1987); Theodore Hamerow, *Reflections on History and Historians* (Madison: University of Wisconsin Press, 1987); Joan Scott, *Gender and the Politics of History*; and Lynn Hunt (ed.), *The New Cultural History* (Berkeley: University of California Press, 1989). A recent issue of the *Times Literary Supplement* (June 23, 1989), also devotes much attention to the nature of history writing, with articles on "its value" and on "where it should go." *The Journal of American History* 76.2 (1989), pp. 393–478, has now entered the debate with a special issue rather less interesting (and more crudely politicized) than the *American Historical Review* symposium.

17. See, for example, Howard Bloch, *Etymologies and Genealogies: A Literary Anthropology of the French Middle Ages* (Chicago: University of Chicago Press, 1983); and the special issue of *Speculum*, vol. 65 (1990), called "The New Philology," edited by Stephen Nicols. Two examples of the use of literary or social science theory by intellectual historians are: Charles M. Radding, "The Evolu-

tion of Medieval Mentalities: A Cognitive-Structural Approach," *American Historical Review* 83 (1978), pp. 577-97; and Nancy F. Partner, "Making Up Lost Time: Writing on the Writing of History," *Speculum* 61 (1986), pp. 909-17. For a critique of uses of literary theory by medievalists, see Norman Cantor, "What has Happened in Medieval Studies?" *Humanities* 5.5 (1984), pp. 16-19. By calling attention to the engagement with literary theory characteristic of a large group of students of medieval literature, I do not mean to evaluate either positively or negatively the quality of the results in individual cases.

18. Peter Novick, *That Noble Dream: The 'Objectivity Question' and the American Historical Profession* (Cambridge: Cambridge University Press, 1988).

19. A crisis in medieval studies was predicted by Geoffrey Barraclough, "What is to be Done about Medieval History?" *The New York Review of Books* 19.11 (June 4, 1970), pp. 51-57, although one can see with hindsight that Barraclough was wrong to associate the *Annales* paradigm so closely with quantitative history or to find an answer in quantification. For an overview of the field in the late seventies that suggests, I think, its lack of direction, see Karl Morrison, "Fragmentation and Unity in 'American Medievalism,' " in M. Kammen (ed.), *The Past Before Us: Contemporary Historical Writing in the United States* (Ithaca: Cornell University Press, 1980), pp. 49-72. To say that medieval historians in the United States have by and large not contributed to the current debate about the nature of historical research (or been cited by the theorists of that debate) is not to imply that no methodologically innovative work is being done. For example, there is reason to think that the early Middle Ages (i.e., the period down to about 1100) is coming to life these days; see Richard E. Sullivan, "The Carolingian Age: Reflections on Its Place in the History of the Middle Ages," *Speculum* 64 (1989), pp. 267-306. Nonetheless, it is clear that, in comparison with early modern historians, medievalists currently make little *general* impact on the historical profession.

20. I rely for my characterization of the new approach on Lynn Hunt, "Introduction: History, Culture and Text," in *The New Cultural History*, pp. 1-22; and David Harlan, "Intellectual History and the Return of Literature," *American Historical Review* 94.3 (June, 1989), pp. 581-609. (I should add here that I

do not find the answer Harlan proposes to the challenge of literary theory satisfactory.)

21. It should be clear, both from what I say here and from what I do in the essays below, that I in no way join the ranks of critics, such as Stanley Fish, who deny the separate existence of the text.

22. For all my emphasis on perspectives, I here clearly make some claim that we can "know" and "judge." The problem of how we ground such knowledge and judgment is a complex one. I find most help with the matter in contemporary philosophy of mind, which admits not only that *objective* judgment of the world outside the mind and the world within is problematic, but also that there are features of our own minds that lie beyond our *subjective* grasp. The problem of historical knowledge and judgment is indeed the philosophical problem of "other minds" and intrinsically related to the mind/body problem, which is the subject (at least obliquely) of my last essay below. The best discussion I have found of all this is Thomas Nagel, *The View from Nowhere* (New York: Oxford University Press, 1986), pp. 3-27, which asserts that true objectivity would have to encompass "all human perspectives, including [one's] own, without depriving them of their character as perspectives" (p. 20). Nagel faces courageously the liabilities consequent upon taking objectivity as a goal, suggests that judgments may lie at various places along a spectrum from subjective to objective, and can be read, I think, as providing a basis for thinking of the historian's aim as true but not universalizing pronouncements.

23. Nagel, *View from Nowhere*, p. 27.

24. Hunt, *The New Cultural History*, introduction, p. 22; for a similar viewpoint, see Lloyd S. Kramer, "Literature, Criticism, and Historical Imagination: The Literary Challenge of Hayden White and Dominick LaCapra," also in *The New Cultural History*, pp. 97-128, especially p. 128. Carolyn G. Heilbrun makes a parallel point about autobiography in *Writing a Woman's Life* (New York: Ballantine Books, 1988), pp. 129-30. In contrast to these authors, however, my use of the term "comic" is based on traditional literary understandings of comedy as a genre. It is therefore not so much a plea for treating history with a sense of humor (although it is that) as a suggestion that the human condition requires

us, both as historians and as human beings, to accept limitation, artifice, compromise and paradox in telling the story of the past.

25. See Wylie Sypher, "The Meanings of Comedy," in Wylie Sypher (ed.), *Comedy: An Essay on Comedy by George Meredith and Laughter by Henri Bergson* (New York: Doubleday, 1956), pp. 193-258, especially p. 255.

26. Although I would not agree entirely with it, there is much that is profound and helpful in Henri Bergson's essay "Laughter" (1900). Bergson argues (p. 93): "Any incident is comic that calls our attention to the physical in a person, when it is the moral side that is concerned." I am grateful to Linda Gregerson for suggesting that I read Bergson.

27. Bergson, "Laughter," p. 77.

28. It is important not to forget that tales of mutilation and fragmentation are about human pain. On this point, see Stephen Greenblatt, *Renaissance Cultures: Essays 1976-1989*, introduction, to appear; and Elaine Scarry, *The Body in Pain: The Making and Unmaking of the World* (New York: Oxford University Press, 1985).

I. *Women's Stories, Women's Symbols*

1. Since I am writing here for an audience of nonmedievalists, I have cited modern translations of medieval texts wherever possible. I have also tried to use examples that will be familiar, or at least accessible, to nonspecialists through secondary literature (see Introduction, n. 14, above). It is obviously not possible in an article of this sort to deal with the technical problems of recensions, authenticity, authorship and so on, associated with medieval texts. I would like to thank Peter Brown, Charles Keyes and Guenther Roth for arguing with me extensively about Victor Turner; I would also like to thank Frank Reynolds for getting me interested in Turner in the first place. [Since I wrote this article, Alison Goddard Elliott, *Roads to Paradise: Reading the Lives of the Early Saints* (Hanover, NH: University Press of New England, 1987), especially pp. 168-80, has applied Turner's processual model to the lives of the early desert saints.]

2. The term "processual symbolic analysis" was coined by Charles Keyes

to describe the theory of symbol held by both Victor Turner and Clifford Geertz; see Keyes, "Notes on the Language of Processual Symbolic Analysis," unpublished paper, 1976. It has been adopted by Turner in *Process, Performance and Pilgrimage: A Study in Comparative Symbology* (New Delhi: Concept, 1979), pp. 143-54, which is reprinted in Victor and Edith Turner, *Image and Pilgrimage in Christian Culture: Anthropological Perspectives* (New York: Columbia University Press, 1978), pp. 243-55. A recent statement which stresses the centrality of social dramas in Turner's perspective is Victor Turner, "Social Dramas and Stories About Them," W. J.T. Mitchell (ed.), *On Narrative* (Chicago: University of Chicago Press, 1981), pp. 137-64.

3. E.E. Evans-Pritchard, *Essays in Social Anthropology* (London: Faber & Faber, 1962), pp. 13-65.

4. Keith Thomas, "The Ferment of Fashion," *Times Literary Supplement* (April 30, 1982), p. 479.

5. See, for example, *Dramas, Fields and Metaphors: Symbolic Action in Human Society* (Ithaca: Cornell University Press, 1974), pp. 33-34, *Image and Pilgrimage*, pp. 249-51, and "Social Dramas and Stories About Them."

6. See, for example, *The Forest of Symbols: Aspects of Ndembu Ritual* (Ithaca: Cornell University Press, 1967), chs. 1, 2, *The Ritual Process: Structure and Anti-Structure* (Chicago: Aldine, 1969), p. 41, and *Dramas, Fields*, pp. 50, 55.

7. See *Forest*, chs. 1, 2, and *Image and Pilgrimage*, pp. 245-49.

8. On Becket, see "Religious Paradigms and Political Action: Thomas Becket at the Council of Northampton," in *Dramas, Fields*, pp. 60-97. On Francis, see "*Communitas*: Model and Process," *Ritual Process*, pp. 131-65 and *passim*.

9. New interpretations of Francis, not available to Turner, would make his ideal more complex than simply poverty. See, for example, E. Randolph Daniel, *The Franciscan Concept of Mission in the High Middle Ages* (Lexington: University Press of Kentucky, 1975); Barbara H. Rosenwein and Lester K. Little, "Social Meaning in the Monastic and Mendicant Spiritualities," *Past and Present* 63 (1974), pp. 4-32; and Lester K. Little, *Religious Poverty and the Profit Economy in Medieval Europe* (Ithaca: Cornell University Press, 1978). [And see now Hester Gelber, "A Theatre of Virtue: The Exemplary World of St. Francis of Assisi," in

J.S. Hawley (ed.), *Saints and Virtues* (Berkeley: University of California Press, 1987), pp. 15-35.]

10. The novel aspect of Turner's analysis seems to me not his notion of the root paradigm of the cross or martyrdom or *imitatio Christi*, an understanding of which seems to have been implicit in all analyses of Becket, but the importance Turner places on Becket's incorporating the model into himself at the votive mass on October 13; see *Dramas, Fields*, pp. 84-85.

11. In "Social Dramas and Stories," Turner writes (p. 147): "I have found that among the Ndembu, for example, prolonged social dramas always revealed the related sets of oppositions that give Ndembu social structure its tensile character: matriliny versus virilocality; the ambitious individual versus the wider interlinking of matrilineal kin; the elementary family versus the uterine sibling group (children of one mother); the forwardness of youth versus the domineering elders; status-seeking versus responsibility; sorcerism (*wuloji*) – that is, hostile feelings, grudges, and intrigues – versus friendly respect and generosity toward others. In the Iranian crisis the divisions and coalitions of interests have become publicly visible, some of which are surprising and revelatory. Crisis constitutes many levels in all cultures." One is struck here by the lack of precision with which the modern analogy is used.

12. On dominant symbols, see also *Dramas, Fields* and *Image and Pilgrimage*, pp. 243-55. On status reversal or elevation, see especially "Humility and Hierarchy: The Liminality of Status Elevation and Reversal," in *Ritual Process*, pp. 166-203.

13. For the four phases of social drama, see "Social Dramas and Stories," p. 145. The model of rites of passage from which Turner derives his notion of social drama has three phases: separation, margin or limen, and reaggregation (see *Image and Pilgrimage*, p. 249); and he frequently seems to assume three phases in social drama. See *Forest*, ch. 4.

14. See Arnold van Gennep, *The Rites of Passage*, trans. M.B. Vizedom and G.L. Caffee (1908; reprint, London: Routledge & Kegan Paul, 1960).

15. See *Forest*, chs. 2, 3.

16. See especially *Process, Performance*.

17. For example, *ibid.*, p. 23.

18. See Hippolyte Delehaye, *The Legends of the Saints: An Introduction to Hagiography*, trans. V. M. Crawford, Westminster Library (London: Longmans, Green, 1907); Simone Roisin, *L'Hagiographie cistercienne dans le diocèse de Liège au XIIIe siècle* (Louvain: Bibliothèque de l'Université, 1947); Charles Williams Jones, *Saints' Lives and Chronicles in Early England* (Ithaca: Cornell University Press, 1947); and Baudoin de Gaiffier, "Hagiographie et historiographie: Quelques aspects du probleme," *La storiografia altomedievale*, Settimane di Studio del Centro italiano de Studi sull'alto medioevo, 17 (Spoleto, 1970), vol. 1, pp. 139-66. [I would now be somewhat less inclined to describe the saint's life as *a* genre or to see its goal as depicting a static model; for criticisms of such formulations, see Michel de Certeau, "Hagiographie," *Encyclopedia Universalis* (Paris, 1968), vol. 8, pp. 207-09; Brigitte Cazelles, *Le Corps de sainteté d'après Jehan Bouche d'Or, Jehan Paulus et quelques vies des XIIe et XIIIe siècles* (Geneva: Libraire Droz, 1982); and Peter Brown, "The Saint as Exemplar in Late Antiquity," *Representations* 1.2 (1983), pp. 1-25.]

19. On the eucharist generally, see Joseph A. Jungmann, *The Mass of the Roman Rite: Its Origins and Development (Missarum Sollemnia)*, trans. F. A. Brunner, 2 vols. (New York: Benziger Brothers, 1955); F. Baix and C. Lambot, *La Dévotion à l'eucharistie et le VIIe centenaire de la Fête-Dieu* (Namur, n.d.); and n. 76, below. An even more obviously processual Christian ritual is baptism.

20. See, for example, *Forest*, and *The Drums of Affliction: A Study of Religious Processes Among the Ndembu of Zambia* (Oxford: Clarendon Press, 1968).

21. For example, *Process, Performance*, pp. 104-05, and *Ritual Process*, pp. 99-105.

22. I am aware that this is a very complicated issue, for it is difficult to sort out how a subgroup relates to the dominant culture; and we cannot *assume* that women will *not* agree with stereotypes of them generated by dominant males. The point is discussed well in Judith Shapiro, "Anthropology and the Study of Gender," *Soundings* 64.4 (1981), pp. 446-65. To "stand with" does not, of course, mean simply to take the view of informants. Turner himself discusses the problems with such an approach, which, he says, makes symbols merely

"signs." See *Forest*, pp. 25-27, and "Symbolic Studies," *Annual Review of Anthropology* 4 (1975), pp. 145-61. What we see when we "stand with" a subculture will no more be simply what its members tell us than what we see when we stand with the dominant culture will be.

23. *Ritual Process*, pp. 192-93.

24. Gustavo Gutierrez, *A Theology of Liberation: History, Politics and Salvation*, trans. Caridad Inda and John Eagleson (Maryknoll, NY: Orbis Books, 1973), especially ch. 3, pp. 287-306.

25. Bonaventure, The Life of St. Francis, in *Bonaventure: The Soul's Journey into God...*, trans. E. Cousins (New York: Paulist Press, 1978), pp. 193-94, 317. On Francis, see also n. 9 above [and Caroline W. Bynum, *Holy Feast and Holy Fast: The Religious Significance of Food to Medieval Women* (Berkeley: University of California Press, 1987), pp. 94-102]. For many other examples of male lives characterized by crisis and abrupt conversion, see Donald Weinstein and Rudolph M. Bell, *Saints and Society: The Two Worlds of Western Christendom, 1000-1700* (Chicago: University of Chicago Press, 1982), pp. 50-79, 109-15.

26. Bonaventure, Life of Francis, pp. 195, 303-07.

27. *Ibid.*, pp. 199-200.

28. *Ibid.*, pp. 204-06.

29. *Ibid.*, p. 243.

30. *Ibid.*, pp. 251-52.

31. *Ibid.*, pp. 257, 278.

32. *Ibid.*, pp. 311-13.

33. *Ibid.*, p. 321.

34. Roisin, *L'Hagiographie*, pp. 108, 111-13 and *passim*.

35. Caroline W. Bynum, *Jesus as Mother: Studies in the Spirituality of the High Middle Ages* (Berkeley: University of California Press, 1982), pp. 110-69.

36. Georges Duby, *The Three Orders: Feudal Society Imagined*, trans. Arthur Goldhammer (Chicago: University of Chicago Press, 1980), pp. 89, 95, 131-33, 145, 209.

37. On Guerric, see *Jesus as Mother*, pp. 120-22 and *passim*.

38. Bernard of Clairvaux, sermon 12 on the Song of Songs, *The Works of*

Bernard of Clairvaux, vol. 2: *On the Song of Songs*, vol. 1, trans. K. Walsh (Kalamazoo, MI: Cistercian Publications, 1976), pp. 77–85. And see *Jesus as Mother*, pp. 115–18, 127–28.

39. Bonaventure, "The Soul's Journey into God," in *Bonaventure...*, p. 93.

40. For example, Bernard of Clairvaux, *The Letters of St. Bernard of Clairvaux*, trans. B.S. James (London: Burns, Oates, 1953), letter 90, p. 135. On clothing, see *RB: 1980: The Rule of St. Benedict*, ed. Timothy Fry *et al.* (Collegeville, MN: Liturgical Press, 1981), pp. 261–63. In the modern world, of course, male religious clothing is a "reversed image" in another sense: monks and priests "wear skirts." On monasticism as institutionalized liminality, see *Ritual Process*, p. 107.

41. See the Office of Richard Rolle, translated from the York Breviary, in Richard Rolle, *The Fire of Love or Melody of Love and The Mending of Life... Translated by Richard Misyn*, ed. and trans. F. M.M. Cowper (London: Methuen, 1914), pp. xlv–lxii, especially p. xlvi.

42. For this argument see *Jesus as Mother*, pp. 257–62, and "Women Mystics," Chapter 4, below. [And see now also Karen Glente, "Mystikerinnenviten aus männlicher und weiblicher Sicht: ein Vergleich zwischen Thomas von Cantimpré und Katherina von Unterlinden," in *Religiöse Frauenbewegung und mystische Frömmigkeit im Mittelalter*, ed. Peter Dinzelbacher and D. Bauer (Cologne and Vienna: Böhlau, 1988), pp. 251-64.]

43. On James and Thomas, see Ernest W. McDonnell, *The Beguines and Beghards in Medieval Culture with Special Emphasis on the Belgian Scene* (1954; reprint, New York: Octagon Books, 1969), pp. 20–40 and *passim*; and Brenda M. Bolton, "*Vitae Matrum*: A Further Aspect of the *Frauenfrage*," in Derek Baker (ed.), *Medieval Women: Dedicated and Presented to Professor Rosalind M.T. Hill*, Studies in Church History: Subsidia 1 (Oxford: Blackwell, 1978), pp. 253–73.

44. *The Book of Divine Consolation of the Blessed Angela of Foligno*, trans. M.G. Steegmann (reprint, New York: Cooper Square, 1966); the Life of Margaret of Cortona, in J. Bollandus and G. Henschius (eds.), *Acta sanctorum...editio novissima*, ed. J. Carnandet *et al.* (Paris: Palmé, etc., 1863-   ) [hereafter AASS], February, vol. 3 (Paris and Rome, 1865), pp. 302–63. [And see now Paul Lachance, *The Spiritual Journey of the Blessed Angela of Foligno According to the*

Memorial of Frater A., Studia Antoniana 29 (Rome: Pontificum Athenaeum Antonianum, 1984); and Ulrich Köpf, "Angela von Foligno: Ein Beitrag zur franziskanischen Frauenbewegung um 1300," in Dinzelbacher and Bauer, *Religiöse Frauenbewegung*, pp. 225-50.]

45. "The Female Saint as Hagiographical Type in the Late Middle Ages," unpublished paper delivered at American Historical Association meeting, December, 1981. See also John Coakley, "The Representation of Sanctity in Late Medieval Hagiography: Evidence from *Lives* of Saints of the Dominican Order," Ph.D. Dissertation, Harvard, 1980; and *Jesus as Mother*, ch. 5.

46. *The Life of Christina of Markyate*, trans. C.H. Talbot (Oxford: Clarendon Press, 1959); the Life of Juliana of Cornillon, AASS, April, vol. 1 (Paris and Rome, 1866), pp. 434-75; *The Book of Divine Consolation of Angela of Foligno*.

47. *Image and Pilgrimage*, pp. 161, 236. See also *Process, Performance*, pp. 104-06, and *Ritual Process*, pp. 105, 183, 200.

48. *The Life of Christina of Markyate*.

49. See John Anson, "The Female Transvestite in Early Monasticism," *Viator* 5 (1974), pp. 1-32; see also Vern Bullough, "Transvestites in the Middle Ages," *American Journal of Sociology* 79 (1974), pp. 1381-94. Caesarius of Heisterbach tells a few such stories from the late twelfth century, but they are imitated from patristic examples: Caesarius of Heisterbach, *The Dialogue on Miracles*, trans. H. von E. Scott and C.C. Swinton Bland (New York: Routledge, 1929), vol. 1, pp. 51-59. One of the problems with the emphasis that Marina Warner places on Joan of Arc's transvestism in her recent book is her failure to give other late medieval examples of women cross-dressing: see Marina Warner, *Joan of Arc: The Image of Female Heroism* (New York: Knopf, 1981). For two examples, see Michael Goodich, "Contours of Female Piety in Later Medieval Hagiography," *Church History* 50 (1981), p. 25. Delehaye, *Legends*, pp. 197-206, traces many of the later stories back to a single prototype.

50. The Life of Margaret of Ypres in appendix to G. Meersseman, "Les frères prêcheurs et le mouvement dévot en Flandre au XIIe siècle," *Archivum Fratrum Praedicatorum* 18 (1948), pp. 106-30; the Life of Mary of Oignies by James of Vitry, AASS, June, vol. 5 (Paris and Rome, 1867), pp. 547-72. On

Mary's inability to adopt complete mendicant poverty, see Bolton, *"Vitae Matrum,"* pp. 257-59. For another parallel story, see Thomas of Cantimpré's Life of Lutgard of Aywières (or of St. Trond), AASS, June, vol. 4 (Paris and Rome, 1867), pp. 189-210.

51. On medieval narrative technique, see William J. Brandt, *The Shape of Medieval History: Studies in Modes of Perception* (New Haven: Yale University Press, 1966).

52. On Joan, see Warner, *Joan of Arc.* On Dorothy of Montau (or of Prussia), see Stephen P. Bensch, "A Cult of the Maternal: Dorothea of Prussia (1347-94)," unpublished paper; Richard Kieckhefer, *Unquiet Souls: Fourteenth-Century Saints and Their Religious Milieu* (Chicago: University of Chicago Press, 1984), pp. 25-26, 210 n. 2, and *passim*; and Ute Stargardt, *The Influence of Dorothea von Montau on the Mysticism of Margery Kempe*, Ph.D. Dissertation, University of Tennessee, 1981. Margery's life is available in a modern English translation: *The Book of Margery Kempe*, trans. W. Butler-Bowdon (New York: Devin-Adair, 1944). On Christina, see *The Life of Christina of Markyate*, and Christopher J. Holdsworth, "Christina of Markyate," *Medieval Women*, pp. 185-204.

53. Anson, "Female Transvestite," argues convincingly that these stories, like the later legend of Pope Joan, were the result of psychological projection. One of the major charges against Joan of Arc, who was accused of heresy (with overtones of witchcraft as well), was cross-dressing; see Warner, *Joan of Arc.*

54. See, for example, the biographies of Christina of Markyate and Juliana of Cornillon cited above, n. 46.

55. Gertrude of Helfta, *Oeuvres spirituelles*, ed. Pierre Doyère, 3 vols., Sources chrétiennes, Série des textes monastiques d'Occident (Paris: Editions du Cerf, 1967-1968); *Hadewijch: The Complete Works*, trans. Columba Hart (New York: Paulist Press, 1980); Mechtild of Magdeburg, *The Revelations...or the Flowing Light of the Godhead*, trans. Lucy Menzies (London: Longmans, 1953); and Beatrice of Nazareth (or Tienen), *Vita Beatricis: De Autobiografie van de Z. Beatrijs van Tienen O. Cist. 1200-1268*, ed. L. Reypens (Antwerp: Ruusbroec-Genootschap, 1964). On Gertrude and Mechtild of Magdeburg, see *Jesus as*

Mother, ch. 5. Hadewijch, who uses intensely erotic language to describe her relationship to God, frequently casts herself in the role of a knight seeking his lady. On androgynous imagery in women's visions, see Elizabeth Petroff, *Consolation of the Blessed* (New York: Alta Gaia Society, 1979), pp. 66-78. [I would now try to avoid the word "androgynous" in formulating this point; see Chapter 5, below, n. 31.]

56. Raymond of Capua, Life of Catherine of Siena, AASS, April, vol. 3 (Paris and Rome, 1866), pp. 892, 884.

57. Catherine of Siena, *The Dialogue*, trans. Suzanne Noffke (New York: Paulist Press, 1980).

58. Marguerite of Oingt, Life of Beatrice of Ornacieux, *Les oeuvres de Marguerite d'Oingt*, ed. Antonin Duraffour, Pierre Gardette and Paulette Durdilly, Publications de l'Institut de linguistique romane de Lyon, 21 (Paris: Belles Lettres, 1965), pp. 104-37.

59. *Ibid.*, pp. 136-37.

60. *Ibid.*, p. 105 (she pierces her hands with nails to achieve stigmata); p. 117 (she sees Christ as a little child at every elevation of the host); p. 122 (the host swells in her mouth until she almost chokes, and after this she can eat no earthly food). For other lives of women *by* women, one can consult the several nuns' books from the early fourteenth century.

61. *The Book of Margery Kempe*, p. 10. It is interesting that the anchorite who advises her here describes Christ as mother and tells her to suck his breast; but Margery herself never uses reversed imagery. Her Christ is always male and she is always female; see, for example, pp. 22-23 and 76-77.

62. *Ibid.*, p. 17.

63. On her need for male protection, see *ibid.*, pp. 25, 28, 32, 98-100. Margery was quite bold about opposing authority figures. This may have been owing in part to her father's status (see Anthony Goodman, "The Piety of John Brunham's Daughter, of Lynn," in Baker, *Medieval Women*, pp. 347-58), although to say this is not to detract from Margery's personal courage and insouciance.

64. *The Book of Margery Kempe*, p. 39.

65. *Ibid.*, p. 192.

66. *Ibid.*, pp. 76, 190; *ibid.*, pp. 74–75, 81.

67. For the texts discussed here see nn. 46 and 52 above. I should empha-size that later medieval women's lives include peasants as well as aristocrats, lay women as well as nuns and quasi-religious.

68. See Petroff, *Consolation of the Blessed*, p. 123; for other examples of circumstances constraining women's decisions, see *ibid.*, p. 42. Weinstein and Bell, *Saints and Society*, pp. 88–97, give a number of examples of saintly women who are unable to determine their marital status and therefore the course of their lives.

69. *The Legend and Writings of Saint Clare of Assisi* (based on German work by E. Grau) (New York: St. Bonaventure, 1953), pp. 35–37; and Jeanne Ancelet-Hustache (ed.), "Les 'Vitae Sororum' d'Unterlinden: Edition critique du Manu-scrit 508 de la Bibliothèque de Colmar," *Archives d'histoire doctrinale et littéraire du moyen âge* 5 (1930), pp. 374–75.

70. See *Legend of Saint Clare*, and Rosalind B. Brooke and Christopher N.L. Brooke, "St. Clare," in Baker, *Medieval Women*, pp. 275–87. For other wom-en's lives in translation, see Petroff, *Consolation of the Blessed*.

71. Weinstein and Bell, *Saints and Society*, Part I, especially pp. 34, 48, 71, 97, 108, 121, 135.

72. A.K. Ramanujan, "On Women Saints," in J. Hawley and D.M. Wulff (eds.), *The Divine Consort: Radha and the Goddesses of India* (Berkeley: Berkeley Religious Studies Series, 1982), pp. 316–24; and Nancy Chodorow, *The Repro-duction of Mothering: Psychoanalysis and the Sociology of Gender* (Berkeley: Uni-versity of California Press, 1978). Ramanujan says about the Indian situation: "The males take on female personae.... Before God all men are women. But no female saint, however she may defy male-oriented relational attitudes, takes on a male persona. It is as if, being already female, she has no need to change anything to turn toward God" (p. 324). See n. 89, below.

73. Examples of excellent scholarship in this vein, which nonetheless result in pejorative assessments of figures like Dorothy, Margery, Marguerite of Oingt and so on, are Edmund Colledge and James Walsh (eds.), *A Book of Showings to the Anchoress Julian of Norwich*, Studies and Texts, 35, 2 parts (Toronto: Pontif-

ical Institute of Mediaeval Studies, 1978), introduction; and Wolfgang Riehle, *The Middle English Mystics*, trans. B. Standring (London: Routledge & Kegan Paul, 1981).

74. André Vauchez, *Le Spiritualité du moyen age occidental VIIIᵉ-XIIᵉ siècles* (Paris: Presses Universitaires de France, 1975); Little, *Religious Poverty*.

75. On the eucharist, see Chapter 4, below.

76. See Jungmann, *Mass*, vol. 2, pp. 120-22, 206ff.; Peter Browe, *Die Verehrung der Eucharistie im Mittelalter* (Munich: Hueber, 1933); and Edouard Dumoutet, *Corpus Domini: Aux sources de la piété eucharistique médiévale* (Paris: Beauchesne, 1942).

77. On women as inferior, according to scientific and theological theory, see Vern Bullough, "Medieval Medical and Scientific Views of Women," *Viator* 4 (1973), pp. 487-93; and the works cited in Chapter 3, n. 46, below.

78. Mechtild of Hackeborn has a vision of herself distributing the chalice; see *Revelationes Gertrudianae ac Mechtildianae*, 2: *Sanctae Mechtildis virginis ordinis sancti Benedicti Liber specialis gratiae*, ed. the monks of Solesmes (Paris: Oudin, 1877), pp. 7-10. More common is the vision in which Christ is priest to the woman recipient; see Peter Browe, *Die eucharistischen Wunder des Mittelalters*, Breslauer Studien zur historischen Theologie, N.F. 4 (Breslau: Müller & Seiffert, 1938), pp. 20-30. On Mechtild of Hackeborn and Gertrude (cited in n. 79 below), see *Jesus as Mother*, ch. 5.

79. Gertrude of Helfta, *Revelationes Gertrudianae ac Mechtildianae* 1: *Sanctae Gertrudis...Legatus divinae Pietatis..* , ed. the monks of Solesmes (Paris: Oudin, 1875), pp. 392-95, and *Oeuvres spirituelles*, vol. 2, pp. 196-98; Angela of Foligno, *Book of Divine Consolation*, p. 223; and the Life of Lukardis of Oberweimar, in *Analecta Bollandiana* 18 (Brussels, 1899), p. 337. See also the Life of Ida of Louvain, AASS, April, vol. 2 (Paris and Rome, 1865), p. 183.

80. For these examples, see the case of the Viennese beguine, Agnes Blannbekin, discussed by Browe, *Die eucharistischen Wunder*, p. 34, and by McDonnell, *Beguines*, pp. 314-17; and the Life of Ida of Léau, AASS, October, vol. 13 (Paris, 1883), pp. 113-14.

81. See Michael Moffatt, *An Untouchable Community in South India: Struc-*

ture and Consensus (Princeton: Princeton University Press, 1979) for data that support Turner's idea of reversal.

82. On the beguines, see the works cited in n. 85, below. In the south of Europe groups like the Humiliati and the mendicant tertiaries paralleled the beguines, who were a Low Country and Rhineland movement.

83. See *Jesus as Mother*, introduction and ch. 3.

84. Brenda Bolton makes this point in *"Vitae Matrum,"* p. 260. And note the number of female saints designated "lay" in Vauchez's list: André Vauchez, *La Sainteté en Occident aux derniers siècles du moyen âge d'après les procès de canonisation et les documents hagiographiques*, Bibliothèque des Ecoles françaises d'Athènes et de Rome, 241 (Rome: Ecole française de Rome, 1981), pp. 656-76; see also pp. 315-18.

85. Joseph Greven, *Die Anfänge der Beginen: ein Beitrag zur Geschichte der Volksfrömmigkeit und des Ordenswesens im Hochmittelalter* (Münster: Aschendorff, 1912); Herbert Grundmann, *Religiöse Bewegungen im Mittelalter* (1935; reprint with additions, Hildesheim: Olms, 1961); R.W. Southern, *Western Society and the Church in the Middle Ages* (Harmondsworth, England: Penguin, 1970), pp. 318-31; Brenda Bolton, *"Mulieres Sanctae,"* in D. Baker (ed.), *Studies in Church History*, 10: *Sanctity and Secularity* (1973), pp. 77-95; and *"Vitae Matrum."* [And see now Carol Neel, "The Origins of the Beguines," *Signs: Journal of Women in Culture and Society* 14.2 (1989), pp. 321-41.]

86. Frederick Stein, "The Religious Women of Cologne: 1120-1320," Ph.D. Dissertation, Yale, 1977. The interpretation which blames male resistance to the religious needs of women must also be modified in light of John B. Freed, "Urban Life and the 'Cura Monialium' in Thirteenth-Century Germany," *Viator* 3 (1972), pp. 311-27.

87. The quotation is from Turner, *Image and Pilgrimage*, p. 251. [Below, in Chapter 2, I suggest that Ernst Troeltsch's idea of the "free groups" characteristic of mystical communities is a better theoretical tool for describing female groups.]

88. The point I raise here parallels the criticism that has been made of certain interpretations of women's symbols that come out of the structuralist camp.

For example, the much-discussed essay by Sherry Ortner, which argues that women are universally imaged as "nature" to the image of man as "culture," has been criticized for, among other things, viewing culture monolithically as the dominant culture; see Ortner, "Is Female to Male as Nature is to Culture?" in Michelle A. Rosaldo and Louise Lamphere (eds.), *Women, Culture and Society* (Stanford: Stanford University Press, 1974), pp. 67-87; Eleanor Leacock and June Nash, "Ideologies of Sex: Archetypes and Stereotypes," *Issues in Cross-Cultural Research*, New York Academy of Sciences, 285 (1977), pp. 618-45; and C.P. MacCormack and M. Strathern (eds.), *Nature, Culture and Gender* (Cambridge: Cambridge University Press, 1980), especially p. 17.

89. For an example of fusion with Christ through eroticism, see *Hadewijch*, trans. Hart; for fusion through eating, see the Life of Ida of Louvain, AASS, April, vol. 2 (Paris and Rome, 1865), pp. 156-89; for fusion through illness, see the Life of Alice of Schaerbeke, AASS, June, vol. 2 (Paris and Rome, 1867), pp. 471-77, and Julian of Norwich, *A Book of Showings*, ed. Colledge and Walsh. See also Ernst Benz, *Die Vision: Erfahrungsformen und Bilderwelt* (Stuttgart, 1969), pp. 17-34 [and Bynum, *Holy Feast*]. Ramanujan's formulation of differences in Indian lives of men and women (see n. 72, above) cannot be completely applied to the medieval tradition exactly because the passivity he implies in women's images does not accurately describe the intensely dynamic aspect of erotic and ascetic images in the West.

90. *The Mirror of Simple Souls*, long known to scholars but discovered only in this century to be Margaret's "heretical" treatise, has been printed in Romana Guarnieri, "Il 'Miroir des simples âmes' di Margherita Porete," *Archivio italiano per la storia della pietà*, vol. 4 (Rome, 1965), pp. 513-635. On the work, see Robert E. Lerner, *The Heresy of the Free Spirit in the Later Middle Ages* (Berkeley: University of California Press, 1972), pp. 72-76, 200-08.

91. Such mysticism is one of Turner's favorite examples of "metaphorical liminality." See *Process, Performance*, p. 125, where he claims that mysticism is interiorized ritual liminality, ritual liminality is exteriorized mysticism.

92. See Little, *Religious Poverty*, and Bynum, *Jesus as Mother*, p. 183. Turner is, of course, aware that reversal is more central in some religions than in oth-

ers; see *Ritual Process*, p. 189. But his paradigm of Christianity seems late medieval, even Franciscan, rather than early modern or antique. In a rather obvious sense, the Reformation was a rejection of elaborate images of reversal – not just of carnival, monks and friars, but of the general notion of world-denial as well.

93. Grundmann, *Religiöse Bewegungen*. On late medieval religiosity as upper class – and especially on conversion as an upper-class phenomenon – see Weinstein and Bell, *Saints and Society*, ch. 7, especially p. 216.

94. See n. 24, above.

95. This writing has been surveyed recently by Rosemary Ruether, "The Feminist Critique in Religious Studies," *Soundings* 64.4 (1981), pp. 388–402; Mark Silk, "Is God a Feminist?" *New York Times Book Review*, April 11, 1982 [and Caroline W. Bynum, "The Complexity of Symbols," in C. Bynum, S. Harrell and P. Richman (eds.), *Gender and Religion: On the Complexity of Symbols* (Boston: Beacon Press, 1986), pp. 1–20]. I should also, however, make the obvious point that conservative historians of religion sometimes use "feminist" quite unfairly as implying biased or poor scholarship and refuse to accept evidence of differences in male and female religiosity, even when the scholars presenting the differences are very careful to refer to specific times, places and texts.

II. *The Mysticism and Asceticism of Medieval Women*

1. This paper was prepared for a conference on Max Weber and the Middle Ages, held at Bad Homburg, West Germany, June 22-24, 1986. I was assigned the task of exploring Weber's and Troeltsch's ideas in the light of the current scholarly attention to women's piety. It appeared in German translation in Wolfgang Schluchter (ed.), *Max Webers Sicht des okzidentalen Christentums: Interpretation und Kritik* (Frankfurt: Suhrkamp, 1988), pp. 355–82. I have been aided by the criticisms of Robert Lerner and Wolfgang Schluchter. I dedicate the paper to my husband, Guenther Roth, who was one of the organizers of the original conference and prepared the German translation.

2. Max Weber, *Economy and Society*, ed. Guenther Roth and Claus Wittich, 3 vols. (New York: Bedminster Press, 1968), vol. 2, pp. 488ff., 504ff. In Max Weber, *The Protestant Ethic and the Spirit of Capitalism*, trans. Talcott Parsons

(New York: Scribner's, 1958), pp. 253-54, n.70, Weber refers to the beguins, or male and female Franciscan tertiaries in the south of France, who may be related to but are also distinct from the beguines in the north of Europe, a female movement. On this, see Robert E. Lerner, "Beguines and Beghards," and "Beguins," *Dictionary of the Middle Ages*, ed. Joseph Strayer (New York: Scribner's, 1983), vol. 2, pp. 157-63. Marianne Weber, *Ehefrau und Mutter in der Rechtsentwicklung: Eine Einführung* (Tübingen: Mohr, 1907), written under Max's influence, treats the beguines; see pp. 273-77. (For Max's influence, see p. 63, n. 1.) Basically she follows the line of Karl Bücher; she explains the movement as the result of a demographic surplus of women, and sees the beguines as primarily an economic phenomenon. See Karl Bücher, *Die Frauenfrage im Mittelalter* (1882; 2nd ed., Tübingen: Laupp, 1910). For a survey of literature from around 1900 that stresses social and economic causation, see Joseph Greven, *Die Anfänge der Beginen: Ein Beitrag zur Geschichte der Volksfrömmigkeit und des Ordenswesens im Hochmittelalter*, Vorreformationsgeschichtliche Forschungen, 8 (Münster: Aschendorff, 1912), pp. 1-27. [A thoughtful survey of twentieth-century German scholarship on medieval women is provided by Martha Howell (with Suzanne Wemple and Denise Kaiser), "A Documented Presence: Medieval Women in Germanic Historiography," in Susan Stuard (ed.), *Women in Medieval History and Historiography* (Philadelphia: University of Pennsylvania Press, 1987), pp. 101-31.]

3. *Economy and Society*, vol. 2, pp. 488-89. Weber is ambivalent about this kind of religiosity; see *ibid.*, p. 571, where he says the "whining cadence of typical Lutheran sermons in Germany...has so often driven strong men out of the church."

4. *Ibid.*, pp. 490, 605.

5. For recent approaches to this question, with appropriate warning against lapsing into essentialist views of male and female differences, see Joan W. Scott, "Gender: A Useful Category of Historical Analysis," *American Historical Review* 91.5 (December, 1986), pp. 1053-75.

6. I.M. Lewis, *Ecstatic Religion: An Anthropological Study of Spirit Possession and Shamanism* (Harmondsworth, England: Penguin, 1971).

7. Herbert Thurston, *The Physical Phenomena of Mysticism* (Chicago: Regnery,

1952); and Rudolph Bell, *Holy Anorexia* (Chicago: University of Chicago Press, 1985). For detailed examination of one case, see Judith C. Brown, *Immodest Acts: The Life of a Lesbian Nun in Renaissance Italy* (New York: Oxford University Press, 1985).

8. See Thurston, *Physical Phenomena*; Bell, *Holy Anorexia*; and Caroline W. Bynum, "Fast, Feast, and Flesh: The Religious Significance of Food to Medieval Women," *Representations* 11 (1985), pp. 1-25.

9. David Herlihy, "The Making of the Medieval Family: Symmetry, Structure and Sentiment," *Journal of Family History* 8.2 (1983), pp. 116-30. See also Diane Owen Hughes, "Representing the Family: Portraits and Purposes in Early Modern Italy," *Journal of Interdisciplinary History* 17.1 (Summer, 1986), pp. 7-38, especially pp. 7-8; and Cynthia Hahn, " 'Joseph Will Perfect, Mary Enlighten, and Jesus Save Thee': The Holy Family as Marriage Model in the Merode Triptych," *The Art Bulletin* 68.1 (1986), pp. 54-66.

10. Elisabeth Vavra, "Bildmotiv und Frauenmystik: Funktion und Rezeption," in Peter Dinzelbacher and D. Bauer (eds.), *Frauenmystik im Mittelalter* (Ostfildern: Schwabenverlag, 1985), pp. 201-30; and Joanna Ziegler, "The Virgin or Mary Magdalen? Artistic Choices and Changing Spiritual Attitudes in the Later Middle Ages," paper presented at the Holy Cross Symposium "The Word Becomes Flesh," November 9, 1985. [See now the superb article by Jeffrey Hamburger, "The Visual and the Visionary: The Image in Late Medieval Monastic Devotions," *Viator* 20 (1989), pp. 161-82.]

11. Gottfried Koch, *Frauenfrage und Ketzertum im Mittelalter: die Frauenbewegung im Rahmen des Katharismus und des Waldensertums und ihre sozialen Wurzeln: 12.-14. Jahrhundert* (Berlin: Akademie-Verlag, 1962). See also Bücher, *Die Frauenfrage*.

12. See Richard Abels and Ellen Harrison, "The Position of Women in Languedocian Catharism," *Mediaeval Studies* 41 (1979), pp. 215-51; Eleanor McLaughlin, "Les Femmes et l'hérésie médiévale: Un problème dans l'histoire de la spiritualité," *Concilium* 111 (1976), pp. 73-90. [And see now Peter Segl, "Die religiöse Frauenbewegung in Südfrankreich im 12. und 13. Jahrhundert zwischen Häresie und Orthodoxie," in Peter Dinzelbacher and Dieter Bauer

(eds.), *Religiöse Frauenbewegung und mystische Frömmigkeit im Mittelalter* (Cologne and Vienna: Böhlau, 1988), pp. 99–116.]

13. See, for example, Rosemary Ruether (ed.), *Religion and Sexism: Images of Women in the Jewish and Christian Traditions* (New York: Simon & Schuster, 1974); Carol P. Christ, "Heretics and Outsiders: The Struggle over Female Power in Western Religion," *Soundings* 61.3: *Dilemmas of Pluralism* (1978), pp. 269–80; and Renée Watkins, "Two Women Visionaries and Death: Catherine of Siena and Julian of Norwich," *Numen* 30.2 (1983), pp. 174–98.

14. Herbert Grundmann, *Religiöse Bewegungen im Mittelalter: Untersuchungen über die geschichtlichen Zusammenhänge zwischen der Ketzerei, den Bettelorden und der religiösen Frauenbewegung im 12. und 13. Jahrhundert* (1935; reprint, with additions, Hildesheim: Olms, 1961).

15. A good example of such an integrated approach is Kaspar Elm, "Die Stellung der Frau in Ordenswesen, Semireligiosentum und Häresie zur Zeit der Elisabeth," in *Sankt Elisabeth: Fürstin, Dienerin, Heilige: Aufsätze, Dokumentation, Katalog* (Sigmaringen: Thorbecke, 1981), pp. 7–28.

16. Michael Goodich, *Vita Perfecta: The Ideal of Sainthood in the Thirteenth Century* (Stuttgart: Hiersemann, 1982); Richard Kieckhefer, *Unquiet Souls: Fourteenth-Century Saints and Their Religious Milieu* (Chicago: University of Chicago Press, 1984); André Vauchez, *La Sainteté en Occident aux derniers siècles du moyen âge d'après les procès de canonisation et les documents hagiographiques* (Rome: Ecole française de Rome, 1981); and Donald Weinstein and Rudolph Bell, *Saints and Society: The Two Worlds of Western Christendom, 1000–1700* (Chicago: University of Chicago Press, 1982).

17. For a brief bibliography and discussion, see Lerner, "Beguines and Beghards." Ernest W. McDonnell, *The Beguines and Beghards in Medieval Culture with Special Emphasis on the Belgian Scene* (Rutgers: Rutgers University Press, 1954; reprint, 1969) remains the basic book, although its organization and presentation are somewhat confused.

18. The best discussion known to me of the state of historical interpretation regarding third orders is a seminar paper written for Yale University in 1985: Cathy Mooney, "Tertiaries and Third Orders in the Middle Ages." See also G.G.

Meersseman, *Dossier de l'ordre de la pénitence au XIIIe siècle* (Fribourg: Editions universitaires, 1961); and Lester Little, *Religious Poverty and the Profit Economy in Medieval Europe* (Ithaca, NY: Cornell University Press, 1978), pp. 206-10.

19. Suzanne F. Wemple, *Women in Frankish Society: Marriage and the Cloister, 500 to 900* (Philadelphia: University of Pennsylvania Press, 1981).

20. See Jo Ann McNamara and Suzanne Wemple, "The Power of Women through the Family in Medieval Europe, 500-1100," *Feminist Studies* 1 (1973), pp. 126-41, and "Sanctity and Power: The Dual Pursuit of Medieval Women," in Renate Bridenthal and Claudia Koonz (eds.), *Becoming Visible: Women in European History* (Boston: Houghton-Mifflin, 1977), pp. 90-118.

21. See Carol P. Christ and Judith Plaskow (eds.), *Womanspirit Rising: A Feminist Reader in Religion* (New York: Harper & Row, 1979), and Charlene Spretnak (ed.), *The Politics of Women's Spirituality: Essays in the Rise of Spiritual Power within the Feminist Movement* (New York: Doubleday-Anchor, 1982). For a lengthier critique of this argument than I can give here, see Caroline Bynum, "The Complexity of Symbols," in C. Bynum, S. Harrell, and P. Richman (eds.), *Gender and Religion: On the Complexity of Symbols* (Boston: Beacon Press, 1986).

22. See Simone Roisin, *L'Hagiographie cistercienne dans le diocèse de Liège au XIIIe siècle* (Louvain: Bibliothèque de l'Université, 1947), pp. 108, 111-20; André Rayez, "Humanité du Christ: La mystique féminine...," *Dictionnaire de spiritualité, ascétique et mystique, doctrine et histoire*, vol. 7, pt. 1 (Paris: Beauchesne, 1969), cols. 1088-90; and Caroline W. Bynum, *Jesus as Mother* (Berkeley: University of California Press, 1982), pp. 110-69, 247-62.

23. The material given in Goodich, *Vita Perfecta*, pp. 163, 209, suggests this, but Goodich does not pursue the point. On the women's movement in general, see Caroline Walker Bynum, *Holy Feast and Holy Fast: The Religious Significance of Food to Medieval Women* (Berkeley: University of California Press, 1987), ch. 1. The best discussion of women's own writings is Peter Dronke, *Women Writers of the Middle Ages: A Critical Study of Texts from Perpetua († 203) to Marguerite Porete († 1310)* (Cambridge: Cambridge University Press, 1984).

24. See Ronald Finucane, *Miracles and Pilgrims: Popular Beliefs in Medieval England* (Totowa, NJ: Rowman & Littlefield, 1977), pp. 130-51.

25. Weinstein and Bell, *Saints*, pp. 220-21; Vauchez, *La Sainteté*, pp. 243-49, 316-18, 402-10; Goodich, *Vita Perfecta*, pp. 173, 211-40; and Jane Tibbetts Schulenberg, "Sexism and the Celestial Gynaeceum from 500 to 1200," *Journal of Medieval History* 4 (1978), pp. 117-33.

26. Vauchez, *La Sainteté*, p. 317.

27. Dinzelbacher and Bauer (eds.), *Frauenmystik*. [The second volume edited by Dinzelbacher and Bauer, *Religiöse Frauenbewegung* (1988) is less satisfactory than the first, in part because it fails to take account of recent, good, non-German scholarship.]

28. Weinstein and Bell, *Saints*, pp. 234-35. See also Ernst Benz, *Die Vision: Erfahrungsformen und Bilderwelt* (Stuttgart: Ernst Klett, 1969), pp. 17-34.

29. See Chapter 4, below.

30. Peter Browe, *Die eucharistischen Wunder des Mittelalters* (Breslau: Müller & Seiffert, 1938); and Chapter 4, below.

31. On Lidwina, see Bynum, "Fast, Feast, and Flesh," pp. 4-8.

32. Hadewijch, *The Complete Works*, trans. Columba Hart (New York: Paulist Press, 1980), vision 5, pp. 276-77. And see Chapter 4, below, n. 78.

33. On this point, see Bynum, *Holy Feast*, ch. 7.

34. See Catherine of Siena, *Il Dialogo della Divina Provvidenza ovvero Libro della Divino Dottrina*, ed. Giuliana Cavallini (Rome: Edizioni Cateriniane, 1968), chs. 14, 23, 113-18, pp. 37-42, 51-54, 274-86. On Dorothy, see Kieckhefer, *Unquiet Souls*, pp. 22-33; and Bynum, *Holy Feast*, ch. 4.

35. Ernst Troeltsch, *The Social Teaching of the Christian Churches*, trans. Olive Wyon, 2 vols. (1931; reprint, New York, Harper, 1960), vol. 1, p. 364.

36. See Bynum, *Holy Feast*, ch. 1; and John B. Freed, "Urban Development and the 'Cura Monialium' in Thirteenth-Century Germany," *Viator* 3 (1972), pp. 311-27.

37. On this point see Chapter 1, above.

38. Brenda M. Bolton, "*Vitae Matrum*: A Further Aspect of the Frauenfrage," in Derek Baker (ed.), *Medieval Women: Dedicated and Presented to Professor Rosalind M.T. Hill*, Studies in Church History, Subsidia 1 (Oxford: Blackwell, 1978), p. 260.

39. See Mooney, "Tertiaries"; and Jean-Claude Schmitt, *Mort d'une hérésie: L'Église et les clercs face aux beguines et aux beghards du Rhin supérieur du XIVᵉ au XVᵉ siècle* (Paris: Mouton, 1978), pp. 207-10. [See also now Anneliese Stoklaska, "Weibliche Religiosität im mittelalterlichen Wien unter besonderer Berücksichtigung der Agnes Blannbekin," in Dinzelbacher and Bauer (eds.), *Religiöse Frauenbewegung*, pp. 165-84.]

40. Troeltsch, *Social Teaching*, vol. 2, p. 730.

41. Ernst Troeltsch, "Epochen und Typen der Sozialphilosophie des Christentums," in *Gesammelte Schriften*, vol. 4: *Aufsätze zur Geistesgeschichte und Religionssoziologie*, ed. Hans Baron (Tübingen: Mohr, 1925), p. 126.

42. Troeltsch, *Social Teaching*, vol. 2, p. 744.

43. *Ibid.*, p. 745.

44. Troeltsch, "Epochen," p. 127, *Social Teaching*, vol. 1, p. 377, and vol. 2, pp. 745-46.

45. In *Social Teaching*, vol. 2, p. 737, Troeltsch mentions as examples of medieval mysticism only Bernard of Clairvaux and the Victorines. The Victorines, proponents of a particular type of allegorical exegesis, are not as a group a very good example of mysticism; on them, see Beryl Smalley, *The Study of the Bible in the Middle Ages*, 3rd ed. (Oxford: Blackwell, 1983).

46. Influential examples of opposition to affective and experiential piety, especially in its female version, are William James, *The Varieties of Religious Experience: A Study in Human Nature* (London: Longmans, Green, 1902), pp. 333-41; William R. Inge, *Studies of English Mystics: St. Margaret's Lectures 1905* (London: John Murray, 1906), pp. 23-26, 52, 74; and Edmund Colledge and James Walsh (eds.), *A Book of Showings to the Anchoress Julian of Norwich*, Studies and Texts, 35, 2 pts. (Toronto: Pontifical Institute of Mediaeval Studies, 1978), introduction and apparatus. See also Evelyn Underhill, *Mysticism: A Study in the Nature and Development of Man's Spiritual Consciousness* (1910; reprint, New York: Meridian, 1955), pp. 52-82, for a contemporary defense against such distrust. Even recent, more phenomenological works on visions tend to suggest that somatic experiences are a lower type: see Benz, *Die Vision*; and Peter Dinzelbacher, *Vision und Visionsliteratur im Mittelalter* (Stuttgart: Hiersemann,

1981). For an approach that avoids this assumption, see Franz Woehrer, "Aspekte der englischen Frauenmystik im späten 14. und beginnenden 15. Jahrhundert," in Dinzelbacher and Bauer (eds.), *Frauenmystik*, pp. 314–40 [and now Hamburger, "Visual and Visionary"].

47. Troeltsch, *Social Teaching*, vol. 2, p. 740.

48. *Ibid.*, pp. 747, 743.

49. It is not possible to recapitulate the full argument here. See Dinzelbacher and Bauer (eds.), *Frauenmystik*, and my *Holy Feast*. Weber, too, underestimates the incarnational emphasis possible in mysticism; see Hans Gerth and C. Wright Mills (eds. and trans.), *From Max Weber: Essays in Sociology* (New York: Oxford University Press, 1946), p. 325, where he says that the mystical quest "has an internal affinity with the depersonalization... of the divine power."

50. See Weber, *Economy and Society*, vol. 2, p. 542ff., and Gerth and Mills, *From Weber*, pp. 324–28.

51. *Economy and Society*, pp. 542, 544, 545, and Gerth and Mills, *From Weber*, p. 325.

52. Gerth and Mills, *From Weber*, p. 325.

53. Gerth and Mills, *From Weber*, p. 326; see also Weber, *Economy and Society*, pp. 545, 547.

54. *Economy and Society*, pp. 544–47, and Gerth and Mills, *From Weber*, p. 326.

55. *Economy and Society*, p. 550. Wolfgang Schluchter, in "Weltflüchtiges Erlösungsstreben und organische Sozialethik," the introduction to *Max Webers Studie über Hinduismus und Buddhismus*, ed. W. Schluchter (Frankfurt: Suhrkamp, 1984), proposes a typology that goes considerably beyond Weber's own. Schluchter suggests that Weber might be read as including under world-rejecting or salvation religion both the impulse to turn away from and the impulse to turn toward the world; each o: these stances would in turn include both active and contemplative (i.e., passive) impulses. Weber's explicit statement (*Economy and Society*, p. 548) that "neither asceticism nor contemplation affirms the world as such" would support such a reading. In any case, although Schluchter's typology does not quite seem to be Weber's, it is useful for analyzing medieval reli-

gious movements, all of which can be seen as both fleeing and turning toward (i.e., trying to convert) the world.

56. Vauchez, *La Sainteté*; and Weinstein and Bell, *Saints.*

57. See Giles Constable, "Twelfth-Century Spirituality and the Later Middle Ages," *Medieval and Renaissance Studies* 5 (1971), pp. 40-45.

58. On these women, see Bolton, "*Vitae Matrum*"; and "*Mulieres sanctae,*" in Derek Baker (ed.), *Studies in Church History*, vol. 10: *Sanctity and Secularity* (1973), pp. 77-95. And, on Clare, see Chapter 1, above.

59. On Lidwina and Lutgard, see Bynum, *Holy Feast*, ch. 4; on Catherine, see *ibid.*, ch. 5. [And see now Karen Scott, "Not Only With Words, But With Deeds: The Role of Speech in Catherine of Siena's Understanding of Her Mission," Ph.D. Dissertation, University of California at Berkeley, 1989.]

60. On theories of the "mixed life," see Constable, "Twelfth-Century Spirituality"; and Bynum, *Jesus as Mother*, pp. 33-34, 51-52.

61. Life of Alice of Schaerbeke, ch. 3, par. 26, in J. Bollandus and G. Henschenius (eds.), *Acta sanctorum...editio novissima*, ed. J. Carnandet *et al.* (Paris: Palmé, etc., 1863-   ) [hereafter AASS], June, vol. 2, p. 476.

62. For this interpretation of Catherine of Genoa, see Bynum, *Holy Feast*, ch. 5.

63. See Chapter 4, below; and Kieckhefer, *Unquiet Souls*, esp. pp. 118-20.

64. Here I adopt some of Schluchter's terminology in "Weltflüchtiges Erlösungsstreben." This aspect of medieval piety would, I think, fit under his category: salvation-religion-turning-toward-the-world/ascetic/world-mastery. He illustrates this category with the Protestant ethic.

65. Weber, *Economy and Society*, vol. 2, p. 542 (translation revised).

66. Life of Ida of Louvain, bk. 1, ch. 5, AASS, April, vol. 2, p. 167.

67. Weber, *Economy and Society*, vol. 2, p. 551ff. In a sense, Troeltsch recognizes this point also; see *Social Teaching*, vol. 2, p. 731. But Troeltsch misses the importance of the ascetic elements in medieval mysticism because he contrasts merely Protestant and Catholic mysticisms rather than Western and non-Western mysticisms.

68. Bernard of Clairvaux, sermon 18 on the Song of Songs, in *The Works*

of Bernard of Clairvaux, vol. 2: *On the Song of Songs*, vol. 1, trans. K. Walsh, Cistercian Fathers Series, 4 (Kalamazoo, MI: Cistercian Publications, 1976), pp. 133-39.

69. On this point, see Bynum, *Holy Feast*, chs. 6, 8. And see Gerth and Mills, *From Weber*, p. 327ff.

70. Marianne Weber's discussion of the beguines (*Ehefrau und Mutter*, pp. 273-77) does take account of their economic activity but the point is a different one from mine. Typical of the German scholarship of her day, her account reduces the life of the beguines to its economic dimension and treats the women's groups simply as guilds. See n. 2, above. The paper by Kathryn Reyerson in Schluchter (ed.), *Max Webers Sicht* agrees with me in criticizing Weber's inattention to medieval caritative activity.

71. David Herlihy, "Women and the Transmission of Religious Knowledge in the Middle Ages," paper given at Rice University Symposium, March, 1986; Sharon Farmer, "Persuasive Voices: Clerical Images of Medieval Wives," *Speculum* 61.3 (1986), pp. 517-43; [Karen Scott, "Catherine of Siena"; and Peter Dinzelbacher, "Das politische Wirken der Mystikerinnen in Kirche und Staat: Hildegard, Birgitta, Katharina," in Dinzelbacher and Bauer (eds.), *Religiöse Frauenbewegung*, pp. 265-302].

72. See n. 32, above. Mechtild of Magdeburg was confident that her suffering with Christ saved 70,000 souls from purgatory: Mechtild, *Offenbarungen der Schwester Mechtild von Magdeburg oder das fliessende Licht der Gottheit*, ed. Gall Morel (1869; reprint, Darmstadt: Wissenschaftliche Buchgesellschaft, 1963), bk. 2, ch. 8, p. 35, and bk. 3, ch. 15, pp. 76-78.

73. Gertrude the Great, *Le Héraut*, bk. 3, ch. 30, in *Oeuvres spirituelles*, ed. Pierre Doyère, vol. 3, Sources chrétiennes, 139 (Paris: Editions du Cerf, 1968), p. 142.

74. This paradoxical quality – the quality of transcending dichotomy – appears to be characteristic of medieval women's piety; see Bynum, "On the Complexity of Symbols."

75. [This point has now been beautifully argued by Scott in "Catherine of Siena."]

76. Michael Goodich, "Contours of Female Piety in Later Medieval Hagiography," *Church History* 50 (1981), pp. 20-32; John Coakley, "The Representation of Sanctity in Late Medieval Hagiography: Evidence from *Lives* of Saints of the Dominican Order," Ph.D. Dissertation, Harvard, 1980; [Scott, "Catherine of Siena"; and the superb article by Karen Glente, "Mystikerinnenviten aus männlicher und weiblicher Sicht: Ein Vergleich zwischen Thomas von Cantimpré und Katherina von Unterlinden," in Dinzelbacher and Bauer (eds.), *Religiöse Frauenbewegung*, pp. 251-64]. And see Chapter 1, above.

77. On this point, see Gerth and Mills, *From Weber*, p. 324.

78. The way in which the Bad Homburg conference was organized and paper topics assigned implies that there is *a* medieval Church structure and *a* medieval theology and ethics that was established in the eleventh to thirteenth centuries and lasted to the Reformation.

79. Georges Duby, *The Three Orders: Feudal Society Imagined*, trans. Arthur Goldhammer (Chicago: University of Chicago Press, 1980), pp. 89, 95, 131-33, 145, 209.

80. Lucien Febvre, *A New Kind of History and Other Essays*, ed. P. Burke, trans. K. Folca (New York: Harper Torchbooks, 1973), pp. 1-26, 44-107; and see n. 8, above.

81. Little, *Religious Poverty*; and Barbara Rosenwein and Lester Little, "Social Meaning in the Monastic and Mendicant Spiritualities," *Past and Present* 63 (May, 1974), pp. 20-32.

82. Reinhard Bendix, *Max Weber: An Intellectual Portrait*, new ed. (Berkeley: University of California Press, 1977), pp. 258-59.

83. Scholars have sometimes suggested that certain women mystics were forerunners of Protestantism or Pietism; see Wilhelm Preger, *Geschichte der deutschen Mystik im Mittelalter...*, 3 vols. (Leipzig: Dörffling & Franke, 1874-1893); and Friedrich-Wilhelm Wentzlaff-Eggebert, *Deutsche Mystik zwischen Mittelalter und Neuzeit: Einheit und Wandlung ihrer Erscheinungsformen* (Berlin: de Gruyter, 1944). This is a different point from the one I make here, since it has to do with the anticlerical implications of mysticism rather than with the innerworldly pattern of late medieval piety. On women in the Reformation, see

Merry Wiesner, "Women's Response to the Reformation," in R. Po-Chia Hsia (ed.), *The German People and the Reformation* (Ithaca, NY: Cornell University Press, 1988), pp. 148-71.

I am aware that I have not proved the bold reperiodization with which I conclude. I intend it merely to suggest the direction of recent scholarship and to provoke Weberian sociologists to give new attention to the late Middle Ages.

84. The papers by Lester Little and Kathryn Reyerson in Schluchter (ed.), *Max Webers Sicht* also suggest that sociologists need to take the lay piety of the late Middle Ages more seriously as background to the Reformation.

III. *The Body of Christ in the Later Middle Ages*

1. This essay was first delivered as a University lecture at Cornell University in November, 1985, and was subsequently presented at Brooklyn College and Columbia University. I am grateful to my hosts at those institutions: Elizabeth A.R. Brown, Joan Jacobs Brumberg, Eugene Rice and Robert Somerville. I would also like to thank Stephen Greenblatt, John Najemy and Richard Trexler for their suggestions and criticisms. I owe special gratitude to Colin Eisler, who read a draft of this article with patient attention to detail and gave sage advice. Finally, I thank Patricia Fortini Brown, Anna Kartsonis and Ruth Mellinkoff, who guided a novice in the field of art history through the complex process of acquiring photographs.

2. Although art historians have long cautioned against doing so, historians and social scientists have tended to read art (often quite creatively) as evidence for social history. See, for example, Philippe Ariès, *Centuries of Childhood: A Social History of Family Life*, trans. Robert Baldick (New York: Knopf, 1962); Jack Goody, *The Development of the Family and Marriage in Europe* (Cambridge: Cambridge University Press, 1983), pp. 153-56; and David Herlihy, *Medieval Households* (Cambridge, MA: Harvard University Press, 1985), p. 12.

3. See Gertrude Schiller, *Ikonographie der christlichen Kunst*, vol. 4, pt. 2: *Maria* (Gütersloh: G. Mohn, 1980), plates 751-56 and pp. 157-60.

4. Mirella Levi d'Ancona, *The Iconography of the Immaculate Conception in the Middle Ages and Early Renaissance*, Monographs on Archeology and Fine

Arts, 7 (New York: College Art Association of America, 1957).

5. On this point generally, see Barbara G. Lane, *The Altar and the Altarpiece: Sacramental Themes in Early Netherlandish Painting* (New York: Harper & Row, 1984).

6. Leo Steinberg, *The Sexuality of Christ in Renaissance Art and in Modern Oblivion* (New York: Pantheon, 1983); first published as a special issue of *October* 25 (Summer, 1983).

7. See, for example, the reviews of Steinberg by Richard Wolheim, *The New York Times Book Review* (April 29, 1984), pp. 13–14; Andre Chastel, *The New York Review of Books*, 31.8 (Nov. 22, 1984), pp. 25–27; David Summers, *Times Literary Supplement* (Nov. 23, 1984), p. 1346; and David Rosand, *The New Republic*, 190 (June 11, 1984), pp. 29–33.

8. Steinberg, *Sexuality*, pp. 98–108.

9. *Ibid.*, pp. 127–30. A particularly fascinating example of this motif, not discussed by Steinberg, is a painting of the vision of St. Bernard by the Master of the Life of the Virgin, now in the Wallraf-Richartz museum; for a reproduction, see *Late Gothic Art from Cologne: A Loan Exhibition, April 5–June 1, 1977* (London: The National Gallery, 1977), plate 14. In this picture, the baby reaches for the breast, which Mary, however, offers not to him but to the viewer. Bernard points to the baby's genitals, which the baby himself covers.

10. Steinberg, *Sexuality*, pp. 58–61, 160–62. And see n. 20, below.

11. On devotion to the holy foreskin, see Robert Fawtier and Louis Canet, *La Double expérience de Catherine Benincasa (sainte Catherine de Sienne)* (Paris: Gallimard, 1948), pp. 245–46; Peter Dinzelbacher, "Die 'Vita et revelationes' der Wiener Begine Agnes Blannbekin (†1315) im Rahmen der Viten- und Offenbarungsliteratur ihrer Zeit," in Peter Dinzelbacher and Dieter Bauer (eds.), *Frauenmystik im Mittelalter* (Ostfildern: Schwabenverlag, 1985), pp. 152–53; and Henri Denifle, *La Désolation des églises, monastères et hôpitaux en France pendant la Guerre de Cent Ans*, vol. 1 (Paris: Impression Anastaltique, 1897), p. 167.

12. In his interpretation of Renaissance preaching, Steinberg has been much influenced by John W. O'Malley, *Praise and Blame in Renaissance Rome: Rhetoric, Doctrine and Reform in the Sacred Orators of the Papal Court. c. 1450–1521*

(Durham: Duke University Press, 1979). The Renaissance sermons Steinberg quotes (*Sexuality*, pp. 61-65) all emphasize pain and bleeding, not sexuality.

13. See, for example, David Toolan, review of Steinberg, *Commonweal* (Dec. 14, 1984), pp. 692-94. And see n. 7, above.

14. See John Boswell, *Christianity, Social Tolerance and Homosexuality: Gay People in Western Europe from the Beginning of the Christian Era to the Fourteenth Century* (Chicago: University of Chicago Press, 1980).

15. Life of Lukardis of Oberweimar in *Analecta Bollandiana* 18 (1899), pp. 337-38. The account of Margaret's kiss is in Life of Benevenuta of Bojano, ch. 10, par. 82, in J. Bollandus and G. Henschenius (eds.), *Acta sanctorum...editio novissima*, ed. J. Carnandet *et al.* (Paris: Palmé, etc., 1863–   ) [hereafter AASS], October, vol. 13, p. 172. Margaret experiences an erotic kiss from Christ in Life of Margaret, ch. 3, par. 15(20), AASS, August, vol. 5, p. 851. On women's erotic relationship with Christ, see Elizabeth Petroff, *Consolation of the Blessed* (New York: Alta Gaia Society, 1979), pp. 66-78.

16. Hadewijch, vision 7, in *Hadewijch: The Complete Works*, trans. Columba Hart (New York: Paulist Press, 1980), pp. 281-82; see also Chapter 4, below, at n. 2.

17. See John H. Van Engen, *Rupert of Deutz*, Publications of the UCLA Center for Medieval and Renaissance Studies, 18 (Berkeley: University of California Press, 1983), pp. 50-53.

18. Catherine of Siena, *Le Lettere de S. Caterina da Siena, ridotte a miglior lezione e in ordine nuovo disposte con note di Niccolo Tommaseo a cura di Piero Misciattelli*, 6 vols. (Siena: Giuntini y Bentivoglio, 1913-22), letter 221, vol. 3, p. 337, letter 50, vol. 1, p. 236, letter 261, vol. 4, p. 146, letter 143, vol. 2, pp. 337-38; and Fawtier and Canet, *Double expérience*, pp. 245-46.

19. E. James Mundy, "Gerard David's *Rest on the Flight into Egypt*: Further Additions to Grape Symbolism," *Simiolus: Netherlands Quarterly for the History of Art* 12.4 (1981-1982), pp. 211-22.

20. There is considerable dispute about the attribution of this pietà. It is usually given to Jean Malouel. For a discussion, see Albert Chatelet, *Early Dutch Painting: Painting in the Northern Netherlands in the Fifteenth Century*, trans.

C. Brown and A. Turner (New York: Rizzoli, 1981), pp. 16-25. For another example of this motif, see Irmgard Hiller and Horst Vey with Tilman Falk, *Katalog der Deutschen und Niederländischen Gemälde bis 1550... im Wallraf-Richartz Museum und im Kunstgewerbemuseum der Stadt Köln*, Kataloge des Wallraf-Richartz Museum, 5 (Cologne, 1969), plate 154.

21. See nn. 49, 50, 78, below.

22. Catherine, *Le Lettere*, ed. Misciattelli, letter 87, vol. 2, pp. 90-92. See also letter 329, vol. 5, pp. 106-07.

23. On Margaret Porete, see Romana Guarnieri (ed.), "Il 'Miroir des simples âmes' di Margherita Porete," *Archivio italiano per la storia della pietà* 4 (1965), pp. 501-635, and Peter Dronke, *Women Writers of the Middle Ages: A Critical Study of Texts from Perpetua (†203) to Marguerite Porete (†1310)* (Cambridge: Cambridge University Press, 1984), pp. 202-28. On Eckhart, see Otto Langer, "Zur dominikanischen Frauenmystik im spätmittelalterlichen Deutschland," in Dinzelbacher and Bauer (eds.), *Frauenmystik*, pp. 341-46. On Gerson, see Caroline Walker Bynum, *Jesus as Mother: Studies in the Spirituality of the High Middle Ages* (Berkeley: University of California Press, 1982), pp. 135-36. See also Johann Tauler, sermons 31 and 33, in *Die Predigten Taulers: aus der Engelberger und der Freiburger Handschrift sowie aus Schmidts Abschriften der ehemaligen Strassburger Handschriften*, ed. Ferdinand Vetter (Berlin: Weidmannsche Buchhandlung, 1910), pp. 310-11, 130. On male suspicion of female religiosity generally, see André Vauchez, *La Sainteté en Occident aux derniers siècles du moyen âge...* (Rome: Ecole française de Rome, 1981), pp. 439-48.

24. See Peter Browe, *Die eucharistischen Wunder des Mittelalters* (Breslau: Müller & Seiffert, 1938), pp. 110-11; and Ernest W. McDonnell, *The Beguines and Beghards in Medieval Culture with Special Emphasis on the Belgian Scene* (New Brunswick, NJ: Rutgers University Press, 1954; reprint, 1969), p. 315.

25. On the prominence of bodily phenomena in women's spirituality, see Peter Dinzelbacher, "Europäische Frauenmystik des Mittelalters," in Dinzelbacher and Bauer (eds.), *Frauenmystik*, pp. 11-23; Franz Wöhrer, "Aspekte der englischen Frauenmystik im späten 14. und beginnenden 15. Jahrhundert," *ibid.*, pp. 314-40; and Herbert Thurston, *The Physical Phenomena of Mysticism* (Chicago:

Regnery, 1952). See also Claude Carozzi, "Douceline et les autres," in *La Reli-gion populaire en Languedoc du XIIIe siècle à la moitié du XIVe siècle*, Cahiers de Fanjeaux, 11 (Toulouse: Privat, 1976), pp. 251–67.

26. For a comment on the modern tendency to reduce all bodily phenom-ena (even mystical) to the sexual, see Simone Weil, *The Notebooks of Simone Weil*, trans. Arthur Wills, 2 vols. (London: Routledge & Kegan Paul, 1956), vol. 2, p. 472: "To reproach mystics with loving God by means of the faculty of sexual love is as though one were to reproach a painter with making pictures by means of colors composed of material substances. We haven't anything else with which to love...."

27. See n. 23, above. Judith C. Brown's *Immodest Acts: The Life of a Lesbian Nun in Renaissance Italy* (New York: Oxford University Press, 1985) is there-fore somewhat misleading. It mistakenly places the behavior it considers in the context of sexual orientation. But what contemporaries asked about the actions of Benedetta Carlini, a seventeenth-century Theatine abbess, was not whether they had an erotic component directed toward a woman, but whether Benedetta Carlini suffered from demonic possession or practiced fraud. "Feigned sanctity" was an important category in seventeenth-century inquisitorial trials, and Benedetta herself retreated, under interrogation, to the claim that she was pos-sessed. See the review of Brown by Mary R. O'Neil, in *Sixteenth-Century Journal* 17.3 (1986), p. 392.

28. Steinberg, *Sexuality*, p. 65. To raise the issue of texts is not to take issue with Steinberg's position that the art object itself is a "primary text," not merely an illustration of a theological tenet. I would myself agree that many of the paint-ings Steinberg discusses are direct evidence about the theological significance of body. But I also hold that the pictures are about a wider range of bodily aspects than Steinberg notices. See, for example, n. 80, below.

29. There is a large amount of recent literature on this topic. See, for exam-ple, Colin Morris, *The Discovery of the Individual: 1050–1200* (New York: Harper & Row, 1972; reprint, 1973); Giles Constable, "Twelfth-Century Spirituality and the Later Middle Ages," *Medieval and Renaissance Studies* 5: *Proceedings of the Southern Institute of Medieval and Renaissance Studies, Summer, 1969* (1971),

pp. 27–60; Bynum, Chapter 4, below; and Richard Kieckhefer, *Unquiet Souls: Fourteenth-Century Saints and Their Religious Milieu* (Chicago: University of Chicago Press, 1984), pp. 89–121. On the increasingly positive sense of body generally in medieval thought, see Alan E. Bernstein, "Political Anatomy," *University Publishing* (Winter, 1978), pp. 8–9.

30. Angela of Foligno, *Le Livre de l'expérience des vrais fidèles: texte latine publié d'après le manuscrit d'Assise*, ed. and trans. M.-J. Ferré and L. Baudry (Paris: Droz, 1927), par. 167, pp. 382–84. [A critical edition of Angela has recently appeared: *Il libro della Beata Angela da Foligno (Edizione critica)*, ed. Ludger Thier and Abele Calufetti (Grottaferrata, 1985). And see Chapter 1, above, n. 44, for other recent scholarship on Angela.]

31. Marguerite of Oingt, *Les Oeuvres de Marguerite d'Oingt*, ed. and trans. Antonin Duraffour, Pierre Gardette and P. Durdilly, Publications de l'Institut de Linguistique Romane de Lyon, 21 (Paris: Belles Lettres, 1965), pp. 147, 139.

32. See Francine Cardman, "The Medieval Question of Women and Orders," *The Thomist* 42 (1978), pp. 582–99; and J. Rézette, "Le Sacerdoce et la femme chez saint Bonaventure," *Antonianum* 51 (1976), pp. 520–27.

33. See *Corpus Iuris Canonici*, ed. E. Friedberg, 2 vols. (Leipzig: Tauchnitz, 1879–1881), vol. 1, pt. 2, causa 33, q. 5, chs. 12–17, cols. 1254–55; Thomas Aquinas, *Summa theologiae*, ed. Blackfriars, 61 vols. (New York: McGraw-Hill, 1964–1981), vol. 13, pt. 1, q. 92, arts. 1–2, pp. 34–41, and q. 93, art. 4, pp. 58–61. It is worth pointing out that neither male nor female theologians argued against the denial of priesthood to women. Indeed, Hildegard of Bingen suggested that women held a different (and complementary) role as brides of Christ (i.e., mystics). See Bynum, *Jesus as Mother*, pp. 91–94, 141–42, and Elisabeth Gössman, "Das Menschenbild der Hildegard von Bingen und Elisabeth von Schönau vor dem Hintergrund der frühscholastischen Anthropologie," in Dinzelbacher and Bauer (eds.), *Frauenmystik*, pp. 24–47.

34. In a now classic study, the great Dutch historian argued that symbolism in the later Middle Ages became florid, mechanical and empty of true experiential content; see Johan Huizinga, *The Waning of the Middle Ages: A Study of the Forms of Life, Thought and Art in France and the Netherlands in the XIVth and XVth*

Centuries, trans. F. Hopman (London: E. Arnold, 1924; reprint, Garden City, NY: Doubleday, 1956). There is, of course, some truth to the argument; see, for example, Francis Rapp, "Zur Spiritualität in elsässischen Frauenklöstern am Ende des Mittelalters," in Dinzelbacher and Bauer (eds.), *Frauenmystik*, pp. 347–65. But it is more accurate to describe late medieval piety as deeply experiential; see Caroline Walker Bynum, *Holy Feast and Holy Feast: The Religious Significance of Food to Medieval Women* (Berkeley: University of California Press, 1987).

35. Schiller, *Ikonographie*, vol. 4, pt. 1: *Die Kirche*, plates 211, 213, 228–40, 260.

36. Bernard of Clairvaux, sermon 9, pars. 5–6, and sermon 10, par. 3, on the Song of Songs, in *Sancti Bernardi opera*, ed. J. Leclercq, C.H. Talbot and H.M. Rochais, vol. 1 (Rome: Editiones Cistercienses, 1957), pp. 45–46, 49–50; see also sermon 23, par. 2, vol. 1, pp. 139–40, and sermon 41, pars. 5–6, vol. 2, pp. 31–32.

37. William of St. Thierry, *Exposé sur le Cantique des Cantiques*, ed. J.M. Déchanet, Sources chrétiennes, 82, Série des textes monastiques d'Occident, 8 (Paris: Editions du Cerf, 1962), ch. 38, pp. 122–24.

38. William of St. Thierry, *Meditativae Orationes*, ch. 8, in J.-P. Migne (ed.), *Patrologiae cursus completus: series latina*, 221 vols. (Paris, 1841–1864) [hereafter PL], vol. 180, col. 236A; trans. Sister Penelope, *The Works of William of St. Thierry*, vol. 1: *On Contemplating God*, Cistercian Fathers Series, 3 (Spencer, MA: Cistercian Publications, 1971), pp. 152–53.

39. Catherine of Siena, *Le Lettere*, ed. Misciattelli, letter 86, vol. 2, pp. 81–82. For a similar use of the metaphor by a male writer, see *The Monk of Farne: The Meditations of a Fourteenth-Century Monk*, ed. Hugh Farmer, trans. a Benedictine of Stanbrook, The Benedictine Studies (Baltimore: Helicon Press, 1961), pp. 64, 73–74. Other examples of the Jesus-as-mother motif may be found in Bynum, *Jesus as Mother*, pp. 110–69; and Valerie Lagorio, "Variations on the Theme of God's Motherhood in Medieval English Mystical and Devotional Writings," *Studia mystica* 8 (1985), pp. 15–37.

40. Ritamary Bradley, "The Motherhood Theme in Julian of Norwich," *Fourteenth-Century English Mystics Newsletter* 2.4 (1976), pp. 25–30; Kari Elizabeth

Børresen, "Christ nôtre mère, la théologie de Julienne de Norwich," *Mitteilungen und Forschungsbeiträge der Cusanus-Gesellschaft* 13 (1978), pp. 320-29; Paula S.D. Barker, "The Motherhood of God in Julian of Norwich's Theology," *Downside Review* 100 (1982), pp. 290-304; and Brant Pelphrey, *Love Was His Meaning: The Theology and Mysticism of Julian of Norwich*, Salzburg Studies in English Literature: Elizabethan and Renaissance Studies, 92.4 (Salzburg, 1982). [And see now Grace M. Jantzen, *Julian of Norwich: Mystic and Theologian* (New York: Paulist Press, 1988).]

41. Julian of Norwich, The Long Text, ch. 57, revelation 14, in *A Book of Showings to the Anchoress Julian of Norwich*, ed. Edmund Colledge and James Walsh, Studies and Texts, 35, 2 parts (Toronto: Pontifical Institute of Mediaeval Studies, 1978), pt. 2, pp. 579-80; trans. by Colledge and Walsh in *Julian· of Norwich: Showings* (New York: Paulist Press, 1978), p. 292.

42. See Chapter 5, below, for a fuller discussion of Julian. Colledge and Walsh have argued, not wholly convincingly, that the motherhood idea has theological roots in William of St. Thierry; see introduction to *A Book of Showings*, pt. 1, pp. 153-62.

43. Marguerite of Oingt, *Oeuvres*, pp. 77-79. And see Chapter 5, below, at n. 36.

44. Schiller, *Ikonographie*, vol. 4, pt. 1: *Die Kirche*, plates 217-19.

45. *Catherine of Siena: The Dialogue*, trans. Suzanne Noffke (New York: Paulist Press, 1980), pp. 206-07; see also p. 210. For other authors who stress the same point, see Chapter 4, below, n. 117.

46. Kari Elisabeth Børresen, *Subordination and Equivalence: The Nature and Role of Women in Augustine and Thomas Aquinas*, trans. Charles H. Talbot (Washington, DC: University Press of America, 1981); Eleanor McLaughlin, "Equality of Souls, Inequality of Sexes: Women in Medieval Theology," in *Religion and Sexism: Images of Women in the Jewish and Christian Traditions*, ed. R. Ruether (New York: Simon & Schuster, 1974), pp. 213-66; and Marie Thérèse d'Alverny, "Comment les théologiens et les philosophes voient la femme?" in *La Femme dans les civilisations des Xe-XIIIe siècles : Actes du colloque tenu à Poitiers les 23-25 septembre 1976*, Cahiers de civilisation médiévale, 20 (1977), pp. 105-29.

47. Hildegard of Bingen, *Liber divinorum operum*, bk. 1, ch. 4, par. 100, PL 197, col. 885, *Liber vitae meritorum*, bk. 4, ch. 32, in *Analecta sacra*, ed. J.-B. Pitra, vol. 8: *Analecta sanctae Hildegardis*... (Monte Cassino, 1882; reprint, Farnborough: Gregg Press, 1966), p. 158; Peter Dronke, *Women Writers*, pp. 144–201; and Gössmann, "Das Menschenbild der Hildegard." For Elizabeth's vision, see *Die Visionen der hl. Elisabeth und die Schriften der Äbte Ekbert und Emecho von Schönau*, ed. F.W.E. Roth (Brünn: "Studien aus dem Benedictiner- und Cistercienser-Orden," 1884), p. 60ff.; and Gertrud Jaron Lewis, "Christus als Frau: Eine Vision Elisabeths von Schönau," *Jahrbuch für internationale Germanistik* 15 (1983), pp. 70–80. [And see now Barbara Newman, *Sister of Wisdom: St. Hildegard's Theology of the Feminine* (Berkeley: University of California Press, 1987); Sabine Flanagan, *Hildegard of Bingen: A Visionary Life* (London: Routledge, 1989); and Anne Clark, "The Spirituality of Elizabeth of Schönau, a Twelfth-Century Visionary," Ph.D. Dissertation, Columbia University, 1989.]

48. Hildegard of Bingen, *Scivias*, pt. 2, vision 6, ed. Adelgundis Führkötter and A. Carlevaris, Corpus christianorum: Continuatio medievalis, 43, 2 vols. (Turnhout: Brepols, 1978), vol. 1, pp. 225–306, esp. p. 231. For *ecclesia* and *humanitas* in miniatures, see Schiller, *Ikonographie*, vol. 4, pt. 1: *Die Kirche*, plates 211, 236, 260. For texts in which Christ marries *humanitas*. see Jan van Ruysbroeck, *The Spiritual Espousals*, trans. Eric Colledge, Classics of the Contemplative Life (New York, n.d.), p. 43; and "Le Miroir du salut éternel," ch. 7, in *Oeuvres de Ruysbroeck l'Admirable*, trans. the Benedictines of St.-Paul of Wisques, vol. 3, 3rd ed. (Brussels: Vromant, 1921), pp. 82–83.

49. Erna Lesky, *Die Zeugungs- und Vererbungslehren der Antike und ihr Nachwirken* (Mainz, 1951); Joseph Needham, *A History of Embryology*, 2nd ed. (Cambridge: Cambridge University Press, 1959), pp. 37–74; Anthony Preus, "Galen's Criticism of Aristotle's Conception Theory," *Journal of the History of Biology* 10 (1977), pp. 65–85; and Thomas Laqueur, "Orgasm, Generation, and the Politics of Reproductive Biology," *Representations* 14 (Spring, 1986), pp. 1–41, and *The Female Orgasm and the Body Politic*, work in progress.

50. Preus, "Galen's Criticism"; Laqueur, "Orgasm, Generation and Reproductive Biology," especially nn. 19, 20; Vern L. Bullough, "Medieval Medical

and Scientific Views of Women," *Viator* 4 (1973), pp. 487–93; John F. Benton, "Clio and Venus: An Historical View of Medieval Love," *The Meaning of Courtly Love*, ed. F.X. Newman (Albany: State University of New York Press, 1969), p. 32; and Charles T. Wood, "The Doctors' Dilemma: Sin, Salvation and The Menstrual Cycle in Medieval Thought," *Speculum* 56 (1981), pp. 710–27.

51. Levi d'Ancona, *Immaculate Conception*.

52. On Mechtild, see Bynum, *Jesus as Mother*, pp. 229, 233–34, 244.

53. See Chapter 4, below, at nn. 118–21; Edouard Dumoutet, *Corpus Domini: Aux sources de la piété eucharistique médiévale* (Paris: Beauchesne, 1942), pp. 77–79; Marguerite of Oingt, *Oeuvres*, pp. 98–99; Henry Suso, *Büchlein der Ewigen Weisheit*, ch. 16, in *Deutsche Schriften im Auftrag der Württembergischen Kommission für Landesgeschichte*, ed. K. Bihlmeyer (Stuttgart: Kohlhammer, 1907), p. 264; Francis of Assisi, *Opuscula sancti patris Francisci Assisiensis*, Bibliotheca Franciscana Ascetica Medii Aevi, 1, 2nd ed. (Quaracchi: Collegium S. Bonaventurae, 1949), p. 123; and Lane, *Altar and Altarpiece*, pp. 12–35.

54. Dumoutet, *Corpus Domini*, pp. 77–79. See also Joseph Braun, *Der christliche Altar in seiner geschichtlichen Entwicklung*, 2 vols. (Munich: Koch, 1924), vol. 2, p. 624. Plates 329, 333, 334, 336, 346, 360 and 361 give a number of examples of the prominence of Mary on retables. This motif tends to associate Mary's conceiving of Christ with the moment of the consecration.

55. Lane, *Altar and Altarpiece*, p. 28. See also Christoph Baumer, "Die Schreinmadonna," *Marian Literary Studies* 9 (1977), pp. 239–72.

56. Lane, *Altar and Altarpiece*, pp. 71–72. Carol J. Purtle, *The Marian Paintings of Jan van Eyck* (Princeton: Princeton University Press, 1982), pp. 13–15, 27–29 and *passim*.

57. James H. Marrow, *Passion Iconography in Northern European Art of the Late Middle Ages and Early Renaissance: A Study of the Transformation of Sacred Metaphor into Descriptive Narrative* (Kortrijk: Van Ghemmert, 1979); and Lionel Rothkrug, "Popular Religion and Holy Shrines: Their Influence on the Origins of the German Reformation and their Role in German Cultural Development," in James Obelkevich (ed.), *Religion and the People, 800–1700* (Chapel Hill, NC: University of North Carolina Press, 1979), p. 29.

58. See Thurston, *Physical Phenomena*; Dinzelbacher, "Europäische Frauen-mystik," *Vision und Visionsliteratur im Mittelalter* (Stuttgart: Hiersemann, 1981); Rudolph M. Bell, *Holy Anorexia* (Chicago: University of Chicago Press, 1985); and Caroline Walker Bynum, "Fast, Feast, and Flesh: The Religious Significance of Food to Medieval Women," *Representations* 11 (Summer, 1985), pp. 1–25.

59. On eucharistic miracles, see Browe, *Die Wunder*, and Chapter 4, below. On stigmata, see Thurston, *Physical Phenomena*; Antoine Imbert Gourbeyre, *La Stigmatisation: L'Extase divine et les miracles de Lourdes: Réponse aux libres-penseurs*, 2 vols. (Clermont-Ferrand: Librairie Catholique, 1894); Pierre Debongnie, "Essai critique sur l'histoire des stigmatisations au moyen âge," *Etudes carméli-taines* 21.2 (1936), pp. 22–59; and E. Amann, "Stigmatisation," *Dictionnaire de théologie catholique*, vol. 14, pt. 1 (Paris, 1939), cols. 2617–19. See also Chapter 6, below, n. 30.

60. For example, this was true of the Flemish saint, Lidwina of Schiedam (d. 1433). See Bynum, "Fast, Feast, and Flesh," pp. 6–7, nn. 24–27.

61. Two saints who stress substituting their suffering for that of others are Alice of Schaerbeke and Catherine of Genoa. See Life of Alice of Schaerbeke, ch. 3, par. 26, AASS, June, vol. 2, p. 476; and Catherine of Genoa, *Il Dialogo spirituale*, in Umile Bonzi da Genova (ed.), *S. Caterina Fieschi Adorno*, vol. 2: *Edizione critica dei manoscritti cateriniani* (Turin: Marietti, 1962), pp. 420–21, 424. See also Catherine, *Trattato del Purgatorio*, in *ibid.*, pp. 343–45. This was also true of Lidwina of Schiedam; see Bynum, "Fast, Feast, and Flesh," p. 6, n. 25.

62. See Mundy, "Gerard David." On the cult of the Virgin's milk in the later Middle Ages, see P.V. Bétérous, "A propos d'une des légendes mariales les plus répandues: le 'lait de la Vierge,' " *Bullétin de l'association Guillaume Budé* 4 (1975), pp. 403–11.

63. Rafael M. Duran, *Iconografia espanola de San Bernardo* (Monasterio de Poblet, 1953); Léon Dewez and Albert van Iterson, "La lactation de saint Bernard: Légende et iconographie," *Cîteaux in de Nederlanden* 7 (1956), pp. 165–89. For two other examples, see Hiller and Vey, *Katalog... Wallraf-Richartz Museum*, plates 126, 159. In the latter (late fifteenth-century) painting, the baby actually pushes the breast toward Bernard. For texts that refer to other lacta-

tions of adults, see Albert Poncelet, "Index miraculorum B.V. Mariae quae saec. VI–XV latine conscripta sunt," *Analecta Bollandiana* 21 (1902), p. 359.

64. See, for example, the miniature from the Milan-Turin Book of Hours in which a stream of milk from Mary's breast goes toward the donor (with whom the viewer presumably identifies) while the baby turns away from the breast; Lane, *Altar and Altarpiece*, p. 6, plate 4.

65. Lane, *Altar and Altarpiece*, pp. 13–23, plate 6; Purtle, *Marian Paintings*, pp. 98–126.

66. Lane, *Altar and Altarpiece*, pp. 1–10, plate 1; Purtle, *Marian Paintings*, p. 100, n. 8; see also Carra Ferguson O'Meara, " 'In the Hearth of the Virginal Womb': The Iconography of the Holocaust in Late Medieval Art," *The Art Bulletin* 63.1 (1981), pp. 75–88. The cupboard and chalice are modern additions to the painting.

67. Lane, *Altar and Altarpiece*, pp. 71–72, plate 47; Purtle, *Marian Paintings*, p. 12, n. 32, and p. 153.

68. Gertrud Schiller, *Iconography of Christian Art*, vol. 2: *The Passion of Jesus Christ*, trans. J. Seligman (London: Humphries, 1972), pp. 228–29, and *Ikonographie*, vol. 4, pt. 1: *Die Kirche*, p. 62. On the related motif of Christ in the winepress, see Marrow, *Passion Iconography*, p. 85, and Braun, *Der Altar*, vol. 2, plate 336.

69. For depictions of Christ bleeding into the chalice, see Schiller, *Iconography*, vol. 2: *Passion*, plates 707, 708, 710, 806; and Lane, *Altar and Altarpiece*, pp. 130–31. On Quirizio's *The Savior*, see Luigi Coletti, *Pittura veneta del Quattrocento* (Novara: Istituto Geografico De Agostini, 1953), pp. xlvii–xlix, 100–01; Sandra Moschini Marconi (ed.), *Gallerie dell'Accademia, Opere d'Arte dei Secoli XIV et XV* (Rome: Istituto Poligrafico dello Stato, Libreria dello Stato, 1955), p. 148; and Louis Gougaud, *Devotional and Ascetic Practices in the Middle Ages*, trans. G.C. Bateman (London: Burns, Oates & Washbourne, 1927), pp. 104–10.

70. Adolphe de Ceuleneer, "La Charité romaine dans la littérature et dans l'art," *Annales de l'Académie Royale d'archéologie de Belgique* 67 (Antwerp, 1919), pp. 175–206.

71. For examples of the double intercession, see Max J. Friedländer, *Early*

Netherlandish Painting, vol. 9, pt. 2, trans. H. Norden with notes by H. Pauwels and M. Gierts (Leyden: Sijthoff, 1973), plate 156; Schiller, *Iconography*, vol. 2: *Passion*, plates 798, 799, 800, 802; Lane, *Altar and Altarpiece*, pp. 7-8, "The 'Symbolic Crucifixion' in the Hours of Catherine of Cleves," *Oud-Holland* 86 (1973), pp. 4-26; Richard C. Trexler, *Public Life in Renaissance Florence*, Studies in Social Discontinuity (New York: Academic Press, 1980), p. 26, plate 8; and A.L. Moir and Malcolm Letts, *The World Map in Hereford Cathedral and The Pictures in the Hereford Mappa Mundi*, 7th ed. (Hereford: The Cathedral, 1975), pp. 11, 19. For the texts on the Holbein, see Schiller, *Iconography*, vol. 2: *Passion*, p. 225.

72. A. Monballieu, "Het Antonius Tsgrooten-triptiekje (1597) uit Tongerloo van Goosen van der Weyden," *Jaarboek van het Koninklijk Museum voor Schone Kunsten Antwerpen* (1967), pp. 13-36.

73. An influential article that projects back into the earlier Western tradition the modern nature/culture contrast is Sherry Ortner, "Is Female to Male as Nature is to Culture?" in Michelle A. Rosaldo and Louise Lamphere (eds.), *Women, Culture and Society* (Stanford: Stanford University Press, 1974), pp. 67-86. For criticisms of Ortner's approach, on these and other grounds, see the works cited in Chapter 1, above, n. 88. For criticism of projecting modern physiological theory onto earlier concepts, see Laqueur, *Female Orgasm and Body Politic*. The point about the mixing of genders has been nicely made by Eleanor McLaughlin, " 'Christ My Mother': Feminine Naming and Metaphor in Medieval Spirituality," *Nashota Review* 15 (1975), pp. 229-48.

74. For examples of hagiographers who praise women as "virile," see Life of Ida of Louvain, AASS, April, vol. 2, p. 159; and Life of Ida of Léau, AASS, October, vol. 13, p. 112. The compliment could, of course, cut both ways.

75. See Bynum, *Jesus as Mother*, pp. 127-28, and Chapter 1, above.

76. Bynum, *Jesus as Mother*, pp. 110-69; Vauchez, *La Sainteté*, p. 446, n. 511; and John Gerson, *Collectorium super Magnificat*, treatise 9, in *Oeuvres completes*, ed. P. Glorieux, vol. 8: *L'Oeuvre spirituelle et pastorale* (Paris: Desclée, 1971), pp. 397-98.

77. Chapter 5, below.

78. Laqueur, "Orgasm, Generation and Reproductive Biology." On the commensurability of bodily fluids, see also Michael Goodich, "Bartholomaeus Angelicus on Child-rearing," *History of Childhood Quarterly: The Journal of Psychohistory* 3 (1975), pp. 75–84, esp. p. 80; Mary M. McLaughlin, "Survivors and Surrogates: Children and Parents from the Ninth to the Thirteenth Centuries," in L. DeMause (ed.), *The History of Childhood* (New York: Psychohistory Press, 1974), pp. 101–81, esp. pp. 115–18; and Wood, "Doctors' Dilemma," p. 719.

79. Such a conception encouraged the exuding miracles (e.g., oil-exuding, miraculous lactation, cures with saliva, ecstatic nosebleeds) that characterized female saints. On such miracles, see Bynum, "Fast, Feast, and Flesh," nn. 14, 15, 81, 82, 83, 85.

80. One thinks of the iconographic tradition associating Mary Magdalene and Francis of Assisi with the toes of Christ: see Joanna Ziegler, "The Virgin or Mary Magdalen? Artistic Choices and Changing Spiritual Attitudes in the Later Middle Ages," paper presented at the Holy Cross Symposium "The Word Becomes Flesh," November 9, 1985; and Roberta J. Schneider, "The Development of Iconographic Manifestations of St. Francis of Assisi as the *Alter Christus* in Late Medieval and Early Renaissance Italian Painting," M.A. Thesis, University of Washington, 1985, plates 8–20. For examples of the Magdalene kissing or hovering over Christ's feet at the Crucifixion or Deposition, see Hiller and Vey, *Katalog... Wallraf-Richartz Museum*, plates 86, 124. For examples of Francis curled around the feet of Christ, see Vincent Moleta, *From St. Francis to Giotto: The Influence of St. Francis on Early Italian Art and Literature* (Chicago: Franciscan Herald Press, 1983), p. 26; and Bernard Berenson, *Italian Pictures of the Renaissance: A List of the Principal Artists and Their Works: Central Italian and Northern Italian Schools*, 3 vols. (London: Phaidon, 1968), vol. 2, plate 448. Margery Kempe was especially devoted to the toes of Christ: see *The Book of Margery Kempe: The Text from the Unique Manuscript Owned by Colonel W. Butler-Bowdon*, ed. Sanford B. Meech and Hope Emily Allen, Early English Text Society, 212 (London, 1940). For a reading of Steinberg (very different from mine) that nonetheless draws attention generally to Christ's bodiliness, see Jane Gallop, "Psy-

choanalytic Criticism: Some Intimate Questions," in *Art in America* (November, 1984), p. 15.

81. See Chapter 4, below; and Kieckhefer, *Unquiet Souls*, pp. 89–121, especially p. 104, for discussion of late medieval notions of using body to approach God. Such an emphasis on body as a means of becoming like Christ is very different from a dualistic rejection of body as the enemy of spirit. To say this is not, however, to deny that medieval thinkers also stressed the disciplining of flesh, especially female flesh. See Kieckhefer, *Unquiet Souls*, pp. 118–20; and Weinstein and Bell, *Saints and Society*, pp. 233–38.

82. See Diane Bornstein, "Antifeminism," *Dictionary of the Middle Ages*, vol. 1 (New York: Scribner's, 1982), pp. 322–25; and n. 46, above.

83. The fact that late medieval theology stressed crucifixion more than resurrection is well known. See Jacques Hourlier and André Rayez, "Humanité du Christ," *Dictionnaire de spiritualité, ascétique et mystique, doctrine et histoire*, vol. 7, pt. 1 (Paris, 1969), cols. 1053–96; Richard W. Southern, *The Making of the Middle Ages* (New Haven: Yale University Press, 1959), pp. 231–40; and Kieckhefer, *Unquiet Souls*, pp. 89–113, esp. p. 96. See also n. 81, above.

IV. *Women Mystics and Eucharistic Devotion*

1. James of Vitry, Life of Mary of Oignies, in J. Bollandus and G. Henschenius (eds.), *Acta sanctorum...editio novissima*, ed. J. Carnandet *et al.* (Paris: Palmé, etc., 1863–) [hereafter AASS], June, vol. 5 (1867), p. 568. I would like to thank Peter Brown, Richard Kieckhefer and Guenther Roth for their help with this essay. [Recent works that provide important context are: Gary Macy, *The Theologies of the Eucharist in the Early Scholastic Period: A Study of the Salvific Function of the Sacrament according to the Theologians, c.1080–c.1220* (Oxford: Oxford University Press, 1984); and Piero Camporesi, *Il Pane selvaggio* (Bologna: Il Mulino, 1980).]

2. Hadewijch, vision 7, in *Hadewych: Visioenen*, ed. J. Van Mierlo, 2 vols., Leuvense Studien en Tekstuitgaven (Louvain, 1924), vol. 1, pp. 74–79; trans. Columba Hart in *Hadewijch: The Complete Works* (New York: Paulist Press, 1980), pp. 280–81.

3. For example, Hadewijch, *Mengeldichten*, ed. J. Van Mierlo, Leuvense Studien en Tekstuitgaven (Antwerp, 1954), pp. 78-85; *Hadewijch*, trans. Hart, pp. 353-55.

4. Life of Margaret of Cortona, AASS, February, vol. 3 (1865), p. 330 and *passim*.

5. Life of Lukardis of Oberweimar, *Analecta Bollandiana* 18 (1899), pp. 337-38.

6. Caroline Walker Bynum, *Jesus as Mother: Studies in the Spirituality of the High Middle Ages* (Berkeley: University of California Press, 1982), pp. 170-72, p. 193, n. 58, p. 257; Joseph Duhr, "Communion fréquente," *Dictionnaire de spiritualité, ascétique et mystique, doctrine et histoire*, ed. M. Viller *et al.* (Paris: Beauchesne, 1932-   ), vol. 2 (1953), cols. 1256-68; Louis Gougaud, *Devotional and Ascetic Practices in the Middle Ages*, trans. G.C. Bateman (London: Burns, Oates & Washbourne, 1927), pp. 113-14; Peter Browe, *Die eucharistischen Wunder des Mittelalters* (Breslau: Müller & Seiffert, 1938), pp. 23-24 and *passim*; F. Baix and C. Lambot, *La Dévotion à l'eucharistie et le VIIᵉ centenaire de la Fête-Dieu* (Namur, n.d.), p. 70; and Emile Bertaud, "Dévotion eucharistique: Esquisse historique," *Dictionnaire de spiritualité*, vol. 4, pt. 2 (1961), cols. 1623-24.

7. Ernst W. McDonnell, *The Beguines and Beghards in Medieval Culture with Special Emphasis on the Belgian Scene* (1954; reprint, New York: Octagon Books, 1969), pp. 305-15; Baix and Lambot, *Dévotion*, pp. 75-80; and the Life of Juliana of Mont-Cornillon, AASS, April, vol. 1 (1866), pp. 442-75.

8. Bynum, *Jesus as Mother*, pp. 170-262; Ursmer Berlière, *La Dévotion au Sacré-Coeur dans l'ordre de saint Benoît*, Collection Pax, 10 (Paris, 1923); and Gougaud, *Practices*, pp. 75-130.

9. McDonnell, *Beguines and Beghards*, p. 313.

10. Joseph Jungmann, *The Mass of the Roman Rite: Its Origins and Development (Missarum Sollemnia)*, trans. F. A. Brunner, 2 vols. (New York: Benziger Brothers, 1955), vol. 2, pp. 20-21; André Vauchez, *La Sainteté en Occident aux derniers siècles du moyen âge d'après les procès de canonisation et les documents hagiographiques* (Rome: Ecole française de Rome, 1981), pp. 431-32; and Duhr, "Communion fréquente," cols. 1256-68.

11. The following discussion is based on Browe, *Die Wunder*.

12. Caesarius of Heisterbach, *Dialogus miraculorum*, ed. Joseph Strange, 2 vols. (Cologne: Heberle, 1851). Although several early collections of *exempla*, addressed to men, contain only male stories, both James of Vitry and Thomas of Cantimpré, writing in the thirteenth century, give female as well as male eucharistic miracles. Frederic C. Tubach, *Index exemplorum: A Handbook of Medieval Religious Tales* (Helsinki: Finnish Academy of Sciences and Letters, 1969), pp. 207-12, lists 32 miracles which concern the host that occurred to men, 20 to women. Of the male miracles, 12 occurred to priests.

13. Richard Rolle's *Form of Living*, like his other two English epistles, was written for a woman. Henry Suso's *Little Book of Eternal Wisdom*, the heart of which is meditations on Christ's death, is addressed chiefly to nuns, as is his *Book of Letters*. The second part of Ruysbroeck's *Mirror of Eternal Salvation*, which is a treatise on the eucharist, was probably written for Marguerite of Meerbeke, to whom he also addressed his *Book of the Seven Cloisters*. All three of these writers had close ties to communities of religious women. On Guiard, see P.C. Boeren, *La Vie et les oeuvres de Guiard de Laon, 1170 env.-1248* (The Hague: Martinus Nijhoff, 1956), pp. 157-58. Most of Tauler's sermons, which stress mysticism and frequent communion, were preached in German to nuns; see Karl Boeckl, *Eucharistielehre der deutschen Mystiker des Mittelalters* (Freiburg: Herder, 1924), pp. 74-122.

14. John of Fécamp, Peter Damian and Gregory VII recommended eucharistic devotion and frequent communion to women; see Baix and Lambot, *Dévotion*, pp. 48-52.

15. *Legenda sanctae Clarae virginis*, ed. Francesco Pennacchi, Società internazionale di studi Francescani in Assisi (Assisi: Tipografia metastasio, 1910), pp. 30-31, 39-40.

16. The eucharist is a major theme in: Life of Mary of Oignies, AASS, June, vol. 5, pp. 547-72; Life of Lutgard of Aywières, AASS, June, vol. 4 (1867), pp. 189-210; Life of Ida of Louvain, AASS, April, vol. 2 (1865), pp. 156-89; Life of Ida of Léau, AASS, October, vol. 13 (1883), pp. 100-35; Life of Christina *Mirabilis* of St. Trond, AASS, July, vol. 5 (1868), pp. 637-60; Life of Alice of

Schaerbeke, AASS, June, vol. 2 (1867), pp. 471-77; Life of Margaret of Ypres, ed. G.G. Meersseman, in "Frères prêcheurs et mouvement dévot en Flandre au XIIIᵉ siècle," *Archivum Fratrum Praedicatorum* 18 (1948), 106-30; and the first book of the Life of Juliana of Cornillon, AASS, April, vol. 1, pp. 442-55.

17. Life of Margaret of Cortona, AASS, February, vol. 3, pp. 302-63; Life of Gherardesca of Pisa, AASS, May, vol. 7 (1866), pp. 161-76; trans. in Elizabeth Petroff, *Consolation of the Blessed* (New York: Alta Gaia Society, 1979), pp. 85-120; Life of Alda or Aldobrandesca of Siena, AASS, April, vol. 3 (1866), pp. 471-76, written, however, in the sixteenth century, trans. in Petroff *Consolation*, pp. 166-78; and Life of Angela of Foligno, for which see Chapter 3, above, n. 30.

18. In addition to the Life of Lukardis (n. 6, above) and the material from Helfta (Bynum, *Jesus as Mother*, pp. 170-262), see Jeanne Ancelet-Hustache (ed.), "Les 'Vitae Sororum' d'Unterlinden: Edition critique du Manuscrit 508 de la Bibliothèque de Colmar," *Archives d'histoire doctrinale et littéraire du moyen âge* 5 (1930), pp. 317-509; Ferdinand Vetter (ed.), *Das Leben der Schwestern zu Töss beschrieben von Elsbet Stagel*, Deutsche Texte des Mittelalters, 6 (Berlin, 1906); and Karl Schröder (ed.), *Der Nonnen von Engelthal Büchlein von der Genaden Überlast*, Bibliothek des litterarischen Vereins in Stuttgart, 108 (Tübingen, 1871). Other *Nonnenbücher* are discussed in Browe, *Die Wunder*; Walter Muschg, *Die Mystik in der Schweiz, 1200-1500* (Frauenfeld: Huber, 1935), pp. 205-41; and Louis Cognet, *Introduction aux mystiques rhéno-flamands* (Paris: Desclée, 1968), pp. 196-201 and *passim*. I am also indebted to an unpublished paper by Frederick M. Stein, "The Mysticism of Engelthal." [And see now Ursula Peters, *Religiöse Erfahrung als literarisches Faktum: Zur Vorgeschichte und Genese frauenmystischer Texte des 13. und 14. Jahrhunderts*, Hermaea germanistische Forschungen, N.F. 56 (Tübingen: Niemeyer, 1988).]

19. Mechtild of Magdeburg, *Offenbarungen der Schwester Mechtild von Magdeburg oder das fliessende Licht der Gottheit*, ed. Gall Morel (1869; reprint, Darmstadt: Wissenschaftliche Buchgesellschaft, 1963), p. 43; trans. Lucy Menzies, *The Revelations of Mechtild of Magdeburg (1210-1297) or The Flowing Light of the Godhead* (London: Longmans, 1953), p. 48.

20. J.-H. Albanés (ed.), *La Vie de sainte Douceline, fondatrice des béguines de Marseille* (Marseilles: Camoin, 1879) [hereafter *Douceline*], pp. 87, 91.

21. Browe, *Die Wunder*, p. 46; and Felix Vernet, *Medieval Spirituality*, trans. the Benedictines of Talacre (London: Sands, 1930), p. 61.

22. Duhr, "Communion fréquente," col. 1240; McDonnell, *Beguines and Beghards*, p. 315.

23. Jules Corblet, *Histoire dogmatique, liturgique et archéologique du sacrement de l'eucharistie*, 2 vols. (Paris: Société Générale de Librairie Catholique, 1885-1886), vol. 1, pp. 188-91; Browe, *Die Wunder*, pp. 97-98; *Die Verehrung der Eucharistie im Mittelalter* (Munich: Hueber, 1933), pp. 28-39, 61-65; and Jungmann, *Mass*, vol. 2, pp. 381-82.

24. Jungmann, *Mass*, vol. 2, pp. 381-85, 412; Archdale A. King, *Liturgies of the Religious Orders* (London: Longmans, Green, 1955), pp. 128-30, 372; and Baix and Lambot, *Dévotion*.

25. Life of Juliana of Cornillon, AASS, April, vol. 1, p. 450; *Douceline*, pp. 133-35; and Life of Ida of Louvain, AASS, April, vol. 2, p. 172.

26. AASS, June, vol. 2, p. 474.

27. AASS, June, vol. 4, pp. 198-99.

28. Browe, *Die Wunder*, pp. 27-28.

29. AASS, October, vol. 13, pp. 113-14. And see also Life of Juliana, AASS, April, vol. 1, pp. 445-46.

30. *Töss*, pp. 32-33. See also "Unterlinden," pp. 442-44.

31. On the Helfta mystics, see Bynum, *Jesus as Mother*, pp. 170-262.

32. Life of Ida of Louvain, AASS, April, vol. 2, pp. 163-65 and *passim*; and Life of Lukardis, *Analecta Bollandiana* 18, pp. 317, 324, 338. See also the Life of Ida of Léau, AASS, October, vol. 13, p. 114.

33. Men used such language too. See, for example, Bernard of Clairvaux, *Sermones super Cantica Canticorum*, sermon 71, *Sancti Bernardi opera*, ed. J. Leclercq, C.H. Talbot and H.M. Rochais, vol. 2 (Rome: Editiones Cistercienses, 1958), pp. 214-24. Wolfgang Riehle, *The Middle English Mystics*, trans. B. Standring (London: Routledge & Kegan Paul, 1981), pp. 107-10, makes it clear that such metaphors are more prevalent in women writers.

34. AASS, June, vol. 4, pp. 192, 193-94.

35. Life of Angela of Foligno, AASS, January, vol. 1, pp. 189, 206.

36. Anna Vorchtlin: "Und het ich dich, ich gez dich vor rehter lieb!" *Engelthal*, p. 36. Mechtild: "das si nut denne got essen mag," quoted in Riehle, *Mystics*, p. 107.

37. AASS, April, vol. 2, pp. 167, 165-66 and 164-65 respectively.

38. Browe, *Die Wunder*, p. 30.

39. Gertrude of Helfta, *Oeuvres spirituelles*, vol. 2: *Le Héraut*, Sources chrétiennes, 139, Série des textes monastiques d'Occident, 25 (Paris: Editions du Cerf, 1968), pp. 256-58, 290-96; *Töss*, pp. 36, 38-39, 45, 47, 87-88; *Engelthal*, pp. 26-27, 31, 36, 39; Life of Angela of Foligno, AASS, January, vol. 1, pp. 205, 206; Antonin Duraffour, Pierre Gardette and P. Durdilly (eds. and trans.), *Les Oeuvres de Marguerite d'Oingt*, Publications de l'Institut de linguistique romane de Lyon, 21 (Paris: Belles Lettres, 1965), pp. 119-21; and Life of Mary of Oignies, AASS, June, vol. 5, pp. 563, 567 and *passim*.

40. Life of Margaret of Faenza, AASS, August, vol. 5, p. 849, and see Petroff, *Consolation*, p. 62.

41. Life of Ida of Louvain, AASS, April, vol. 2, p. 177. In this vision, which lasted from the reading of the epistle until the moment of elevation, Ida bathes the baby, hugs him to her breast and at first refuses to return him to Mary.

42. McDonnell, *Beguines and Beghards*, p. 328; and Browe, *Die Wunder*, p. 106.

43. Life of Lukardis, *Analecta Bollandiana* 18, p. 324; Life of Lutgard, AASS, June, vol. 4, pp. 191-92; Life of Margaret of Ypres in Meersseman, "Frères prêcheurs," pp. 107-09, 117-18, 120; Life of Ida of Louvain, AASS, April, vol. 2, p. 173; *Oeuvres de Marguerite*, pp. 98-99; Life of Angela of Foligno, AASS, January, vol. 1, p. 205; and Philipp Strauch (ed.), *Die Offenbarungen der Adelheid Langmann*, Quellen und Forschungen zur Sprach- und Kulturgeschichte der germanischen Völker, 26 (Strasbourg: Trübner, 1878), pp. 11-12. See also "Unterlinden," pp. 442-44.

44. Ernst Benz, *Die Vision: Ergahrungsformen und Bilderwelt* (Stuttgart: Ernst Klett, 1969), pp. 17-34. See also Donald Weinstein and Rudolph M. Bell, *Saints*

and Society: The Two Worlds of Western Christendom, 1000–1700 (Chicago: University of Chicago Press, 1982), pp. 234–35.

45. AASS, June, vol. 5, p. 552.

46. *Analecta Bollandiana* 18, pp. 312–17.

47. Life of Beatrice, in *Oeuvres de Marguerite*, p. 105.

48. Life of Mary of Oignies, AASS, June, vol. 5, p. 564; Gertrude, *Oeuvres*, vol. 2: *Héraut*, bk. 2, pp. 226–353; L. Reypens (ed.), *Vita Beatricis: De Autobiografie van de Z. Beatrijs van Tienen O. Cist. 1200–1268* (Antwerp: Ruusbroec-Genootschap, 1964) [hereafter *Beatrijs*], p. 64; and Life of Margaret of Ypres in Meersseman, "Frères prêcheurs," pp. 125–26.

49. *Töss*, pp. 37, 50–51. One of the sisters composed a poem which said: "Ie siecher du bist, ie lieber du mir bist" (*ibid.*, p. 37).

50. *Hadewijch*, trans. Hart; see especially letters 1, 2, 22, 26, 29. On Mechtild, see Bynum, *Jesus as Mother*, pp. 235–47.

51. Life of Angela, AASS, January, vol. 1, p. 208. See also Life of Aldobrandesca, AASS, April, vol. 3, pp. 473–74.

52. Mechtild of Hackeborn, *Revelationes Gertrudianae ac Mechtildianae*, vol. 2: *Sanctae Mechtildis...Liber specialis gratiae*, ed. the Monks of Solesmes (Paris: Oudin, 1877), pp. 365–66.

53. Life of Christina *Mirabilis*, AASS, July, vol. 5, pp. 637–60.

54. Life of Lukardis, *Analecta Bollandiana* 18, p. 312.

55. "Unterlinden," pp. 340–42. Weinstein and Bell, *Saints and Society*, pp. 233–35, demonstrate that penitential asceticism was more common among female saints than among male in the later Middle Ages. [And see now Peter Ochsenbein, "Leidensmystik in dominikanischen Frauenklöstern des 14. Jahrhunderts am Beispiel der Elsbeth von Oye," in Peter Dinzelbacher and Dieter Bauer (eds.), *Religiöse Frauenbewegung und mystische Frömmigkeit im Mittelalter* (Cologne and Vienna: Böhlau, 1988), pp. 353–72.]

56. AASS, June, vol. 2, pp. 473–74. See also Life of Juliana of Cornillon, AASS, April, vol. 1, p. 449.

57. For other examples of the fusion of suffering and ecstasy, see Chapter 5, below, nn. 53, 71.

58. See n. 2, above.

59. Browe, *Die Wunder*, pp. 110–11.

60. AASS, April, vol. 2, p. 164; *Beatrijs*, pp. 134–37, 142–43, 173–75.

61. Letter of Abbess T[engswich] of Andernach to Hildegard, epistle 116, in J.-P. Migne (ed.), *Patrologiae cursus completus: series latina*, 221 vols. (Paris, 1841–1864) [hereafter PL], vol. 197, col. 336C.

62. Bynum, *Jesus as Mother*, pp. 9–21, 247–62. See also Weinstein and Bell, *Saints and Society*, pp. 228–29.

63. See Bynum, *Jesus as Mother*, pp. 15–16, 247–62.

64. Life of Juliana, AASS, April, vol. 1, p. 475.

65. Life of Angela of Foligno, AASS, January, vol. 1, p. 204.

66. Life of Benevenuta of Bojano, AASS, October, vol. 13, p. 163.

67. See nn. 25–32, above.

68. Life of Margaret, AASS, February, vol. 3, pp. 340–43; Life of Mary of Oignies, AASS, June, vol. 5, pp. 566 and 567; and Life of Ida of Louvain, AASS, April, vol. 2, pp. 178–79. And see Browe, *Die Wunder*, pp. 31–40.

69. See Bynum, *Jesus as Mother*, pp. 240–42, 245.

70. See Mark Reuel Silk, "*Scientia Rerum*: The Place of Example in Later Medieval Thought," Ph.D. Dissertation, Harvard, 1982, pp. 213–42.

71. Vauchez, *La Sainteté*, pp. 249, 317–18, 419–27. Vauchez points out that the few male *lay* saints also show eucharistic fervor (although not to the extent of some of the women).

72. See Chapter 1, above.

73. *The Life of Christina of Markyate: A Twelfth Century Recluse*, ed. C.H. Talbot (Oxford: Clarendon Press, 1959), pp. 134–56, 160–70; *Douceline*, pp. 155–57; Life of Margaret of Faenza, AASS, August, vol. 5 (1868), p. 850; and Bynum, *Jesus as Mother*, p. 245, n. 281.

74. Stephen E. Wessley, "The Thirteenth-Century Guglielmites: Salvation through Women," *Medieval Women: Dedicated and Presented to Professor Rosalind M.T. Hill*, ed. Derek Baker, Studies in Church History, Subsidia 1 (Oxford: Basil Blackwell, 1978), pp. 289–303; McDonnell, *Beguines and Beghards*, pp. 492–96; and Marjorie Reeves, *The Influence of Prophecy in the Later Mid-*

dle Ages (Oxford: Oxford University Press, 1969), pp. 248-50.

75. Bynum, *Jesus as Mother*, pp. 240-42, 245; and Life of Juliana, AASS, April, vol. 1, pp. 457-58.

76. Gertrude, *Oeuvres*, vol. 3: *Héraut*, p. 176; and see Bynum, *Jesus as Mother*, pp. 196-209, 255-56.

77. Hildegard of Bingen, *Scivias*, ed. Adelgundis Führkötter and Angela Carlevaris, Corpus christianorum: Continuatio medievalis, 43, 2 vols. (Turnhout: Brepols, 1978), vol. 1, pp. 19-21, 147-48, 290-91.

78. Jungmann, *Mass*, vol. 2, pp. 364-65.

79. AASS, June, vol. 2, p. 476.

80. AASS, April, vol. 1, p. 453. [A great deal of what the fourteenth-century saint Catherine of Siena says about receiving and eating implies that reception *is* service; see Chapter 5, below, n. 65. On the need to take women's own emphasis on service seriously, see Chapter 2, above.]

81. Browe, *Die Wunder*, p. 34.

82. AASS, April, vol. 2, p. 183.

83. To cite an obvious example: William James, *The Varieties of Religious Experience: A Study in Human Nature* (1902; reprint, New York: New American Library, Mentor, 1958), pp. 267-71.

84. On anorexia nervosa, see Hilde Bruch, *The Golden Cage* (Cambridge, MA: Harvard University Press, 1978); *Eating Disorders: Obesity, Anorexia Nervosa and the Person Within* (New York: Basic Books, 1973); and Sheila MacLeod, *The Art of Starvation: A Story of Anorexia and Survival* (New York: Schocken Books, 1981). [For discussion of the applicability of the modern category to medieval material, see now Rudolph Bell, *Holy Anorexia* (Chicago: University of Chicago, 1985); Caroline Walker Bynum, *Holy Feast and Holy Fast: The Religious Significance of Food to Medieval Women* (Berkeley: University of California Press, 1987); and Joan Jacobs Brumberg, *Fasting Girls: The History of Anorexia Nervosa* (Cambridge, MA: Harvard University Press, 1988). I have commented on this discussion and explained my differences from Bell in "Holy Anorexia in Modern Portugal," *Culture, Medicine and Psychiatry* 12 (1988), pp. 259-68. It makes a great deal of difference whether one treats not-eating as an isolated phenomenon, as

does Bell, or locates it, as I do, among other religious food practices. It also makes considerable difference whether one looks at women's own words or primarily at contemporary male descriptions of them. Ignoring women's self-understanding leads to neglect of what they considered to be the evangelical implications of their food practices. See n. 80, above.]

85. Browe, *Die Wunder*, pp. 49–54; Corblet, *Histoire de l'eucharistie*, vol. 1, pp. 430–33; and T.E. Bridgett, *History of the Holy Eucharist in Great Britain*, 2 vols. (London: Kegan Paul, 1881), vol. 2, p. 195. Ebenezer Cobham Brewer, *A Dictionary of Miracles: Imitative, Realistic and Dogmatic* (Philadelphia: Lippincott, 1884), lists one other male case: John the Good of Mantua (d. 1222). [For a slightly different count, see now Bynum, *Holy Feast*; and Bell, *Holy Anorexia*.]

86. Browe, *Die Wunder*, pp. 44–48, 36–40.

87. AASS, June, vol. 5, pp. 551–52; and see n. 45, above. Although disgusted by earthly food, Mary frequently received grace palpably as food or drink. For example, she saw milk flow from relics (p. 567).

88. AASS, April, vol. 2, pp. 158–163. Food imagery runs throughout Ida's life. In one non-eucharistic miracle, for example, she changes beer into wine to bring a wavering young girl back to the religious life (p. 165).

89. AASS, July, vol. 5, pp. 652–53, 654.

90. AASS, April, vol. 1, pp. 443–47.

91. Raymond of Capua, Life of Catherine of Siena, AASS, April, vol. 3 (1866), pp. 862–967 *passim*, especially pt. 1, chs. 4–6, and pt. 2, ch. 5, pp. 879–87, 903–07.

92. Although there appears to be no cross-cultural literature on anorexia, it is clear that food preparation is a female role in most cultures and that, in a number of cultures (for example, India), fasting is a particularly popular form of asceticism for women; see *Popular Hinduism and Hindu Mythology: An Annotated Bibliography*, compiled by Barron Holland (Westport, CT: Greenwood Press, 1979), pp. 120–21.

93. Life of Angela, AASS, January, vol. 1, pp. 191–92, 205, 207. Christ explicitly tells Angela, in a warning against excessive asceticism, that sleeping, eating and drinking are acceptable if done in love for him (p. 193).

94. James of Vitry, *The Historia Occidentalis of Jacques de Vitry: A Critical Edition*, ed. John F. Hinnebusch, Spicilegium Friburgense, 17 (Fribourg: The University Press, 1972), pp. 87-88; and the Life of Alpaïs of Cudot, AASS, November, vol. 2, pp. 174-209.

95. McDonnell, *Beguines and Beghards*, p. 310.

96. *Ibid.*, pp. 310, 315, 330, 415; Brenda M. Bolton, "*Vitae Matrum*: A Further Aspect of the Frauenfrage," in Derek Baker (ed.), *Medieval Women*, pp. 267-68; and Robert I. Moore, *The Origins of European Dissent* (New York: St. Martin's Press, 1977), pp. 168-96. [Cathars were also understood to oppose bodily resurrection; see Chapter 6, nn. 124, 125, below. Miracles of incorrupt cadavers and theological discussions of the resurrection of bones and body parts were thus closely related to eucharistic theology and eucharistic miracles, both because these aspects of theory and practice all deal with the part/whole issue and because they all have implications for the positive valuation of matter.]

97. For example, Life of Mary of Oignies, AASS, June, vol. 5, pp. 547-50, 562-63, 565-66.

98. Life of Juliana, AASS, April, vol. 1, pp. 461-62.

99. "Unterlinden," p. 352; *Oeuvres de Marguerite*, p. 101; Life of Gherardesca, AASS, May, vol. 7, pp. 175-76.

100. Mechtild of Hackeborn, *Liber specialis gratiae*, p. 260. In another vision John the Evangelist told her that those who are married and own property are no further from Christ than those who renounce such things "because the Word is made flesh" (*ibid.*, p. 265).

101. Edouard Dumoutet, *Corpus Domini: Aux sources de la piété eucharistique médiévale* (Paris: Beauchesne, 1942), pp. 51-100, especially pp. 50-61, 88-96; Bertaud, "Dévotion," col. 1624; Ronald C. Finucane, *Miracles and Pilgrims: Popular Beliefs in Medieval England* (Totowa, NJ: Rowman & Littlefield, 1977), pp. 197-98; and Benedicta Ward, *Miracles and the Medieval Mind: Theory, Record and Event, 1000-1215* (Philadelphia: University of Pennsylvania Press, 1982), pp. 15-18.

102. Bynum, *Jesus as Mother*, pp. 82-109.

103. Bernard of Clairvaux, *De gradibus humilitatis*, in *Sancti Bernardi opera*, vol. 3, pp. 20-21; Bonaventure, *Legenda maior*, ch. 13, in *Analecta Franciscana*, 10: *Legendae S. Francisci Assisiensis saeculis XIII et XIV conscriptae* (Quaracchi, 1926-41), pp. 615-20; and Life of Mary of Oignies, AASS, June, vol. 5, pp. 551-52.

104. Life of Margaret of Cortona, AASS, February, vol. 3, p. 330; Life of Lukardis, *Analecta Bollandiana* 18, p. 314. [See Chapter 6, below, at n. 2.]

105. Life of Margaret of Ypres, ed. Meersseman, "Frères prêcheurs," p. 108.

106. *Beatrijs*, pp. 138-39. Male theologians occasionally show doubts about such literal imitation. James of Vitry says we should admire but *not* imitate Mary of Oignies (AASS, June, vol. 5, p. 550). But this is an exception. The author of Beatrice's life wants her model *imprinted on* her sisters (*Beatrijs*, p. 185) and Margaret of Cortona was enjoined to *be an example* (AASS, February, vol. 3, p. 342).

107. Mark 3.35. For the use of this metaphor by Guerric of Igny in the twelfth century, see Bynum, *Jesus as Mother*, pp. 120-22.

108. Caesarius, *Dialogus*, bk. 9, ch. 32, p. 189; and Life of Ida of Louvain, AASS, April, vol. 2, pp. 165, 166-67. Hadewijch, *Mengeldichten*, pp. 65-71, in *Hadewijch*, trans. Hart, pp. 345-49, works out an extended allegory of the soul pregnant with Christ. On Dorothy of Montau, I am indebted to an unpublished paper by Stephen P. Bensch, "A Cult of the Maternal: Dorothea of Prussia (1347-94)."

109. See, for example, Julia O'Faolain and Lauro Martines (eds.), *Not in God's Image* (New York: Harper & Row, 1973).

110. See Chapter 3, above, n. 33.

111. For the image in Gertrude the Great and Mechtild of Hackeborn, see Bynum, *Jesus as Mother*, pp. 194, 210, 255; see also *Oeuvres de Marguerite*, pp. 73, 101; *Douceline*, p. 91 ("Ques es arma? *Speculum divine majestatis*; en la qual Dieus a pauzat son sagell"); and *Beatrijs*, pp. 71, 99-100, 110-11. See also Chapter 5, below, nn. 17-18.

112. John F. Benton, "Clio and Venus: An Historical View of Medieval Love," in *The Meaning of Courtly Love*, ed. F.X. Newman (Albany: State University of New York Press, 1969), p. 32; and the works cited in Chapter 5, n. 1, below.

113. For example, Life of Juliana of Cornillon, AASS, April, vol. 1, pp. 454, 457-58. On this point see also Bynum, *Jesus as Mother*, pp. 135-36, and Chapter 1, above.

114. On Gertrude, see Bynum, *Jesus as Mother*, pp. 196-209, 225-27. Throughout her poems, Hadewijch uses male *personae* more frequently than female.

115. Peter Dronke, *Women Writers of the Middle Ages: A Critical Study of Texts from Perpetua († 203) to Marguerite Porete († 1310)* (Cambridge: Cambridge University Press, 1984.)

116. See Chapter 3, above, n. 47. Medieval authors use both *homo* and *Eva* to stand for "humanity"; see "Underlinden," p. 352, and Life of Juliana of Cornillon, AASS, April, vol. 1, p. 450, respectively.

117. For women's emphasis on Christ's divinity and on the human Jesus as soul and body, see Bynum, *Jesus as Mother*, pp. 170-262; *Hadewijch*, trans. Hart, pp. 61-63; Angela of Foligno, AASS, January, vol. 1, p. 231; and Catherine of Siena, *The Dialogue*, trans. Suzanne Noffke (New York: Paulist Press, 1980), p. 210.

118. *Scivias*, vol. 1, pp. 225-306, especially p. 231 and plate 15.

119. See Bynum, *Jesus as Mother*, pp. 229, 233-34, 244.

120. Dumoutet, *Corpus Domini*, pp. 77-79. Dumoutet quotes William Durandus who says in his *Rationale* that the reliquary (*capsa*) into which one puts the consecrated host *is* the body of Mary. See Figures 6.10 and 6.11 below for other devotional objects that depict Mary as the container or clothing of Christ.

121. Barbara Jane Newman, "*O Feminea Forma*: God and Woman in the Works of St. Hildegard (1098-1179)," Ph.D. Dissertation, Yale, 1981, pp. 131-34; and *Oeuvres de Marguerite*, pp. 98-99. [See now the works cited in Chapter 3. above, nn. 33 and 47.]

122. *Douceline*, pp. 19, 43 and *passim*. Marguerite of Oingt identifies both with Christ and with his mother; see *Oeuvres de Marguerite*, p. 77 and *passim*. For the theme in Italian lives, see Petroff, *Consolation*. The author of the Life of Clare (Thomas of Celano?) holds Clare up as a model to women; see *Legenda Clarae*, p. 3: "Sequantur ergo viri viros Verbi incarnati novos discipulos: imitentur feminae Claram, Dei matris vestigium, novam capitaneam mulierum."

123. For example, Life of Benevenuta of Bojano, AASS, October, vol. 13, pp. 164–65. See also Life of Ida of Louvain, AASS, April, vol. 2, pp. 164–65, where Ida's "eating" of both communion and Scripture is seen as being parallel to Mary's bearing Christ in her uterus.

124. Recent feminist theology, some of which makes such assertions, is discussed in Bynum, "The Complexity of Symbols," in C. Bynum, S. Harrell and P. Richman (eds.), *Gender and Religion: On the Complexity of Symbols* (Boston: Beacon, 1986).

[My effort, in this essay, to understand sympathetically the piety of medieval women is not intended either to advocate such piety for modern women or to deny the substantial limitations imposed on women in the thirteenth century by patriarchal structures and attitudes. This essay explores the creativity with which women used fundamental Christian motifs; "Women's Stories" and "The Female Body and Religious Practice" (Chapters 1 and 6 respectively) give attention to the factors that constricted their creativity.]

V. *"...And Woman His Humanity"*

1. Julia O'Faolain and Lauro Martines (eds.), *Not in God's Image* (New York: Harper & Row, 1973); Vern L. Bullough, "Medieval Medical and Scientific Views of Women," *Viator* 4 (1973), pp. 487–93; Eleanor C. McLaughlin, "Equality of Souls, Inequality of Sexes: Women in Medieval Theology," in *Religion and Sexism: Images of Women in the Jewish and Christian Traditions*, ed. Rosemary Ruether (New York: Simon & Schuster, 1974), pp. 213–66; and Marie-Thérèse d'Alverny, "Comment les théologiens et les philosophes voient la femme?" *La Femme dans les civilisations des Xᵉ–XIIIᵉ siècles: Actes du colloque tenu à Poitiers les 23–25 septembre 1976, Cahiers de civilisation médiévale* 20 (1977), pp. 105–29. Because this article was written for an audience of nonspecialists, primary sources are cited in English translation where possible.

2. David Herlihy, "Women in Medieval Society," reprinted in *The Social History of Italy and Western Europe 700–1500* (London: Variorum Reprints 1978).

3. Natalie Z. Davis, *Society and Culture in Early Modern France* (Stanford: Stanford University Press, 1975), pp. 124–31.

4. André Vauchez, *La Sainteté en Occident aux derniers siècles du moyen âge d'après les procès de canonisation et les documents hagiographiques* (Rome: Ecole française de Rome, 1981), pp. 427-35; Donald Weinstein and Rudolph M. Bell, *Saints and Society: The Two Worlds of Western Christendom, 1000 to 1700* (Chicago: University of Chicago Press, 1983), *passim*, especially p. 87; and Elizabeth Petroff, *Consolation of the Blessed* (New York: Alta Gaia Society, 1979). For an interesting recent example of this interpretation, see Hope P. Weissman, "Margery Kempe in Jerusalem: *Hysteria Compassio* in the Late Middle Ages," in M.J. Carruthers and E.D. Kirk (eds.), *Acts of Interpretation: The Text in its Context, 700-1600: Essays in Honor of E. Talbot Donaldson* (Norman, OK: Pilgrim Books, 1982), pp. 201-17.

5. Caroline Walker Bynum, *Jesus as Mother: Studies in the Spirituality of the High Middle Ages* (Berkeley: University of California Press, 1982), pp. 135-46; Joan M. Ferrante, *Woman as Image in Medieval Literature from the Twelfth Century to Dante* (New York: Columbia University Press, 1975); Vauchez, *La Sainteté*; Weinstein and Bell, *Saints and Society*; Jane Tibbets Schulenburg, "Sexism and the Celestial Gynaeceum from 500 to 1200," *Journal of Medieval History* 4 (1978), pp. 117-33; Stephen E. Wessley, "The Thirteenth-Century Guglielmites: Salvation through Women," in Derek Baker (ed.), *Medieval Women: Dedicated and Presented to Professor Rosalind M.T. Hill*, Studies in Church History: Subsidia 1 (Oxford: Blackwell, 1978), pp. 289-303; and Marjorie Reeves, *The Influence of Prophecy in the Later Middle Ages* (Oxford: Oxford University Press, 1969), pp. 248-50.

6. Simone Roisin, *L'Hagiographie cistercienne dans le diocèse de Liège au XIIIe siècle* (Louvain: Bibliothèque de l'Université, 1947), pp. 108, 111-13.

7. See Weinstein and Bell, *Saints and Society*, tables on pp. 123-37. According to Weinstein and Bell, women (who represented about 17.5 percent of the saints canonized or revered between 1000 and 1700) accounted for about half of the saints who were especially devoted to Jesus. They represented only about a third of the saints characterized by devotion to Mary, however. Since women's piety was more affective than men's, we expect devotion to all members of the holy family to be disproportionately represented in their spirituality. Such

357

affectivity perhaps accounts for their devotion to Mary, which may have nothing to do with Mary's gender (although it may).

8. See Life of Columba of Rieti, in J. Bollandus and G. Henschenius (eds.), *Acta sanctorum*, ed. J. Carnandet *et al.* (Paris: Palmé, etc., 1863-   ) [hereafter AASS], May, vol. 5 (1866), pp. 149-226; and cf. Thomas of Celano's(?) Life of Clare with Clare's own writings in *Legenda sanctae Clarae virginis*, ed. Francesco Pennacchi, Società internazionale di studi Francescani in Assisi (Assisi: Tipografia metastasio, 1910).

9. Bynum, *Jesus as Mother*, pp. 110-69.

10. Douceline of Marseilles and Umiliana Cerchi performed miracles predominantly for women; so did Richard Rolle and Henry Suso. See Claude Carozzi, "Douceline et les autres," in *La Religion populaire en Languedoc du XIIIᵉ siècle à la moitié du XIVᵉ siècle* (Toulouse: Edouard Privat, 1976), pp. 251-67; Weinstein and Bell, *Saints and Society*, p. 53; and Chapter 1, above, n. 41. On Suso, see nn. 43, 44, 45 in this chapter.

11. Ronald C. Finucane, *Miracles and Pilgrims: Popular Beliefs in Medieval England* (Totowa, NJ: Rowman & Littlefield, 1977).

12. This is true of Catherine of Siena, Angela of Foligno and Margaret of Cortona; see Life of Catherine, AASS, April, vol. 3 (1866), pp. 862-967; Life of Angela, AASS, Jan., vol. 1 (1863), pp. 186-234; and Life of Margaret, AASS, Feb., vol. 3 (1865), pp. 302-63. [For better editions of the Angela material than were available to me when I wrote this article, see Chapter 3, above, n. 30.]

13. Weinstein and Bell, *Saints and Society*, pp. 220-38. And see Peter Dinzelbacher, "Europäische Frauenmystik des Mittelalters: Ein Überlick," in Peter Dinzelbacher and Dieter Bauer (eds.), *Frauenmystik im Mittelalter* (Ostfildern: Schwabenverlag, 1985), pp. 11-23.

14. Weinstein and Bell, *Saints and Society*, pp. 228-32; Bynum, *Jesus as Mother*, pp. 247-62.

15. Derived from Weinstein and Bell, *Saints and Society*, tables on pp. 123-37. Peter Dinzelbacher, *Vision und Visionsliteratur im Mittelalter* (Stuttgart: Anton Hiersemann, 1981), p. 229, sums up differences between early medieval visions characteristic of men and later visions characteristic of women in a way that

underlines this point. Women's visions were expected and sought for; men's occurred suddenly. Women's visions confirmed them in an already chosen way of life; men's marked the onset of a new life.

16. Chapter 1, above.

17. For example, *Vita Beatricis: De Autobiografie van de Z. Beatrijs van Tienen O. Cist. 1200-1268*, ed. L. Reypens (Antwerp: Ruusbroec-Genootschap, 1964), pp. 71, 99-100, 110-11; *Les Oeuvres de Marguerite d'Oingt*, ed. and trans. Antonin Duraffour, P. Gardette and P. Durdilly, Publications de l'Institut de linguistique romane de Lyon 21 (Paris: Belles Lettres, 1965), pp. 73, 101; and see Bynum, *Jesus as Mother*, pp. 136, 170-262. For the negative idea, see O'Faolain and Martines, *Not in God's Image*, which sometimes misleads by quoting out of context.

18. *La vie de sainte Douceline, fondatrice des beguines de Marseilles*, ed. J.-H. Albanés (Marseilles: Camoin, 1897), p. 91. And on Mechtild of Hackeborn see Bynum, *Jesus as Mother*, pp. 210, 215.

19. Herbert Grundmann, "Die Frauen und die Literatur im Mittelalter: Ein Beitrag zur Frage nach der Entstehung des Schrifttums in der Volkssprache," *Archiv für Kulturgeschichte* 26 (1936), pp. 129-61; Simone Roisin, "L'Efflorescence cistercienne et le courant féminin de piété au XIIIe siècle," *Revue d'histoire ecclésiastique* 39 (1943), pp. 342-78; Bynum, *Jesus as Mother*, pp. 170-74; n. 67, below; and Life of Lukardis of Oberweimar, *Analecta Bollandiana* 18 (1899), pp. 340-41.

20. Bynum, *Jesus as Mother*, pp. 91-92, 141-42.

21. *Ibid.*, pp. 235-47. See *Lettres de sainte Catherine de Sienne*, trans. E. Cartier, 4 vols., Bibliothèque Dominicaine, 2nd ed. (Paris: Editions P. Tequin, 1886), letter 147, p. 907, and letter 268, p. 1380, where Catherine calls weakness "female" and urges "virility." Peter Dronke, *Women Writers of the Middle Ages: A Critical Study of Texts from Perpetua († 203) to Marguerite Porete († 1310)* (Cambridge: Cambridge University Press, 1984) argues throughout that the topos of the "poor little woman" was often used by women writers as an ironic and assertive statement of female ability.

22. Bynum, *Jesus as Mother*, pp. 203-09, 221, 259-61. For women who felt vulnerable before the control over the eucharist that priests exercised, see Life

of Ida of Louvain, AASS, April, vol. 2 (1865), pp. 164–65, and Life of Margaret of Cortona, AASS, Feb., vol. 3, pp. 311, 316, 339–44. Catherine of Siena venerated priests for their ability to consecrate the eucharist.

23. On the various types of spiritual literature produced in the Middle Ages and the major writers, the best discussion is still Jean Leclercq, François Vandenbroucke and Louis Bouyer, *La Spiritualité du moyen âge* (Paris: Aubier, 1961), which is vol. 2 of *Histoire de la spiritualité chrétienne*, ed. Bouyer, Leclercq, Vandenbroucke and Cognet.

24. Bynum, *Jesus as Mother*, pp. 110–69. See also André Cabassut, "Une Dévotion médiévale peu connue: La Dévotion à 'Jesus Nôtre Mère,' " *Mélanges Marcel Viller, Revue d'ascétique et de mystique* 25 (1949), pp. 234–45; Eleanor C. McLaughlin, " 'Christ My Mother': Feminine Naming and Metaphor in Medieval Spirituality," *Nashota Review* 15 (1975), pp. 228–48; and Valerie Lagorio, "Variations on the Theme of God's Motherhood in Medieval English Mystical and Devotional Writings," *Studia mystica* 8 (1985), pp. 15–37.

25. *The Works of Aelred of Rievaulx*, vol. 1: *Treatises and Pastoral Prayer*, trans. M.P. Mcpherson, Cistercian Fathers Series, 2 (Spencer, MA: Cistercian Publications, 1971), p. 73.

26. *The Monk of Farne: The Meditations of a Fourteenth-Century Monk*, trans. a Benedictine nun of Stanbrook (Baltimore: Helicon Press, 1961), p. 64.

27. Second sermon for Saints Peter and Paul, ch. 2, in *Liturgical Sermons*, 2 vols., trans. the monks of Mount St. Bernard Abbey, Cistercian Fathers Series, 8, 32 (Spencer, MA: Cistercian Publications, 1970-1971), vol. 2, p. 155.

28. Sermons 9 and 10, in *The Works of Bernard of Clairvaux*, vol. 2: *On the Song of Songs*, vol. 1, trans. Kilian Walsh (Kalamazoo, MI: Cistercian Publications, 1976), pp. 57–58, 62–63.

29. *The Letters of St. Bernard of Clairvaux*, trans. Bruno Scott James (London: Burns, Oates, 1953), pp. 3, 7, with my changes. For other examples of male usage, see Bynum, *Jesus as Mother*, pp. 113–54.

30. *Ibid.*, pp. 211–15.

31. *Ibid.*, pp. 186–96, especially nn. 47, 48. For other examples of mixed-gender imagery in women's lives, see Petroff, *Consolation*, pp. 66–78; and n. 57,

below. [When I first wrote this article, I called such imagery androgynous; I now drop the term because it might be taken to imply a self-consciousness about mixing the sexes, which is *not* what I mean.]

32. *Hadewijch: The Complete Works*, trans. Columba Hart (New York: Paulist Press, 1980), p. 16, n. 57, and p. 87; cf. pp. 47, 114, 119.

33. Life of Lutgard, AASS, June, vol. 4 (1867), pp. 189-210, especially pp. 191-93.

34. Life of Angela, AASS, Jan., vol. 1, pp. 189, 206; and Life of Catherine, AASS, April, vol. 3, p. 903.

35. Life of Alda or Aldobrandesca of Siena, AASS, April, vol. 3 (1866), pp. 471-76, written in the sixteenth century.

36. *Oeuvres de Marguerite d'Oingt*, pp. 77-79.

37. *Julian of Norwich: Showings*, trans. Edmund Colledge and James Walsh (New York: Paulist Press, 1978), long text, ch. 58, p. 294. On Julian, see Brant Pelphrey, *Love Was His Meaning: The Theology and Mysticism of Julian of Norwich*, Salzburg Studies in English Literature: Elizabethan and Renaissance Studies, 92.4 (Salzburg: Institut für Anglistik und Amerikanistik, Universität Salzburg, 1982). [See now Grace M. Jantzen, *Julian of Norwich: Mystic and Theologian* (New York: Paulist Press, 1988)]. When Julian says that we are "substantial and sensual," she means (very roughly translated) that we are soul and body; but this is not simple soul/body dualism. As both Pelphrey and Jantzen suggest, Julian is best understood as meaning that we combine being a person (substantiality) with a physicalness that needs to be shaped (sensuality); both substantiality and sensuality are created and saved (or recreated) by mother Jesus.

It is worth noting that the pronouns that refer to mother Jesus remain male in the original Middle English, thus enhancing the extent to which Julian's image of Jesus mixes the sexes.

38. Julian, *Showings*, long text, ch. 60, pp. 298-99.

39. Helinand of Froidmont, sermon 27, in J.-P. Migne (ed.), *Patrologiae cursus completus: series latina*, 221 vols. (Paris, 1841-1864) [hereafter PL], vol. 212, col. 622B; see also sermon 20, cols. 646-52.

40. Bynum, *Jesus as Mother*, p. 128, n. 63.

41. Bonaventure, The Life of Francis, in *Bonaventure: The Soul's Journey into God*, trans. E. Cousins (New York: Paulist Press, 1978) pp. 204-06, 243, 251-52, 257, 278.

42. On Bernard's female image of himself, see Bynum, *Jesus as Mother*, pp. 115-18. [On Francis, see now Hester Gelber, "A Theatre of Virtue: The Exemplary World of St. Francis of Assisi," in *Saints and Virtues*, ed. J.S. Hawley (Berkeley: University of California Press, 1987), pp. 15-35.] For saints influenced by their mothers, see Weinstein and Bell, *Saints and Society*, p. 23.

43. *The Exemplar: Life and Writings of Blessed Henry Suso, O.P.: Complete Edition based on Manuscripts*, trans. M. Ann Edwards, 2 vols. (Dubuque, IO: Priory Press, 1962), vol. 1, pp. xxxviii, 12, 45-46, 51-52, 54. And see Caroline W. Bynum, *Holy Feast and Holy Fast: The Religious Significance of Food to Medieval Women* (Berkeley: University of California Press, 1987), pp. 94-112, for an extended discussion of feminine imagery in Suso and Rolle.

44. Suso, *Exemplar*, vol. 1, pp. xxxiv-xxxv, 95-98, 103-06; for assessments of Abelard's attitudes toward women, see Robert Javelet, *Image et ressemblance au douzième siècle, de saint Anselme à Alain de Lille*, 2 vols. (Paris: Letouzey et Ané, 1967), vol. 1, pp. 241-42; and Mary M. McLaughlin, "Peter Abelard and the Dignity of Women: Twelfth-Century 'Feminism' in Theory and Practice," in *Pierre Abélard, Pierre le Vénérable: Les courants philosophiques, littéraires et artistiques en Occident au milieu du XIIe siècle*, Colloques internationaux du Centre National de la Recherche Scientifique, 546 (Paris: Editions du Centre National de la Recherche Scientifique, 1975), pp. 282-333.

45. Suso, *Exemplar*, vol. 1, pp. 103-06. Another woman-oriented Dominican of the fourteenth century was similarly critical of the penitential asceticism and eucharistic devotion that he correctly saw as characteristic of women: see John Tauler, *Spiritual Conferences*, ed. and trans. E. Colledge and Sister M. Jane (St. Louis: Herder, 1961), sermon 33, pp. 269-76.

46. Chapter 1, above. Tauler, *Spiritual Conferences*, p. 274, urges women not to be "womanly."

47. John Anson, "The Female Transvestite in Early Monasticism: The Origin and Development of a Motif," *Viator* 5 (1974), pp. 1-32.

48. Raymond of Capua, Life of Catherine, AASS, April, vol. 3, p. 892.

49. Bynum, *Jesus as Mother*, pp. 208-09, 226-27; Julian, *Showings*, short text, ch. 6, p. 135, deleted in long text.

50. *The Book of Margery Kempe*, trans. W. Butler-Bowdon (New York: Devin-Adair, 1944), ch. 52, pp. 110-15.

51. See Bynum, *Jesus as Mother*, pp. 240-47, and Chapter 1, above.

52. *Book of Margery Kempe*, pp. 22-23, 74-77.

53. *Oeuvres de Marguerite d'Oingt*, p. 139.

54. *Hadewijch*, trans. Hart, pp. 280-81. Quoted in Chapter 4, above, at n. 3.

55. Jo Ann McNamara, "Sexual Equality and the Cult of Virginity in Early Christian Thought," *Feminist Studies* 3.3/4 (1976), pp. 145-58.

56. Letter 116, from Abbess T[engswich] of Andernach to Hildegard, PL 197, col. 336C.

57. AASS, April, vol. 3, p. 884. Catherine's own images for herself are female and for Christ mixed-gender. Her Christ is bridegroom and mother; see Catherine of Siena, *The Dialogue*, trans. Suzanne Noffke (New York: Paulist Press, 1980).

58. See n. 21, above.

59. Chapter 4, above, nn. 39-43.

60. Davis, *Society and Culture*, chs. 4, 5, pp. 97-151; Vern L. Bullough, "Transvestites in the Middle Ages," *American Journal of Sociology* 79 (1974), pp. 1381-94; Marie Delcourt, "Les Complexe de Diane dans l'hagiographie chrétienne," *Revue de l'histoire des religions* 153 (1958), pp. 1-33; and Evelyne Patlagean, "L'histoire de la femme déguisée en moine et l'évolution de la sainteté féminine à Byzance," *Studi medievali*, 3rd ser., 17, fasc. 2 (1976), pp. 597-623. See also Anson, "Female Transvestite."

61. See Bynum, *Holy Feast*, p. 417, n. 44, for a list of cases.

62. See Chapter 3, above, nn. 47, 48, and Chapter 4, above, n. 118.

63. On Mechtild, see Bynum, *Jesus as Mother*, pp. 229, 233-34, 244. And see Catherine, *Lettres*, letter 196, p. 1098. For Catherine, unlike Mechtild and Hildegard, humanity is more frequently Adam — that is, a male image (see *ibid.*, p. 319).

64. Hildegard, *Scivias*, vol. 1, pp. 19–21, 147–48, 290–91.

65. See Catherine, *Lettres*, letter 36, pp. 316–17, letter 198, pp. 1112–13, letter 231, p. 1234, letter 322, p. 1538; Robert Fawtier and Louis Canet, *La Double expérience de Catherine Benincasa (Sainte Catherine de Sienne)*, Bibliothèque des Idées (Paris: Gallimard, 1948), pp. 245–46; and Bynum, *Holy Feast*, pp. 165–80.

66. Life of Ida of Louvain, AASS, April, vol. 2, pp. 165, 166–67. On Dorothy, see Richard Kieckhefer, *Unquiet Souls: Fourteenth-Century Saints and Their Religious Milieu* (Chicago: University of Chicago Press, 1985), pp. 22–33. And see Chapter 4, above, n. 108.

67. On stigmata, see E. Amann, "Stigmatisation," in *Dictionnaire de théologie catholique*, 15 vols. (Paris, 1909–1950), vol. 14, pt. 2, cols. 2616–24; Vauchez, *La Sainteté*, pp. 514–18; and Chapter 3, above, n. 59.

68. *Hadewijch*, trans. Hart, pp. 353–55. Bynum, *Holy Feast*, explores this theme more fully.

69. See Chapter 2, above, at n. 28.

70. Life of Mary of Oignies, AASS, June, vol. 5 (1867), p. 552. On Gertrude, see Bynum, *Jesus as Mother*, pp. 192, 253, n. 295. On Villana de' Botti and Dauphine of Puimichel, see Kieckhefer, *Unquiet Souls*, p. 57, and Process of canonization, art. 33, in Jacques Cambell (ed.), *Enquête pour le procès de canonisation de Dauphine de Puimichel, comtesse d'Ariano († 26-xi-1360)* (Turin: Erasmo, 1978), p. 52. For other examples, see Chapter 4, above, nn. 45–49.

71. Julian, *Showings*, long text, chs. 2, 3, 4, pp. 177–81.

72. For the prominence of poverty as a theme in male spirituality, see Lester K. Little, *Religious Poverty and the Profit Economy in Medieval Europe* (Ithaca, NY: Cornell University Press, 1978). There is some evidence that food is a theme in women's piety cross-culturally; see Chapter 4, above, especially nn. 84, 92; Jack Goody, *Cooking, Cuisine and Class: A Study in Comparative Sociology* (Cambridge: Cambridge University Press, 1982), p. 193; and Peggy Reeves Sanday, *Female Power and Male Dominance: On the Origins of Sexual Inequality* (Cambridge: Cambridge University Press, 1981), pp. 76–77.

73. Brenda Bolton, "*Vitae Matrum*: A Further Aspect of the *Frauenfrage*,"

in Baker (ed.), *Medieval Women*, pp. 253-73; Rosalind B. Brooke and Christopher N.L. Brooke, "St. Clare," in *ibid.*, pp. 275-87; and Weinstein and Bell, *Saints and Society*, p. 88-97.

74. Weinstein and Bell, *Saints and Society*, p. 235. Pelphrey, *Love Was His Meaning*, suggests that Julian of Norwich saw sin as a painful and necessary part of being human and that her theory of union with God did not involve "stages" the soul "passed beyond" but rather a continuity of self, a becoming fully human with Jesus. This reading of Julian would make her *Showings* a more conceptually and theologically subtle statement of the kind of "continuity" I find in other women's writing from the period.

75. Nancy Chodorow, *The Reproduction of Mothering: Psychoanalysis and the Sociology of Gender* (Berkeley: University of California Press, 1978). A.K. Ramanujan, "On Women Saints," in J.S. Hawley and D.M. Wulff (eds.), *The Divine Consort: Radha and the Goddesses of India* (Berkeley: Graduate Theological Union, 1982), pp. 316-24, applies these ideas to Indian saints. See Chapter 1, above, nn. 72, 89, for differences and similarities in the Indian and Western usages. See also Bynum, "The Complexity of Symbols," in C. Bynum, S. Harrell and P. Richman (eds.), *Gender and Religion: On the Complexity of Symbols* (Boston: Beacon, 1986), n. 23.

76. Weinstein and Bell, *Saints and Society*, pp. 235-36.

77. This suggestion runs counter to the literature that argues that women need, and tend to create, female images: see, for example, Elaine Pagels, "What Became of God the Mother?" *Signs* 2 (1976), pp. 293-303; and Carol P. Christ, "Heretics and Outsiders: The Struggle over Female Power in Western Religion," *Soundings* 61.3: *Dilemmas of Pluralism* (1978), pp. 260-80. See Bynum, "The Complexity of Symbols," nn. 1, 2, 13, 15.

78. See nn. 21, 45, 46, 55, above.

VI. *The Female Body and Religious Practice*

1. Peter of Vaux, Life of Colette of Corbie, trans. Stephen Juliacus, ch. 10, par. 84, in J. Bollandus and G. Henschenius (eds.), *Acta sanctorum...editio novissima*, ed. J. Carnandet *et al.* (Paris: Palmé, etc., 1863-   ) [hereafter

AASS], March, vol. 1 (1865), p. 558. See Caroline Walker Bynum, *Holy Feast and Holy Fast: The Religious Significance of Food to Medieval Women* (Berkeley: University of California Press, 1987), p. 67.

2. Life of Lukardis, ch. 55, *Analecta Bollandiana* 18 (1899), p. 340.

3. Johan Huizinga, *The Waning of the Middle Ages: A Study of Forms of Life, Thought and Art in France and the Netherlands in the XIVth and XVth Centuries*, trans. F. Hopman (1924; reprint, Garden City, NJ: Doubleday, 1956); and Barbara W. Tuchman, *A Distant Mirror: The Calamitous Fourteenth Century* (New York: Knopf, 1978).

4. [See now Francis Barker, *The Tremulous Private Body: Essays on Subjection* (London: Methuen, 1984); and Piero Camporesi, *The Incorruptible Flesh: Bodily Mutation and Mortification in Religion and Folklore*, trans. T. Croft-Murray and H. Elsom (Cambridge: Cambridge University Press, 1988).]

5. For discussion of the modern period, see Catherine Gallagher and Thomas Laqueur (eds.), *The Making of the Modern Body: Sexuality and Society in the Nineteenth Century* (Berkeley: University of California Press, 1987). For discussion of the Middle Ages, see Danielle Jacquart and Claude Thomasset, *Sexualité et savoir médical au Moyen Age* (Paris: Presses Universitaires de France, 1985); Jacques Le Goff, "Corps et idéologie dans l'Occident médiéval: La Révolution corporelle," in *L'Imaginaire médiéval: Essais* (Paris: Gallimard, 1985), pp. 123–27 [*The Medieval Imagination*, trans. Arthur Goldhammer (Chicago: University of Chicago Press, 1989]; and Michel Sot, "Mépris du monde et résistance des corps aux XIe et XIIe siècles," and Jacques Dalarun, "Eve, Marie ou Madeleine? La Dignité du corps féminin dans hagiographie médiévale," in *Médiévales* 8: *Le Souci du corps* (1985), pp. 6–32.

6. A close reading of the evidence Le Goff presents in "Corps et idéologie" makes this clear. In the twelfth- and thirteenth-century literature he cites, disease and deformity are symbols of sin or of the corruption of society (not primarily of sex); the disgust displayed toward body is ultimately a disgust toward the putrefaction that will be manifest most clearly in the grave. [And see now Camporesi, *Incorruptible Flesh*.]

7. I have discussed this in Chapter 4, above, in "Fast, Feast and Flesh: The

Religious Significance of Food to Medieval Women," *Representations* 11 (Summer, 1985), pp. 1-25, and in *Holy Feast*. The point is also made by Peter Dinzelbacher, "Europäische Frauenmystik des Mittelalters: Ein Überblick," in Peter Dinzelbacher and Dieter Bauer (eds.), *Frauenmystik im Mittelalter* (Ostfildern: Schwabenverlag, 1985), pp. 11-23; by Peter Brown, *The Cult of the Saints: Its Rise and Function in Latin Christianity* (Chicago: University of Chicago Press, 1981); by Jacques Gélis and Odile Redon, "Preface," and Michel Bouvier, "De l'incorruptibilité des corps saints," in Jacques Gélis and Odile Redon (eds.), *Les Miracles miroirs des corps* (Paris: Presses et Publications de l'Université de Paris VIII, 1983), pp. 9-20, 193-221; by Marie-Christine Pouchelle, "Représentations du corps dans la *Légende dorée*," *Ethnologie française* 6 (1976), pp. 293-308, and *Corps et chirurgie à l'apogée du moyen âge: Savoir et imaginaire du corps chez Henri de Mondeville, chirurgien de Philippe le Bel* (Paris: Flammarion, 1983); by Dominique de Courcelles, "Les Corps des saints dans les cantiques catalans de la fin du moyen âge," *Médiévales* 8: *Le souci du corps* (1985), pp. 43-56; and, in a different way, by Herbert Thurston, *The Physical Phenomena of Mysticism* (Chicago: Henry Regnery, 1952). [See now Camporesi, *Incorruptible Flesh*, and Jeffrey Hamburger, "The Visual and the Visionary: The Image in Late Medieval Monastic Devotions," *Viator* 20 (1989), pp. 161-82.]

8. P. Séjourné, "Reliques," *Dictionnaire de théologie catholique* [hereafter DTC] (Paris: Letouzey et Ané, 1903-1972), vol. 13, pt. 2, cols. 2330-65; Patrick J. Geary, *Furta Sacra: Thefts of Relics in the Central Middle Ages* (Princeton: Princeton University Press, 1978), esp. pp. 152-54; and E.A.R. Brown, "Death and the Human Body in the Later Middle Ages: The Legislation of Boniface VIII on the Division of the Corpse," *Viator* 12 (1981), pp. 221-70, especially pp. 223-24.

9. See Peter the Venerable, sermon 4, in J.-P. Migne (ed.), *Patrologiae cursus completus: series latina*, 221 vols. (Paris, 1841-1864) [hereafter PL], vol. 189, cols. 1001-03; reedited by Giles Constable, "Petri Venerabilis Sermones Tres," *Revue Bénédictine* 64 (1954), pp. 269-70. See also Caesarius of Heisterbach, *Dialogus miraculorum*, ed. Joseph Strange, 2 vols. (Cologne: Heberle, 1851), bk. 8, ch. 87, vol. 2, pp. 145-46.

Medieval theologians and hagiographers never, however, assumed that the saint was *only* the relic; see Caroline W. Bynum, "Bodily Miracles and the Resurrection of the Body in the High Middle Ages," in Thomas Kselman (ed.), *Belief in History* (Notre Dame, IN: University of Notre Dame Press, forthcoming, 1990), nn. 89-92.

10. See, for example, the case of Lukardis, *Holy Feast*, pp. 113-14. See also Life of Lutgard of Aywières, bk. 1, chs. 1-2, and bk. 2, ch. 1, AASS, June, vol. 4 (Paris and Rome, 1867), pp. 192-94; and Life of Benevenuta of Bojano, ch. 10, par. 82, AASS, October, vol. 13 (1883), p. 172.

11. Nicole Hermann-Mascard, *Les Reliques des saints: Formation coutumière d'un droit*, Société d'Histoire du Droit: Collection d'histoire institutionnelle et sociale, 6 (Paris: Edition Klincksieck, 1975), p. 274, n. 21. As examples, see the process of canonization of 1276 for Margaret of Hungary in Vilmos Fraknoi, *Monumenta romana episcopatus vesprimiensis (1103-1526)*, vol. 1 (Budapest: Collegium Historicorum Hungarorum Romanum, 1896), pp. 237-38, 266, 267, 288; and the case of Lidwina of Schiedam, "Fast, Feast and Flesh," p. 5.

12. Angela of Foligno, *Le Livre de l'expérience des vrais fideles: Texte latin publié d'après le manuscrit d'Assise*, ed. and trans. M.-J. Ferré and L. Baudry (Paris: Editions Droz, 1927), par. 53, p. 106 (cf. *ibid.*, par. 80, p. 166); Raymond of Capua, *Legenda maior* of Catherine of Siena, pt. 2, ch. 4, pars. 155, 162-63, and pt. 3, ch. 7, pars. 412, 414, AASS, April, vol. 3 (1866), pp. 901, 902-03, 963; and Catherine of Genoa, *Il Dialogo spirituale* and *Vita*, ch. 12, ed. Umile Bonzi da Genova, *S. Caterina Fieschi Adorno*, vol. 2: *Edizione critica dei manoscritti cateriniani* (Turin: Marietti, 1962), pp. 422-27, 140-41. And see Thomas of Celano, First Life of Francis of Assisi, bk. 1, ch. 7, par. 17, in *Analecta Franciscana* 10 (Quaracchi: Collegium S. Bonaventurae, 1941), p. 16; Celano, Second Life, bk. 1, ch. 5, par. 9, in *ibid.*, pp. 135-63; Bonaventure, *Legenda maior* of Francis, pt. 1, ch. 1, pars. 5, 6, in *ibid.*, pp. 562-63; and Bonaventure, *Legenda minor*, ch. 1, 8th lesson, in *ibid.*, pp. 657-58. On Angela, see Chapter 1, above, n. 44, and Chapter 3, above, n. 30.

13. *Holy Feast*, pp. 122-23, 126, 211, 273-75.

14. Giles Constable, *Attitudes Toward Self-Inflicted Suffering in the Middle*

Ages, Ninth Stephen J. Brademas Sr. Lecture (Brookline, MA: Hellenic College Press, 1982); Richard Kieckhefer, *Unquiet Souls: Fourteenth-Century Saints and Their Religious Milieu* (Chicago: University of Chicago Press, 1984), chs. 3-5; and Brenda Bolton, *"Mulieres sanctae,"* in Derek Baker (ed.), *Studies in Church History* 10: *Sanctity and Secularity: The Church and the World* (1973), pp. 77-93, and *"Vitae Matrum*: A Further Aspect of the *Frauenfrage,"* in Derek Baker (ed.), *Medieval Women: Dedicated and Presented to Professor Rosalind M.T. Hill* (Oxford: Blackwell, 1978), pp. 253-73.

15. Life of Suso, ch. 31, in Henry Suso, *Deutsche Schriften. Im Auftrag der Württembergischen Kommission für Landesgeschichte,* ed. Karl Bihlmeyer (Stuttgart: Kohlhammer, 1907), pp. 91-92; trans. M. Ann Edwards, *The Exemplar: Life and Writings of Blessed Henry Suso, O.P.,* ed. Nicholas Heller, 2 vols. (Dubuque: Priory Press, 1962), vol. 1, pp. 87-88.

16. Angela of Foligno, *Le Livre,* par. 75, pp. 156-58.

17. Peter Browe, *Die eucharistischen Wunder des Mittelalters* (Breslau: Müller & Seiffert, 1938).

18. Peggy Reeves Sanday, *Divine Hunger: Cannibalism as a Cultural System* (New York: Cambridge University Press, 1986); and Louis-Vincent Thomas, *Le Cadavre: De la biologie à l'anthropologie* (Brussels: Editions Complexe, 1980), pp. 159-69.

19. Ronald C. Finucane, *Miracles and Pilgrims: Popular Beliefs in Medieval England* (Totowa, NJ: Rowman & Littlefield, 1977), pp. 197-98; Benedicta Ward, *Miracles and the Medieval Mind: Record and Event, 1000-1215* (Philadelphia: University of Pennsylvania Press, 1982), pp. 15-18; Gary Macy, *The Theologies of the Eucharist in the Early Scholastic Period: A Study of the Salvific Function of the Sacrament According to the Theologians, c.1080-c.1220* (Oxford: Oxford University Press, 1984), pp. 87-95; and *Holy Feast,* p. 255.

20. Adam of Eynsham, *Life of Hugh of Lincoln,* ed. D. Douie and H. Farmer, 2 vols. (London: Thomas Nelson, 1961), bk. 5, ch. 15, vol. 2, p. 170.

21. Leo Steinberg, *The Sexuality of Christ in Renaissance Art and in Modern Oblivion* (New York: Pantheon, 1983). And see Chapter 3, above.

22. See Louis Canet in Robert Fawtier and Louis Canet, *La Double expérience*

de Catherine Benincasa (sainte Catherine de Siene) (Paris: Gallimard, 1948), pp. 245-46. [See now Karen Scott, "Not Only With Words, But With Deeds: The Role of Speech in Catherine of Siena's Understanding of Her Mission," Ph.D. Dissertation, University of California at Berkeley, 1989.]

23. Peter Dinzelbacher, "Die 'Vita et Revelationes' der Wiener Begine Agnes Blannbekin (✝1315) im Rahmen der Viten- und Offenbarungsliteratur ihrer Zeit," in Dinzelbacher and Bauer (eds.), *Frauenmystik*, pp. 152-77. And see Chapter 3, above, n. 11.

24. See Thurston, *Physical Phenomena*; Dinzelbacher, "Überblick,"; *Vision und Visionsliteratur im Mittelalter* (Stuttgart: Hiersemann, 1981); Rudolph M. Bell, *Holy Anorexia* (Chicago: University of Chicago Press, 1985); and *Holy Feast*. As all four of the important recent books on saints make clear, these phenomena are particularly documented for Low Country women in the thirteenth century, for women in the Rhineland in the late thirteenth and early fourteenth centuries, and for northern Italian women in the fourteenth and fifteenth centuries: see André Vauchez, *La Sainteté en Occident aux derniers siècles du moyen âge d'après les procès de canonisation et les documents hagiographiques* (Rome: Ecole française de Rome, 1981); Donald Weinstein and Rudolph M. Bell, *Saints and Society: The Two Worlds of Western Christendom, 1000-1700* (Chicago: University of Chicago Press, 1982); Michael Goodich, *Vita Perfecta: The Ideal of Sainthood in the Thirteenth Century* (Stuttgart: Hiersemann, 1982); and Kieckhefer, *Unquiet Souls*.

25. Thurston, *Physical Phenomena*, especially pp. 69, 95-99, 123; Antoine Imbert-Gourbeyre, *La Stigmatisation: L'Extase divine et les miracles de Lourdes: Réponse aux libres-penseurs*, 2 vols. (Clermont-Ferrand, 1894), which must be used with caution; Pierre Debongnie, "Essai critique sur l'histoire des stigmatisations au moyen âge," *Etudes carmélitaines* 21.2 (1936), pp. 22-59; and E. Amann, "Stigmatisation," DTC 14, pt. 1, cols. 2617-19.

26. J.-K. Huysmans, *Sainte Lydwine de Schiedam* (Paris, 1901), pp. 288-91, which, however, contains no documentation; Thurston, *Physical Phenomena*, pp. 268-70; Hermann-Mascard, *Les Reliques*, pp. 68-69; Charles W. Jones, *Saint Nicolas of Myra, Bari and Manhattan: Biography of a Legend* (Chicago: Univer-

sity of Chicago Press, 1978), pp. 144-53; and Bynum, "Fast, Feast and Flesh," nn. 22, 81, 82, 85. Women also account for most of the cases of exuding sweet odors: see Thurston, *Physical Phenomena*, pp. 222-32.

27. *Holy Feast*, pp. 203-04, 257, 268-69; Chapter 4, above, at nn. 107-08.

28. Clare of Montefalco's spiritual sisters tore out her heart after her death and found the insignia of the Passion incised upon it; see Vauchez, *La Sainteté*, p. 408. Three precious stones, with images of the Holy Family on them, were supposedly found in the heart of Margaret of Città di Castello; see Life of Margaret, ch. 8, *Analecta Bollandiana* 19 (1900), pp. 27-28. On mystical espousal rings and miraculous bodily elongation, see Thurston, *Physical Phenomena*, pp. 139, 200. [On Clare, see now Camporesi, *Incorruptible Flesh*, pp. 4-6, and Giulia Barone, "Probleme um Klara von Montefalco," in Peter Dinzelbacher and Dieter Bauer (eds.), *Religiöse Frauenbewegung und mystische Frömmigkeit im Mittelalter* (Cologne and Vienna: Böhlau, 1988), pp. 215-24.]

29. See Pouchelle, *Corps et chirurgie*, pp. 132-36. Pouchelle claims that the earliest official dissections (in 1315) were dissections of female bodies. The dissections to which she refers were clearly not the first dissections or autopsies of any sort. Dissections arising out of embalming or for the purpose of determining the cause of death in legal cases were practiced at least from the early thirteenth century; dissections of the human body for teaching purposes were practiced at Bologna about 1300. See Walter Artelt, *Die ältesten Nachrichten über die Sektion menschlicher Leichen im mittelalterlichen Abendland*, Abhandlungen zur Geschichte der Medizin und der Naturwissenschaften, 34 (Berlin: Ebering, 1940), pp. 3-25; Mary Niven Alston, "The Attitude of the Church Towards Dissection Before 1500," *Bulletin of the History of Medicine* 16 (1944), pp. 221-38; Ynez Viole O'Neill, "Innocent III and the Evolution of Anatomy," *Medical History* 20.4 (1976), pp. 429-33; Nancy G. Siraisi, "The Medical Learning of Albertus Magnus," in James A. Weisheipl (ed.), *Albertus Magnus and the Sciences: Commemorative Essays, 1980* (Toronto: Pontifical Institute of Mediaeval Studies, 1980), p. 395; and Jacquart and Thomasset, *Sexualité*, p. 49.

30. According to the tables in Weinstein and Bell, *Saints and Society*, women provide 27 percent of the wonder-working relics although only 17.5 per-

cent of the saints. On blood prodigies, see Thurston, *Physical Phenomena*, pp. 283-93.

31. Claude Carozzi, "Douceline et les autres," in *La Religion populaire en Languedoc du XIIIe siècle à la moitie du XIVe siècle*, Cahiers de Fanjeaux 11 (Toulouse, 1967), pp. 251-67; and see de Courcelles, "Les Corps des saints," especially p. 51.

32. Thurston, *Physical Phenomena*, pp. 233-82, especially pp. 246-52. Of the 42 saints living between 1400 and 1900 whose feasts are kept by the universal Church, there are claims of incorruption in 22 cases and in seven more there are reports of odd phenomena which imply nondecay. Seventeen of the incorrupt are male, but of the six females among the 42 five are incorrupt and for the sixth (Jane Frances de Chantal), who was embalmed, there appears to be a claim for extraordinary survival. There are thus more incorrupt male bodies, but all the female bodies are claimed to be incorrupt. On incorruption, see also Bouvier, "De l'incorruptibilité"; João de Pina-Cabral, *Sons of Adam, Daughters of Eve: The Peasant World of the Alto Minho* (Oxford: Clarendon Press, 1986), pp. 230-38; and Bynum, "Holy Anorexia in Modern Portugal," in *Culture, Medicine and Psychiatry* 12 (1988), pp. 259-68. For examples of miraculous bodily closure in women saints, see Bynum, "Fast, Feast and Flesh," n. 54.

33. Weinstein and Bell, *Saints and Society*, pp. 234-35.

34. Ernst Benz, *Die Vision: Erfahrungsformen und Bilderwelt* (Stuttgart: Ernst Klett, 1969), pp. 17-34; Kieckhefer, *Unquiet Souls*, pp. 57-58; and Elizabeth A. Petroff, *Medieval Women's Visionary Literature* (Oxford: Oxford University Press, 1986), pp. 37-44.

35. Julian of Norwich, *A Book of Showings to the Anchoress Julian of Norwich*, long text, chs. 2-4, ed. E. Colledge and J. Walsh, Studies and Texts, 35, 2 parts (Toronto: Pontifical Institute of Mediaeval Studies, 1978), pt. 2, pp. 285-98; Life of Villana de' Botti, ch. 1, pars. 11-12, AASS, August, vol. 5 (1868), pp. 866-67; Caroline Walker Bynum, *Jesus as Mother: Studies in the Spirituality of the High Middle Ages* (Berkeley: University of California Press, 1982), pp. 192, 253 n. 295; L. Reypens (ed.), *Vita Beatricis: De Autobiografie van de Z. Beatrijs van Tienen O. Cist. 1200-1268* (Antwerp: Ruusbroec-Genootschap, 1964), p. 64; Life of

Margaret of Ypres, in G.G. Meersseman (ed.), "Frères prêcheurs et mouvement dévot en Flandre au XIIIe siècle," *Archivum Fratrum Praedicatorum* 18 (1948), pp. 125-26; Bynum, "Fast, Feast and Flesh," pp. 4-8; Kieckhefer, *Unquiet Souls*, pp. 22-33; Life of Alpaïs of Cudot, AASS, November, vol. 2, pt. 1 (1894), pp. 167-209; and Life of Serafina of San Gimignano, AASS, March, vol. 2 (1865), pp. 232-38. And see Chapter 5, above, nn. 70, 71.

36. *Vita Beatricis*, bk. 3, ch. 6, pp. 134-36. See also pp. 45-49, 63, 99, 154-55. The poet Hadewijch also speaks of ecstasy as "insanity"; see poem 15, Poems in Couplets, in Hadewijch, *The Complete Works*, trans. Columba Hart (New York: Paulist Press, 1980), pp. 350-52. Philip of Clairvaux in his Life of Elisabeth of Spalbeek calls her ecstasy *imbecillitas*; see *Catalogus codicum hagiographicorum Bibliothecae regiae Bruxellensis*, Subsidia hagiographica 1, vol. 1, pt. 1 (Brussels, 1886), p. 364.

37. Life of Alice, ch. 3, par. 26, AASS, June, vol. 2 (1867), p. 476. And see Life of Lutgard of Aywières, bk. 3, ch. 1, AASS, June, vol. 4, p. 204. The emphasis on service is important. Even those women who languished alone in illness thought of themselves as saving others through their suffering. Although all recent works on saints (Vauchez, *La Sainteté*, Weinsten and Bell, *Saints and Society*, Goodich, *Vita Perfecta*, and Kieckhefer, *Unquiet Souls*) have contrasted contemplative women with active ones and have seen the active form of life to be more characteristic of Italian women, I take issue with this dichotomy; see Chapter 2, above, especially n. 61.

38. See Jerome Kroll and Bernard Bachrach, "Sin and the Etiology of Disease in Pre-Crusade Europe," *Journal of the History of Medicine and Allied Sciences* 41 (1986), pp. 395-414; Alain Saint-Denis, "Soins du corps et médecine contre la souffrance à l'Hôtel-Dieu de Laon au XIIIe siècle," *Médiévales* 8:*Le souci du corps* (1985), pp. 33-42; and Katharine Park, "Medicine and Society in Medieval Europe, 500-1500," in Andrew Wear (ed.), *Medicine in Society* (Cambridge: Cambridge University Press, forthcoming, 1990), ch. 2.

39. Life of Alpaïs, bk. 3, ch. 4, and bk. 4, ch. 1, AASS November, vol. 2, pt. 1 (Brussels, 1894), pp. 196-97, 198. For Elsbeth Achler, see Karl Bihlmeyer (ed.), "Die Schwäbische Mystikerin Elsbeth Achler von Reute († 1420)...," in

G. Baesecke and F. J. Schneider (eds.), *Festgabe Philipp Strauch zum 80. Geburtstag am 23. September 1932* (Halle: Niemeyer, 1932), pp. 88–109. On Catherine, see Raymond, Life, pt. 2, ch. 5, par. 167, AASS, p. 904.

40. Elsbet Stagel, *Das Leben der Schwestern zu Töss beschrieben von Elsbet Stagel*, ed. Ferdinand Vetter, Deutsche Texte des Mittelalters, 6 (Berlin: Weidmann, 1906), p. 37.

41. Life of Walburga (d. 779) by Wolfhard of Eichstadt in AASS, February, vol. 3 (Antwerp, 1658), pp. 528, 540–42.

42. Pierre-André Sigal, *L'Homme et les miracles dans la France médiévale (XIe–XIIe siècle)* (Paris: Editions du Cerf, 1985), especially pp. 259–61.

43. Dinzelbacher, "Überblick"; and Peter Dronke, *Women Writers of the Middle Ages: A Critical Study of Texts from Perpetua (†203) to Marguerite Porete (†1310)* (Cambridge; Cambridge University Press, 1984), pp. x–xi.

44. See, for example, Bernard of Clairvaux, *Sermones super Cantica Canticorum*, sermon 71, *Sancti Bernardi opera*, ed. J. Leclercq, C.H. Talbot and H.M. Rochais, vol. 2 (Rome: Editiones Cistercienses, 1958), pp. 214–24; and John Tauler, sermon 31, in *Die Predigten Taulers*, ed. Ferdinand Vetter (Berlin: Wiedmann, 1910), p. 310. See also Huizinga, *Waning*, pp. 197–200.

45. This point is made in a number of the papers in Dinzelbacher and Bauer (eds.), *Frauenmystik*. See especially Franz Wöhrer, "Aspekte der englischen Frauenmystik im späten 14. und beginnenden 15. Jahrhundert," pp. 314–40.

46. See above nn. 10, 13, 26, 27, 36; Hadewijch, vision 7, *Hadewijch*, trans. Hart, pp. 280–81; and Chapter 4, above, at n. 2.

47. See Siegfried Ringler, "Die Rezeption mittelalterlicher Frauenmystik als wissenschaftliches Problem, dargestellt am Werk der Christine Ebner," and Dinzelbacher, "Agnes Blannbekin," in Dinzelbacher and Bauer (eds.), *Frauenmystik*, pp. 178–200 and 152–77; and Chapter 4, above. Miraculous elements tend to be more or less stressed in accounts of visions depending on the audience for which they are composed; see Simone Roisin, *L'Hagiographie cistercienne dans le diocèse de Liège au XIIIe siècle* (Louvain: Bibliothèque de l'Université, 1947). [On the nuns' books, see now Ursula Peters, "Frauenliteratur im Mittelalter? Überlegungen zur Trobairitzpoesie, zur Frauenmystik und zur femi-

nistischen Literaturbetrachtung," *Germanisch-Romanische Monatsschrift* N.F. 38 (1988), pp. 35–56; *Religiöse Erfahrung als literarisches Faktum: Zur Vorgeschichte und Genese frauenmystischer Texte des 13. und 14. Jahrhunderts* (Tübingen: Niemeyer, 1988); Peter Dinzelbacher, "Zur Interpretation erlebnismystischer Texte des Mittelalters," *Zeitschrift für deutsches Altertum und deutsche Literatur* 117 (1988), pp. 1–23; and Hamburger, "Visual and Visionary," especially n. 70.]

48. [See Hamburger, "Visual and Visionary."]

49. For a comparison of male and female visions, see Dinzelbacher, *Vision*, pp. 151–55, 226–28; and Kieckhefer, *Unquiet Souls*, p. 172. [And see now Karen Glente, "Mystikerinnenviten aus männlicher und weiblicher Sicht: Ein Vergleich zwischen Thomas von Cantimpré und Katherina von Unterlinden," in Dinzelbacher and Bauer (eds.), *Religiöse Frauenbewegung*, pp. 251–64.]

50. Bynum, *Jesus as Mother*, pp. 110–69; *Holy Feast*, ch. 3; and Hester G. Gelber, "A Theatre of Virtue: The Exemplary World of St. Francis of Assisi," in J.S. Hawley (ed.), *Saints and Virtues* (Berkeley: University of California Press, 1987), pp. 15–35.

51. Browe, *Die Wunder*, pp. 110–11; and Tauler, sermon 31, *Die Predigten*, pp. 310–11.

52. Wöhrer, "Aspekte der englischen Frauenmystik."

53. For Hadewijch, see *Hadewijch*, trans. Hart. For Margaret Porete, see Romana Guarnieri (ed.), "Il 'Miroir des simples ames' di Margherita Porete," *Archivio italiano per la storia della pietà* 4 (1965), pp. 501–635; Dronke, *Women Writers*, pp. 202–28; [and see now Ulrich Heid, "Studien zu Marguerite Porete und ihrem 'Miroir des simples ames' " in Dinzelbacher and Bauer (eds.), *Religiöse Frauenbewegung*, pp. 185–214.]

54. Marguerite of Oingt, *Les Oeuvres de Marguerite d'Oingt*, ed. and trans. Antonin Duraffour, Pierre Gardette and P. Durdilly (Paris: Belles Lettres, 1965), p. 147. See Chapter 3, above, at n. 31.

55. [See Chapter 3, above, at n. 30.]

56. Angela of Foligno, *Le Livre*, par. 66, pp. 138–40.

57. *Ibid.*, par. 151, p. 326. For the contrast between Eckhart and women mystics, see Otto Langer, "Zur dominikanischen Frauenmystik im spätmit-

telalterlichen Deutschland," in Dinzelbacher and Bauer (eds.), *Frauenmystik*, pp. 341-46.

58. See *Holy Feast*, p. 210.

59. This difference cuts across differences of class or region. The few female saints we know of from poorer groups in society are remarkably similar in their pious practices to the saintly princesses and noblewomen of the period; see Weinstein and Bell, *Saints and Society*, pp. 216, 220-38. The class difference shows up, of course, in the numbers from various classes canonized and in the religious opportunities open to different economic statuses. On regional differences, see the point about Italian women at n. 37, above.

60. For helpful remarks on this topic, see Barbara Duden's Introduction to her "Repertory on Body History: An Annotated Bibliography," in *Zone 5: Fragments for a History of the Human Body*, Part 3 (New York: Urzone, 1989), pp. 471-73.

61. *Jesus as Mother*, pp. 9-21, 170-262; and Chapter 4, above, pp. 134-39. The argument is implied in the title of a recent collection, *Women of Spirit: Female Leadership in the Jewish and Christian Traditions*, ed. Rosemary Ruether and Eleanor McLaughlin (New York: Simon & Schuster, 1979). Petroff, *Women's Visionary Literature*, p. 27, argues that writing itself was considered a male activity; therefore women needed direct divine inspiration to call a writing and speaking voice into existence.

62. *Holy Feast*, pp. 76-77, 229, 253. Eucharistic visions, especially visions of the bleeding host, occurred to women more frequently than to men; see Browe, *Die Wunder*; and Chapter 4, above.

63. Herbert Grundmann, "Die Frauen und die Literatur im Mittelalter: Ein Beitrag zur Frage nach der Entstehung des Schrifttums in der Volksprache," *Archiv für Kulturgeschichte* 26 (1936), pp. 129-61.

64. Margot Schmidt, "Elemente der Schau bei Mechtild von Magdeburg und Mechtild von Hackeborn: Zur Bedeutung der geistlichen Sinne," in Dinzelbacher and Bauer (eds.), *Frauenmystik*, pp. 123-51.

65. Petroff, *Women's Visionary Literature*, pp. 28-32; and Walter J. Ong, *Orality and Literacy: The Technologizing of the Word* (London: Methuen, 1982).

66. David Herlihy, "Women in Medieval Society," in Herlihy, *The Social History of Italy and Western Europe, 700–1500* (London: Variorum Reprints, 1978), "The Making of the Medieval Family: Symmetry, Structure and Sentiment," *Journal of Family History* 8.2 (1983), pp. 116–30, *Medieval Households* (Cambridge, MA: Harvard University Press, 1985), especially ch. 5; and Elizabeth Petroff, *Consolation of the Blessed* (New York: Alta Gaia Society, 1979), pp. 61–62. Although it is clearly true that religious women responded both to personal deprivation and to the patriarchal structure of society, which denied to them many social roles available to men, religious imagery cannot ever be read simply either as compensation or as projection. See Bynum, *Holy Feast, passim* and especially chs. 9, 10, and "The Complexity of Symbols," in C. Bynum, S. Harrell and P. Richman (eds.), *Gender and Religion: On the Complexity of Symbols* (Boston: Beacon Press, 1986), pp. 1–20.

67. See *Holy Feast*, ch. 4, nn. 174, 212, and ch. 7, nn. 15, 21. [On child abandonment, see now John Boswell, *The Kindness of Strangers: The Abandonment of Children in Western Europe from Late Antiquity to the Renaissance* (New York: Pantheon Books, 1988).]

68. *Holy Feast*, ch. 7, nn. 11, 21, and ch. 8, nn. 4, 8.

69. Muriel Joy Hughes, *Women Healers in Medieval Life and Literature* (New York: King's Crown Press, 1943); John F. Benton, "Trotula, Women's Problems, and the Professionalization of Medicine in the Middle Ages," *Bulletin of the History of Medicine* 59 (1985), pp. 30–53; Margaret Wade Labarge, *A Small Sound of the Trumpet: Women in Medieval Life* (Boston: Beacon Press, 1986), ch. 8; and Monica Green, "Women's Medical Practice and Health Care in Medieval Europe: Review Essay," *Signs: Journal of Women in Culture and Society* 14.2 (1989), pp. 434–73.

70. Charles Singer, "The Scientific Views and Visions of Saint Hildegard (1098–1180)," in C. Singer (ed.), *Studies in the History and Method of Science*, vol. 1 (Oxford: Clarendon Press, 1917); Gertrude M. Engbring, "Saint Hildegard, Twelfth-Century Physician," *Bulletin of the History of Medicine* 8 (1940), pp. 770–84; Dronke, *Women Writers*, pp. 144–201; Barbara Newman, *Sister of Wisdom: St. Hildegard's Theology of the Feminine* (Berkeley: Univer-

sity of California Press, 1987), pp. 121-55; and see n. 113, below.

71. For Hildegard of Bingen dressing her nuns as brides to receive communion, see Chapter 4, above, n. 61. For examples of cradles and baby Christ figures used by women in the liturgy, see Elisabeth Vavra, "Bildmotiv und Frauenmystik – Funktion und Rezeption," in Dinzelbacher and Bauer (eds.), *Frauenmystik*, pp. 201-30; Ursula Schlegel, "The Christchild as Devotional Image in Medieval Italian Sculpture: A Contribution to Ambrogio Lorenzetti Studies," *The Art Bulletin* 52.1 (March, 1970), pp. 1-10; and Petroff, *Women's Visionary Literature*, p. 54, n. 22.

72. [Hamburger, "Visual and Visionary," p. 168, plate 3.]

73. Susan Groag Bell, "Medieval Women Book Owners: Arbiters of Lay Piety and Ambassadors of Culture," *Signs* 7.4 (Summer, 1982), pp. 742-68; and Kathleen Ashley and Pamela Scheingorn (eds.), *Interpreting Cultural Symbols: St. Anne in Late Medieval Society* (Athens, GA: University of Georgia Press, forthcoming, 1990). As I have argued elsewhere (Chapter 3, above), such images are not by any means limited to reflecting social roles. Moreover, as I have argued in all my work, there is no reason to assume that people are attracted only to images of their own sex; see especially Bynum, "Complexity of Symbols." It is a well-known fact, for example, that the "Christ and St. John group" (a devotional object depicting male love) is found predominantly in late medieval convents.

74. Thurston, *Physical Phenomena*; I.M. Lewis, *Ecstatic Religion: An Anthropological Study of Spirit Possession and Shamanism* (Harmondsworth, England: Penguin, 1971); Bynum, "Holy Anorexia in Modern Portugal"; Katherine Carlitz, "Private Suffering as a Public Statement: Biographies of Virtuous Women in Sixteenth-Century China," paper delivered at Seventh Berkshire Conference on the History of Women, June, 1987; and Robert McClory, "Cutters: Mutilation: The New Wave in Female Self-Abuse," *Reader: Chicago's Free Weekly* 15.48 (September 5, 1986), pp. 29-38.

75. Le Goff, "Corps et idéologie," pp. 123-25.

76. Robert W. Ackerman, "*The Debate of the Body and the Soul* and Parochial Christianity," *Speculum* 37 (1962), pp. 541-65, especially pp. 552-53. In the Dialogue, Flesh does try to retaliate by suggesting that sin lies rather in the

will – that is, that it should really be charged to Soul's account.

77. Clarissa Atkinson, " 'Precious Balsam in a Fragile Glass': The Ideology of Virginity in the Later Middle Ages," *Journal of Family History* 8.2 (Summer, 1982), pp. 131–43; and Marc Glasser, "Marriage in Medieval Hagiography," *Studies in Medieval and Renaissance History* n.s. 4 (1981), pp. 3–34.

78. Kari Elisabeth Børresen, *Subordination et équivalence: nature et rôle de la femme d'après Augustin et Thomas d'Aquin* (Oslo, 1968); Natalie Z. Davis, *Society and Culture in Early Modern France* (Stanford: Stanford University Press, 1975), pp. 124–31; and the works cited in Chapter 5, n. 1, above.

79. Medieval theologians sometimes carried the dichotomy further, suggesting that the mother was responsible for the nurture of the child's body but the father was charged with its *educatio* – that is, the nourishing of its soul. See John T. Noonan, Jr., *Contraception: A History of Its Treatment by the Catholic Theologians and Canonists*, enlarged ed. (Cambridge, MA: Harvard University Press, 1986), p. 280. Female theologians agreed with male about the dichotomy but sometimes used it in unusual ways. See, for example, the discussion of Hildegard of Bingen in Prudence Allen, *The Concept of Woman: The Aristotelian Revolution 750 B.C.–A.D.1250* (Montreal and London: Eden Press, 1985), p. 297; and the works on Hildegard cited in n. 113, below.

80. Weinstein and Bell, *Saints and Society*, pp. 234–36; Dalarun, "Eve, Marie ou Madeleine?"

81. James of Voragine, *Legenda aurea vulgo historia lombardica dicta*, ed. Th. Graesse (Dresden and Leipzig: Libraria Arnoldiana, 1846). According to my very rough count, 23 of 24 female martyrs defend their virginity (12 die). There are only six cases of male saints whose virginity is threatened (only one dies). In contrast, there are 48 temporary resurrections of men, only nine of women. Such an emphasis on the inviolability of the living female body should be placed against the background of the culture's similar emphasis on the incorruptibility of the female dead and in the context also of various miracles of miraculous body closure; see n. 32, above and n. 98, below. On the extraordinary popularity and diffusion of the *Golden Legend*, see Brenda Dunn-Lardeau, *Legenda Aurea: Sept siècles de diffusion* (Montreal and Paris: Bellarmin and J. Vrin, 1986).

82. See Chapter 3, above, n. 73.

83. See Valerie Lagorio, "Variations on the Theme of God's Motherhood in Medieval English Mystical and Devotional Writings," *Studia mystica* 8 (1985), pp. 15–37, which gives citations to earlier literature on the subject.

84. *Holy Feast*, pp. 266–67; *Jesus as Mother*, pp. 113–29.

85. Gertrud Schiller, *Ikonographie der christlichen Kunst*, vol. 4, pt. 1: *Die Kirche* (Gütersloh: Gerd Mohn, 1976), plates 217–19; and Robert Zapperi, *L'Homme enceint: L'Homme, la femme et le pouvoir*, trans. M.-A. M. Vigueur (Paris: Presses Universitaires de France, 1983), pp. 19–46.

86. For Christ bleeding into the chalice (either in the so-called "Mass of St. Gregory" or the "Eucharistic Man of Sorrows"), see Gertrud Schiller, *Iconography of Christian Art*, trans. J. Seligman, vol. 2: *The Passion of Jesus Christ* (London: Humphries, 1972), plates 707, 708, 710, 806; and Ewald M. Vetter, "Mulier amicta sole und mater salvatoris," *Münchner Jahrbuch der bildenden Kunst*, ser. 3, vols. 9, 10 (1958–1959), pp. 32–71, especially p. 51. For the so-called "Double Intercession," in which Christ's wound is made parallel to Mary's lactating breast, see Schiller, *Iconography*, vol. 2: *Passion*, plates 798, 802; Barbara G. Lane, *The Altar and the Altarpiece: Sacramental Themes in Early Netherlandish Painting* (New York: Harper & Row, 1984), pp. 7–8; and A. Monballieu, "Het Antonius Tsgrooten-triptiekje (1507) uit Tongerloo van Goosen van der Weyden," *Jaarboek van het Koninklijk Museum voor Schone Kunsten Antwerpen* (1967), pp. 13–36. I am grateful to Stephen Wight and James Marrow for help with this point and with the material in the next two notes.

87. *Holy Feast*, pp. 165–80. By the sixteenth century, artists often showed Catherine drinking from Christ's side while he lifted the open wound toward her mouth with his fingers in the same gesture *Maria lactans* usually employs to present her nipple to her baby son. See engravings by M. Florini (1597) and Pieter de Jode (1600 or 1606), after Francisco Vanni: W. Pleister, "Katharina von Siena," *Lexikon der christlichen Ikonographie*, ed. W. Braunfels, vol. 7 (Vienna: Herder, 1974), col. 305, plate 4; and "Peeter de Jode I," *Niederländisches Künstler-Lexikon*, ed. Wurzbach (Leipzig: Halm & Goldmann, 1906), vol. 1, p. 759, item 12. See also the painting of Catherine's vision by Ludovico Gimignani (1643–

1697) reproduced in Jean-Noel Vuarnet, *Extases féminines* (Paris: Artaud, 1980), and the eighteenth-century painting of the same scene by Gaetano Lapis reproduced in Giuliana Zandri, "Documenti per Santa Caterina da Siena in Via Giulia," *Commentari* 22 (1971), p. 242 fig. 2.

88. The picture reproduced in Figure 6.9 exists in at least four versions; the best (signed and dated to 1527) is in Munich. See *Le Siècle de Bruegel: La Peinture en Belgique au XVIᵉ siècle*, 2nd ed. (Brussels: Musées Royaux des Beaux-Arts de Belgique, 1963), pp. 106–07, item 115; and Max J. Friedländer, *Early Netherlandish Painting*, vol. 8: *Jan Gossart and Bernart van Orley*, trans. Heinz Norden, notes by H. Pauwels and S. Herzog (Leyden: Sijhoff, 1972), plate 29. Several other depictions of the Virgin and child by Gossaert show a similar enlarging of the child's breasts: see Friedländer, *Jan Gossart*, plate 31, number 30; plate 36, numbers 38a, b; and Larry Silver, *"Figure nude, historie e poesie*: Jan Gossaert and the Renaissance Nude in the Netherlands," *Nederlands kunsthistorisch Jaarboek* 37 (1986), pp. 25–28. One of these uses the two-fingered lifting gesture by which the Virgin calls attention to the child's nipple: Friedländer, *Jan Gossart*, plate 31, number 30. Gossaert also draws attention to the Virgin's breast, especially by having the child lean on it, stroke it or cuddle against it as he sleeps; see *ibid.*, plates 33, 36, 38; and Silver, *"Figure nude*," p. 28, plate 45. Perhaps one should not seek a Christological explanation for this iconographic emphasis, since Gossaert appears in at least one place to represent *putti* with engorged breasts; see the *putti* on the base of the columns depicted on shutters now in the Toledo Museum (Friedländer, *Jan Gossart*, plate 17). Gossaert shared the late medieval–Renaissance fascination with hermaphrodites; he drew the famous statue of the *Resting Apollo* or *Hermaphrodite* on his trip to Rome in 1508 and illustrated the story of Hermaphroditus and Salmacis: see Max J. Friedländer, *Early Netherlandish Painting: From Van Eyck to Bruegel*, trans. Marguerite Kay (New York: Phaidon, 1965), p. 96, plate 210; and Silver, *"Figure nude*," p. 17. His hermaphroditic infants may reflect this interest or may indeed simply be Mannerist efforts to shock. Critical discussion of Gossaert always emphasizes the "massive," "heavy," "carnal" quality of the bodies he depicts; his attention to the breast and especially to the engorged male breast has not been commented on.

NOTES TO PAGES 206–214

89. Pouchelle, *Corps*, pp. 157–60 [and Camporesi, *Incorruptible Flesh*]. It is a truism that medical and theological opinion were not, in the Middle Ages, fully compatible; this was especially true of opinion about sexual practice and abstinence. See Joan Cadden, "Medieval Scientific and Medical Views of Sexuality: Questions of Propriety," *Medievalia et Humanistica* n.s. 14 (1986), pp. 157–71; and Jacquart and Thomasset, *Sexualité*, p. 265ff. Nonetheless, in the ideas about gender that I discuss here, medical, theological and folk conceptions were quite often compatible and similar. See also Park, "Medicine and Society in Medieval Europe."

90. Chapter 3, above.

91. Thomas Aquinas, *Summa theologiae*, ed. Blackfriars, 61 vols. (New York: McGraw-Hill, 1964–1981), pt. 3a, q. 28, article 1, vol. 51, p. 41, and pt. 3a, q. 32, art. 4, vol. 52, p. 55. Bonaventure, *De assumptione B. Virginis Mariae*, sermon 1, sect. 2, in *S. Bonaventurae opera omnia*, ed. Collegium S. Bonaventurae, vol. 9 (Quarrachi: Collegium S. Bonaventurae, 1901), p. 690.

92. Lane, *Altar*, pp. 71–72; Carol J. Purtle, *The Marian Paintings of Jan van Eyck* (Princeton: Princeton University Press, 1982), pp. 13–15, 27–29 and *passim*; and Vetter, "Mulier amicta sole und mater salvatoris." And see Chapter 4, above, nn. 118–21.

93. See references in Chapter 3, above, nn. 49, 50; and Pouchelle, *Corps*. Galen's two-seed theory holds that both male and female contribute to the matter of the fetus; Galen is unclear, however, on what the female seed is – that is, on whether it is the menstruum or a female lubricant; see Anthony Preus, "Galen's Criticism of Aristotle's Conception Theory," *Journal of the History of Biology* 10 (1977), 65–85. The situation in the Middle Ages was further complicated by the fact that Galen was known partly in spurious texts; see Luke Demaitre and Anthony A. Travill, "Human Embryology and Development in the Works of Albertus Magnus," in Weisheipl (ed.), *Albertus Magnus and the Sciences*, pp. 414–16. The account of Galen and his influence in Allen, *Concept of Woman*, is oversimplified.

94. Pouchelle, *Corps*, p. 234 and *passim*.

95. M. Anthony Hewson, *Giles of Rome and the Medieval Theory of Concep-*

tion: A Study of the De formatione corporis humani in utero (London: Athlone Press, 1975); and Jacquart and Thomasset, *Sexualité*, pp. 87–92.

96. See Mary McLaughlin, "Survivors and Surrogates: Children and Parents from the Ninth to the Thirteenth Centuries," in L. DeMause (ed.), *The History of Childhood* (New York: The Psychohistory Press, 1974), pp. 115–18; Charles T. Wood, "The Doctors' Dilemma: Sin, Salvation and The Menstrual Cycle in Medieval Thought," *Speculum* 56 (1981), pp. 710–27, especially p. 719; and Pouchelle, *Corps*, pp. 263–66. The Aristotelian idea that blood is the basic fluid, concocted into milk, semen and so forth, is a partial departure from the earlier theory of the four humors and not fully compatible with it; see Preus, "Galen's Criticism," pp. 76–78.

97. Pouchelle, *Corps*, p. 264. Some anatomists actually held that the womb and breasts were connected by a blood vessel; see Jacquart and Thomasset, *Sexualité*, pp. 59–60, 71–72.

98. See Jacquart and Thomasset, *Sexualité*, p. 100.

99. Blood was a highly ambiguous symbol. But exactly because the culture held it to be in some ways impure, the shedding of blood, either naturally or through cauterization or leeching, was purgative. Thus, although menstrual blood was taboo, menstruation was a necessary and positive function. See Pouchelle, *Corps*, pp. 115–23; Jacquart and Thomasset, *Sexualité*, pp. 99–108; Kroll and Bachrach, "Sin and...Disease," especially p. 409; and L. Gougaud, "La Pratique de la phlébotomie dans les cloîtres," *Revue Mabillon* 53 (1924), pp. 1–13.

100. Male suspicion of women's visionary and charismatic experiences, like male distrust of the female body, was never absent. It seems to have increased in the later fourteenth, fifteenth and sixteenth centuries. See Vauchez, *La Sainteté*, pp. 439–48; Weinstein and Bell, *Saints and Society*, pp. 228–32; and Edouard Dumoutet, *Corpus Domini: Aux sources de la piété eucharistique médiévale* (Paris: Beauchesne, 1942), p. 125. The increase in witchcraft accusations in the same period is an aspect of this mistrust.

101. Francine Cardman, "The Medieval Question of Women and Orders," *The Thomist* 42 (October, 1978), pp. 582–99.

102. According to Christ and Paul, the first shall be last, the meek shall inherit the earth, and the foolishness of men is wisdom before God. See Bynum, *Jesus as Mother*, pp. 127-28, and Chapter 1, above.

103. For examples of hagiographers who praise women as "virile," see Chapter 3, above, n. 75.

104. Dronke, *Women Writers*; and Barbara Newman, *Sister of Wisdom*, pp. 34-41. See also Bynum, *Jesus as Mother*, pp. 110-69, *Holy Feast*, pp. 80, 281; and Vauchez, *La Sainteté*, p. 446, n. 511.

105. See Chapter 5, above, pp. 165-70; and Barbara Newman, *Sister of Wisdom*, *passim*, and especially pp. 250-71.

106. Thomas Laqueur, "Orgasm, Generation, and the Politics of Reproductive Biology," *Representations* 14 (Spring, 1986), pp. 1-41; Pouchelle, *Corps*, pp. 223-27, 307-10, 323-25; Jacquart and Thomasset, *Sexualité*, pp. 50-52; and Claude Thomasset, "La Représentation de la sexualité et de la génération dans la pensée scientifique médiévale," in Willy Van Hoecke and A. Welkenhuysen (eds.), *Love and Marriage in the Twelfth Century*, Mediaevalia Lovaniensia, series 1, studia 8 (Louvain: The University Press, 1981), pp. 1-17, especially pp. 7-8.

107. In discussing women's right to drink wine in the monastery, Abelard claims that women are rarely inebriated, because their bodies are humid and pierced with many holes; see Allen, *Concept of Woman*, p. 281. See also Pouchelle, *Corps*, pp. 310, 323-27, and Jacquart and Thomasset, *Sexualité*, p. 66, on the general sense in the culture that the female body is full of openings. Such assumptions are part of the background to the emphasis in saints' lives on miraculous closure; see nn. 24, 32, above; and Pouchelle, *Corps*, pp. 224-28. To religious writers, the good female body is closed and intact; the bad woman's body is open, windy and breachable. At the same time, the closed, secret and virgin body of a woman is fascinating and threatening, inviting investigation.

108. See n. 93, above.

109. There is much about this in Allen, *Concept of Woman* (although the individual accounts are not always correct). See also Jacquart and Thomasset, *Sexualité*, pp. 193-95; and Thomasset, "La Représentation."

110. See Demaitre and Travill, "Albertus Magnus," pp. 432-34; Thomasset,

"La Représentation," pp. 5-7; J. M. Thijssen, "Twins as Monsters: Albertus Magnus's Theory of the Generation of Twins and Its Philosophical Context," *Bulletin of the History of Medicine* 61 (1967), pp. 237-46; and André Pecker, *Hygiène et maladie de la femme au cours des siècles* (Paris: Dacosta, 1961), ch. 5 — a quasi-popular account which nonetheless makes the interest in hermaphrodites quite clear. Stories of bearded women were also popular at the close of the Middle Ages.

111. Zapperi, *L'Homme enceint*; and Pouchelle, *Corps*, pp. 142, 223.

112. On the increased attention to the physicality of Christ in the later Middle Ages, see Kieckhefer, *Unquiet Souls*, pp. 89-121. On the increasingly positive sense of body generally, see Alan E. Bernstein, "Political Anatomy," *University Publishing* (Winter, 1978), pp. 8-9.

113. On Hildegard, see Newman, *Sister of Wisdom*; Elisabeth Gössmann, "Das Menschenbild der Hildegard von Bingen und Elisabeth von Schönau vor dem Hintergrund der frühscholastischen Anthropologie," in Dinzelbacher and Bauer (eds.), *Frauenmystik*, pp. 24-47; and Chapter 3, above, n. 47. On Julian, see Eleanor McLaughlin, " 'Christ my Mother': Feminine Naming and Metaphor in Medieval Spirituality," *Nashota Review* 15 (1975). On Margery Kempe, see Clarissa W. Atkinson, *Mystic and Pilgrim: The Book and the World of Margery Kempe* (Ithaca, NY: Cornell University Press, 1983).

114. See nn. 4, 5, 75-81, above.

115. Allen, *Concept of Woman*. See also Maryanne Cline Horowitz, "Aristotle and Women," *Journal of the History of Biology* 9 (1976), pp. 186-213.

116. A recent nonscholarly book that argues this position is Frank Bottomley, *Attitudes Toward the Body in Western Christendom* (London: Lepus Books, 1979).

117. See Oscar Cullmann, "Immortality of the Soul or Resurrection of the Dead? The Witness of the New Testament," in Terence Penelhum (ed.), *Immortality* (Belmont, CA: Wadsworth, 1973), pp. 53-84; and Robert H. Gundry, *Soma in Biblical Theology with Emphasis on Pauline Anthropology* (Cambridge: Cambridge University Press, 1976). [And see now Paula Fredriksen, "Beyond the Body/Soul Dichotomy: Augustine on Paul against the Manichees and the

Pelagians," *Recherches augustiniennes* 23 (1988), pp. 87-114; and Chapter 7, below, n. 2].

118. Richard Heinzmann, *Die Unsterblichkeit der Seele und die Auferstehung des Leibes: Eine problemgeschichtliche Untersuchung der frühscholastischen Sentenzen- und Summenliteratur von Anselm von Laon bis Wilhelm von Auxerre*, Beiträge zur Geschichte der Philosophie und Theologie des Mittelalters: Texte und Unter-suchungen, 40.3 (Münster: Aschendorff, 1965); and Hermann J. Weber, *Die Lehre von der Auferstehung der Toten in den Haupttraktaten der scholastischen Theologie von Alexander von Hales zu Duns Skotus*, Freiburger Theologische Studien (Frei-burg: Herder, 1973). Thomas Aquinas, *Quaestiones disputatae de potentia Dei abso-luta*, q. 5. art. 10, ed. P.M. Pession, in Thomas Aquinas, *Quaestiones disputatae*, vol. 2, ed. P. Bazzi *et al.*, 8th ed. (Rome: Marietti, 1949), pp. 43-44, says explicitly that Porphyry's idea that the soul is happiest without the body, and Plato's idea that the body is a tool of the soul, are wrong; the soul is more like God when it is united to the body than when it is separated, because it is then more perfect.

119. Hewson, *Giles of Rome*, p. 56, n. 21.

120. See the works cited in n. 118, above.

121. See Chapter 7, below, n. 44.

122. A. Michel, "Résurrection des morts," DTC 13, pt. 2, cols. 2501-03. Benedict XII, in the bull *Benedictus Deus*, cited the profession of faith of Michael Paleologus at the Second Council of Lyon of 1274 which asserted that *omnes homines* appear before the tribunal of Christ in the Last Judgment *cum suis corporibus*. See n. 153, below.

123. Michel, "Résurrection des morts," cols. 2501-71. And see Aquinas, *On the Truth of the Catholic Faith: Summa contra Gentiles*, trans. Anton Pegis *et al.*, 4 vols. in 5 (New York: Image Books, 1955-1957), bk. 4, ch. 85, par. 4, vol. 4, pp. 323-24; and Wilhelm Kübel, "Die Lehre von der Auferstehung der Toten nach Albertus Magnus," *Studia Albertina: Festschrift für Bernhard Geyer zum 70. Geburtstage*, ed. H. Ostlender, Beiträge zur Geschichte der Philosophie und Theologie der Mittelalters, Supplementband 4 (Münster: Aschendorff, 1952), pp. 279-318. For the position that *all* must rise and that *body* must be rewarded

or punished for good or evil deeds, theologians regularly cited II Cor. 5.10.

124. See, for example, Moneta of Cremona, *Adversus Catharos et Valdenses Libri quinque* (Rome, 1743; reprint, Ridgewood, NJ: Gregg Press, 1964), bk. 4, chs. 8-12, pp. 346-88; and, on Moneta, Georg Schmitz-Valckenberg, *Grundlehren katharischer Sekten des 13. Jahrhunderts: Eine theologische Untersuchung mit besonderer Berücksichtigung von Adversus Catharos et Valdenses des Moneta von Cremona*, Münchener Universitäts-Schriften: Kath. Theologische Fakultät: Veröffentlichungen des Grabmann-Institutes zur Erforschung der mittelalterlichen Theologie und Philosophie, N.F. 11 (Munich: Schöningh, 1971), pp. 196-207.

125. Many of the extant sources on the Cathar position (both anti-Cathar polemic and Cathar material itself) suggest that the dualists' insistence on "spiritual body" and their denial of any resurrection of physical body was based in their abhorrence of matter – its tangibility, putrefiability, dissolvability. One has the sense that, to the Cathars (at least as they appeared to orthodox eyes), the paradigmatic body was the cadaver. See Walter L. Wakefield and Austin P. Evans (eds.), *Heresies of the High Middle Ages: Selected Sources Translated and Annotated*, Records of Civilization, 81 (New York: Columbia University Press, 1969), pp. 167, 231, 238-39, 297, 311-13, 321-23, 337, 339-42, 343-45, 353, 357, 361, 380. See also M.D. Lambert, "The Motives of the Cathars: Some Reflections...," in *Studies in Church History* 15: *Religious Motivation: Biographical and Sociological Problems for the Church Historian* (1978), pp. 49-59.

126. Wood, "Doctors' Dilemma"; and Edward D. O'Connor (ed.), *The Dogma of the Immaculate Conception: History and Significance* (Notre Dame, IN: University of Notre Dame Press, 1958).

127. Albert the Great, *De animalibus libri XXVI nach der Cölner Urschrift*, vol. 1, Beiträge zur Geschichte der Philosophie des Mittelalters: Texte und Untersuchungen, 15 (Münster: Aschendorff, 1916), bk. 9, tract. 1, ch. 2, p. 682.

128. Weber, *Auferstehung*, pp. 13-41, 235-36; Hewson, *Giles of Rome*, pp. 38-58; and Kübel, "Die Lehre...nach Albertus," especially p. 299.

129. Aquinas, *De potentia Dei*, q. 6, arts. 5-10, pp. 49-54. Aquinas argues (art. 8) that Christ willed to eat after the resurrection to show the reality of his

body; angels cannot, however, really eat and speak (i.e., move the organs and the air or divide food and send it throughout the body). The analysis makes it quite clear that the human body/soul nexus is far closer than that suggested by any model of a spirit using a material object (as the angels do). See especially article 8, reply to objection 8, where Aquinas explains why Christ's eating after the resurrection is different from the angels' eating, even though in neither case can food be changed into flesh and blood.

130. Thomas wrote, probably in the following order, four lives of women saints, all of which are characterized by somatic miracles and highly experiential piety: a supplement to James of Vitry's Life of Mary of Oignies, AASS, June, vol. 5 (1867), pp. 572–81; a Life of Christina *Mirabilis* (which contains the most remarkable somatic miracles of any thirteenth-century woman's *vita*) AASS, July, vol. 5 (1868), pp. 637–60; a Life of Margaret of Ypres (see n. 35, above); and a Life of Lutgard of Aywières (which he composed in order to obtain her finger as a relic), AASS, June, vol. 4, pp. 187–210. He also composed a *vita* of John, first abbot of Cantimpré. His *Bonum universale de apibus*, ed. Georges Colvener (Douai, 1627), is a collection of miracle stories, many of which display a concern for body. On this, see Henri Platelle, "Le Recueil des miracles de Thomas de Cantimpré et la vie religieuse dans les Pays-Bas et le nord de la France au XIIIe siècle," in *Assistance et Assistés jusqu'à 1610*, Actes du 97e Congrès National des Sociétés Savantes, Nantes, 1972 (Paris: Bibliothèque Nationale, 1979), pp. 469–98; and Alexander Murray, "Confession as a Historical Source in the Thirteenth Century," in *The Writing of History in the Middle Ages: Essays Presented to Richard William Southern* (Oxford: Clarendon Press, 1981), pp. 275–322, especially pp. 286–305.

131. *Die Gynäkologie des Thomas von Brabant: Ein Beitrag zur Kenntnis der mittelalterlichen Gynäkologie und ihrer Quellen*, ed. C. Ferckel (Munich: Carl Kuhn, 1912), an edition of part of book 1 of Thomas of Cantimpré's *De naturis rerum*; there is a new edition by Helmut Boese, *Liber de natura rerum: Editio princeps secundum codices manuscriptos*, vol. 1: *Text* (New York and Berlin: De Gruyter, 1973). On Thomas's encyclopedia, see Pierre Michaud-Quantin, "Les Petites encyclopédies du XIIIe siècle," *Cahiers d'histoire mondiale* 9.2: *Encyclopédies et*

civilisations (1966), pp. 580-95; G.J.J. Walstra "Thomas de Cantimpré, *De naturis rerum*: Etat de la question," *Vivarium* 5 (1967), pp. 146-71, and 6 (1968), pp. 46-61; and Helmut Bocsc, "Zur Textüberlieferung von Thomas Cantimpratensis' Liber de natura rerum," *Archivum fratrum praedicatorum* 39 (1969), pp. 53-68.

132. See Katharine Park and Eckhart Kessler, "The Concept of Psychology," and K. Park, "The Organic Soul," in Charles B. Schmitt (ed.), *The Cambridge History of Renaissance Philosophy* (Cambridge: Cambridge University Press, 1987) chs. 13, 14; and E. Ruth Harvey, *The Inward Wits: Psychological Theory in the Middle Ages and the Renaissance*, Warburg Institute Surveys, 6 (London: Warburg Institute, 1975).

133. See Preus, "Galen's Criticism." See also Michael Boylan, "The Galenic and Hippocratic Challenges to Aristotle's Conception Theory," *Journal of the History of Biology* 17 (1984), pp. 83-112.

134. See Hewson, *Giles of Rome.*

135. See the works cited in n. 118, above, and Michel, "Résurrection des morts."

136. Aquinas, Commentary on I Cor. 15, lect. 2, quoted in Emile Mersch and Robert Brunet, "Corps mystique et spiritualité," *Dictionnaire de spiritualité, ascétique et mystique: doctrine et histoire*, vol. 2, pt. 2 (Paris: Beauchesne, 1953), col. 2352.

137. In general, see Heinzmann, *Unsterblichkeit*, pt. 2 *passim*; and Weber, *Auferstehung*, *passim*, especially pp. 125-57, 217-54. On the question of the necessity of material continuity for numerical continuity, answers ranged from William of Auxerre (in the early thirteenth century), who argued that the ashes of Paul must rise as the body of Paul (Heinzmann, *Unsterblichkeit*, p. 243, n. 11), to Durandus (in the early fourteenth century) who held that God can make the body of Peter out of dust that was once the body of Paul (Weber, *Auferstehung*, p. 228ff., especially p. 241, n. 400).

138. [I have discussed this in much greater detail in Chapter 7, below.]

139. Because of this telescoping of body into soul, some recent interpreters have debated how important body is to Thomas. See Chapter 7, below, n. 48. Nonetheless, Aquinas did argue that, without body, the soul in heaven before

the end of time would in a certain sense lack memory and other passions; see *Summa contra Gentiles*, bk. 2, ch. 81, pars. 12, 14, 15, vol. 2, pp. 264-66.

140. *Summa contra Gentiles*, bk. 4, ch. 81, par. 7, vol. 4, p. 303: "Corporeity, however, can be taken in two ways. In one way, it can be taken as the substantial form of a body.... Therefore, corporeity, as the substantial form in man, cannot be other than the rational soul...." See Bernardo C. Bazan, "La Corporalité selon saint Thomas," *Revue philosophique de Louvain* 81, 4th series 49 (1983), pp. 369-409, especially pp. 407-08. Bazan says that, according to Thomas, "Notre corporalité est toute penetrée de spiritualité, car sa source est l'âme rationnelle."

141. Bonaventure, *De assumptione B. Virginis Mariae*, sermon 1, sect. 2, p. 690; fuller citation in Chapter 7, below, at n. 55. See also Aquinas, *Summa contra Gentiles*, bk. 4, ch. 79, par. 11, vol. 4, p. 299; and the passage from *De potentia Dei* cited in n. 118, above.

142. See Chapter 7, below, n. 52.

143. See Chapter 7, below, nn. 56, 57.

144. Weber, *Auferstehung*, p. 304, n. 197, and see *ibid.*, pp. 266, 135-36.

145. Weber, *Auferstehung*, pp. 255-63. Thomas held that risen bodies will not eat but will have the capacity for touch; see Chapter 7, below, n. 16. [On the senses in heaven, see now Camporesi, *Incorruptible Flesh*, pp. 243-57.]

146. Nikolaus Wicki, *Die Lehre von der himmlischen Seligkeit in der mittelalterlichen Scholastik von Petrus Lombardus bis Thomas von Aquinas*, Studia Friburgensia N.F. 9 (Freiburg: Universitätsverlag, 1954); Joseph Goering, "The *De Dotibus* of Robert Grosseteste," *Mediaeval Studies* 44 (1982), pp. 83-109; and Weber, *Auferstehung*, pp. 314-42.

147. See, for example, Hugh of St. Victor, *De sacramentis*, bk. 2, pt. 18, ch. 18, PL 176 (1854), col. 616A; Peter Lombard, *Sententiae in IV libris distinctae*, vol. 2, 3rd ed., Spicilegium Bonaventurianum, 5 (Grottaferrata: Collegium Bonaventurae ad Claras Aquas, 1981), bk. 4, distinctio 44, pp. 510-22; and Aquinas, *Summa contra Gentiles*, bk. 4, ch. 90, par. 9, vol. 4, p. 334.

148. See, for example, *Summa contra Gentiles*, bk. 4, ch. 88, vol. 4, pp. 328-30, and *Summa theologiae*, pt. 3a, q. 54, art. 4, vol. 55, pp. 30-35. See also Sup-

plement to *Summa theologiae*, pt. 3, q. 96, art. 10, on whether the scars of the martyrs are an *aureole*; *Supplementum*, compiled and edited by the Brothers of the Order, in *Sancti Thomae Aquinatis Opera omnia*, vol. 12 (Rome: S.C. de Propaganda Fide, 1906), p. 238. In general, thirteenth-century theologians drew on Augustine's *City of God*, bk. 22, ch. 17 ("vitia detrahentur, natura servabitur") on this matter; see Weber, *Auferstehung*, p. 79, n. 194.

149. Allen, *Concept of Woman*; and Weber, *Auferstehung*, pp. 256-59. Weber quotes Augustinus Triumphus, writing on the resurrection, to the effect that, if persons were to rise in the opposite sex, they would not be the same persons. "Non omnes resurgentes eundem sexum habebunt, nam masculinus sexus et femininus, quamvis non sint differentiae formales facientes differentiam in specie, sunt tamen differentiae materiales facientes differentiam in numero. Et quia in resurrectione quilibet resurget non solum quantum ad id quod est de identitate specifica, secundum habet esse in specie humana, verum etiam resurget quantum ad id, quod est de identitate numerali, secundum quam habet esse in tali individuo. Ideo oportet unumquodque cum sexu proprio et cum aliis pertinentibus ad integritatem suae individualis naturae resurgere, propter quod femina resurget cum sexu femineo et homo cum masculino, remota omni libidine et omni vitiositate naturae." Moneta of Cremona, writing against the Cathars, argued that God created sex difference; see Moneta, *Adversus Catharos*, bk. 1, ch. 2, sect. 4, and bk. 4, ch. 7, sect. 1, pp. 121, 315.

150. The resurrected bodies of the damned will be incapable of corruption (i.e., of dissolution or of loss of their matter), but not incapable of suffering. See n. 153, below.

151. Theologians were aware that some of the particular issues they raised in debates over eschatology had implications for the cult of relics – particularly the issue of whether the cadaver of John is still the body of John and whether its specific matter must rise in John at the Last Judgment. See Weber, *Auferstehung*, pp. 76-78, 150-153, 239; and n. 137, above.

152. *Summa theologiae*, pt. 3a, q. 14, arts. 1-4, vol. 49, pp. 170-87, especially p. 174.

153. Indeed, scholastic theologians held that the damned also receive their

NOTES TO PAGES 231-234

bodies *whole* after the resurrection, because only the permanence (i.e., the perfect balance or wholeness) of these bodies insures that their punishment will be permanent and perpetual; see Kübel, "Die Lehre...nach Albertus," pp. 316-17.

154. After fierce debate, the issue was finally settled by Benedict XII in the bull *Benedictus Deus* of January 29, 1336; see Henry Denzinger, *Enchiridion symbolorum: Definitionum et declarationum de rebus fidei et morum*, 31st ed., ed. C. Rahner (Freiburg: Herder, 1957), pp. 229-30. For a brief overview, see M.J. Redle, "Beatific Vision," *New Catholic Encyclopedia* (Washington, DC: Catholic University of America, 1967), vol. 2, pp. 186-93.

155. A. Challet, "Corps glorieux," DTC 3, cols. 1879-1906.

156. See, for example, the cases of Jane Mary of Maillé and Columba of Rieti in *Holy Feast*, pp. 131-34, 148.

157. *Summa theologiae*, pt. 3a, q. 15, art. 5, obj. 3 and reply to obj. 3, vol. 49, pp. 204-07, and see also 3a, q. 14, art. 1, obj. 2 and reply to obj. 2, pp. 170-75. Bernard of Clairvaux expresses the same opinion in *De diligendo Deo*, sect. 10, par. 29, *Tractatus et opuscula*, p. 144.

158. [See Chapter 7, below; and Caroline W. Bynum, "Bodily Miracles and the Resurrection of the Body in the High Middle Ages," in Thomas Kselman (ed.), *Belief in History* (Notre Dame, IN: University of Notre Dame Press, forthcoming, 1990), especially nn. 68-73, 76-85. The picture of Agatha reproduced here can (and *should*) also be read as representing the sadism frequent in late medieval depictions of the female nude; see Gill Saunders, *The Nude: A New Perspective* (London: Herbert Press, 1989), p. 15.]

159. Caesarius, *Dialogus*, bk. 12, ch. 47, vol. 2, p. 354.

160. *Ibid.*, ch. 50, pp. 355-56; see also *ibid.*, ch. 54, p. 358. For the importance of marks of healing visible on the body, see Judith-Danielle Jacquet, "Le Miracle de la jambe noire," in *Les Miracles miroirs des corps*, pp. 23-52.

161. See n. 32, above. A related issue is the incorruptibility of the bodies of great sinners; see Chapter 7, below, n. 120.

162. *Summa theologiae*, pt. 3a, q. 15, art. 4, vol. 49, p. 202 (my translation).

163. Doctors showed their own awareness of such psychosomatic unity. For example, Henri de Mondeville, skeptical about miraculous cures, explained

their apparent success thus: "If the human spirit believes that a thing is useful (which in itself is of no help), it may happen that by the imagination alone this thing aids the body." See Pouchelle, *Corps*, p. 107. Mondeville shows by many examples how "in acting on the soul one acts on the body" (*ibid.*, p. 108).

164. Henri Platelle, "La Voix du sang: Le Cadavre qui saigne en présence de son meutrier," *La Piété populaire au Moyen Age*, Actes du 99e Congrès National des Sociétés Savantes, Besançon, 1974 (Paris: Bibliothèque Nationale, 1977), pp. 161–79; Finucane, *Miracles and Pilgrims*, pp. 73–75; Bouvier, "De l'incorruptibilité"; Philippe Ariès, *The Hour of Our Death*, trans. Helen Weaver (New York: Knopf, 1981), pp. 261–68, 353ff.; and Jacques Gélis, "De la mort à la vie: Les 'Sanctuaires à reprit,' " *Ethnologie française* II (1981), pp. 211–24.

165. Life of Christina *Mirabilis*, ch. 5, number 36, pars. 47–48, AASS, July, vol. 5, p. 658–59; trans. Margot H. King, *The Life of Christina Mirabilis*, Matrologia latina, 2 (Saskatoon: Peregrina, 1986), pp. 27–28. This little dialogue was supposedly witnessed by Thomas, abbot of St. Trond; see ch. 5, number 36, par. 47, p. 658. See also Petroff, *Women's Visionary Literature*, p. 36; and Ackerman, "*Debate of the Body and Soul* and Parochial Christianity."

166. For the text, see Karl Brunner, "Mittelenglische Todesgedichte," *Archiv für das Studium der neueren Sprachen* 167, N.F. 67 (1935), pp. 30–35. See also Marjorie M. Malvern, "An Earnest 'Monyscyon' and 'thinge Delectabyll' Realized Verbally and Visually in 'A Disputacion Betwyx the Body and Wormes,' A Middle English Poem Inspired by Tomb Art and Northern Spirituality," *Viator* 13 (1982), pp. 415–43.

167. See Malvern, " 'Monyscyon'," pp. 427, 432ff.

168. Stanzas 24, 28, 29 in Brunner, "Mittelenglische Todesgedichte," p. 34.

VII. *Material Continuity, Personal Survival and Resurrection*

1. I have considered some of this material from another point of view in "Bodily Miracles and the Resurrection of the Body in the High Middle Ages," in Thomas Kselman (ed.), *Belief in History* (South Bend, IN: University of Notre Dame Press, forthcoming, 1990). I am grateful to Steven P. Marrone, Guenther Roth, Robert Somerville and Stephen D. White for their helpful readings of

earlier drafts; to Elizabeth A.R. Brown for sharing her unpublished work; and to Arthur Danto, Hester Gelber and Isaac Levi for several very illuminating remarks dropped in the course of conversation. This article is dedicated to Donald J. Wilcox, whose ideas about the resurrection of the body have influenced my research profoundly and whose friendship has sustained me intellectually over the years since we were graduate students together.

2. See Gisbert Greshake and Jacob Kremer, *Resurrectio mortuorum: Zum theologischen Verständnis der leiblichen Auferstehung* (Darmstadt: Wissenschaftliche Buchgesellschaft, 1986); A. Michel, "Résurrection des morts," in *Dictionnaire de théologie catholique*, ed. A. Vacant *et al.* (Paris: Letouzey et Ane, 1909-1950) [hereafter DTC], vol. 13, pt. 2, cols. 2501-571; H. Cornélis, J. Guillet, Th. Camelot and M.A. Genevois, *The Resurrection of the Body*, Themes of Theology (Notre Dame: Fides, 1964); Ton H.C. Van Eijk, *La Résurrection des morts chez les Pères Apostoliques* (Paris: Beauchesne, 1974); R.M. Grant, "The Resurrection of the Body," *Journal of Religion* 28 (1948), pp. 120-30, 188-208; Henry Chadwick, "Origen, Celsus, and the Resurrection of the Body," *The Harvard Theological Review* 41 (1948), pp. 83-102; Joanne E. McWilliam Dewart, *Death and Resurrection*, Message of the Fathers of the Church, 22 (Wilmington, DE: Michael Glazier, 1986); and Gedaliahu G. Stroumsa, "Emergence of the Reflexive Self in Early Christian Thought," *History of Religions* (forthcoming, 1990).

3. Henry Denzinger, *Enchiridion symbolorum definitionum et declarationum de rebus fidei et morum*, 11th ed., ed. C. Bannwart (Freiburg: Herder, 1911), pp. 189, 202-03.

4. *Chartularium universitatis Parisiensis...*, ed. H. Denifle and A. Chatelain, vol. 1 (Paris: Delalain, 1889), p. 544, and see nn. 72-74, below.

5. For this interpretation of heresy for the medieval period see R.I. Moore, *The Formation of a Persecuting Society: Power and Deviance in Western Europe, 950-1250* (New York: Blackwell, 1987). And see Chapter 6, nn. 124, 125, above.

6. On Robert, see Richard Heinzmann, *Die Unsterblichkeit der Seele und die Auferstehung des Leibes: Eine problemgeschichtliche Untersuchung der frühscholastischen Sentenzen- und Summenliteratur von Anselm von Laon bis Wilhelm von Auxerre*, Beiträge zur Geschichte der Philosophie und Theologie des Mittel-

alters: Texte und Untersuchungen, 40.3 (Münster: Aschendorff, 1965), p. 163ff. Honorius Augustodunensis, *Elucidarium*, in J.-P. Migne (ed.), *Patrologiae cursus completus: series latina* (Paris, 1841-1864) [hereafter PL], vol. 172, cols. 1109-76, begins with an extremely materialist and literal consideration of last things, only to conclude his treatise by spiritualizing them to an astonishing extent.

7. Jacques Le Goff, *La Naissance du purgatoire*, Bibliothèque des histoires (Paris: Gallimard, 1981) [*The Birth of Purgatory*, trans. Arthur Goldhammer (Chicago: University of Chicago Press, 1984)]. For a brief overview of the controversy concerning the beatific vision, see M.J. Redle, "Beatific Vision," *New Catholic Encyclopedia* (Washington, DC: Catholic University of America, 1967) vol. 2, pp. 186-93.

8. Kieran Nolan, *The Immortality of the Soul and the Resurrection of the Body According to Giles of Rome: A Historical Study of a Thirteenth Century Theological Problem*, Studia Ephemeridis 'Augustinianum,' 1 (Rome: Studium Theologicum Augustinianum, 1967), pp. 69-75, 90-96, 105-13, 124-30, edits Giles's *Quaestiones* on the resurrection; see n. 69, below. Albert's *De resurrectione* is edited by W. Kübel, in Albert, *Opera omnia*, ed. Institutum Alberti Magni Coloniense, vol. 26 (Münster: Aschendorff, 1958).

9. See the indices to Palémon Glorieux's great study of quodlibetal literature: *La Littérature quodlibétique de 1260 à 1320*, Bibliothèque Thomiste, 5 and 21 (Le Saulchoir: Kain, 1925; and Paris: J. Vrin, 1935).

10. Peter Lombard, *Sententiae in IV libris distinctae*, ed. Collegium S. Bonaventurae, Spicilegium Bonaventurianum, 4 and 5, 2 vols. (Grottaferrata: Collegium S. Bonaventurae ad Claras Aquas, 1971 and 1981) [hereafter Lombard, *Sentences*], bk. 4, dist. 43-50, vol. 2, pp. 510-60. Peter's treatment is quite ad hoc and disorganized; even the summary I give here imposes on it a coherence it does not have.

11. Hugh of St. Victor, *De sacramentis*, bk. 2, pt. 18, c. 18, PL 176, col. 616.

12. Honorius Augustodunensis, *Elucidarium*, PL 172, cols. 1164-65, 1169; and Herrad of Hohenbourg, *Hortus deliciarum*, chs. 850-52, 855, 887, 1090; see *Hortus deliciarum: Reconstruction*, ed. Rosalie Green *et al.* (London and Leiden: Warburg Institute/University of London and Brill, 1979), pp. 423-35, 447, 481.

See also the texts edited and discussed in Odon Lottin, *Psychologie et morale aux XII*e *et XIII*e *siècles*, vol. 5: *Problèmes d'histoire littéraire: L'Ecole d'Anselme de Laon et de Guillaume de Champeaux* (Gembloux: J. Duculot, 1959), pp. 321, 374.

13. Guibert, *De pignoribus*, PL 156 (Paris, 1853), especially bk. 1, cols. 611-30. On Guibert's treatise, see Bynum, "Bodily Miracles and Resurrection."

14. See Heinzmann, *Die Unsterblichkeit der Seele*, pp. 148-55; Lottin, *Psychologie*, vol. 5, pp. 35, 265-66, 320-21, 393-96, and vol. 4, pt. 1, pp. 55; and Nolan, *Giles of Rome*, pp. 116-23.

15. Hermann J. Weber, *Die Lehre von der Auferstehung der Toten in den Haupttraktaten der scholastischen Theologie von Alexander von Hales zu Duns Skotus* (Freiburg: Herder, 1973), pp. 331-32.

16. Thomas Aquinas held that risen bodies will have the capacity for touch; see *Summa contra Gentiles*, bk. 4, ch. 84, in *Sancti Thomae Aquinatis Opera Omnia...*, vols. 13-15 (Rome: Apud Sedem Commissionis Leoninae, 1918-1930), vol. 15, pp. 268-69. Risen bodies will not, however, eat: see *Summa contra Gentiles*, bk. 4, ch. 83, vol. 15, pp. 262-66. In *Quaestiones disputatae de potentia*, q. 6, art. 8, in *Thomae Aquinatis...Opera omnia*, ed. S.E. Frette, vol. 13 (Paris: Vives, 1875), p. 205, Aquinas argues that Christ willed to eat after the resurrection in order to show the reality of his body; see also Aquinas, *Summa theologiae*, ed. Blackfriars, 61 vols. (New York: McGraw-Hill, 1964-1981) 3a, q. 55, art. 6, vol. 55, pp. 56-65, and Chapter 6, above, n. 129. Albert the Great (*De resurrectione*, tract. 2, q. 8, art. 5, p. 278) argues that, in order to demonstrate his resurrected body, the resurrected Christ ate without the food becoming of his substance; we too could eat that way in the glorified body but have no need to, since we need not demonstrate the resurrection. Weber, *Auferstehung*, pp. 259-60, shows how thirteenth-century theologians vacillated in their treatments of whether there is tasting in heaven. Basic principles conflicted: on the one hand, vegetative functions were seen as eliminated in heaven; on the other hand, as Albert said, "Nulla potestate nobili destituentur."

17. Michael Allyn Taylor, "Human Generation in the Thought of Thomas Aquinas: A Case Study on the Role of Biological Fact in Theological Science," Ph.D. Dissertation, Catholic University of America, 1982; on thirteenth-cen-

tury discussions of the cannibalism problem, see also Nolan, *Giles of Rome*, pp. 114-23.

18. A good deal of modern scholarship on the resurrection question has been deeply influenced by the work of the Swiss theologian, Oscar Cullmann, who argued that immortality (a Greek concept) and resurrection (a Judeo-Christian concept) are fundamentally incompatible in the history of Christian thought; see Cullmann, *Christ and Time: The Primitive Christian Conception of Time and History*, trans. F. Filson, 3rd ed. (London: SCM, 1962), "Immortality and Resurrection," in Krister Stendahl (ed.), *Immortality and Resurrection* (New York: Macmillan, 1965), pp. 9-53, and "Immortality of the Soul or Resurrection of the Dead? The Witness of the New Testament," in Terence Penelhum (ed.), *Immortality* (Belmont, CA: Wadsworth, 1973), pp. 53-84. For discussions of medieval thought influenced by Cullmann, see Heinzmann, *Die Unsterblichkeit der Seele*; Weber, *Auferstehung*; and Greshake and Kremer, *Resurrectio mortuorum*. I have chosen to ignore Cullmann's concerns, which are not relevant to the issues I raise in this paper.

19. For example, Herbert Thurston, *The Physical Phenomena of Mysticism* (Chicago: Henry Regnery, 1952); and Piero Camporesi, *The Incorruptible Flesh: Bodily Mutation and Mortification in Religion and Folklore*, trans. T. Croft-Murray and H. Elsom (Cambridge: Cambridge University Press, 1988).

20. Occasionally, also, scholars have defended the doctrine of resurrection by insisting that it involved a positive assessment of the body and even of sexuality; see Frank Bottomley, *Attitudes Toward the Body in Western Christendom* (London: Lepus Books, 1979). See also Prudence Allen, *The Concept of Woman: The Aristotelian Revolution 750 B.C.–A.D. 1250* (Montreal and London: Eden Press, 1985), which views the rise of Aristotle as a victory for sexism but argues that medieval teaching on the resurrection of the body, with its assertion that human beings will rise in two sexes, undercuts the negative Aristotelian position.

21. For disapproving assessments of the medieval interest and the suggestion that modern scholars should turn their attention not to the offensive examples but to the fundamental issues behind them, see H.M. McElwain, "Resurrection of the Dead, theology of," *New Catholic Encyclopedia*, (New York: McGraw-

Hill, 1967) vol. 12, p. 425; and J.A. MacCulloch, "Eschatology," in *Encyclopedia of Religion and Ethics*, ed. J. Hastings, (New York: Scribner's, 1914), vol. 5, pp. 386, 391.

22. For teletransportation, see Robert Nozick, *Philosophical Explanations* (Cambridge, MA: Harvard University Press, 1981), pp. 29–70, especially pp. 41–42, 58–59; Derek Parfit, *Reasons and Persons* (Oxford: Clarendon Press, 1984), pp. 199–347, especially pp. 199–204, 241–42; and Thomas Nagel, *The View From Nowhere* (New York: Oxford University Press, 1986), pp. 28–53, especially pp. 42–44. For brain transplants, see Sydney Shoemaker, *Self-Knowledge and Self-Identity* (Ithaca, NY: Cornell University Press, 1963), p. 23ff.; Bernard Williams, *Problems of the Self: Philosophical Papers 1956–1972* (Cambridge: Cambridge University Press, 1973), pp. 46–63; George Rey, "Survival," in *The Identities of Persons*, ed. Amelie O. Rorty (Berkeley: University of California Press, 1976), pp. 41–66; and John Perry, "The Importance of Being Identical," in *ibid.*, pp. 67–89. The works by Nagel, Parfit and Nozick just cited as well as the essay by Perry cited in the note below also use brain transplant examples.

23. John Perry, *A Dialogue on Personal Identity and Immortality* (Indianapolis: Hackett, 1978).

24. Nozick, *Philosophical Explanations*, pp. 58–59.

25. J.L. Austin, *Sense and Sensibilia* (New York: Oxford University Press, 1962), p. 3, quoted in Nancy Struever, "Philosophical Problems and Historical Solutions," in B. Danenhauer (ed.), *At the Nexus of Philosophy and History* (Athens, GA: University of Georgia Press, 1987), p. 76. Parfit, *Reasons and Persons*, p. 200, points out that Wittgenstein and Quine have similar doubts about whether we learn anything from these science fiction stories. (Parfit rejoins that what is important is the fact that we have reactions to them; therefore they help us think about what we think we are.)

26. Struever, "Philosophical Problems," p. 76.

27. Although I wish to argue that this is true for medieval examples as well, I should point out here that the classic examples in medieval philosophical discussion had, in some cases, a long history. The example of the statue, melted and reforged, came into medieval discussion via Peter Lombard from Augustine's

City of God and came to Augustine, of course, from the common fund of Greek philosophy. Tracing how the example is used, however, tells us, as we shall see in n. 61, below, precisely how identity theory changes and fails to change in the late thirteenth century.

28. Richard Swinburne, *The Evolution of the Soul* (Oxford: Clarendon Press, 1986), pp. 7-10, 298-312. See also Sydney Shoemaker and Richard Swinburne, *Personal Identity* (Oxford: Blackwell, 1984).

29. H.H. Price, "Survival and the Idea of 'Another World' " and "Mediumship and Human Survival" (originally published 1953), used in Penelhum (ed.), *Immortality*, pp. 21-52, 103-18. The same articles are used in Peter A. French (ed.), *Philosophers in Wonderland: Philosophy and Psychical Research* (St. Paul, MN: Llewellyn, 1975), pp. 297-308; and see French's prefatory note in *ibid.*, pp. 289-96.

30. For explanations of Locke's argument see Swinburne, "The Dualist Theory," in Shoemaker and Swinburne (eds.), *Personal Identity*, pp. 8-10; or Perry, *Dialogue*, pp. 314-20, 325.

31. For readable summaries of recent debate that suggest the prominence of these two theories, see Perry, *Dialogue*; Penelhum (ed.), *Immortality*, introduction; or Rorty, *Identities*, introduction.

32. See Perry, *Dialogue*, p. 325.

33. See the works by Parfit and Nozick cited in n. 22, above. Charles Coburn, "Personal Identity Revisited," *Canadian Journal of Philosophy* 15.3 (1985), pp. 379-403, disagrees with Nozick's "closest continuer" theory by arguing that the notion of personal identity is simply unanalyzable; identity cannot be reduced to some element of continuity. Even Coburn, however, spends a great deal of time discussing brain transplant operations, which appear to him the best argument against his position. It is also worth noting that Swinburne, who argues for soul, devotes much attention to brain transplant cases; see *Evolution of Soul*, pp. 299-301.

34. *The Man Who Mistook His Wife for a Hat and Other Clinical Tales* (New York: Summit Books, 1985). See also Oliver Sacks, "Tics," *New York Review of Books*, January 29, 1987, pp. 37-41; and Jonathan Glover, "Am I My Brain?" *New*

York Review of Books, April 9, 1987, pp. 31-34, a review of Nagel's *View from Nowhere* that makes issues of bodily continuity even more central in Nagel's discussion than I think Nagel does. A recent work in psychology that stresses, in revolutionary ways, the "embodied-ness" of knowing is George Lakoff, *Women, Fire and Dangerous Things: What Categories Reveal about the Mind* (Chicago: University of Chicago Press, 1987).

35. Nancy Weber, *Broken-Hearted* (New York: Dutton, 1989); and see nn. 37-40, below.

36. The September 25, 1987 episode of *Max Headroom*, "Deities," in which Christian ideas about resurrection of the body are parodied through depiction of a group like the Los Angeles cryonics sect, is a particularly good example. I am indebted to Stephen Wight and Antonia Walker for advice about contemporary movies.

37. Renée C. Fox and Judith P. Swazey, *The Courage to Fail: A Social View of Organ Transplants and Dialysis*, 2nd ed. (Chicago: University of Chicago Press, 1974), pp. 27-32; and Renée C. Fox, "Organ Transplantation: Sociocultural Aspects," *Encyclopedia of Bioethics*, ed. W. T. Reich (New York: Free Press, 1978), pp. 1166-69.

38. Fox and Swazey, *Courage to Fail*, p. 32.

39. W.A. Crammond, "Renal Homotransplantation: Some Observations on Recipients and Donors," *British Journal of Psychiatry* 113 (1967), p. 1226; quoted in Fox and Swazey, *Courage to Fail*, p. 27.

40. Louis Sahagun and T.W. McGarry, "Investigators Seek Severed Head at Cryonics Center," *L.A. Times*, Saturday, January 9, 1988, pt. 1, p. 35.

41. I am indebted to Paula Fredriksen for this reference.

42. Barbara Harris, *Who Is Julia?* (New York: D. McKay, 1972). A recent novel that plays with such questions is Lawrence Shainberg, *Memories of Amnesia* (New York: Paris Review Editions/British American Publishing, 1988). Sydney Shoemaker in Shoemaker and Swinburne, *Personal Identity*, p. 69, also calls attention to the relevance of examples from popular fiction.

43. See Rey, "Survival," pp. 41-46.

44. Heinzmann, *Die Unsterblichkeit der Seele*, p. 208; and Weber, *Auferste-*

hung, pp. 80–106. Simon of Tournai, William of Auxerre, Aquinas, Bonaventure and Giles of Rome all held that the resurrection of the body was both natural and supernatural; see Nolan, *Giles of Rome*, pp. 96–104, 140.

45. Etienne Gilson, *History of Christian Philosophy in the Middle Ages* (New York: Random House, 1955); and Frederick Copleston, *A History of Philosophy*, vol. 2, pts. 1, 2: *Medieval Philosophy* (Westminster, MD: Newman Press, 1950). Even those intellectual historians who have disagreed with Gilson have done so on other grounds than the one I raise here; see Fernand van Steenbergen, *Aristotle in the West: The Origins of Latin Aristotelianism*, trans. L. Johnston (Louvain: Nauwelaerts, 1955); and M.-D. Chenu, *La Théologie au douzième siècle*, Etudes de philosophie médiévale, 45 (Paris: J. Vrin, 1957). The basic Catholic position has been to see a growing awareness of and positive appreciation of "nature" and "the natural" in the twelfth century, which prepared for the reception of Aristotle in the thirteenth.

46. The burden of Heinzmann's *Die Unsterblichkeit der Seele* is to show the emergence in the twelfth century with Gilbert de la Porrée of a more Aristotelian conception of person over against Platonic definitions of man as soul found, for example, in Hugh of St. Victor. This argument is, however, to some extent misleading. Although technical definitions may have shifted from Platonic to Aristotelian, thinkers such as Hugh and Bernard of Clairvaux actually treated the human being as an entity composed of body and soul (see n. 50, below, and Weber, *Auferstehung*, p. 123ff.). So indeed did the Fathers. Among patristic treatises on the resurrection, I find only Ambrose's *De excessu fratris sui Satyri*, bk. 2, ch. 20, PL 16 (Paris, 1880), cols. 1377–78, adhering to a strictly Platonic definition. For recent revisionist opinion about Augustine's anthropology, see Peter Brown, *The Body and Society: Men, Women and Sexual Renunciation in Early Christianity* (New York: Columbia University Press, 1988); Joyce Salisbury, "The Latin Doctors of the Church on Sexuality," *Journal of Medieval History* 12 (1986), pp. 279–89; Paula Fredriksen, "Beyond the Body/Soul Dichotomy: Augustine on Paul against the Manichees and the Pelagians," *Recherches augustiniennes* 23 (1988), pp. 87–114; and G. Stroumsa, "Reflexive Self."

47. Aquinas, *In epistolam I ad Corinthios commentaria*, ch. 15, lect. 2, in

Opera omnia, ed. Frette, vol. 21 (1876), pp. 33-34: "...si negetur resurrectio corporis, non de facili, imo difficile est sustinere immortalitatem animae. Constat enim quod anima naturaliter unitur corpori.... Unde anima exuta corpore, quamdiu est sine corpore, est imperfecta. Impossibile autem est quod illud quod est naturale et per se, sit finitum et quasi nihil, et illud quod est contra naturam et per accidens, sit infinitum, si anima semper duret sine corpore.... Et ideo si mortui non resurgunt, solum in hac vita confidentes erimus. Alio modo, quia constat quod homo naturaliter desiderat salutem suiipsius; anima autem, cum sit pars corporis homini, non est totus homo, et anima mea non est ego; unde, licet anima consequatur salutem in alia vita, non tamen ego vel quilibet homo." See Emile Mersch and Robert Brunet, "Corps mystique et spiritualité," *Dictionnaire de spiritualité, ascétique et mystique, doctrine et histoire*, ed. M. Viller *et al.* (Paris: Beauchesne, 1932–   ), vol. 2, col. 2352; and A. Michel, "Résurrection des morts," DTC 13, pt. 2, cols. 2501-71. For a modern position on the survival issue that agrees with Aquinas, see Peter Geach, "Immortality," in Penelhum (ed.), *Immortality*, p. 11ff.

48. They include Norbert Luyten, "The Significance of the Body in a Thomistic Anthropology," *Philosophy Today* 7 (1963), pp. 175-93; Bernardo C. Bazan, "La Corporalité selon saint Thomas," *Revue philosophique de Louvain* 81, 4 ser. 49 (1983), pp. 369-409; J. Giles Milhaven, "Physical Experience: Contrasting Appraisals by Male Theologians and Women Mystics in the Middle Ages," paper given at the Holy Cross Symposium "The Word Becomes Flesh," November 9, 1985; and Swinburne, *Evolution of the Soul*, pp. 299-306, especially n. 9.

49. See Weber, *Auferstehung*, pp. 228-29. According to most interpreters, Aquinas does not go all the way toward seeing matter as potency. In his early writing, he holds that individuated matter in some sense subsists after the soul and body are separated. It is not that this matter is individuated by determined dimensions; rather, it retains in flux a certain relation (undetermined dimensions) to the individuality it had when it was formed by the human soul. See Michel, "Résurrection," in DTC, cols. 2557-58; and Weber, *Auferstehung*, pp. 220-21. However one understands this teaching, it further supports the

impression that Aquinas is not willing to abandon material continuity entirely as an element in identity.

50. *Summa contra Gentiles*, bk. 4, ch. 81, vol. 15, pp. 252-53; Bazan, "La Corporalité selon saint Thomas," pp. 407-08; and see Chapter 6, above, n. 140.

51. A perceptive exception to the ignoring of positive conceptions of the body among twelfth-century thinkers is John Sommerfeldt, "The Body in Bernard of Clairvaux's Anthropology," paper delivered at the International Conference on Medieval Studies, Kalamazoo, Michigan, May, 1988.

52. Quoted in Gerhart B. Ladner, "Terms and Ideas of Renewal," in Robert L. Benson and Giles Constable (eds.), *Renaissance and Renewal in the Twelfth Century* (Cambridge, MA: UCLA Center for Medieval and Renaissance Studies and Harvard University Press, 1982), p. 6. For an example of soul yearning for body, see Caesarius of Heisterbach, *Dialogus miraculorum*, ed. Joseph Strange, 2 vols. (Cologne: Heberle, 1851), dist. 12, ch. 50, vol. 2, p. 356. Heinzmann, *Die Unsterblichkeit der Seele*, p. 188, quotes a passage from the summa called *Breves dies hominis* in which Plato is represented as supporting the position that resurrection is natural because of the longing of soul for body. This suggests that contemporaries were aware that a Platonic position tends in some ways to give more weight to body than an Aristotelian one (and not necessarily negative weight).

53. On this point generally, see Caroline W. Bynum, *Holy Feast and Holy Fast: The Religious Significance of Food to Medieval Women* (Berkeley: University of California Press, 1987). I suggest there that asceticism in the later Middle Ages treated body less as a trap or hindrance than a means of access to the divine; for a similar point of view, see *Les Miracles miroirs des corps*, ed. Jacques Gélis and Odile Redon (Paris: Presses et Publications de l'Université de Paris VIII – Vincennes à St. Denis, 1983).

54. Bernard, *De diligendo Deo*, sect. 11, pars. 30-33, in *Sancti Bernardi opera*, ed. J. Leclercq, C.H. Talbot and H.M. Rochais (Rome: Editiones Cisterciensis, 1957–   ), vol. 3: *Tractatus et Opuscula*, pp. 145-47; trans. Robert Walton, *The Works of Bernard of Clairvaux*, vol. 5: *Treatises*, vol. 2, Cistercian Fathers Series 13 (Washington, DC: Cistercian Publications, 1974), pp. 122-24.

55. Bonaventure, *De assumptione B. Virginis Mariae*, sermon 1, sect. 2, in

S. Bonaventurae Opera omnia, ed. Collegium S. Bonaventurae, vol. 9 (Quarrachi: Collegium S. Bonaventurae, 1901), p. 690. See also Aquinas, *Summa contra Gentiles*, bk. 4, ch. 79, vol. 15, p. 249, and Aquinas, *De potentia*, q. 5, art. 10, pp. 176-77, which says explicitly that Porphyry's idea that the soul is happiest without the body, and Plato's idea that the body is a tool of the soul, are wrong; the soul is more like God when it is united to the body than when it is separated, because it is then more perfect.

56. Weber, *Auferstehung*, p. 326. The doctrine of the plurality of forms seems to lurk behind much Franciscan teaching on the dowries (*dotes*) of the glorified body, for thinkers such as Bonaventure and Richard of Middleton hold that body is in some way predisposed for the flowing over of glory into it before it receives the *dotes*; see *ibid.*, p. 314ff.

57. Weber, *Auferstehung*, p. 304, n. 197, and see *ibid.*, pp. 266 and 135-36. The idea that the soul is held back from full enjoyment of God when it is without the body comes from Augustine. It is also found in Dominican theologians, for example Giles of Rome; see Nolan, *Giles of Rome*, pp. 46, 78.

58. Weber, *Auferstehung*, pp. 243-44.

59. Heinzmann, *Die Unsterblichkeit der Seele*, p. 147ff.; and Weber, *Auferstehung*, pp. 217-19. I would place the change in emphasis in the patristic notion of resurrection – a change toward a materialist interpretation – at the time of the debate between Methodius and the Origenists.

60. John of Damascus, *In librum de fide orthodoxa*, bk. 4, ch. 27, in J.-P. Migne (ed.), *Patrologiae cursus completus: series graeca* (Paris, 1857-1866), vol. 94, col. 1220; see Weber, *Auferstehung*, p. 62, n. 99, and p. 218, n. 261. For Hugh of St. Victor's use of the idea, see Heinzmann, *Die Unsterblichkeit der Seele*, p. 159.

61. This is made clear in their use of the example of the statue, taken from Augustine (see *Enchiridion*, ch. 23, par. 89, Corpus christianorum: Series latina 46, ed. E. Evans [Turnhout: Brepols, 1969], p. 97) and treated in Lombard's *Sentences*, bk. 4, dist. 44, chs. 2-4, vol. 2, pp. 517-19. Bodily resurrection is, they argue, like the melting down and reconstituting of a statue: it is the same statue because it is made of the same matter. although the material bits need not be returned to exactly the same place in the whole. See Heinzmann, *Die Unsterb-*

lichkeit der Seele, pt. 2 *passim*. By the later thirteenth century, some who adopt the new identity theory reject the analogy to a statue altogether. They argue that a reforged statue is not the same statue (even if the matter is the same) because it does not have the same form – the form of a statue (unlike the soul) not being substantial. See Weber, *Auferstehung*, p. 244ff.

62. Heinzmann, *Die Unsterblichkeit der Seele*, p. 150ff.

63. Hugh, *De sacramentis*, bk. 1, pt. 6, chs. 35–37, PL 176, col. 284–88. Growth continued to be hard for scholastic natural philosophers to explain, and Aristotelian categories did not necessarily provide the answer. See Joan Cadden, "The Medieval Philosophy and Biology of Growth: Albertus Magnus, Thomas Aquinas, Albert of Saxony and Marsilius of Inghen on Book I, c. V of Aristotle's *De Generatione et Corruptione*, with Translated Texts of Albertus Magnus and Thomas Aquinas," Ph.D. Dissertation, Indiana University, 1971.

64. See n. 14, above; and Weber, *Auferstehung*, p. 217ff.

65. Heinzmann, *Die Unsterblichkeit der Seele*, p. 243, n. 11.

66. Durandus of St. Pourçain, *In Sententias theologicas Petri Lombardi commentariorum libri quatuor* (Lyon: Apud Gasparem, 1556), dist. 44, q. 1, fol. 340v–341r: "Utrum ad hoc quod idem homo numero resurgat, requiratur quod formetur corpus eius eisdem pulueribus in quos fuit resolutum." (The printed edition of the commentary is the third and last redaction, moderate in comparison to earlier ones; see Gilson, *History*, p. 774, n. 81.)

67. In answer to the question whether the soul of Peter can be in the body of Paul (which he says is misformulated), Durandus argues (*In Sententias*, dist. 44, q. 1, pars. 4, 5, fol. 341r): "...quaestio implicat contradictionem: quia corpus Petri non potest esse nisi compositum ex materia et anima Petri...ergo anima Petri non potest esse in corpore Pauli nec econverso, nisi anima Petri fiat anima Pauli.... Restat ergo quod alio modo formetur quaestio...: supposito quod anima Petri fieret in materia quae fuit in corpore Pauli, utrum esset idem Petrus qui prius erat." He concludes (*ibid.*, par. 6, fol. 341r): "...cuicumque materiae vniatur anima Petri in resurrectione, ex quo est eadem forma secundum numerum, per consequens erit idem Petrus secundum numero." For the background to Durandus's position, see Weber, *Auferstehung*, pp. 217-53, 76-78.

Weber's basic argument is that there were a number of precursors to Durandus's position, the originality of which has been overestimated.

68. Weber, *Auferstehung*, p. 234.

69. Giles of Rome's Sentence commentary never reaches book 4. His major statement on the resurrection, in the *Quaestiones de resurrectione mortuorum et de poena damnatorum*, has been edited by Nolan, *Giles of Rome*, pp. 69-75, 90-96, 105-13, 124-30. Giles's position clearly foreshadows Durandus's; see *Quaestiones* in Nolan, *Giles*, pp. 73-74, and Nolan's discussion, pp. 88, 120. What guarantees the identity of earthly body and risen body (and therefore the identity of person) is not matter but form. As Weber points out, however (*Auferstehung*, pp. 234-36), Giles does not go all the way to Durandus's position. When Giles discusses Christ's body in the *triduum* he makes it clear that, although the body is not man, the material cadaver continues and is Christ's body; Nolan, *Giles*, p. 60. Moreover, like Aquinas, Giles devotes much attention to the question of whether the body that rises is a body into which food was converted and to related questions about the resurrection of eaten flesh; see Nolan, *Giles*, pp. 114-23. For Giles's embryological theory, see M. Anthony Hewson, *Giles of Rome and the Medieval Theory of Conception: A Study of the* De formatione corporis humani in utero (London: University of London, The Athlone Press, 1975). For a similar interpretation of John of Paris, see nn. 78, 80, below.

70. *Summa contra Gentiles*, bk. 4, chs. 80-81, vol. 15, pp. 251-54. Aquinas holds that risen body will be reconstituted out of all of the former matter of the body; but it is not impossible for it to be reconstituted out of some other matter. Interpretation of this passage has been controversial. See Weber, *Auferstehung*, p. 229; and E. Hugueny, "Résurrection et identité corporelle selon les philosophies de l'individuation," *Revue des sciences philosophiques et théologiques* 23 (1934), pp. 94-106. Hugueny argues that Thomas's thought developed away from the idea of material continuity and toward formal identity.

71. See n. 17, above.

72. *Chartularium universitatis Parisiensis*, vol. 1, p. 487.

73. Proposition 17, *ibid.*, p. 544, quoted above, at n. 4.

74. Propositions 25, 148, 155, 178 in *ibid.*, pp. 544-55; and see Roland

Hissette, *Enquête sur les 219 articles condamnés à Paris le 7 Mars 1277*, Philosophes médiévaux, 22 (Louvain and Paris: Publications Universitaires de Louvain and Vander-Oyez, 1977), pp. 187, 294, 307–08.

75. Debate over whether Christ was a man in the *triduum* went back into the twelfth century. By the mid-thirteenth century, theologians generally agreed that living union was necessary for humanness (i.e., for being a man). Aquinas's theory, however, raised the question whether Christ's body on the cross and in the grave were the same body. Giles of Lessines in 1278 raised the issue in a treatise on the unicity of form which he sent to Albert the Great. (Indeed, he added the thesis of the equivocality of body to the list of those condemned in 1270, but it is not clear that it was in fact condemned.) Perhaps because of Albert's defense, the unicity of form was not condemned in 1277 in Paris, but in 1277 in Oxford the position was condemned that: "corpus vivum et mortuum est equivoce corpus..." Weber, *Auferstehung*, pp. 76–78, 150–51. John Quidort (John of Paris) also got into trouble for the implications of his teaching on identity for the body of Christ; see *ibid.*, p. 239. On the condemnation of the doctrine of the unicity of form in England, see *Chartularium universitatis Parisiensis*, vol. 1, pp. 558–59; Copleston, *History*, vol. 2, pt. 2, pp. 153–54; and Hewson, *Giles of Rome and Conception*, pp. 6–11.

76. Elizabeth A.R. Brown, "Authority, the Family, and the Dead in Late Medieval France," unpublished paper, especially nn. 41–46; and Francesco Santi, "Il cadavre e Bonifacio VIII, tra Stefano Tempier e Avicenna, inforno ad un saggio di Elizabeth Brown," *Studi Medievali*, 3rd ser., 28.2 (1987), pp. 861–78.

77. Weber, *Auferstehung*, p. 242, n. 404.

78. Lottin, *Psychologie*, vol. 5, pp. 214–18, 320–21. John of Paris, in his *De unitate formae*, dealt explicitly with the objection that the unicity of form threatened the belief that Christ's body was Christ in the *triduum*; see Franz Pelster, "Ein anonymer Traktat des Johannes v. Paris O.P. über das Formenproblem in Cod. Vat. lat. 862," *Divus Thomas* 24 (1946), pp. 26–27.

79. See n. 76, above.

80. Pelster, "Ein anonymer Traktat des Johannes v. Paris," p. 26.

81. Aquinas, *Summa theologiae*, pt. 3a, q. 25, art. 6, vol. 50, pp. 202–05.

82. E. Brown, "Authority, the Family, and the Dead," quite rightly argues that neither the unicity nor the plurality of forms dictated a particular approach to burial, although theologians in the 1280s took radically different positions on the advisability of partition of corpses.

83. Peter the Venerable, "Sermo in honore sancti illius cuius reliquiae sunt in presenti," ed. in Giles Constable, "Petri Venerabilis Sermones Tres," *Revue bénédictine* 64 (1954), pp. 265-72.

84. *Dialogus*, ed. Strange, dist. 8, ch. 87, vol. 2, p. 155.

85. For another example, see Bernard of Clairvaux, *Vita S. Malachiae*, in PL 182, col. 1118, which closes with this description of the holy body: "Tuum es, Jesu bone, depositum, quod nobis creditum est; tuus thesaurus, qui reconditur penes nos. Servamus illum resignandum in tempore, quo reposcendum censueris: tantum ut absque contubernalibus suis non egrediatur, sed quem habuimus hospitem, habeamus ducem, tecum et cum ipso pariter regnaturi in saecula saeculorum. Amen." The lines make it clear that the body is a body, a treasure and pledge of the saint whose soul is in heaven; but they also speak of the body as the saint himself, who will go forth to meet Christ at the Last Judgment, accompanied by Bernard and his companion monks.

86. See Chapter 6, above, n. 164.

87. Philippe Ariès, *The Hour of Our Death*, trans. Helen Weaver (New York: Knopf, 1981), pp. 261-68, 353ff. (Although some people today still believe such stories, growth of hair and nails does not occur in corpses.)

88. Thurston, *Physical Phenomena*, pp. 246-52; and Chapter 6, above, n. 32.

89. Agostino Paravicini Bagliani, "Rajeunir au Moyen Age: Roger Bacon et le mythe de la prolongation de la vie," in *Revue médicale de la Suisse romande* 106 (1986), pp. 9-23, and "Storia della scienza e storia della mentalità: Ruggero Bacone, Bonifacio VIII e la teoria della 'prolongatio vitae,' " in C. Leonardi and G. Orlandi (eds.), *Aspetti della Letteratura latina nel secolo XIII: Atti del primo Convegno internazionale di studi dell' Associazione per il Medioevo e l'Umanesimo latini (AMUL) Perugia 3-5 ottobre 1983*, Quaderni del Centro per il Collegamento degli Studi Medievali e Umanistici nell' Università di Perugia, 15 (Florence and Perugia: "La Nuova Italia," 1985), pp. 243-80; and, for useful

NOTES TO PAGES 267-268

background on thirteenth-century notions of "physic," see Faye Marie Getz, "Medicine at Medieval Oxford," in *The History of Oxford University*, vol. 2 (Oxford: Clarendon Press, forthcoming, 1990).

90. Aquinas, *Summa theologiae*, pt. 3a, q. 15, art. 5, obj. 3 and reply to obj. 3, vol. 49, pp. 204-07, suggests that beatific vision flows over naturally into body; therefore the martyrs bore up under pain. See also *ibid.*, pt. 3a, q. 14, art. 1, obj. 2 and reply to obj. 2, vol. 49, pp. 170-77; Bynum, "Bodily Miracles and Resurrection," n. 64; the references to Eusebius in nn. 91, 95, 96, below; and Caesarius, *Dialogus*, dist. 12, chs. 47, 50, 54, vol. 2, pp. 354, 355-56, 358. Artistic depictions of martyrdoms, which became steadily more gory, more detailed and more numerous in the course of the thirteenth and fourteenth centuries, continued to represent the tortured saints as if they did not feel the cruelties inflicted upon them (see Chapter 6, above, Figures 6.14, 6.15). Since painters, sculptors and illuminators at this period felt no hesitation in depicting Christ as suffering, dying or dead, we should view the serenity of artistic representations of tortured saints as deliberate and theologically significant. It seems, paradoxically, that thirteenth- and fourteenth-century artists presented in Christ the suffering of humanity and, in his saints, the power of divinity.

91. Eusebius, *The Ecclesiastical History*, bk. 5, ch. 1, trans. Kirsopp Lake, 2 vols. (Cambridge, MA: Loeb Classical Library, Heinemann and Harvard University Press, 1926; reprint, 1980), vol. 1, pp. 435-37. Throughout book 5, chapter 1, Eusebius displays a fascination with the details of torture similar to that found in James of Voragine.

92. Minucius Felix, *Octavius*, chs. 11, 34, 37-38, trans. R.E. Wallis in A. Roberts and J. Donaldson (eds.), *The Ante-Nicene Fathers: Translations of the Writings of the Fathers Down to A.D. 325*, vol. 4 (Edinburgh, 1885; reprint, Grand Rapids, MI: Eerdmans, 1982), pp. 178-79, 194, 196-97; on this passage see Arthur Darby Nock, "Cremation and Burial in the Roman Empire," *Harvard Theological Review* 25.4 (1932), p. 334. The accounts of both Eusebius and Minucius Felix imply, of course, that some Christians did assume that bodily partition threatened resurrection.

93. Tertullian, *De Resurrectione mortuorum*, chs. 32, 57, in *Tertulliani Opera*,

vol. 2, Corpus christianorum: Series latina (Turnhout: Brepols, 1954), pp. 961–62, 1004–05; trans. Holmes, in Roberts and Donaldson (eds.), *Ante-Nicene Fathers*, vol. 3 (1885; reprint, New York: Scribner's, 1926), pp. 567–68, 590.

94. Augustine, *De cura pro mortuis gerenda*, PL 40, cols. 591–610.

95. Eusebius reports this in the same passage where he cites with scorn the Roman conviction that scattering bodies prevents resurrection; he also tells us that the Romans had to post guards to prevent the faithful from stealing the remains to bury them; see *Ecclesiastical History*, bk. 5, ch. 1, vol. 1, pp. 435–37. For stories of early Christians caring for remains, see Nicole Hermann-Mascard, *Les Reliques des saints: Formation coutumière d'un droit*, Société d'Histoire du Droit: Collection d'histoire institutionnelle et sociale 6 (Paris: Editions Klincksieck, 1975), pp. 23–26. James of Voragine repeats such stories in the *Golden Legend*, where they gain considerably greater prominence.

Many scholars have pointed out that a belief in resurrection tends to emerge in situations of persecution, for adherents want to claim that those who die for the faith will be rewarded in another life with the good fortune they have clearly in some sense been denied in this life. Lionel Rothkrug gives a more profound version of this argument when he suggests that, to Jews of the Maccabee period and to early Christians, resurrection was a substitute for the burial owed to the pious; see Lionel Rothkrug, "German Holiness and Western Sanctity in Medieval and Modern History," *Historical Reflections/Réflexions historiques* 15.1 (1988), pp. 161–249, especially pp. 215–29. Thus, early Christians could adhere to the hope of resurrection and yet display intense concern for the remains (relics) of their heroes.

96. Eusebius, bk. 5, ch. 1, vol. 1, p. 419.

97. See nn. 133–145, below.

98. E.A.R. Brown, "Death and the Human Body in the Later Middle Ages: The Legislation of Boniface VIII on the Division of the Corpse," *Viator* 12 (1981), pp. 238–40.

99. E. Brown, "Authority, the Family, and the Dead," typescript, pp. 11–12.

100. See E. Brown, "Death and the Human Body," "Authority, the Family, and the Dead"; Paravicini Bagliani, "Rajeunir au Moyen Age," "Ruggero Bacone,

Bonifacio VIII e la teoria della 'prolongatio.vitae' "; and Pierre Duparc, "Dilaceratio corporis," *Bulletin de la Société Nationale des Antiquaires de France 1980–1981* (Paris: Boccard, 1981), pp. 360-72.

101. E. Brown, "Authority, the Family, and the Dead," typescript, p. 16. Brown argues that Boniface's personal fear of death and skepticism about the resurrection were basic motives for the bull.

102. Paravicini Bagliani, "Rajeunir au Moyen Age," and "Ruggero Bacone, Bonifacio VIII e la teoria della 'prolongatio vitae.' "

103. See Brigitte Cazelles, *Le Corps de sainteté d'après Jehan Bouche d'Or, Jehan Paulus, et quelques Vies des XIIe et XIIIe siècles* (Geneva: Droz, 1982), pp. 55-56.

104. Judith-Danielle Jacquet, "Le Miracle de la Jambe Noire," in Gélis and Redon (eds.), *Les Miracles miroirs*, pp. 23-52.

105. Ariès, *Hour of Our Death*, p. 29ff.; Peter Brown, *The Cult of the Saints: Its Rise and Function in Latin Christianity* (Chicago: University of Chicago Press, 1981); P. Séjourné, "Reliques," DTC 13, pt. 2, cols. 2330-65; Hermann-Mascard, *Les Reliques*; Patrick J. Geary, *Furta Sacra: Thefts of Relics in the Central Middle Ages* (Princeton: Princeton University Press, 1978), especially pp. 152-54; Joan M. Petersen, *The Dialogues of Gregory the Great in Their Late Antique Cultural Background*, Studies and Texts 69 (Toronto: Pontifical Institute of Mediaeval Studies, 1984'), pp. 140-50; and Rothkrug, "German Holiness and Western Sanctity."

106. E. Brown, "Death and the Human Body" and Duparc, "Dilaceratio corporis."

107. E. Brown, "Authority, the Family, and the Dead," typescript, pp. 16-17.

108. *Ibid.*, p. 14.

109. See Marie-Christine Pouchelle, *Corps et chirurgie à l'apogée du Moyen Age: Savoir et imaginaire du corps chez Henri de Mondeville...* (Paris: Flammarion, 1983), pp. 132-36; and Chapter 6, above, n. 29.

110. See, for example, the cases of Clare of Montefalco and Margaret of Città di Castello cited in Chapter 6, above, n. 28.

111. Edward Peters, *Torture* (Oxford: Blackwell, 1985); J.G. Bellamy, *The*

Law of Treason in England in the Later Middle Ages (Cambridge: Cambridge University Press, 1970); and Camporesi, *Incorruptible Flesh*, pp. 19–24.

112. *Wallraf-Richartz-Museum, Köln: Vollständiges Verzeichnis der Gemäldesammlung* (Cologne: Electa, 1986), p. 147, plate 157; and see also p. 58. It is also worth noting that the drawing, in Herrad of Hohenbourg's *Hortus deliciarum*, of corpses rising from their tombs for the resurrection labels the bodies "ossa mortuorum," although they are drawn as bodies, not bones. See Herrad of Hohenbourg, *Hortus deliciarum: Reconstruction*, ed. Rosalie Green *et al.* (London and Leiden: Warburg Institute/University of London and Brill, 1979), p. 427, plate 141, number 326, of fol. 251r. For canon law concerning relics, see Duparc, "Dilaceratio corporis," and Hermann-Mascard, *Les Reliques*.

113. Sixten Ringbom, *Icon to Narrative: The Rise of the Dramatic Close-Up in Fifteenth-Century Devotional Painting*, Acta Academiae Aboensis, ser. A: Humaniora, 31.2 (Abo, 1965), pp. 48–52; quoted passage on p. 50. See also Gertrud Schiller, *Iconography of Christian Art*, vol. 2: *The Passion of Jesus Christ*, trans. Janet Seligman (Greenwich, CT: New York Graphic Society, 1972), pp. 184–97, plates 664–73.

114. Elizabeth M. Hallam, "Royal Burial and the Cult of Kingship in France and England, 1060–1330," *Journal of Medieval History* 8.4 (1982), pp. 359–80; I am also indebted to an unpublished paper by Edward Peters, "Courtly Death."

115. E. Brown, "Authority, the Family, and the Dead," typescript, pp. 11–12.

116. Hallam, "Royal Burial."

117. See Chapter 6, above, n. 29.

118. Peters, *Torture*, pp. 67–68; and Bellamy, *Law of Treason*, pp. 9, 13, 20–21, 26, 39, 45–47, 52, 226–27. Bellamy points out that historians today sometimes know a medieval verdict only from the nature of the punishment inflicted. We know, for example, that a homicide had been adjudged petty treason in fourteenth-century England if the male perpetrator was drawn and hanged, or the female perpetrator burned.

119. Saul N. Brody, *The Disease of the Soul: Leprosy in Medieval Literature* (Ithaca, NY: Cornell University Press, 1974), pp. 64–66, 79, 85–86. See also R.I. Moore, *The Formation of a Persecuting Society: Power and Deviance in Western*

Europe, 950-1250 (New York: Blackwell, 1987), pp. 58-63, "Heresy as Disease," in W. Lourdaux and D. Verhelst (eds.), *The Concept of Heresy in the Middle Ages (11th-13th Century): Proceedings of the International Conference, Louvain, May 13-16, 1973* (Louvain: University Press, 1976), pp. 1-11; and Camporesi, *Incorruptible Flesh*, pp. 90-96.

120. A related issue concerning incorruptibility is the incorruptibility of the bodies of great sinners; see Ariès, *Hour of Our Death*, p. 360, and Louis-Vincent Thomas, *Le Cadavre: De la biologie à l'anthropologie* (Brussels: Editions Complexe, 1980), pp. 39-44, 199, who however underestimates the positive value given to incorruptibility in the Western Middle Ages. See also Camporesi, *Incorruptible Flesh*. The fact that the earth is reported to refuse the normal process of decay to the extraordinarily evil suggests that there is in this culture an accepting, as well as an abhorring, of natural decay. Normal, organic corruption may be good, because it is a prelude to fertility; hence the analogy drawn in patristic writing between the naturally germinating seed and the resurrected bodies of the martyrs, "seeds of the church." These natural analogies, however, mostly drop out of theological writing in the high Middle Ages; see my unpublished paper, "Seeds, Statues and Whales: Metaphors for the Resurrection of the Body in the Twelfth Century," plenary address to the Medieval Academy of America, April 13, 1989.

121. Caesarius, *Dialogus*, ed. Strange, dist. 8, chs. 53, 60, vol. 2, pp. 125-26, 133. He also tells (*ibid.*, dist. 8, ch. 88, vol. 2, pp. 155-56) of bones that sort themselves out so that the false relics are eliminated. For stories of bones that, however, invite their disturbance, see *ibid.*, dist. 8, chs. 85-87, vol. 2, pp. 151-55.

122. See E. Brown, "Death and the Human Body," pp. 227, 243. Guibert of Nogent in the *De pignoribus* tells several earlier tales that are intended to indicate that relics do not wish to be dismembered; see *De pignoribus*, bk. 1, ch. 4, PL 156, cols. 626-30, and my Introduction, above, nn. 1, 2.

123. Thomas of Cantimpré, *Supplementum* [to Life of Mary], ch. 1, pars. 6-7, and ch. 3, par. 14, in J. Bollandus and G. Henschenius (eds.), *Acta sanctorum ... editio novissima*, ed. J. Carnandet *et al.* (Paris: Palmé, 1863-   ), June, vol. 5, pp. 574-78.

124. The insistence that a relic is the saint or that the heart of a king buried among his people is their sovereign seems parallel to modern statements that a donor lives on in a transplanted organ.

125. On the miniatures from the *Hortus deliciarum*, see my Introduction, above, nn. 3–5. On the tempera painting from the Vatican that uses the motif, see Deoclecio Redig de Campos, "Eine unbekannte Darstellung des Jüngsten Gerichts aus dem elften Jahrhundert," *Zeitschrift für Kunstgeschichte* N.F. 5 (1936), pp. 124–33; and Wilhelm Paeseler, "Die römische Weltgerichtstafel im Vatikan (Ihre Stellung in der Geschichte des Weltgerichtsbildes und in der römischen Malerei des 13. Jahrhunderts)," *Kunstgeschichtliches Jahrbuch der Bibliotheca Hertziana* 2 (1938), pp. 311–94.

126. B. Brenk, "Die Anfänge der Byzantinischen Weltgerichtsdarstellung," *Byzantinische Zeitschrift* 57 (1964), pp. 106–26; *Tradition und Neuerung in der christlichen Kunst des ersten Jahrtausends: Studien zur Geschichte des Weltgerichtsbildes*, Wiener Byzantinische Studien, 3 (Vienna: Hermann Böhlau, 1966); and Kurt Weitzmann, "Byzantine Miniatures and Icon Painting in the Eleventh Century" (1966), reprinted in H.L. Kessler (ed.), *Studies in Classical and Byzantine Manuscript Illuminations* (Chicago: University of Chicago Press, 1971), pp. 271–313.

127. For later uses of the Byzantine program that underline the themes of both assembled fragments and regurgitation, see Gabriel Millet, *Monuments de l'Athos relevés avec le concours de l'Armée française d'Orient et de l'Ecole française d'Athènes*, vol. 1: *Les Peintures* (Paris: Librairie Ernest Leroux, 1927), plates 149, 247; and Paul Underwood, "Third Preliminary Report on the Restoration of the Frescoes in the Kariye Camii at Istanbul by the Byzantine Institute, 1956," *Dumbarton Oaks Papers* 12 (1958), pp. 237–87, especially pp. 242, 252–60.

128. Selma Jonsdottir, *An Eleventh-Century Byzantine Last Judgement in Iceland* (Reykjavik: Almenna Bokafelagio, 1959).

129. Fol. 109v of Melk MS 1833 makes use of the Byzantine motif of regurgitated parts in isolation from the total program; see Hanns Swarzenski, *Die lateinischen illuminierten Handschriften des XIII. Jahrhunderts in den Ländern an Rhein, Main und Donau*, 2 vols., Die deutsche Buchmalerei des XIII. Jahrhunderts

(Berlin: Deutscher Verein für Kunstwissenschaft, 1936), vol. 1, p. 163, especially n. 8.

130. And see also the Ottonian book cover from mid-ninth-century Reichnau reproduced in Schiller, *Iconography*, vol. 2: *Passion*, p. 456, plate 365.

131. On the Trier Apocalypse, see Richard Laufner and Peter Klein (eds.), *Trierer Apokalypse: Vollständige Faksimile-Ausgabe im Originalformat des Codex 31 der Stadtbibliothek Trier: Kommentarband* (Graz: Akademische Druck- und Verlagsanstalt, 1975); and James Snyder, "The Reconstruction of an Early Christian Cycle of Illustrations for the Book of Revelation: The Trier Apocalypse," *Vigiliae Christianae* 18 (1964), pp. 142-62. On the closely related Cambrai Apocalypse, see H. Omont, "Manuscrits illustrés de l'Apocalypse aux IXe et Xe siècles," *Bullétin de la Société de Reproductions de Manuscrits à Peintures* 6 (1922), pp. 62-64, 84-86, 93-94, plate 31.

132. Hans Posse, *Die Gemäldegalerie des Kaiser-Friedrich-Museums: Vollständiger beschreibender Katalog…*, pt. 2: *Die Germanischen Länder* (Berlin: Julius Bared, 1911), pp. 147-48.

133. Caesarius of Heisterbach describes a corpse that was revered as a saint simply because it was found miraculously reassembled after execution for robbery; see Caesarius, *Dialogus*, dist. 7, ch. 58, vol. 2, pp. 76-79.

134. See Cazelles, *Le Corps de sainteté*, pp. 219-20 and *passim*; and G. Philippart, *Les Légendiers latins et autres manuscrits hagiographiques*, Typologie des sources du moyen âge occidental, 24-25 (Turnhout: Brepols, 1977), pp. 40, 47.

135. Konrad Kunze, "Jacobus a (de) Voragine," *Die deutsche Literatur des Mittelalters: Verfasserlexikon* (Berlin: de Gruyter, 1983), vol. 4, col. 454; and see Chapter 6, above, n. 81.

136. See Giselle Huot-Girard, "La Justice immanente dans la *Légende dorée*," *Cahiers d'études médiévales* 1 (1974), pp. 135-47; Alain Boureau, *La Légende dorée: Le Système narratif de Jacques de Voragine († 1298)* (Paris: Editions du Cerf, 1984); Sherry L. Reames, *The Legenda Aurea: A Reexamination of Its Paradoxical History* (Madison, WI: University of Wisconsin Press, 1985); and Marie-Christine Pouchelle, "Représentations du corps dans la Légende dorée," *Ethnologie française* 6 (1976), pp. 293-308. André Vauchez, "Jacques de Voragine et les saints

du XIIIe siècle dans la Légende dorée," in B. Dunn-Lardeau (ed.), *Legenda Aurea: Sept siècles de diffusion: Actes du colloque international... à l'Université du Québec à Montréal 11–12 mai 1983* (Montreal and Paris: Bellarmin and J. Vrin, 1986), pp. 27-56, gives an interpretation opposed to that of Boureau and Reames.

137. Of the 153 chapters (many of which tell several stories), 91 treat martyrs; the majority of the martyrs discussed are not merely killed but are in some way dismembered. As Boureau notes (*La Légende dorée*, p. 116), James details 81 kinds of torture.

138. Boureau, *La Légende dorée*, pp. 60-61, 115-33.

139. Hippolyte Delehaye, *The Legends of the Saints*, trans. V.M. Crawford, Westminster Library (London: Longmans, Green, 1907), pp. 97, 130-34; René Aigrain, *L'Hagiographie: Ses sources, ses methodes, son histoire* (Paris: Bloud & Gay, 1953), p. 146; Baudouin de Gaiffier, "La Mort par le glaive dans les Passions des martyrs," *Recherches d'hagiographie latine*, Subsidia hagiographica, 52 (Brussels: Société des Bollandistes, 1971), pp. 70-76; Cazelles, *Le Corps de sainteté*, pp. 50-60; Boureau, *La Légende dorée*, pp. 126-33; and Alison Goddard Elliott, *Roads to Paradise: Reading the Lives of the Early Saints* (Hanover, NH: University Press of New England, 1987), pp. 14-15, 151.

140. James of Voragine, *Legenda aurea vulgo historia lombardica dicta*, 3rd ed., ed. Th. Graesse (Breslau: Köbner, 1890), pp. 400-03.

141. *Ibid.*, pp. 740-41, 597-601, 601-02.

142. *Ibid.*, pp. 203-04. It is worth noting that Sophia is said to have gathered up the remains of her daughters and buried them, with the help of bystanders; she was then buried with her children. This chapter, not found in the 1283 manuscript, is probably a later interpolation, but is fully in the spirit of the other chapters; see Boureau, *La Légende dorée*, pp. 27-28.

143. James, *Legenda aurea*, ed. Graesse, pp. 799-803; trans. G. Ryan and H. Ripperger, *The Golden Legend*, 2 parts (London: Longmans, Green, 1941), pt. 2, p. 719.

144. James also uses the seed metaphor in his discussion of the death of the contemporary saint, Peter Martyr; see *Legenda aurea*, ed. Graesse, p. 282: "Sic granum frumenti cadens in terram et infidelium manibus comprehensum

et mortuum uberem consurgit in spicam, sic botrus in torculari calcatus liquoris redundat in copiam, sic aromata pilo contusa odorem plenius circumfundunt, sic granum sinapis contritum virtutem suam multipliciter demonstravit." The metaphor was extremely important in the earliest Christian discussions of resurrection (see A. Michel, "Résurrection des morts," cols. 2515-32), but eclipsed in the high Middle Ages (see Bynum, "Seeds, Statues and Whales").

145. My reading agrees with those of Boureau, *La Légende dorée*, p. 126, and Cazelles, *Le Corps de sainteté*, pp. 48-61.

146. Thomas, *Le Cadavre*.

147. For such miracles see Chapter 6, above, nn. 13, 25-27, 30-32, 96-100, 107.

148. Nock, "Cremation and Burial"; and Jocelyn M.C. Toynbee, *Death and Burial in the Roman World* (Ithaca, NY: Cornell University Press, 1971). I am at work on a study of the doctrine of bodily resurrection in the patristic period that will make clearer both its relationship to previous Mediterranean attitudes to the cadaver and the changes between patristic discussion and that of the thirteenth century.

149. To say this is not, of course, to deny the importance of the introduction of new texts and terminology (especially those of Aristotle); see above, at n. 45.

Index

419

Bell, Rudolph, 56, 75, 186, 351–52
n.84. *See also* Weinstein and Bell.
Bellegambe, Jean, 285, 293.
Benedetta Carlini, 333 n.27.
Benedictus Deus, 392 n.154.
Benevenuta of Bojano, 136.
Benz, Ernst, 131, 188.
Bergson, Henri, 25.
Bernard of Clairvaux, 36, 72, 93, 103,
108, 109, 145, 157–60, 165, 190–
92, 218, 256–57, 408 n.85.
Bible, moralized, 97, 99, 206.
Birgitta of Sweden, 36, 137, 186.
Blannbekin, Agnes, 122, 126, 139, 186.
Bloch, Marc, 20, 27.
Bloemardine, 59.
Blood: as basic body fluid, 100, 109,
114, 214–15, 220–21; as symbol,
87, 91–92, 101–03, 108, 172, 383
n.99; miracles, 101–02.
Bodily Assumption, 210.
Body: as matter, 228–29; history
of, 19–20, 182–83, 194–95, 366
nn.4–7; relationship to soul, 182,
222–35 *passim*; women especially
associated with, 98–102, 146–50,
171–75, 203, 204–05, 206–22,
236–38, 332 n.25. *See also* Resur-
rection of the body.
Bonaventure, 36, 49, 212, 218, 229,
257; *Life of Francis*, 34–35.
Boniface VIII, 269, 270.
Bossy, John, 20.
Bourdieu, Pierre, 16.
Brizio chapel, *see* Signorelli.
Browe, Peter, 122–23.
Brown, Elizabeth, 261.
Brown, Peter, 19.
Bücher, Karl, 57.
Burial practices, 266–72, 280, 295,
417 n.148; burial *ad sanctos*, 269,
270, 272.
Butler, Joseph, 248.
Byzantine Last Judgment, icono-
graphic program of, 12–13, 280–84,

286–87, 414 nn.127, 129.

CADAVER, 259, 266, 270–72, 295,
408 n.87. *See also* Dissection,
Incorruptibility of cadaver.
Caesarius of Heisterbach, 123–24, 146,
234, 265, 275, 276.
Campin, Robert, *Madonna and Child
before a Firescreen*, 103, 104.
Cannibalism, 185, 243–44, 260.
Carozzi, Claude, 187.
Cathars, 39, 63, 143, 195–96, 240,
387 n.125.
Catherine of Genoa, 66, 69, 188.
Catherine of Siena, 36, 39, 54, 62,
66, 69, 87, 96, 97–98, 167–69,
172–73, 185–86, 189, 212, 222,
363 n.57; and care of sick, 197;
and eucharist, 98, 141; nursed by
Christ, 162, 206, 211, 380–81 n.87.
Certeau, Michel de, 16.
Chalcidius, 255.
Charroux, abbey of, 272.
Chauliac, Guy de, 220.
Chodorow, Nancy, 43.
Christ and St. John Group, *see*
Devotional objects.
Christchild, statues of, *see* Devotional
objects.
Christina Ebner, 126.
Christina of Markyate, 37–38, 42, 137.
Christina *Mirabilis* of St. Trond, 141,
142, 236–37.
Circumcision, 84, 87ff., 114.
Cistercians, 47, 59, 63, 71, 121, 128.
Clare of Assisi, 42, 124, 153, 176.
Clement VI, 270.
Colette of Corbie, 181.
Columba of Rieti, 153.
Comedy, as model for writing history,
24–26, 304 n.24, 305 n.26.
communitas, Victor Turner's theory
of, 47, 49.
Conception, theories of, 214, 226–
27, 337 nn.49–50, 382 n.93.

Pilgrimage, 38, 40, 42, 60.
Pisano, Giovanni, 95.
Platonism, 223, 254–56, 401 n.46,
  403 n.52.
Pouchelle, Marie-Christine, 218, 272.
Premonstratensians, 47.
Priesthood of the Virgin, iconographic
  motif of, 101, 212, 219.
Purgatory, 62–63, 102, 231, 267.

QUASI-RELIGIOUS STATUS, 46–48, 59,
  64. See also Beguines, Tertiaries.
Quirizio of Murano, The Savior, 106,
  110.
Quodlibetal disputations, 224, 241.

RAYMOND OF CAPUA, 39, 167–69,
  185.
Recluses, 121, 122.
Reformation, relation to Middle Ages,
  18, 77–78.
Regurgitation: as iconographic and
  literary motif, 11–13, 267–68,
  280–89; as metaphor for writing
  history, 14, 24–26.
Relics, 183–84, 185, 230, 254, 261,
  272, 276, 367–68 n.9, 371–72 n.30,
  391 n.151, 412 n.112, 414 n.124.
Reliquaries, 145, 273–75, 277, 295,
  355 n.120.
Resurrection of the body, 11–13, 204,
  224, 227–31, 234–35, 239–97
  passim; and persecution, 410 n.95.
Richard I, 272.
Richard of Middleton, 226, 257.
Robert of Melun, 240, 255.
Roger of Wendover, 272.
Roisin, Simone, 35, 153.
Rolle, Richard, 36, 124, 153, 157,
  163, 191, 345 n.13.
Rothkrug, Lionel, 101, 410 n.95.
Rupert of Deutz, 86.
Ruysbroeck, Jan van, 124, 191, 345
  n.13.

SACKS, OLIVER, 249.
Sacred Heart, devotion to, 122.
Saints' lives, see Hagiography.
Science fiction, as evidence of mod-
  ern attitudes toward body, 245–52,
  398 nn.22, 25.
Scott, Joan, 21.
Sect, Troeltsch's theory of, 61–65.
Sexuality, 41, 43, 204, 333 n.26; of
  Christ, 82–88, 92, 114; expressed
  in religious ecstasy, 133–34.
Sigal, Pierre-André, 189.
Siger of Lille, 125.
Signorelli, 285, 292.
Song of Songs, 44, 93, 106, 124,
  159–60, 190.
Soul: Aristotelian theory of, 227;
  between death and resurrection,
  242; female images for, 165–70;
  relationship to body, 182, 222–35
  passim. See also Form.
Southern, R.W., 47.
Sperry experiments, 252.
Star Trek, 245, 297.
Steinberg, Leo, 15, 16, 79ff., 185, 195.
Stigmata, 34, 56, 60, 102, 125, 131,
  132, 133, 173, 186–87, 231, 370
  n.25.
Suso, Henry, 101, 124, 153, 157, 158,
  165–66, 184, 191, 345 n.13.
Sylvestris, Bernard, 256.

TABERNACLES FOR RESERVATION OF
  HOST, 144–45.
Tauler, John, 66, 67, 70, 72, 124,
  153, 157, 190, 191, 345 n.13.
Teresa of Avila, 66.
Tertiaries, 16, 57, 59, 61, 64, 65, 68,
  71, 74, 78, 120, 122, 128, 156.
Tertullian, 239, 260, 267–68.
Thomas, Keith, 20, 27.
Thomas of Cantimpré, 36, 138, 143,
  157, 196, 226, 237, 388 nn.130–31.
Thurston, Herbert, 55–56, 187.
Tiedala of Nivelles, 130.

Zone Books series designed by Bruce Mau

Type composed by Archetype

Printed and bound Smythe-sewn by Arcata Graphics/Kingsport
    using Sebago acid-free paper